Cooperatives

and Local

Development

Theory and
Applications for the
21st Century

Edited by
Christopher D. Merrett
and Norman Walzer

M.E.Sharpe
Armonk, New York
London, England

Library of Congress Cataloging-in-Publication Data

Cooperatives and local development : theory and applications for the 21st century / edited
by Christopher D. Merrett and Norman Walzer.
    p. cm.
   Includes bibliographical references and index.
   ISBN 0-7656-1123-6 (cloth : alk. paper) ISBN 0-7656-1124-4 (pbk. : alk. paper)
    1. Cooperation—United States. 2. Agriculture, Cooperative—United States. 3. Rural
development—United States. 4. Rural industries—United States. 5. Cooperation—
Government policy—United States. 6. Cooperative societies—Law and legislation—
United States. I. Merrett, Christopher D. II. Walzer, Norman.

HD3444.C635 2003
334′.0973—dc21

               2003045422

Dedication

Cooperatives offer hope for the revitalization of rural and urban communities across North America. Consequently, we dedicate this book to future generations, including our children and grandchildren: Grace Merrett, Alastair Merrett, Mark Walzer, Steven Walzer, and Emma Walzer.

Contents

List of Tables, Figures, and Boxes

Tables

Figures

Boxes

Preface

The market economy has changed profoundly over the past two centuries. In the nineteenth century, business enterprises were largely single-product ventures, managed directly by the owners and rooted within national economies. In the twentieth century, firms employed managers who were not owners. Firms also evolved into multiproduct, multiunit entities that could employ thousands of workers. In the twenty-first century, many firms operate on a global scale, taking advantage of free trade policies and rapidly evolving computer and telecommunications technologies.

These changes have included at least two constants. First, markets continue to create social inequalities because of differential access to scarce resources or because of market inefficiencies. Second, marginalized participants in the market system have formed cooperatives to increase their market power. In the nineteenth century, impoverished English factory workers formed the Rochdale consumer cooperative. In the twentieth century, American farmers formed co-ops to increase their power in monopolistic markets. At the beginning of the twenty-first century, small businesses, agricultural producers, and consumers are participating in an increasingly competitive global marketplace, and, as in previous eras, they have created a variety of cooperative businesses to increase their market presence.

While co-ops have had a constant market presence, their internal structure has had to evolve due to changes in the global economy. Furthermore, there is a growing recognition among researchers and policymakers that co-ops are not isolated economic firms. Rather, they are viewed as economic development tools that can help a group of producers generate start-up capital, jobs, and tax revenues in a community.

Given this potential, it is crucial that producers, consumers, economic developers, and researchers realize how co-ops can promote local economic and community development. Hence, this book includes the perceptions of experts on a variety of cooperative issues, including the challenges involved in starting a co-op and in understanding its impact on surrounding communities. This book can be especially useful because it provides the theoretical foundations and practical applications of cooperative behavior.

Many people have supported this project and deserve special thanks. Without the financial support provided by the Illinois Council on Food and Agricultural Research (C-FAR), this book would not have been possible. Thanks to the contributing authors who stayed on task and made this project a priority. Special thanks are extended to Karen Poncin and the staff of the Curriculum Publications Clearinghouse, and to Susan Rescigno and the editorial staff at M.E. Sharpe, who worked with the editors to guide this manuscript through the editing and production process. As always, responsibility for any errors or omissions belongs solely to the editors.

Cooperatives

and Local

Development

1

Introduction: Cooperative Theory and Its Applications for the Twenty-First Century

Christopher D. Merrett and Norman Walzer

We live in paradoxical times. On the one hand, laissez-faire policymakers advocate the expansion of global markets through free trade agreements (Cohen 1995; Hufbauer and Schott 1992), which necessarily exposes local communities and national economies to intensified economic competition (Harvey 1989). Consequently, local producers and workers must increase their efficiency and scale of operations to compete (McMichael 1996).

In rural areas, farm producers have been pressured to either get big or get out, prompting the vertical integration of production, mergers, and the concentration of agribusiness ownership (Goodman and Watts 1997; Heffernan, Gronski, and Hendrickson 1999). In urban areas, grocery stores, pharmacies, and other locally owned enterprises have been forced by the same market pressures to expand their operations or face bankruptcy. Large discount stores, home improvement centers, and drugstore chains threaten neighborhood grocers, pharmacists, and other community-based entrepreneurs (Williams 2002; Wrigley 2001).

On the other hand, advocates of free markets also tout the merits of personal responsibility, community, and local control (Shuman 2000). These conflicting policy prescriptions confront community and economic developers with a conundrum. How can communities comprised of family farms, locally owned enterprises, and place-bound consumers survive in the face of increasingly intense global economic pressures that corrode community relations?

This book argues that individuals in rural communities can achieve economic and social objectives as a group that they could not achieve as sole producers, workers, or consumers. The case is made as authors in this edited volume review classic texts, current literature, and case studies relevant to

3

co-ops and community-based economic development. The rest of this chapter details the objectives of the book. It then provides an overview of each chapter, and concludes with a brief section describing where further research is needed in cooperative theory and development.

Objectives of the Book

One might wonder why a book on cooperative theory matters at the beginning of the twenty-first century. Some might view the co-op as an inefficient anachronism—a prisoner of its eighteenth-century origins (Booth 1987). Commentators have described a series of internal inefficiencies in the cooperative model, such as the free rider problem, that have undermined the ability of co-ops to compete in a capitalist economy (Cook 1995; Fulton 2001). During the twentieth century, the number of agricultural co-ops steadily declined, roughly proportionate to the declining number of farms (Sexton 1986, 1170).

Producer and consumer co-ops have restructured in several ways in order to cope with increasing market pressures. Some co-ops merged or were forced to form alliances with investor-owned firms (IOFs) to survive. Other co-ops were purchased by IOFs outright. For example, members of Blooming Prairie (2002), an organic and natural product distributor based in Iowa City, Iowa, and Mounds City, Minnesota, with an annual sales exceeding $130 million, recently voted to sell the co-op to United Natural Foods—a publicly traded IOF with sales exceeding $1 billion. Other co-ops simply went out of business because they could not adapt to economic change (North Farm Cooperative 2002).

At the dawn of the twenty-first century, some writers suggest that the globalization of markets and the increasing reliance on flexible production processes further undermine the ability of producer and consumer co-ops to compete (Cooke and Morgan 1994). Elster (1989) captures the essence of the skeptic's view when he asks, "If cooperative ownership is so desirable, why are there so few cooperatives?" (93).

By this logic, one might assume that the number of co-ops has declined so much that they no longer have a significant role to play in the twenty-first century. It is true that many producer and consumer co-ops have struggled. Not surprisingly, however, so have many IOFs in a range of economic sectors. As Joseph Schumpeter (1950) noted, capitalism is a process of "creative destruction" (81). As economic change occurs, new firms emerge that can profit in the new business environment, while companies such as Polaroid and Pan American Airlines have filed for bankruptcy or no longer exist.

New firms and products emerge in the niches created by bankrupted businesses, as is exemplified by Southwest Airlines and the expanding digital camera business. This same process also affects the cooperative business model. Some co-ops fail while others restructure to cope with change. New cooperative structures emerge that are better adapted to the new economic conditions. This book sheds light on recent innovations in the theory and application of the co-op model.

Proponents of the cooperative enterprise approach justify its continuing importance by pointing to the significant economic and community development roles it has played over the past two centuries (Cheney 1999; Fitch 1996; Wilkinson and Quarter 1996). These roles can be readily seen by looking at how the co-op as a formal business entity emerged in the nineteenth century during the Industrial Revolution (Melnyk 1985). Underpaid English factory workers could not afford to purchase enough food to keep their families from going hungry. In 1844, one enterprising group of workers formed the Rochdale purchasing co-op to buy food in bulk (Melnyk 1985). By doing so, these consumers lowered the unit costs of buying groceries, enabling them to purchase more for their hard-earned wages. In the early twentieth century, farmers in the United States confronted monopsonistic market conditions. The concentrated ownership of commodity processors and distributors meant that farmers did not receive a fair price for their commodities (Fulton 2001; McLaughlin 1996). Hence, American farmers and their political supporters were spurred to action, culminating with the passage of the federal Capper-Volstead Act in 1922. This legislation has been described as the "Magna Carta" for cooperative development because it permits small-scale farm producers, consumers, and workers to achieve economies of scale through co-ops, protecting them from charges of anti-trust behavior (Williams and Merrett 2001, 150). In many instances, family farms, community grocery stores, or local factories could not survive if they had not incorporated cooperative principles into their daily operations.

At the beginning of the twenty-first century, co-ops still have an enormous impact on the North American and global economy, even though the contributions that co-ops make have changed in qualitative and quantitative ways over the past two centuries, as the following figures reveal. To see the dynamic nature of the cooperative sector, note how many co-ops began and how many existing co-ops closed each year during the past four decades (Figure 1.1). Clearly, the overall number of farmer co-ops has declined due to the overall declining number of farmers who can participate as co-op members, as well as the aforementioned mergers, acquisitions, and bankruptcies (Figure 1.2).

Offsetting this somewhat negative news is the fact that agricultural co-ops report growing net profits. In 1954, an estimated 10,072 farmer co-ops

Figure 1.1 **Co-ops Organized and Discontinued in the United States, 1960 to 1996**

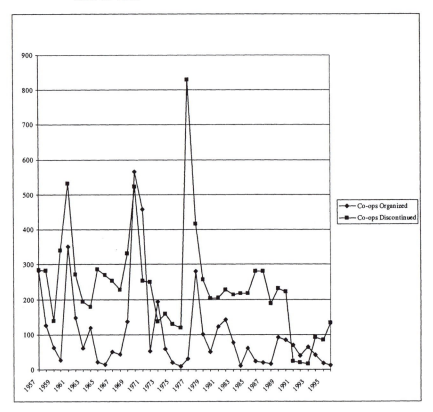

Source: USDA (1998), 48–51.

generated $332 million in net income. By 1996, the number of co-ops had declined to 3,884, but they collectively earned over $2.2 billion in net income ($380 million in real terms) (USDA 1998, 67).

Farmer co-ops also play a substantial role in the commodity market. In 1998, co-ops accounted for 27 percent of all farm marketings in the United States (Kraenzle 2001, 7). An examination of specific commodity sectors confirms the extent to which farmer co-ops contribute to the U.S. economy. For example, the USDA estimates that co-ops earned 90 percent of cash receipts from milk sales in the United States (Table 1.1). Agricultural co-ops also have a growing international role. In 1995, co-ops produced 12.3 percent of U.S. agricultural exports, which is worth an estimated value of $5.6 billion (USDA 1997).

Consumer co-ops also play a major role in the United States. For example,

Figure 1.2 **Farms and Farmer Cooperative Memberships in the United States, 1930 to 1995**

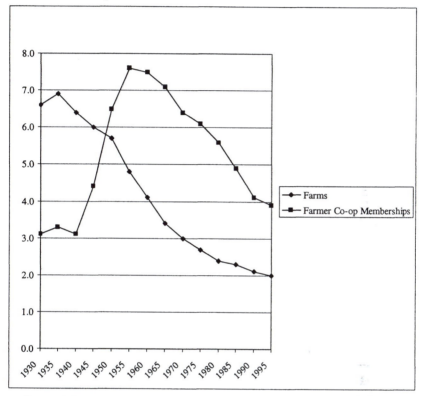

Source: USDA (1998), 17.

credit unions are a form of cooperative savings and loan enterprise, where depositors are also partial owners. In 2001, there were 9,984 federally in-sured credit unions in the United States, representing 79.4 million members, holding assets worth $501.6 billion (NCUA 2001, 7). In short, almost one-third of the American population belonged to a cooperative enterprise.

Consumer food co-ops have a much smaller presence in the United States than farmer co-ops or credit unions, but even here, the numbers are impres-sive. The National Cooperative Grocers Association (NCGA 2002) serves 80 cooperative grocery stores with 200,000 members across 26 states. These stores generate more than $400 million in annual sales.

Consumer food co-ops have a much larger market presence in many West-ern European countries. Co-ops represent 25 percent of the consumer food market in Norway and 30 percent in Denmark (United Nations 1996). In Switzerland, co-ops constitute 50 percent of the consumer food market (United

Table 1.1

Cooperative Share of U.S. Farm Marketings, 1999

Commodity group	Percentage of U.S. cash receipts
Milk	89
Grains and oilseeds	34
Cotton and cottonseed	29
Fruits and vegetables	18
Livestock and wool	13
All other (including poultry and eggs, dry edible beans and peas, nuts, rice, tobacco, sugarcane, sugar beets, honey, and other commodities)	12
Total (all farm commodities weighted by value)	27

Source: Kraenzle (2001, 7).

Nations 1996). The broader point is that at the beginning of the twenty-first century, co-ops are, in many ways, more relevant than ever.

Overview of the Book

This volume has at least two intended audiences: (1) researchers and (2) policymakers. First, it targets researchers interested in the debates about cooperative theory and applications. Existing reviews focus on narrowly defined topics such as agriculture (e.g., Cobia 1989; Leistritz 1997; Royer 1994), a specific geographic region such as Europe (e.g., Schilthuis and Van Bekkum 2000), a special type of co-op such as New Generation or worker (e.g., Fairbairn 1989; Fulton, Popp, and Gray 1998; Merrett and Walzer 2001; Schaffner 1995; Torgerson 1970), or reference manuals and reviews designed for community developers or the general public (Nadeau and Thompson 1996; NCFC 1999). In contrast, this volume focuses on a broad range of cooperatives.

Second, this volume provides information to help political and economic leaders make informed public policy decisions by educating them about the role that co-ops might play in promoting economic and community development. The aim is to recognize the important research that has been completed in the past, while embracing the fact that in a globalizing economy, business forms can be expected to emerge, including new cooperative forms and new applications of existing cooperative models.

A discussion of the theoretical underpinnings of cooperative behavior will be augmented by case studies of cooperative ventures. In order to accomplish these goals, the book is divided into five broad sections: (1) Understanding

Cooperative Theory, (2) Public Policy Issues, (3) Management Issues, (4) Cooperatives in Economic Development, and (5) Cooperatives in Community Development.

Understanding Cooperative Theory

In order to provide a context for the book, the first section includes three chapters that discuss the history and underlying theory of cooperative behavior. In chapter 2, Brett Fairbairn argues that co-ops have had an important and long-standing role in the economic development of both the United States and Canada. He begins by tracing the origins of the cooperative movement to the eighteenth-century Age of Enlightenment. With its appeal to reason and individualism, this social and intellectual ferment gave birth to two social organizations: the voluntary association and the business enterprise. The co-op represents an amalgam of these two entities.

During the next two centuries, the cooperative model evolved to cope with changing socioeconomic conditions. Fairbairn documents the role of co-ops in colonial North America and in nineteenth-century agriculture. He further explores the legislation that expanded the role of co-ops during the twentieth century before plunging into a discussion of credit unions and consumer co-ops. The chapter concludes by revisiting the theme of economic change. Economic hardship during the depression prompted many working-class individuals to join co-ops. The economic crisis of the 1970s and the social movements unleashed during this period sparked social change within co-ops as well.

In chapter 3, Kim Zeuli builds on the historical perspective by presenting an overview of cooperative theory. She begins by arguing that co-ops come in myriad forms. This fact makes it difficult to simply define a co-op, yet a good starting point might be to consider the principles first established by the Rochdale cooperative in nineteenth-century England. With this set of benchmark principles in mind, Zeuli describes how the cooperative model, as well as theory to explain cooperative behavior, has evolved due to changes in the economy and society.

Zeuli's key contribution is to provide a "property rights" analysis of cooperative change. A co-op is a firm with resources owned by many members. The shared ownership raises a series of "property rights" questions pertaining to who controls resources owned by the co-op, who makes decisions, and how net profits and equity are managed. Previous research on property rights within cooperative firms (co-ops) has focused on how a "property rights" perspective can explain why co-ops fail. Zeuli turns this approach around to ask why, from a "property rights" perspective, do owners of capital embrace the cooperative model in the first place? She then goes on to investigate how internal and external pressures have prompted changes to the cooperative enterprise, comparing how the different cooperative models (e.g., Rochdale, traditional, or New Generation) address property rights issues.

In the final chapter of this section, chapter 4, Lee Egerstrom focuses on the internal and external obstacles that co-ops must simultaneously manage if they are going to succeed. Co-ops have a more complex internal structure than traditional IOFs. Egerstrom focuses on so-called agency problems—the often conflicting goals among cooperative members, as well as the tensions that sometimes exist between co-op members and managers. He then draws on the work of Michael Porter and others to describe a set of external challenges such as access to market information and the political culture of a region in which the co-op operates. Egerstrom concludes that if co-ops are going to manage these internal and external threats, they must adopt new organizational forms such as New Generation Cooperatives (NGCs), joint ventures, and partnerships, along with a range of other cooperative business forms.

Public Policy Issues

The second section contains two chapters that focus on the legal and tax policy environment in which co-ops must operate. In chapter 5, Mark Hanson outlines the development of cooperative law in the United States. He traces the roots of American cooperative law to the principles underpinning the Rochdale cooperative and the Grange. Hanson then argues that in order to understand the legal status of co-ops, federal and state statutes must be considered. At first, important federal legislation, including the Capper–Volstead Act of 1922 and the Agricultural Marketing Act of 1929, protected co-ops from anti-trust lawsuits. As the American economy changed during the twentieth century, state cooperative law evolved to provide producers more flexibility to participate in cooperative enterprises. These new legal forms include NGCs, limited liability companies (LLCs), Iowa Chapter 501 Statute firms, and firms organized under the Wyoming Processing Cooperative Law. Despite recent changes to state cooperative law, Hanson argues that more legal changes are needed to help co-ops compete effectively with IOFs.

In chapter 6, Jeff Royer argues that there is an important connection between cooperative legal issues, finance, and taxation policy. Specifically, the legal structure adopted by a specific cooperative enterprise determines in large part how start-up capital can be raised and how the co-op and its members will shoulder their tax burden. Consequently, Royer provides a primer on the models used to resolve problems of cooperative finance and taxation. Specific topics addressed include equity acquisition, liquidity and retirement, models used to measure the implication of changing tax policy, and fiscal challenges embedded in nontraditional co-ops such as NGCs and LLCs.

Management Issues

The two chapters that make up the third section investigate in greater detail some of the agency problems elucidated in previous chapters. In chapter 7, Joan Fulton asks why individuals agree to cooperate? More importantly, why do individual co-op members engage in disloyal behavior by patronizing other firms? When co-op members do business outside their co-op, they are acting as "free riders" by taking advantage of the benefits of the co-op while benefiting from better prices offered by competing firms.

In a related development, there has been a spate of corporate mergers among agribusiness giants such as Cargill and Continental Grain. As these IOFs merge, co-ops must restructure in order to compete. The dilemma co-op members must resolve is how to expand their scale. Do co-ops merge with other co-ops to preserve their cooperative structure, or do they enter into strategic alliances with noncooperative business entities? In these two scenarios, the issue is whether individuals or co-ops should, in fact, cooperate or if they should act individually.

Fulton uses a game theory approach to investigate the external conditions and internal decisions that prompt individuals and firms to either cooperate or act alone. This discussion provides an overview of alternative forms of game theory, including the Prisoners' Dilemma, the Assurance Problem, and the Chicken Game, to show how we can simulate individual and corporate responses to various restructuring scenarios.

In chapter 8, Peter Goldsmith incorporates elements of game theory plus a model of why co-ops fail to explain why there has been a recent increase in the number of value-adding producer co-ops. Goldsmith begins by explaining that co-ops have played an important role in the past by serving as a pricing benchmark for producers and consumers. He further argues that in a changing global economy, traditional co-ops are inherently inefficient. An econometric model is used to show where these inefficiencies lie. In essence, Goldsmith quantifies the agency problems that develop. To wit, by using game theory, he shows how the objective functions of co-op members diverge over time. This phenomenon hinders coalition maintenance within an open-membership co-op where the exit of unhappy members is a plausible threat. Cooperative management has few strategies to retain dissatisfied members.

Goldsmith then offers the closed-membership co-op as a possible alternative. His unique contribution, however, is to theorize how co-ops can remain viable during uncertain economic times by incorporating ideas from relationship management theory. Goldsmith argues that in order to succeed, co-ops must identify their core competencies, including those assets that make them uniquely competitive in specific markets. Assets certainly include the fixed capital investments, but they also include the "tacit knowledge" and soft knowledge of co-op members and employees that enable the co-op to offer inimitable goods and services.

Special attention must be paid to relationships along the value chain. A producer co-op must nurture relationships with suppliers as well as with consumers to gain continuous feedback. As Goldsmith argues, the product exchange must also be a knowledge exchange so that trust-based relationships evolve along the supply chain. In order to flesh out these concepts, Goldsmith describes a successful New Zealand producer co-op that supplies high-quality meat to upscale restaurants in San Francisco. He concludes that co-ops may reap better returns by investing in "soft knowledge" rather than hard assets because of the greater flexibility it affords them in turbulent economic times.

Cooperatives in Economic Development

The previous sections have presented abstract concepts associated with the formation and management of co-ops; however, co-ops are often touted for their ability to unite communities while promoting economic growth, particularly in disadvantaged areas (Merrett and Walzer 2001; Trechtor and King 2002). Consequently, the fourth section of the book includes three chapters that focus specifically on the applications of cooperative theory in the real world of economic development.

In chapter 9, David Schaffner discusses the role played by commodity marketing co-ops. He begins by arguing that marketing co-ops, while representing a large market share, have experienced recent declines in that share. These declines have occurred because of the increasingly global reach of IOF commodity marketing firms such as Cargill, ConAgra, and Archer Daniels Midland.

Schaffer further argues that co-ops have not increased their transnational reach to the same extent as IOFs for several reasons. First, open-membership co-ops have more interest in providing a market for co-op members than in paying attention to consumer demands. This limits their ability to develop long-term marketing strategies.

Second, property rights conflicts limit the ability of a co-op to deploy assets overseas, again limiting the global reach that co-ops might have. Finally, agency problems emerge in open-membership co-ops, making it difficult to unify co-op membership behind a single, long-term strategy. In order to address these and other problems, Schaffner explores closed membership co-ops such as Dakota Growers Pasta; branded product marketing co-ops such as Citrus World; and bargaining co-ops such as CherrCo, a "super cooperative" that bargains on behalf of cherry producers in several U.S. states and Canadian provinces.

In chapter 10, Randall Torgerson examines the role played by producer co-ops in the United States. He argues that farmers are prompted to form or join co-ops because of market inequalities. Individual farmers lack power to bargain against more powerful suppliers and processors. The issue of economic inequality prompts Torgerson to address a more weighty idea, namely, that co-ops and other forms of collective action serve an important institutional role in sustaining democracy. Co-ops allow disenfranchised individuals to wield market or political power as a group that they could not brandish as individuals. By linking collective action to political power, Torgerson is then able to investigate the public policy implications of cooperative behavior.

The chapter achieves this goal by first providing a taxonomy of collective action by farmers, including professional associations (e.g., Illinois Corn Growers or Kansas Association of Wheat Growers), which represent farmer interests in the political arena, and marketing co-ops that integrate vertically and/or horizontally along a commodity chain or into other commodity sectors, which represent farmer interests in the marketplace. Torgerson then explains how co-ops and the practice of "pooling" provide a public good by enhancing competition, serving as a check against monopolistic pricing, maintaining quality standards, and potentially reducing the dependence that farmers might have on government price supports.

The final section of the chapter explores how the cooperative model has evolved to become more competitive, while retaining some of its democratic attributes. Torgerson compares aspects of the traditional, open-membership marketing co-op versus the NGC model. He acknowledges the economic and employment benefits an NGC can bring to a region, but cautions that many new cooperative models are "works in progress." Care must be taken to ensure that producer co-ops continue to serve the needs of farmers in a changing global marketplace.

Torgerson further implies that co-ops benefit more than the co-op members and employees. Communities that host the co-op also receive economic impacts. This might be especially true in the case of processing co-ops that require investment in a local processing facility, the hiring of local workers, and the potential for increased farm income to be spent within the local community.

In chapter 11, Larry Leistritz discusses how to measure the potential that a producer co-op might have to reinvigorate economically struggling rural regions. He does so by discussing the underlying theory and applications of economic impact analysis. The chapter introduces readers to fundamental concepts, including economic base theory, the measurement of multiplier effects, and input–output analysis. The idea is that when a firm begins operations in a community, it generates an initial economic impact or direct effect due to initial construction costs, purchase of local utilities, and wages paid to workers. The firm also generates so-called indirect effects as it purchases inputs from other firms in the community.

Finally, the induced effects can be measured as workers throughout the community spend more money due to the increased income generated. Leistritz takes this general input–output model to measure the economic impact of NGCs such as Dakota Growers Pasta and North American Bison Cooperative. He concludes that NGCs can make a substantial economic impact on a community, but warns that estimating the economic impact must be done carefully. When measuring the indirect impacts, one must understand whether inputs are purchased locally or from afar. The answer will determine the size of the indirect and induced effects in the community. Despite this caveat, economic impact analysis is an important tool because it can help communities decide whether infrastructural improvements, capital investments, or other policy changes enacted to build an NGC are worth the effort.

Cooperatives in Community Development

Thus far, this volume has emphasized agricultural marketing and producer co-ops. While they are enormously important, it is imperative to address other cooperative forms because of their vital role in providing goods and services to consumers. This section elaborates on consumer and worker co-ops, paying special attention to their role in promoting economic goals as well as community development. The implication is that co-ops exist and even thrive for both monetary and nonmonetary reasons.

In chapter 12, Ann Hoyt explores the origins and development of consumer co-ops, beginning with the economic justification for such co-ops. Reasons include the failure of markets to provide goods or services, to counter the effects of oligopolies, and to provide a measure of consumer protection, among other justifications. Hoyt also argues that there are nonmonetary reasons why people create and join consumer co-ops, such as for a political rationale. Consumers may want to maintain control over an essential local enterprise. They may be concerned about environmental issues and may prefer to conduct business with a firm that shares their values about sustainable use of resources.

Hoyt's most significant contribution is to argue that social objectives can be obtained through co-ops. Specifically, she shows that consumer co-ops can help a community develop social capital. Writers such as Pierre Bourdieu (1999) and Robert Putnam (2000) argue that communities within industrial democracies have experienced the erosion of social networks, interpersonal trust, and attachment to place. These losses have contributed to declining voter turnout, diminishing rates of volunteerism, and reduced civic engagement in community affairs.

Hoyt claims that co-ops are by definition a network of social relations with a sense of purpose and identity. Consequently, co-ops can strengthen the social capital within a community by increasing the social interaction and trust. The broader implication is that Hoyt, like Torgerson, agrees that marketing and consumer co-ops both have the potential to bolster democratic behavior in capitalist societies.

Finally, chapter 13 also investigates the link between democracy and co-operative behavior. In this instance, Greg MacLeod concentrates on the nexus of social capital, democracy, and worker co-ops. Advocates of laissez-faire capitalism argue that free markets promote democratic politics while generating economic benefits for all. MacLeod argues to the contrary that unfettered market capitalism leads to the concentration of capital. This necessarily causes greater social and regional inequality, to say nothing of environmental degradation and the erosion of social capital in communities where workers have lost their jobs due to firm relocation or restructuring.

Capitalist enterprises do not have to operate in such a callous manner, however. MacLeod shows that co-ops such as the Mondragon firms in the Basque region of Spain, the cooperative networks in the Emilia-Romagna region of northern Italy, or the community-owned enterprises in the Canadian province of Quebec represent successful examples of worker-owned firms.

Arguments have been made that co-ops cannot compete with IOFs (Elster 1989; Kibbe 1998; Shrader 2002). MacLeod responds that worker co-ops have a lower business failure rate than traditional business startups, and that co-ops such as the Mondragon, with 100,000 employee-owners, effectively compete with the largest IOFs in Western Europe. These firms succeed because they pay attention to the interrelationships between worker-owners, the firm, and the communities in which they operate. The more important point is that these co-ops succeed without laying workers off or threatening relocation to wrest concessions out of workers or communities during economic recessions.

Looking Toward the Future

At the outset, this chapter claimed that, despite some internal problems, co-ops continue to evolve and succeed while competing in a global capitalist economy. The stated purpose of the book is to revisit the established theory of cooperative behavior while suggesting new theories to explain the new cooperative models that have evolved over the past two centuries. Case studies are offered to better illustrate how innovative co-ops and communities have employed new forms of collective action to succeed in the global economy of the twenty-first century. These are rather modest objectives.

There is also a more ambitious, yet implicit subtext to this volume, however. Hopefully, the reader will be able to identify at least three broad themes that run through the 13 chapters. First, critics abound who argue that co-ops are increasingly irrelevant as a business model or as a vehicle for promoting economic or community development (Elster 1989). By the end of the volume, the hope is that you will be convinced otherwise. The authors argue, using many examples, that co-ops are vital for monetary and non-monetary reasons.

Second, this book has an optimistic message. The message is that in an era of capital concentration and corporate malfeasance, grassroots community responses can make a major contribution to providing a better living environment. Whether the authors are discussing the Rochdale consumer co-ops of nineteenth-century England, the farm marketing co-ops of the early twentieth century, the Mondragon worker co-ops that emerged in the middle of the twentieth century, or NGCs coming on line at the beginning of the twenty-first century, it is clear that farmers, workers, consumers, and communities are working together to achieve economic and social goals that they could not achieve as individual actors. The problem for grassroots organizations is that they often lack the technical resources to respond effectively. Hopefully, the theory and case studies offered in this book can redress this deficiency.

The third and final theme is that co-ops have an important role to play in sustaining democracy. Several chapters claim that co-ops play an important role in ensuring that markets operate fairly and that marginalized producers, workers, and consumers can effectively participate in the marketplace. Furthermore, co-ops and other forms of collective action can effectively generate political change, as exemplified in the evolution of laws related to co-ops. As we move further into the twenty-first century, the authors conclude that co-ops will continue to support the principles of economic and political fairness within industrial capitalism.

References

Blooming Prairie. 2002. *Current News: Proposal Results*. Press release, September 28. Available at www.bpco-op.com/news (October 28, 2002).

Booth, Douglas. 1987. *Regional Long Waves, Uneven Growth, and the Cooperative Alternative*. Westport, CT: Praeger.

Bourdieu, Pierre. 1999. "Site Effects." In *The Weight of the World: Social Suffering in Contemporary Society*, ed. Pierre Bourdieu, 123–129. Stanford, CA: Stanford University Press.

Cheney, George. 1999. *Values at Work: Employee Participation Meets Market Pressure at Mondragon*. Ithaca, NY: Cornell University Press.

Cobia, David, ed. 1989. *Cooperatives in Agriculture*. Englewood Cliffs, NJ: Prentice-Hall.

Cohen, Isaac. 1995. "The NAFTA's Winners and Losers: A Focus on Investment." In *NAFTA as a Model of Development: The Benefits and Costs of Merging High- and Low-Wage Areas*, ed. Richard Belous and Jonathan Lemco, 37–40. Albany: State University of New York Press.

Cook, Michael. 1995. "The Future of U.S. Agricultural Cooperatives: A Neo-institutional Approach." *American Journal of Agricultural Economics* 77 (December): 1153–1159.

Cooke, Philip, and Kevin Morgan. 1994. "Growth Regions Under Duress: Renewal Strategies in Baden Württemburg and Emilia-Romagna." In *Globalization, Institutions, and Regional Development in Europe*, ed. Ash Amin and Nigel Thrift, 91–117. New York: Oxford University Press.

Elster, Jon. 1989. "From Here to There; or, if Cooperative Ownership Is So Desirable, Why Are There So Few Cooperatives?" *Social Philosophy and Policy* 6, no. 2: 93–111.

Fairbairn, Brett. 1989. *Building a Dream: The Co-operative Retailing System in Western Canada, 1928–1988*. Saskatoon, Saskatchewan: Western Producer Prairie Books.

Fitch, Robert. 1996. "In Bologna, Small Is Beautiful: The Cooperative Economics of Italy's Emilia-Romagna Holds a Lesson for the U.S." *The Nation*, May 13, 18–21.

Fulton, Joan, Michael Popp, and Carolyn Gray. 1998. "Evolving Business Arrangements in Local Grain Marketing Cooperatives." *Review of Agricultural Economics* 20, no. 1: 54–68.

Fulton, Murray. 2001. "Traditional Versus New Generation Cooperatives." In *A Cooperative Approach to Local Economic Development*, ed. Christopher D. Merrett and Norman Walzer, 11–24. Westport, CT: Quorum Books.

Goodman, David, and Michael Watts, eds. 1997. *Globalising Food: Agrarian Questions and Global Restructuring*. New York: Routledge.

Harvey, David. 1989. "From Managerialism to Entrepreneurialism: The Transformation in Urban Governance in Late Capitalism." *Geografiska Annaler* 71B, no. 1: 3–17.

Heffernan, William, Robert Gronski, and Mary Hendrickson. 1999. *Report to the National Farmers Union: Consolidation in the Food and Agricultural System*. Washington, DC: National Farmers Union. Available at www.nfu.org/images/heffernan_1999.pdf. (November 25, 2002).

Hufbauer, Gary, and Jeffrey Schott. 1992. *North American Free Trade: Issues and Recommendations*. Washington, DC: Institute for International Economics.

Kibbe, Theron. 1998. "Value-added Contract Cooperatives: Investor and Non-investor Differences." *American Cooperation* 8, no. 3: 193–197.

Kraenzle, Charles. 2001. "Co-op's Share of Farm Market, Major Cash Expenditures Down in '99." *Rural Cooperatives Magazine* 61, no. 1: 7–9.

Leistritz, F. Larry. 1997. "Assessing Local Socioeconomic Impacts of Rural Manufacturing Facilities: The Case of a Proposed Agricultural Processing Plant." *Journal of the Community Development Society* 28: 43–64.

McLaughlin, Paul. 1996. "Resource Mobilization and Density Dependence in Cooperative Purchasing Associations in Saskatchewan, Canada." *Rural Sociology* 61, no. 2: 326–348.

McMichael, Philip. 1996. "Globalization: Myths and Realities." *Rural Sociology* 61, no. 1: 25–55.

Melnyk, George. 1985. *The Search for Community: From Utopia to a Co-operative Society*. Montreal: Black Rose Books.

Merrett, Christopher D., and Norman Walzer, eds. 2001. *A Cooperative Approach to Local Economic Development*. Westport, CT: Quorum Books.

Nadeau, E.G., and David Thompson. 1996. *Cooperation Works*. Rochester, MN: Lone Oak Press.

National Cooperative Grocers Association (NCGA). 2002. "About US: Basic Facts." Available at www.nationalgrocers.com/about_facts.html (November 25, 2002).

National Council of Farmer Cooperatives (NCFC). 1999. *American cooperation online*. Washington, DC: NCFC. Available at www.ncfc.org/resources/index.htm (November 25, 2002).

National Credit Union Administration (NCUA). 2001. *Year-end Statistics for Federally Insured Credit Unions*. Alexandria, VA: NCUA. Available at www.ncua.gov/ref/statistics/statistics.html (November 25, 2002).

North Farm Cooperative. 2002. *Bankruptcy Notification to Membership* (August 2). Available at www.northfarm.com (October 28, 2002).

Putnam, Robert. 2000. *Bowling Alone: The Collapse and Revival of American Community*. New York: Simon and Schuster.

Royer, Jeffrey S. 1994. "Economic Nature of the Cooperative Association: A Retrospective Appraisal." *Journal of Agricultural Cooperation* 9: 86–94.

Schaffner, David. 1995. *Agricultural Marketing Cooperatives: An Annotated Bibliography*. Davis: Center for Cooperatives, University of California at Davis.

Schilthuis, Gijs, and Onno-Frank Van Bekkum. 2000. *Agricultural Cooperatives in Central Europe*. Assen, The Netherlands: Van Gorcum.

Schumpeter, Joseph. 1950. *Capitalism, Socialism and Democracy*. New York: Harper and Row.

Sexton, Richard. 1986. "Cooperatives and the Forces Shaping Agricultural Marketing." *American Journal of Agricultural Economics* 68: 1167–1172.

Shrader, Robynn. 2002. "Blooming Prairie Proposal Offers Opportunity to Strengthen Our Retailer Network." *Cooperative Grocer Online* 102 (September–October). Available at www.cooperativegrocer.com/cg2002/bloomingprairieprop.shtml (November 25, 2002).

Shuman, Michael. 2000. *Going Local: Creating Self-Reliant Communities in a Global Age*. New York: Routledge.

Torgerson, Randall E. 1970. *Producer Power at the Bargain Table*. Columbia: University of Missouri Press.

Trechtor, David, and Robert King, eds. 2002. *The Impact of New Generation Cooperatives on Their Communities* (RBS Research Report 177). Washington, DC: U.S. Department of Agriculture (USDA).

United Nations. 1996. *Status and Role of Cooperatives in the Light of New Economic and Social Trends*. Report of the Secretary General. Available at www.un.org/documents/ga/docs/51/plenary/a51-267.htm (November 25, 2002).

U.S. Department of Agriculture (USDA). 1997. *Cooperatives in International Trade* (Cooperative Information Report 1, Section 27). Washington, DC: USDA.

———. 1998. *Cooperative Historical Statistics* (Cooperative Information Report 1, Section 26). Washington, DC: USDA.

Wilkinson, Paul, and Jack Quarter. 1996. *Building a Community-controlled Economy: The Evangaline Co-operative Experience*. Toronto: University of Toronto Press.

Williams, Chris, and Christopher D. Merrett. 2001. "Putting Cooperative Theory into Practice: The 21st Century Alliance." In *A Cooperative Approach to Local Economic Development*, ed. Christopher D. Merrett and Norman Walzer, 147–166. Westport, CT: Quorum Books.

Williams, Melissa. 2002. "Wal-Mart Battle Moves to Asheville City Council." *Asheville* (NC) *Citizen-Times*, June 23. Available at http://cgi.citizen-times.com/cgi-bin/story/news/15251 (November 25, 2002).

Wrigley, Neil. 2001. "The Consolidation Wave in U.S. Food Retailing: A European Perspective." *Agribusiness* 17, no. 4: 489–513.

PART I

UNDERSTANDING COOPERATIVE THEORY

$$2$$

History of Cooperatives

Brett Fairbairn

Cooperatives and Economic Transformations in the United States and Canada, c. 1800–Present

Cooperatives emerged as part of a sweeping socioeconomic transformation, changing the lives of countless people in North America throughout the past two centuries. They are neither the causes of basic transformations in society nor an oppositional reaction to such changes; rather, they are attempts by people to steer and guide, to influence developments, and to shape their own futures within a changing world.

This chapter will give a broad, introductory overview of the nature of co-ops, the phases and sectors of their development, and the connections to their times and societies. Two related points are that co-ops are now, and have always been, part of economic transformations. Economic stress and change—industrialization in 1880 or globalization in 2001—are reasons for the existence of co-ops. Also, co-ops (like all organizations) do not stand on their own but are reflections of and reactions to broad social processes. Members and leaders cannot understand co-ops unless they understand the wider economy and society of which co-ops are one part.

Cooperatives and Modernism

"Modernism" (or modernization) is a hotly contested term. Not enough perspective on the European/North American world between the late eighteenth and twentieth centuries exists to agree on what made up the essential characteristics of the world we have known. It seems provisionally clear, however, that the modern era was characterized by rational pragmatism, secularism, growing urbanism, the power of nation-states, the economization of many aspects of society, and other related mentalities and behaviors. In simple terms, the modern era was increasingly dominated by the twin institutions of the state (i.e., government) and the market—the unconstrained, spreading, "free" market. Modernism involved the remaking of society to meet the requirements of the state and of the market (Polanyi 1944). These processes had immense impacts on the lives of ordinary people, and it is in these impacts that we see the origins of co-ops.

Co-ops were typically formed by those experiencing difficulty dealing with an aspect of economic change. Their creation came about partly because they offered practical advantages. Behind this practical activity, however, there was often a broader vision. Cooperatives were a way to contest the meaning of modernity—farmers protesting urban-centered policies, regions or classes resisting economic domination by others, idealists fighting secular values, or citizens revitalizing their communities in the face of adverse forces. These kinds of efforts can take many forms, including interest and pressure groups, political parties, philanthropic and cultural organizations, and social and educational movements of many kinds. Where citizens' concerns were primarily economic in nature, a co-op was a logical response. Co-ops can even be seen as an *inevitable* type of response, given the problems people faced and the tools available.

In the wake of the eighteenth-century European Enlightenment—the age of reason and the critique of absolutism, one of whose expressions was the American Revolution—there were two new forms of participation available to free citizens in a free society. There was, on the one hand, the voluntary association: a democratic combination of citizens for a common aim, often one with public or community implications. The association was a main mechanism by which people could participate in the public sphere of society.

An alternative was the business enterprise form, also voluntary, as a means for people to participate in a free economy. The combination of these two forms, the association and the enterprise, created the co-op as a kind of hybrid. In retrospect, it seems inevitable that this combination would emerge, and, indeed, co-ops were independently invented by many groups.

The International Co-operative Alliance (ICA) defines a co-op as "an autonomous association of persons united voluntarily to meet their common economic, social, and cultural needs and aspirations through a jointly-owned and democratically-controlled enterprise" (MacPherson 1996, 1). The association–enterprise duality of co-ops is embedded in this definition and in more than a century of European and international cooperative thought. Co-ops are both associations and business enterprises. They must be understood in both lights, and they must succeed in both dimensions to thrive.

Other definitions of co-ops are generally compatible with the ICA definition and use similar language. The National Cooperative Business Association (NCBA), the apex organization for U.S. co-ops (2001), defines a co-op as a business "owned and democratically controlled by its members." The Canadian Co-operative Association (CCA 2001) begins its description of co-ops by stating that they are "business organizations owned by the members who use their services."

A widely quoted definition used by the U.S. Department of Agriculture (USDA) identifies a co-op as an organization characterized by member ownership, member control, and member benefit. What all of these definitions have in common is that they stress the business focus of co-ops, combined with a democratic ownership/control linkage to a group of users and/or employees.

It is important to understand the cooperative concept behind these definitions because it is not always easy to decide, in practice, whether any given organization is a co-op or not. The question is not a legalistic, black-and-white one, but rather a matter of strategy, purpose, control structures, and connections to defined communities of people. There are many shades of gray, or better, a whole rainbow of colors.

The diversity of co-ops relates to the fact that they have emerged in many different regions, classes, communities, economic sectors, and time periods, with a wide variety of different approaches and ways of thinking despite some similarities in structure. In North America, the most prominent types of co-ops include agricultural co-ops, credit unions, and consumer cooperative stores (three types highly developed by the mid-twentieth century) as well as other types such as housing, health, worker, and various other service co-ops that have, for the most part, developed more recently. This chapter will survey the historical development of these different sectors of cooperative activity.

Co-ops, like other innovations, tend to follow a normal pattern of expansion and diffusion. Typically, within each sector and each region where co-ops develop, there is a long initial phase of buildup and experimentation. To contemporaries, it may not appear that there is progress since short-term fluctuations and failures of particular models and organizations loom large.

At some point, however, successful movements enter into a take-off phase of geometric expansion. The number of organizations multiplies; organizations spread to new areas; and the membership increases vastly in a few decades. During such a take-off phase, leaders are confident and optimistic, often to the point of predicting the transformation of the whole of society; however, all movements eventually enter a stabilization phase, in which they have saturated the niches they can easily fill in the economy and society. A period of consolidation of organizations sets in; co-ops, having spread widely, now sink deeper organizational roots and become more tightly knit (Fairbairn 1995–1996).

It is important to remember that all these phases are normal. Co-ops have not failed when they enter a stabilization phase—quite the opposite. They are consolidating because of the extent of their success, and this is not the end of the story. New cycles of expansion or contraction may follow, and, frequently, cooperative movements are regenerated by the introduction of new kinds of co-ops alongside the old.

Stages and periods are also an important framework of analysis. Each type of co-op and each region may follow its own independent timeline of experimentation, expansion, and consolidation, and these might not be synchronized with each other; however, broad social and economic trends and interconnections between different cooperative movements might mean that at least some cooperative movements are at similar stages in similar time periods. In terms of large-scale economic trends as they have affected various co-ops in the United States and Canada, several general phases of development and evolution exist:

- the period of eastern colonization and early industrial development before about 1860;
- the opening, settlement, and closing of the West, from the 1860s to the turn of the century (a decade or two later in Canada) and, connected with this, the maturing of new industrial economies from the 1880s to the 1920s;
- the rise of new forms of corporate organization and control from the 1920s to the 1950s;
- the consolidation of organizations and the impact of urbanization and consumerism from the 1950s to the 1970s;
- the decline of the industrial model of organization beginning in the 1970s; the rise of the service economy, information technology, and the new economy; the beginnings of postindustrialism or postmodernism.

Within each of these broad periods, co-ops both reflected the contemporary assumptions, concerns, and models, and also constituted conscious and unconscious reactions against selected, undesirable aspects of the contemporary economy.

Cooperatives and the Colonization of North America

Co-ops did not exist in North America prior to the arrival from Europe of the market and the state as forms of social organization. Native Americans and early colonists traded, but most of them traded only incidentally within an economy largely oriented toward individual or group subsistence. It was only during the nineteenth century that market relations spread more pervasively, and the unregulated or self-regulated market became a central form of social organization, one that destabilized and remade almost every other institution in society. Milestones in the development of the modern state included the independence of the thirteen colonies and the creation of the United States of America, which opened a wave of westward expansionism. Equally striking is the decade of the 1860s, which saw new western settlement policies, the first transcontinental railroad, land-grant universities, the Civil War, Reconstruction, and the beginnings of industrial take-off. North of the U.S. border, milestones included the confederation of Canada in 1867 and the beginnings of its own political and industrial development as well as westward expansion.

Co-ops emerged as part of colonialism in North America—they emerged as European institutions and as tools for Europeans to establish themselves as settlers in a world that was new to them. Co-ops did not exist (until much later) for the benefit of the aboriginal population (which was immensely reduced by disease, devastated, and swept aside), but, rather, for the colonists. More specifically, co-ops were a response to tensions and problems in the colonial economy that became more apparent as it underwent industrialization. Ordinary settlers and working people found that the economic system did not serve their needs; not infrequently, they saw themselves opposed by businesses, monopolies, and political elites. From the perspective of colonialism, co-ops were the tools of the "small colonizers" to resist their own exploitation by the economic and political elites of the new society (Memmi 1991, 10). The idea of the co-op was both imported by the colonists from Europe and also independently developed and adapted by settlers of European origin under North American conditions.

The first co-ops in both Canada and the United States were near replicas of European models, often started by immigrants with experience in European cooperative movements. Initially, these immigrants and their ideas of cooperation came mainly from Britain, home of the world's first and leading cooperative movement.

The Philadelphia Contributionship of 1752, organized with the participation of Benjamin Franklin, was one of the earliest mutual fire-insurance associations; it was based directly on a London association of 1696 (Knapp 1969, 8). As in Europe, mutuals were related precursors of co-ops but were not the same as co-ops. Farmers' mutual fire-insurance companies spread widely in rural areas in the nineteenth century.

Reforming factory owner Robert Owen came from Britain to found a co-op community at New Harmony, Indiana, in 1825. The Owenite Movement also inspired a series of labor-exchange stores in the 1820s (Knapp 1969, 18). Followers of French socialist Charles Fourier founded cooperative "phalanxes" in the 1840s; among the best-known cooperative colonies of that era was Brook Farm near Boston (Spann 1989).

As in Britain, there was a general sequence of development from mutuals to cooperative communities and Owenite associations to consumer cooperative stores based on or resembling the famous Rochdale, England, cooperative of 1844. Also as in Britain, the first formal co-ops in Canada and the United States were consumer co-ops formed by urban workers. The Workingmen's Protective Union stores, of which the first was established in Boston in 1845, grew into a regional movement with 403 local divisions by 1852 and sales exceeding $1 million per year. Due to schism and mismanagement, however, these collapsed a few years later (Knapp 1969, 23).

The last large-scale effort at urban, working-class co-ops was seen in the workshops and stores of the Knights of Labor in the 1880s; however, working-class stores continued to emerge in scattered mining communities until the twentieth century. Of these, the largest was the British Canadian Cooperative in Sydney Mines, Nova Scotia, created in 1906. For decades, it was the largest consumer co-op in North America (MacPherson 1979, 22).

Specific European ethnic groups played important roles at various stages in the development of cooperation in the Americas. The British were important, especially in Canada, where some key local, provincial, and national leaders came with direct personal experience of a mature cooperative movement in their home country. George Keen, long-time general secretary of the Co-operative Union of Canada, was exemplary of the British connection (MacPherson 1979, 26). Such co-proponents actively promoted Rochdale-style cooperative ideas, including strong local stores, cooperative education, and the creation of federated centrals. Scandinavians were also prominent, especially in the Upper Midwest. Swedes, Danes, and Norwegians led many local cooperative efforts from the 1860s on. In this case, they were not importing cooperative models from their home countries, where cooperation was as yet weakly developed; rather, they were picking up North American and Rochdale models of cooperation, which appear to have found special resonance in their cultures and communities (Keillor 2000, 297).

The Finns, who came later into New England and the Great Lakes region, may have had knowledge of co-ops in their home country and were certainly inspired to cooperative action by the political ideals they carried from Europe (Turner 1968, 51). The fact that many Europeans migrated to North America to escape oppression contributed to their enthusiasm for cooperative projects to build a better society in their new homeland.

At the same time, ethnic exclusion—the dominance of older immigrants and their defensive reaction against new arrivals—also helped push some of the new immigrants to form their own co-ops. This was perhaps especially true of the Eastern Europeans who came in the early twentieth century—for example, the Ukrainian miners in northern Ontario who formed co-ops based on the triple identity of their ethnicity, their occupation, and their socialist politics. Co-ops often played a role in uniting different ethnic groups in their new communities (indeed, they were often the only institutions to do so), but it was also true that specific ethnic groups dominated the leadership in certain regions.

Although European models and European immigrant cultures remained influential, it was in agriculture that co-ops began to take root in new and distinctive North American forms. They did so in connection with powerful social and political movements that sought to reform some inequities of the nineteenth-century economy.

Adaptation in Nineteenth-Century Agriculture

Agriculture was the foundation of the nineteenth-century North American economy; thus, it could not help but be strongly affected by general economic change. It employed the great bulk of the population, so that changes in agriculture had widespread and powerful social effects. The pace of change in agriculture accelerated in the 1860s as railroads and steamships connected world commodity markets more closely. Grain from America, Canada, Argentina, and Australia began to flood into European markets, and world prices began to fall.

At the same time, new technologies, new crop varieties, and new industries arose. From about the 1880s, the dairy industry became an important sector for farmers who were displaced from grain markets or who sought higher returns. A ceaseless process of shifting pressures and opportunities, competition, new technology, diversification, and integration had begun. North American farmers, especially in the West, were both market-oriented and exposed to fluctuations and monopolistic abuses. From these circumstances arose the distinctive strength of North American agricultural cooperation.

The Grange (or to use the official name, the Patrons of Husbandry) constituted the first large-scale farm organization in North America. It was started in 1869 by Oliver H. Kelley and other government employees in Washington, DC, to promote self-help and improvement for farmers. The Grange organization was founded on the example of secret societies such as the Masons. Local clubs or societies sprang up in rural communities, spreading to the midwestern plains in the 1870s. The hard times after the crash of 1873 gave a boost to the movement; by 1875, there were 858,000 members and state organizations in thirty-two states (Shannon 1957, 55). All told, there were some 25,000 local Grange organizations created during the 1870s (Wieting 1952, 7).

Local Granges sponsored farmer-owned stores based on the Rochdale model, and in various locales they set up grain elevator, central wholesale (Iowa, Illinois), bank (California), fire-insurance, meat packing, or flour milling co-ops. These co-ops were strongest in Iowa, though many encountered economic difficulties during the downturns of the 1870s; they were weakest in the South.

Among early forms of co-ops, those in the dairy sector were widespread and long-lasting. Handling and transporting milk to urban markets (and as co-ops expanded and new technology was introduced, processing the milk as well) were tasks that went beyond the capabilities of small farmers since the perishability of the product and the poor infrastructure created special challenges. Also, many farmers entered the dairy industry as the frontier moved westward, closing new lands for grain and cattle. The developing dairy industry offered new opportunities but also required more sophisticated technology (centrifugal separators became common in the 1880s), knowledge, and market connections. Dairy co-ops facilitated the adaptation of farms and the development of a new industry. It is not surprising that such co-ops were among the earliest in many regions, including the Canadian Prairies (better known for wheat and cattle), and that dairying has remained a strong sector of agricultural cooperation.

Self-help among farmers was frequently connected with political activity. Farmers' political parties emerged with names like Reform, Independent, or Anti-Monopoly; often such parties were organized by Grange members and held their meetings in Grange halls. Farmer candidates strove for legislation and regulation to control railroads and other monopolies but often ended up back in the mainstream Republican and Democratic parties (Shannon 1957).

Both cooperative and political action reached a new height in the 1880s. On the cooperative side, the Farmers' Alliance movement sprang out of farmer protests against the crop-lien system in the South. The movement began with the organization of the Knights of Reliance, soon renamed The Farmers' Alliance, in Texas in 1877. The Farmers' Alliance engaged traveling lecturers and organizers who crossed the countryside to mobilize farmers into suballiances and co-ops. The Farmers' Alliance's cotton "bulking" plans (cooperative marketing) culminated in the opening of the Texas Exchange in 1887. In the same year, the Farmers' Alliance organized on a national basis and spread more systematically into other states, beginning most notably with Illinois, the Dakotas, and Minnesota (1887–1889), followed by the key breakthrough into Kansas.

The Dakotas' success came in connection with a club movement started in 1884 as a protest against rail and elevator monopolies; from this movement, about thirty-five cooperative warehouses and a statewide cooperative farmers' exchange came into existence. Radicalization of this movement in the face of opposition from merchants led to a close partnership with the Farmers' Alliance movement in 1888. The Dakotas and the Farmers' Alliance together launched a cooperative crop-insurance plan, the Alliance Hail Association, which turned into a multistate venture.

Following the other successes, the Farmers' Alliance organizing drive in Kansas saw more than 75,000 farmers join during a nine-month period in 1889–1890. Local, county, and state co-ops were created in marketing and warehousing and soon in many other activities as well. A cooperative livestock marketing plan spread from Kansas to Missouri, Nebraska, and the Dakotas, with 125,000 members involved by 1890. Meanwhile, on the political side, Farmers' Alliance–affiliated candidates scored huge successes in the 1890 Kansas state elections, capturing 96 seats of 125 in the legislature. Such efforts were reflected nationally in the development of the national People's Party, which contested federal elections in 1892–1896 as one of the most successful third-party movements in American history (Goodwyn 1978).

This early history of the cooperative movement is worth considering in some detail because of four characteristics that remained basic to the farm cooperative movement for many decades. First, from an early date, the driving force behind farmer cooperation was the struggle against monopolies and, more generally, for a better balance between the interests of farmers and agriculture on one hand and business on the other.

Second, these movements were strongly regional in nature; they were centered in specific states and groups of states at various times. These regional concentrations reflected to some degree the regional development of the continental economy; most importantly, it was farmers in the relatively newly settled midwestern region who protested their place in the emerging industrial order.

Third, political and cooperative actions were intertwined at every stage; farmers' interest organizations, political parties, and co-ops developed in synergy with one another. Finally, in the distinction between the Grange in the 1870s and the Farmers' Alliance in the 1880s, we can see a duality that has long remained a part of farm politics and farm co-ops.

The Grange was more of a nonpolitical, less radical organization, started in fact by public servants. It sponsored relatively small-scale or limited co-ops of fairly conventional types. The Farmers' Alliance stood for a more ambitious approach and was more sweeping in its aspirations to direct national and international marketing, more risky, more controversial, and more political. These two different approaches have coexisted ever since in North American farm movements, expressed in competing structures like the later Farm Bureau and Farmers' Union organizations in the United States or the Grain Growers and Farmers' Union organizations in Canada and their respective styles of co-ops.

Prior to World War I, farmer co-ops were enmeshed in a broad, agrarian reform movement that included important political and cultural dimensions. The contributions of this reform movement to both American and Canadian society and politics have certainly been underestimated, in part due to the urban bias of historians (Sanders 1999, 2). Its co-ops, however, were not long-lived and were for the most part only indirect ancestors of today's organizations. The movement was an experimental era, a period of local action and tremendous variety and innovation, which can be said of many small and transitory but instructive successes. More lasting forms of agricultural cooperation emerged in the interwar era and were associated with greater attention to corporate structure, scale and power, efficiency, and management. In many cases, the support of farm organizations and government agencies was pivotal to this success.

Cooperatives, Agriculture, and the State in the Twentieth Century

The twentieth century brought the further development of modern management and corporate ownership of big business as well as democratic politics and the modern state. This was a more organized kind of capitalism, and in response co-ops became more organized and more systematic.

A new period of farmer organization began in the early twentieth century with the creation of a variety of new institutions. The Farmers' Union movement began in 1902 with the creation in Texas of what was first known as the Farmers' Educational and Cooperative Union of America. Like the earlier Farmers' Alliance, farmers' unions actively promoted co-ops and spread through the South, the Midwest, and into the West and Northwest.

Also important was the Society of Equity, created in Indiana in 1902 by farm magazine editor J.A. Everitt, who had a vision of farmers organized as a "third power" alongside capital and labor. The Wisconsin chapter of the Society of Equity became aligned with the progressive movement of Robert M. La Follette. Wisconsin's broad cooperative movement helped enact a new cooperative law in 1911 that became a model for other states.

Finally, the farm bureau movement emerged during this same period. The first farm bureau was created by New York state agents in 1911, and farm bureaus were created in many other states in the years that followed. They remained linked to the New York state and to the concepts of technical and managerial improvement in agriculture (Knapp 1969, 176ff).

The role of state extension agents in cooperative development signaled the start of a new stage in agricultural cooperation with growing government activity in the decades that followed. A significant step was the appointment in 1908 of a Country Life Commission by President Theodore Roosevelt. He later said that he had been inspired by the work of Irish cooperative leader and rural-development advocate Horace Plunkett (Knapp 1969, 111).

The Country Life Commission reflected a growing concern among public leaders and intellectuals that rural society was suffering under the impact of industrialization and urbanization and that voluntary action by rural people was needed to revitalize their communities. In subsequent years, government became increasingly active in building an extension service to support rural modernization. The Smith–Lever Act of 1914 was an important step in formalizing a framework for extension as a partnership among state and federal governments as well as universities.

In the 1920s, farmers made important gains in organizing cooperative control of agricultural marketing with the aid of a supportive federal government. A sign of growing approval of co-ops was the passage of the Clayton Act in 1914 exempting nonprofit marketing co-ops from federal antitrust laws. This was followed by the more extensive immunity for co-ops embodied in the Capper–Volstead Act of 1922. In effect, Capper–Volstead recognized the cooperation of farmers to control the marketing of their products as a form of economic combination more worthy than others.

The significance of the Capper–Volstead Act is a subject of some disagreement. On one hand, its practical legal importance for most co-ops was small; however, symbolically, it was huge because it recognized and sanctioned a new, large-scale, corporate form of agricultural cooperation (Woeste 1998, 233). Similar thinking went into the Cooperative Marketing Act of 1926, which for the first time formally pledged the USDA to promote cooperation. The USDA retains this active educational and developmental mandate to the present day, primarily exercised through the Rural Business Cooperative Services agency.

Even though governments supported cooperation, farmers still had to organize the co-ops. It was the collapse of commodity prices after World War I that motivated farmers to take marketing into their own hands, and they did so through a range of marketing co-ops created during the 1920s. Many of these followed the popular "pooling" model, based on the original 1895 experience of the Southern California Fruit Exchange and popularized during the 1920s by California lawyer Aaron Sapiro. The idea of pooling was to create large, centralized co-ops to control markets and prices of key commodities. By 1925, pools had been created for wheat, cotton, tobacco, and other products. Efforts to obtain more supportive legislation for larger and more comprehensive pools continued, and by 1928, so-called "Uniform Marketing Laws" had passed in forty-six states (Wieting 1952, 9). The pooling movement was cut short by the depression, however, and the collapse of world commodity markets and prices, and it was never revived to its original ambitious proportions.

Further development and change was brought to American agricultural co-ops during the depression. The Franklin Roosevelt administration established the Farm Credit System (FCS) in 1933 to expand and formalize earlier programs for cooperative credit. The FCS funneled capital through central banks for co-ops to local Production Credit Associations (later organized as co-ops) to meet production-related credit needs.

Also, in 1935, as part of the New Deal, the government offered low-interest credit for rural electrification. Private for-profit companies and municipal utilities benefited from the program as did new rural electric co-ops. A new sector of utility co-ops emerged with ongoing support provided through the USDA, which by 2001 served over 1 million Americans.

Meanwhile, in Canada, both similar and different kinds of co-ops had emerged. In the 1890s and 1900s, farmers from coast to coast began to be involved in producers' movements and co-ops. Many early organizations, like the Grange in Ontario or the Society of Equity in Alberta, spread from south of the border (often assisted by immigrants from the United States to Canada) or were copied by Canadian farmers from American examples. Grain growers' organizations sprang up in the West (the first being the Territorial Grain Growers' Association founded in 1901 at Indian Head in what was later Saskatchewan), and by the time of World War I, there were strong United Farmers' organizations in most of the anglophone provinces.

In three provinces, United Farmers' organizations ran political candidates and captured government alone or as part of coalitions (Ontario Farmer–Labour government, 1919; Alberta United Farmers government, 1921; Manitoba Progressives, 1922), while in a fourth province, Saskatchewan, the farm organization worked in partnership with the Liberal party and elected from its ranks several cabinet ministers and one premier in Liberal governments (Wood 1975). As in the United States, these regional movements supported a short-lived federal party—in this case, the Progressives of the 1920s. Later forms of rural populism, left and right, included the Cooperative Commonwealth Federation (CCF), which governed in Saskatchewan 1944–1964, and the Social Credit Party, which governed in Alberta from 1935 through 1970. Like their predecessors, these movements were connected to co-ops.

The first large-scale, formal agricultural co-op in Canada was the Grain Growers' Grain Company of 1906 (later United Grain Growers [UGG]), a grain-marketing co-op that, after some difficulty with the merchants, obtained a seat to trade grain on the Winnipeg Commodity Exchange. Grain Growers' and United Farmers' organizations created local buying clubs and marketing co-ops and eventually central co-ops to serve them such as United Farmers Co-operative of Ontario (later UCO), which was purchased by U.S.-based Growmark in 1994 to form one of the first cross-border cooperative systems, and United Farmers of Alberta Cooperative (UFA), which still exists as a farm supply organization.

Next came cooperative grain handling through farmer-owned elevator systems. While Manitoba bowed to farmer pressure and created a system of government-owned grain elevators in 1909, in Saskatchewan (1911) and Alberta (1913), governments deflected calls for state ownership by creating cooperative elevator companies.

Despite the success in creating these large co-ops, farmers remained dissatisfied with what they saw as the conservative and unambitious leadership. Their spirit was captured better by the pooling movement of the 1920s, which sought not only to trade grain in Winnipeg and handle it in country elevators, but also to create an integrated national/international marketing system under centralized farmer control.

Wheat pools were created in Alberta (1923) and Manitoba and Saskatchewan (1924). Immediately, the pools set up a central selling agency to coordinate their overseas sale of grain (G. Fairbairn 1984). Also in the mid-1920s, pools were established for other commodities, such as milk and wool. Such voluntary pools were not, however, the first choice of farmers. Their experience with the federal government's compulsory Canadian Wheat Board during World War I led them to favor government-run pooling. After many trials and tribulations during the depression, and considerable political maneuvering, they got what they wanted by the 1940s when a monopoly for western Canadian grains, the Canadian Wheat Board, was reestablished. After the 1930s, the "wheat pools" remained as co-ops for handling board grain, purchasing farm inputs, and marketing nonboard crops and livestock; however, they no longer existed in their original role.

Different but roughly parallel developments occurred in Quebec, where the first agricultural co-op was created in 1903 with the assistance of Catholic clergyman J.A.B. Allaire, inspired by the Catholic farmers' co-ops of Belgium. By World War I, there were about 100 local co-ops and three centrals. Local dairy co-ops began to emerge and laid the foundation for a strong sector of cooperation.

The agricultural co-ops were built up and centralized by intervention of the provincial government in the 1920s, which amalgamated the three centrals to form Coopérative Fédérée du Québec in 1922, a central farm supply and agricultural marketing co-op. The government's heavy-handed control was contested by the 1924 farmers' union, the Union Catholique des Cultivateurs. Farmers regained control, and the movement expanded in the 1930s and 1940s.

By the mid-twentieth century, strong agricultural co-ops existed in most regions of the United States and Canada, created through a combination of farmer political activism, economic mobilization, and government involvement or support.

Financial Cooperatives, 1900–1950

Financial cooperation came comparatively late in North America. While scattered cooperative banks had been created, especially by working-class people in New England cities, the widespread development of cooperative savings and credit in North America occurred only in the twentieth century. The popular need for credit was linked to economic change as producers sought capital to modernize farming, fishing, or other business activities. Consumers needed to manage their finances and to handle unforeseen expenditures in an emerging consumer society.

Credit unions began with the deliberate study and adaptation of European models by a clerk of the Canadian House of Commons, Alphonse Desjardins. In listening to parliamentary debates in the 1890s, Desjardins became concerned about the problems of usury and lack of access to credit for ordinary people. Desjardins read everything he could find, corresponded with European cooperative leaders, and, in 1900, introduced a new cooperative model called the *caisse populaire* (meaning "people's bank").

The first example was created in Desjardins's hometown of Lévis, Quebec (across the river from Quebec City), and like many *caisses* created in the years that followed, it was set up with the active help of the Catholic clergy. Desjardins's model consisted of a small, parish-based savings-and-loan, taking shares and deposits from local people and lending the funds for primarily productive purposes—to improve the businesses or farms of local members.

By strengthening local economies, Desjardins and his followers hoped to preserve and reinforce the closely knit identity of French Catholic communities, especially in small towns and rural areas (Rudin 1990). Desjardins's credit unions multiplied rapidly and began to knit together into federated and central organizations following his death in 1920 and especially during the difficult years of the depression.

Against a backdrop of local and regional autonomy, the powerful central institutions of the Desjardins movement—central banking, insurance, investment, and more—emerged gradually, and after the 1960s, they became prominent enterprises in the Quebec economy. By the 1990s, more than two-thirds of the Quebec people were members of *caisses populaires*, which had become the dominant retail banking institutions and leading commercial lenders for small and medium enterprises.

Meanwhile, Desjardins's original idea had spread far and wide and had been adapted into new forms. Desjardins had been invited to speak in New Hampshire and Massachusetts in 1908. One of his hosts was Pierre Jay, state commissioner of banks for Massachusetts, who wrote to approximately 150 major employers urging them to create credit co-ops for their employees. Jay was also able to cite the successful example of the Globe Savings and Loan in Boston (Moody and Fite 1984, 23).

Workplace credit unions offered numerous advantages to both employers and employees. They helped employees avoid financial problems, reduced pressures on employers for salary advances, and were seen as a fringe benefit for employees. This approach differed from Desjardins's model in that it was secular rather than parish-based and in that it focused on wage employees, whose needs were more for consumer credit rather than productive loans; however, Desjardins's advice and symbolic support was still important. Jay invited Desjardins to help draft a credit union act for Massachusetts (1909), one of the first on the continent.

The widespread development of credit unions across the United States came in the 1920s because of a partnership between a Boston merchant with inherited wealth and social-reform ideals, Edward A. Filene, and a talented organizer, Roy Bergengren. From 1921 to 1934, Filene supported credit unions with huge amounts of his own time and with nearly $1 million of his own money (Sekerak and Danforth 1980, 14). The centerpiece was a Credit Union Extension Bureau, financed with Filene's money from 1921 through 1934 and directed by Bergengren.

The bureau's purpose was to promote the credit union model, to obtain appropriate legislation in different states, and to encourage the formation of state and national credit union leagues. It was hugely successful in these objectives. By 1930, there were more than 1,000 credit unions; legislation was passed in almost all states and federally by the Roosevelt administration in 1934; also in 1934, credit unions were strong enough to start their own federation, the Credit Union National Association (CUNA), which was based in Madison, Wisconsin.

Credit unions on the Filene/Bergengren model were to be institutions organized tightly around a "common bond" among members—membership in another co-op, in a church, in a labor union, or as employees of the same firm. At least three-quarters of the credit unions were based on workplace affinity. Credit unions continued to multiply; by 1940, there were more than 9,000 with almost 3 million members. By the late twentieth century, more than 20,000 credit unions had over 80 million members (NCBA 2001).

Just as the credit union idea changed when taken across the border from Quebec to New England, it changed again as it was imported back from the United States into anglophone parts of Canada. In Nova Scotia, the Antigonish Movement, which developed in the 1920s–1930s, centered on the Extension Department of St. Francis Xavier University. Catholic priests Jimmy Tompkins and Moses Coady organized fishermen to form unions and processing plants and started a broad adult education movement (MacPherson 1979; Welton 2001).

The Antigonish Movement's approach to adult education centered on study circles in which participants discussed problems facing their communities and developed plans of action. Frequently, these plans involved creating a credit union, an agricultural or fishing co-op, or a cooperative store. The study-circle method combined with Coady's rhetoric and leadership turned the movement into an effective mechanism for widespread cooperative development (Alexander 1997; MacPherson 1979, 100ff.; Welton 2001). The credit unions, in particular, were an innovation in anglophone Canada. As defined by the Antigonish Movement, they were community institutions mobilizing local savings for investment in local development. Bergengren helped draft a new Nova Scotian credit-union law, passed in 1932, setting an example for the rest of anglophone Canada. By 1938, there were enough credit unions in existence to form their own provincial league, which affiliated with CUNA.

Credit unions also spread into other parts of anglophone Canada in the 1930s, usually following efforts by cooperative leaders and sympathetic government officials to establish appropriate legislation. Credit unions were a project undertaken by existing co-ops and other institutions, often initiated, organized, and housed by sponsor organizations. Most often, they explained their purpose in terms of consumer lending (helping ordinary people deal with extraordinary purchases, medical expenses, and so on) rather than production lending.

In Ontario, something more like the American model prevailed, with a mix of workplace and community credit unions emerging. In the West, the first credit unions were often urban employees' credit unions, but by the late 1930s, credit unions were developing in rural communities. These rural credit unions gave the movement a new twist because they were based on open community membership and an orientation toward the farm community; over time, they became important agricultural lenders. Leagues affiliated with CUNA were created in the early 1940s for purposes of educational and political representation, as were central banks (cooperative credit societies) based on federated structures of credit unions. While credit unions emerged later than other major kinds of co-op, by mid-century they were well organized and rapidly growing.

Consumer Cooperatives, 1900–1950

The term "consumer cooperative" can be applied widely to all co-ops that organize people in their capacity as consumers rather than as producers. This category includes credit unions (consumption of financial services), housing co-ops, medical co-ops, and many others.

The term can also be used in a narrow sense to mean co-ops formed to purchase goods, typically in the form of cooperative retail stores. To begin with, it is appropriate to use the second, narrower sense since it is the basic model of nineteenth- and early twentieth-century cooperation. It involves one further ambiguity, however. Many early cooperative stores were started by farmers who wanted to use them both for purchase of household necessities like food and for purchase of farm inputs like seed, feed, twine, and building materials (and sometimes also for marketing farm products). A "producer" mentality permeated many early consumer co-ops, making it difficult to draw a clear line between the two kinds of cooperation.

As noted, the first consumer co-ops came from farm and labor organizations as offshoots of these wider movements. By the end of the nineteenth century, cooperative stores were widely known thanks to the Grange, the Knights of Labor, and so on, though they were not necessarily well understood.

In the United States, urban groups, employers, and employees began to establish more lasting foundations for consumer cooperation. As in other countries, industrialists founded consumer co-ops for their workers. A successful example is the progressive St. Louis manufacturer N.O. Nelson in 1892 (Sekerak and Danforth 1980, 37–38). In other places, entrepreneurs, individual trade unions, and labor leaders sponsored co-op (frequently, pseudo co-op) schemes, with mixed success.

Other impulses came from a variety of sources, often specific immigrant groups. One of the most successful regional consumer movements was created by Finnish cooperators in the Great Lakes region, who built one of the strongest cooperative wholesalers in the United States by the 1930s–1940s. The co-op's "Red Star" coffee, with a hammer and sickle on the package, is an indication of the politics of the time (Sekerak and Danforth 1980, 45). Elsewhere, other immigrant groups were involved. For example, in New York City, Americans of Russian and Jewish ancestry played a key role in starting local co-ops and laying a basis for later cooperative federations.

The period before World War I was one of wide experimentation and diversity of consumer cooperation in many kinds of communities. Between World War I and the Great Depression of the 1930s, the movement acquired ideological and organizational focus. A series of visionary leaders conceived of consumer cooperation as a general answer to numerous social ills. Their vision, though it drew on the experiences of working-class and farm movements, was not strongly tied to class or to social milieu but was instead a general doctrine of consumer sovereignty and democracy through co-ops. Without a doubt, the most important advocate was James Peter Warbasse, a driving force in the 1916 creation of the Cooperative League of the United States. Warbasse's sweeping rhetoric fed the presses of growing cooperative movements across the continent until the 1940s (Donohue 1999, 121ff.).

The social protest of the 1930s also fed the movement, as people disillusioned with the prevailing economic system and desperate for economic relief turned to consumer co-ops as an answer. Social-reformist theology, notably the Social Gospel movement, added to intellectual justification of the movement. A prominent role was played by Japanese cooperator and Christian cleric Kagawa Toyohiko, who visited the United States in the mid-1930s to spread his teachings of "Brotherhood Economics" (Schildgen 1988). By the end of the 1930s, the Cooperative League had swelled to 2,175 member co-ops, representing over 1 million Americans. Besides conventional consumer co-ops, the movement expanded into housing, health care, credit, rural electricity, and many other fields (Sekerak and Danforth 1980, 63).

In Canada, as in the United States, consumer cooperative stores were an early form of cooperation that emerged in connection with trade unions in eastern manufacturing cities, in mining communities, and in rural towns connected with agrarian movements. More often than in the United States, there was a direct connection to British ideals and examples; the famous British Canadian cooperative in Nova Scotia even traded directly with the Cooperative Wholesale Society of the mother country (MacPherson 1979, 129).

Keen's Co-operative Union of Canada (predecessor of the Canadian Cooperative Association) was created in 1909 to promote Rochdale's ideas of consumer cooperation. Possibly because of the influence of particular cooperative leaders familiar with the British movement, consumer co-ops in the West strove at a comparatively early stage of their development to break away from the producers' movement to create their own wholesale co-ops.

Cooperative wholesale companies emerged in the three Prairie provinces in the late 1920s, but not without conflicts with the producers' organizations. Though they defined themselves as consumer organizations, they still served mainly farmers, with farm supply as a major line of business. Indeed, the mechanization of farming and rising input costs were a major impetus for the development of consumer cooperative systems. In 1935, Saskatchewan farmers created a consumer-owned cooperative oil refinery (Fairbairn 1989). Similarly, in the East, agricultural and consumer cooperation were combined. Canadian Livestock Co-operatives (Maritimes) became Maritime Co-operative Services in 1945 (ancestor of present-day Co-op Atlantic), combining livestock marketing with farm supply and general cooperative wholesaling (MacPherson 1979, 200).

The economic crisis after World War I and during the 1930s had given a major impetus to consumer cooperation. Cooperative stores now existed widely and were at least loosely united in leagues or wholesales. Consumers were learning new roles in an advanced modern economy; the cooperative movement held out the prospect that one role was to reshape the economy by wielding collective power in the marketplace. Other types of consumer co-ops—using the broader definition—also emerged in the 1920s and the depression years, but took off only in the postwar era.

Consolidation, Professionalization, and New Waves: Cooperative Systems from the 1950s

The postwar era saw two kinds of developments. First, among the older and by now reasonably well-established co-ops, this was an era of consolidation. Co-ops amalgamated, merged, and grew larger and fewer in number as they tried to match economic trends and better-integrated competitors. They created larger and more powerful central co-ops and began to become better integrated as regional and sectoral systems. Together with these changes, they cultivated better modern management, marketing, and services. Characteristic of the period were new publications and leaders stressing the importance of management and new associations and networks of cooperative managers (Voorhis 1961, 161). This was a defensive adjustment, a narrowing in on business success, but it was, at the same time, a rapid period of growth and a confident and optimistic assertion of cooperative power and ambition. In these ways, co-ops mirrored changes in the wider society. Second—also mirroring wider social changes—there were new waves of cooperative development, dealing with new issues.

By the mid-twentieth century, the widest extent of agricultural cooperation had been established in both the United States and Canada, and key institutions were in place that dominated the sector until the end of the century. The institutions were at first larger in scale and more stable in Canada, where strong, centralized provincial/regional co-ops like UGG, UCO, UFA, and the Wheat Pools existed already by the 1920s and remained fixtures of the agricultural scene into the 1990s and beyond.

While the ideas were similar, the United States had a much wider variety of local co-ops and federated systems. These entered into a prolonged process of amalgamation, merger, and consolidation, creating a network of large regional companies by the late twentieth century. By the end of the century, the largest of these resulting co-ops—the four largest co-ops of any type in the United States—were Farmland Industries (headquarters in Kansas City, Missouri; revenues $10 billion), Dairy Farmers of America (Kansas City, Missouri; $7.6 billion), Cenex Harvest States (St. Paul, Minnesota; $6.3 billion), and Land O'Lakes Inc. (St. Paul, Minnesota; $5.3 billion) (National Cooperative Bank 2001).

Financial co-ops also consolidated. In the United States, with the merger of the St. Paul Bank for Cooperatives in 1999, CoBank of Denver became the dominant institution for agricultural cooperative financing and for the Farm Credit System. For financing the consumer cooperative sector, Congress created a National Cooperative Bank in 1978, which privatized in 1981. Individual credit unions grew, the largest ones including employee credit unions such as for the armed forces; community credit unions also grew geographically larger to the extent that they could under American law.

Federal legislation in 1998 facilitated the consolidation process. In Canada, there was consolidation within but not between provinces. Credit union leagues merged with provincial credit societies (central banks) to form Credit Union Centrals in the 1970s that united the representative/educational and commercial functions; these focused increasingly on better management and improved integration (MacPherson 1995). The various centrals are loosely connected in a Credit Union Central of Canada.

Other financial co-ops in Canada were created within the credit unions and the wider cooperative movement. The Desjardins system in Quebec developed powerful central insurance companies and, in the 1960s, an investment arm. The integration of the Desjardins system was carried further in 2000 with the abolition of regional federations to create a two-tier federated structure. Elsewhere in Canada, cooperative and credit-union leaders launched a series of ventures and subsidiaries. Insurance companies created in the 1940s grew (now the Co-operators Insurance Group), while in the 1950s a trust company (Co-op Trust) was created, as well as funds and corporations for guaranteeing credit-union deposits. Canada does not have cooperative banks as the United States and other countries do.

Among consumer co-ops, the postwar era was marked by the local and regional successes of prominent, individual consumer co-ops, the largest being the famous Berkeley, California, Co-op; the Greenbelt Co-op outside Washington, DC; and UNICOOP in Puerto Rico. Many new co-ops entered the field in the 1970s, associated with ecological and organic-foods movements, especially in urban areas of the northwestern United States from Minneapolis across to Seattle.

The enduring weakness of American consumer co-ops, however, has been the failure to form strong central wholesalers. Perhaps this contributed to cooperative failures in the 1980s and 1990s, notably of the flagship Berkeley and Greenbelt co-ops. In contrast to traditional, locally controlled consumer co-ops, a new model of co-op, REI Co-op of Seattle, which sells outdoor sporting equipment and clothing, emerged in the 1920s and has grown since the war into an immense enterprise with more than 2 million members. This centralized co-op draws direct membership from across the United States, defining its members not by geography but by common interest in outdoor recreation and environmental values.

Mountain Equipment Co-op, with over 1 million members, is the Canadian counterpart to REI. In addition, western Canada has strong conventional consumer co-ops. These include, notably, the Calgary Co-op, which has over 300,000 members and is the largest of its type on the continent, and Federated Co-operatives Limited (FCL), a successful central wholesaler and manufacturer serving both urban and rural consumer markets. FCL is the result of a long process of mergers among the provincial cooperative wholesalers in the West as well as the Saskatchewan cooperative refinery that took place from the 1940s to the 1970s (Fairbairn 1989). In the East, Co-op Atlantic has developed as a similar, integrated central wholesaler for a regional consumer cooperative movement.

The postwar era was also the period in which housing co-ops, which had started earlier, finally blossomed. In 1920, there had been three housing co-ops in the United States. Co-ops run by Finnish and Jewish immigrants in New York City were prominent in the early years (Birchall 1997, 195). In the years that followed, more co-ops emerged, still mainly in New York City where labor unions and especially organizer Abraham Kazan launched a variety of projects. One of the largest was the East River Housing Cooperative of 1955.

The real spread of the movement began with the introduction of reduced-interest government loans for co-ops serving low-income groups (through 1961 and 1968 legislation). Cooperative housing foundations also played a key role. By 1980, there were some 2,000 co-ops housing 530,000 families, and by the 1990s, more than 1 million units of cooperative housing existed in the United States (NCBA 2001; Sekerak and Danforth 1980, 66–67).

In Canada, both the timing and the connection to public policy initiatives were roughly similar. The first housing co-ops emerged in the Atlantic provinces and in Quebec during the interwar period but mainly in the form of house-building co-ops in rural communities. Continuing housing co-ops emerged for students beginning in the 1930s, but the first continuing family housing was not developed until 1966 with the Willow Park Housing Cooperative in Winnipeg, Manitoba. Beginning in 1969, lobbying by cooperative, labor, and student organizations persuaded the federal government to fund a cooperative housing program, which helped create a national movement of thousands of housing co-ops with about a quarter of a million members throughout the 1970s and 1980s (Co-operative Housing Federation of Canada 2001).

Health co-ops also began in the interwar era and spread after World War II. Female garment workers established a health center in New York City in 1919, and other unions joined or organized health centers in the years that followed. Dr. Michael Shadid, a Lebanese immigrant, organized a farmers' cooperative hospital in Elk City, Oklahoma, in 1929, starting a new wave of development.

The Cooperative League of the United States began to promote health co-ops in 1937, and new group health associations and mutuals were organized in many cities beginning in that year. Some direct-service, group-practice health-care plans in the United States (Health Maintenance Organizations [HMOs]) are organized as co-ops, serving in total 1.4 million Americans (NCBA 2001; Sekerak and Danforth 1980, 60ff.).

In Canada, some health centers also emerged from labor unions, notably the Group Health Centre in Sault Ste. Marie, Ontario; however, the main development was in Saskatchewan, where health activists and members of the cooperative movement organized a number of consumer-run health co-ops (community clinics) in the 1960s. Because Canada has mandatory public health insurance for all citizens, there are no HMOs.

Worker co-ops (companies owned and democratically controlled by their employees) are less common in both the United States and Canada than in some other countries. In the United States, about 10,000 employee stock-ownership plans developed since the 1970s (with tax benefits from the government) to cover almost 10 percent of the workforce. Employees own a majority of the shares in only about 1,500 cases; and in only a handful do the employees have the full, democratic control associated with the cooperative model. One estimate is that there are approximately 500 worker co-ops in the United States, scattered across many regions and industrial sectors (ICA Group 2001).

In Canada, worker co-ops also emerged mainly since the 1970s; they were widely scattered for the most part with systematic development mainly in Quebec where development programs by the provincial government have encouraged them, especially in the forestry, transportation, and service sectors. One estimate is that several hundred worker co-ops exist in Canada, probably 60 percent of them in Quebec. A national federation was formed in 1991.

As cooperative systems consolidated and became more formalized, and as new co-ops emerged, the fields of cooperative education and development became more formal. Co-ops stressed competence of directors, management, and staff, and built systematic training programs for these groups.

At the same time, they struggled to find better ways to educate members and the wider public. This reflected a growing perception on the part of cooperative leaders that education was still urgently needed, perhaps more so than ever given the new complexity of co-ops. Also, old methods such as extension agents, field workers, community meetings, summer institutes, camps and picnics, and newspapers were no longer as effective as they once were.

Gradually, new agencies, new centers, and new associations emerged. The Association of Cooperative Educators, a binational organization, was created in the 1950s to promote and professionalize cooperative education. Other formal associations and training institutes emerged in many sectors and regions. In the late 1950s, Canadian cooperators started a Cooperative College of Canada in Saskatoon to offer courses and certificates by correspondence as well as by residential programs.

University research centers emerged in numerous locations, beginning initially with international education centers at St. Francis Xavier University in Nova Scotia (Coady Institute, 1959); the University of Wisconsin (1962); and the Université de Sherbrooke, Quebec (1976). The University of Wisconsin's Center for Cooperatives broadened into a full-blown domestic and international research and training center. Other university centers followed, including those at the University of Saskatchewan (1984), the Université de Montréal (1987), University of California at Davis (1987), North Dakota State University (1994), and the University of Victoria (2000).

A variety of development agencies also started from federations and foundations (as in the case of cooperative housing) to regional consulting services and regional cooperative development councils. These often reflected partnerships among co-ops, frequently with public support or funding. In the United States, a network of Cooperative Development Centers developed as government-sector partnerships in the 1990s. Successful government relations work by NCBA led to federal funding for such development centers starting in 1993. Partners and sponsors for such centers include university institutes, specialized cooperative development agencies, business-development and training centers, farm organizations, and cooperative federations. A group of eight such centers formed a Cooperation Works network in 1999.

In Canada, the most effective development partnerships emerged in Quebec, mainly in connection with a network of regional development co-ops formed by existing co-ops through which the provincial government funneled funds in the 1990s for development of new co-ops.

From the 1950s onward, cooperative sectors developed stronger, more consolidated, and more formal organizations as a way to meet the needs and adapt to the world around them. A growing awareness of change and of the need to approach it with professional competence was characteristic of the postwar era. Even as co-ops adapted, however, the world was changing around them.

Postindustrialism and Postmodernism, 1970s to the Present

Beginning in about the 1970s, the world's industrial economies began to undergo an important transformation. The watershed was marked by several international economic events: the first oil crisis, the collapse of international monetary arrangements in favor of a less regulated system of currencies, and the economic crisis of high inflation combined with high unemployment. These changes were followed by the recession of the early 1980s. Old industries that had been the mainstays of economies for a century were downsizing, closing, or mechanizing in new ways, with tens of thousands thrown out of work at a time. There were trade wars, with new rounds of free trade, protectionism, and bloc-building. Commodities faced falling prices on world markets. Growth was in the services sector; part-time work, multiple employments, and career changes became more frequent. With these trends came the information revolution embodied in the widespread introduction of personal computer systems and the emergence of the Internet. The information economy that has emerged during this new era has been characterized as one of globalization, turbulence, and unpredictability.

These changes affected North American co-ops in a variety of immediate as well as indirect ways. In inflationary periods like the 1970s, the challenge was to manage expansion and limit debt; recessions such as what took place in the 1980s called for cost cutting and efficiency. In both environments, innovations and new forms of service were required, from automated banking machines to cardlock fuel depots.

Some co-ops failed in one period or the other; some merged; and some came through economically stronger than they had been. Even though co-ops had in some cases become quite large organizations, they also had to respond more nimbly to changing conditions. New competitors appeared, as mergers, acquisitions, and economic restructuring built up bigger and better integrated groups of companies in many sectors in which co-ops were active, notably food and agriculture, but also banking. In the 1990s, many large co-ops faced the challenge of how to deal with these new or larger competitors. Importantly, a new model of the private firm has emerged. Instead of a single monolithic corporation, many firms have reinvented themselves as networks of holdings, joint ventures, subsidiaries, contracts, and outsourced services. By doing this, they have expanded their vertical reach within marketing channels while at the same time retaining flexibility. Co-ops that evolved in many cases to deal with big centralized monopolies now find themselves facing a different form of corporate power concentration.

There were also important indirect effects. The new, postindustrial society affected the members of co-ops and the communities in which they live. Changing issues, attitudes, and priorities led to less commitment by members to old kinds of co-ops; co-ops perceived this as a decline in member loyalty and an increase in individualism.

Many formerly easy assumptions were put in question, including occupational, racial, ethnic, religious, and gender identities that had previously formed a basis for cooperative action. Gender provides a good example: before about the 1970s, it was unremarkable to have co-ops in which women made crucial member-level decisions but where men filled all leadership roles. Since at least the 1970s, co-ops in which this is the case appear to be increasingly anachronistic, disconnected from social realities, and no longer innovative or progressive (Neal 1998; *Proceedings from the Women in Cooperatives Forum* 1998).

Social and economic changes in communities led to new economic challenges for established co-ops—for example, continued mergers in declining or depopulated rural areas—and also to the emergence of new co-ops. Since the 1970s, many of the new or expanding kinds of co-ops have been those dealing with values, lifestyles, or services rather than with basic material goods. Much of the growth in housing co-ops, worker co-ops, community-development organizations, women's co-ops, aboriginal co-ops, co-ops associated with ecological ideas or health, and others has occurred within the new postindustrial framework.

Agriculture provides a good case study of the transitions among co-ops. Centralized, multipurpose co-ops such as those that had been built up by amalgamation in the 1950s–1970s encountered increasing difficulties, largely because of lack of focus, transparency, and connection with members. Though many co-ops encountered difficulties, Canadian grain co-ops were especially hard-pressed, with UGG converting to private ownership by the 1990s, Saskatchewan Wheat Pool adopting a unique capital structure of nonmember ownership in 1995, and Alberta and Manitoba wheat pools amalgamating with each other and then, in 2001, with UGG.

By contrast, new co-ops emerged that featured strong vertical integration around a narrow focus of activities, with heavy member investment and commitment. The New Generation Cooperatives (NGCs) epitomized this trend. The first co-op of this type was created in 1971, and after a lapse of some years, the model took off in the 1980s–1990s with the creation of nearly 200 such co-ops, mainly in the Upper Midwest (Egerstrom 1994; Egerstrom, Bos, and Van Dijk 1996).

NGCs are not a universal solution to problems in agriculture, but they demonstrate important principles that other co-ops can learn from: transparency, close integration between the cooperative and members' own economic activities, heavy member involvement and investment, and a more consumer- and quality-oriented focus along the marketing chain. Other successful co-ops of a more conventional structure, such as the Agropur dairy cooperative in Quebec, exhibit a number of these features without being NGCs.

As these examples indicate, the two broad challenges for co-ops in the new environment are, first, to reinvent themselves structurally, and, second, to reconnect with members. The two challenges are related. Large co-ops must develop—and are beginning to evolve—an approach that counters the new structures of their competitors. Many have indeed undertaken joint ventures, strategic alliances, mergers, and acquisitions, but it might be said that these have often produced firms that are not as flexible as their competitors, not always well-integrated, and not transparent to members. For members to "buy into" a large cooperative organization—literally—they may have to be able to buy into and participate directly in those parts of it that concern them.

Co-ops may develop into something more like umbrellas for groups of interrelated ventures, with greater involvement and commitment of particular groups of members to the specific issues that concern them within the wider organization. Perhaps we will see a renaissance of federated cooperative models, because these can allow for more flexibility and more effective combination of local knowledge and innovation with central economies of scale.

For federations to be healthy, however, they need *both* strong locals *and* strong centrals. Some cooperative systems lack one or the other dimension. Whatever the forms that new co-ops take, the successful ones are likely to be firms built around information—around value added, quality assurance, knowledge of production conditions, and knowledge of consumer preferences—rather than around commodities or things. Not incidentally, this implies a growing need for continuous education of decision makers and members.

In every era, co-ops have changed. It is safe to predict that they will change again. When this happens, what we think we know about co-ops may turn out not to be true after all. The new economy in which co-ops operate is postindustrial and requires a shift away from industrial models of the firm and industrial modes of thinking—away, in other words, from rigidity and compartmentalization, toward teams, innovation, knowledge, and networks. This shift is not only postindustrial but, in breaking down intellectual and organizational boundaries, it is also cultural and postmodern.

The future for co-ops will involve the removal of barriers within minds and communities as well as those between units, firms, and regions. Like other institutions, co-ops will need to bring to bear the talents, energies, and commitment of more diverse groups of people, both among their staff and among their members. This will happen not only because it is socially desirable, but also because it is economically necessary to have innovation, stakeholder commitment, and teamwork.

Co-ops have learned and must remember enduring lessons from each stage of their development. From their earliest days comes the lesson of how important it is to be linked to specific communities of people and to specific needs analyzed and understood by groups. From the early industrial era comes their role as opponents of monopoly, as counterweights to concentration.

Through the first half of the twentieth century, co-ops practiced improved and modern management and marketing; through the second half, they involved the consolidation of larger and more integrated systems. All of these lessons remain important, and co-ops forget any of them at their own peril. The *culture* of co-ops—the stories cooperators tell about themselves—must continue to incorporate all of the hard-won experiences of their history.

The most important challenge for co-ops is to remember who and what they are while also innovating and changing. There is nothing sacred about the way co-ops were structured or the things they did in the 1880s, the 1920s, or the 1950s. Each cooperative model is an adaptation to a specific set of circumstances and to the needs associated with a particular wave of economic transformation. The economic idea behind the structures of co-ops is essential: the idea of voluntary association among members for mutual investment and advantage, functional integration between members and their enterprises, and member engagement in a co-op that connects them transparently with final sources or destinations of products and services. Cooperators ultimately need to be loyal to this idea and not to any particular manifestation of it.

One of the striking features of North American cooperative history is the openness to borrowing, imitating, and adapting foreign ideas and models of cooperation. Many groups displayed great energy, creativity, and enterprise in creating co-ops, but they rarely did so from scratch. Inspiration came from Britain, Ireland, and Central Europe; from Japan; from Canada into the United States in some cases, and from the United States into Canada in others. The combination of creativity and openness explains much of the current and future success of North American co-ops.

References

Alexander, Anne. 1997. *The Antigonish Movement: Moses Coady and Adult Education Today.* Toronto: Thompson Educational.

Birchall, Johnston. 1997. *The International Co-operative Movement.* Manchester, UK: Manchester University Press.

Canadian Co-operative Association (CCA). 2001. "Ottawa. Ontario. Canada: Candiana Cooperative Association." Available at www.coopcca.com (October 30, 2001).

Centre for the Study of Co-operatives. 1998. *Proceedings from the Women in Cooperatives Forum, 7–8 November 1997.* Saskatoon, Saskatchewan: Centre for the Study of Co-operatives.

Co-operative Housing Federation of Canada. 2001. "Bookmarks in Our History." Available at www.chfc.ca (November 1, 2001).

Donohue, Kathleen. 1999. "From Cooperative Commonwealth to Cooperative Democracy: The American Cooperative Ideal." In *Consumers Against Capitalism? Consumer Cooperation in Europe, North America, and Japan, 1840–1990,* ed. Ellen Furlough and Carl Strikwerda, 115–134. Lanham, MD: Rowman and Littlefield.

Egerstrom, Lee. 1994. *Make No Small Plans: A Cooperative Revival for Rural America.* Rochester, MN: Lone Oak Press.

Egerstrom, Lee, Pieter Bos, and Gert Van Dijk, eds. 1996. *Seizing Control: The International Market Power of Cooperatives.* Rochester, MN: Lone Oak Press.

Fairbairn, Brett. 1989. *Building a Dream: The Co-operative Retailing System in Western Canada, 1928–1988.* Saskatoon, Saskatchewan: Western Producer Prairie Books.

———. 1995–1996. "Constructing an Alternative Language for Co-operative Growth: An Ecological Metaphor." *Coopératives et Développement* 27, nos. 1–2, 77–103.

Fairbairn, Garry. 1984. *From Prairie Roots. The Remarkable Story of Saskatchewan Wheat Pool.* Saskatoon, Saskatchewan: Western Producer Prairie Books.

Goodwyn, Lawrence. 1978. *The Populist Moment: A Short History of the Agrarian Revolt in America.* New York: Oxford University Press.

The ICA Group. 2001. "Frequently Asked Questions about Employee Ownership." Available at www.ica-group.org (November 1, 2001).

Keillor, Steven J. 2000. *Cooperative Commonwealth: Co-ops in Rural Minnesota, 1859–1939.* St. Paul: Minnesota Historical Society Press.

Knapp, Joseph. 1969. *The Rise of American Cooperative Enterprise, 1620–1920.* Danville, IL: Interstate.

MacPherson, Ian. 1979. *Each for All: A History of the Co-operative Movement in English Canada, 1900–1945.* Toronto: Macmillan.

———. 1995. *Co-operation, Conflict, and Consensus: B.C. Central and the Credit Union Movement to 1994.* Vancouver, British Columbia: B.C. Central Credit Union.

———. 1996. *Co-operative Principles for the 21st Century.* Geneva: International Co-operative Alliance.

Memmi, Albert. 1991. *The Colonizer and the Colonized.* Boston: Beacon Press.

Moody, J. Carroll, and Gilbert C. Fite. 1984. *The Credit Union Movement: Origins and Development, 1850–1980.* 2d ed. Dubuque, IA: Kendall/Hunt.

National Cooperative Bank. 2001. *Cooperative Top 100.* Available at www.ncb.com (October 30, 2001).

National Cooperative Business Association (NCBA). 2001. "Co-op Primer." Available at www.ncba.coop/stats.cfm (November 1, 2001).

Neal, Rusty. 1998. *Brotherhood Economics: Women and Co-operatives in Nova Scotia.* Sydney, Nova Scotia: UCCB Press.

Polanyi, Karl. 1944. *The Great Transformation: The Political and Economic Origins of Our Time.* Boston: Beacon Press.

Rudin, Ronald. 1990. *In Whose Interest? Quebec's Caisses Populaires 1900–1945.* Montreal: McGill-Queen's University Press.

Sanders, Elizabeth. 1999. *Roots of Reform: Farmers, Workers, and the American State 1877–1817.* Chicago: University of Chicago Press.

Schildgen, Robert. 1988. *Toyohiko Kagawa: Apostle of Love and Social Justice.* Berkeley, CA: Centenary Books.

Sekerak, Emil, and Art Danforth. 1980. *Consumer Cooperation: The Heritage and the Dream.* Santa Clara, CA: Consumers Cooperative Publishing Association.

Shannon, Fred A. 1957. *American Farmers' Movements.* Princeton, NJ: Van Nostrand.

Spann, Edward K. 1989. *Brotherly Tomorrows: Movements for a Cooperative Society in America, 1820–1920.* New York: Columbia University Press.

Turner, Howard Haines. 1968. *Case Studies of Consumers' Cooperatives: Successful Cooperatives Started by Finnish Groups in the United States Studied in Relation to Their Social and Economic Environment.* New York: AMS Press.

Voorhis, Jerry. 1961. *American Cooperatives: Where They Came From, What They Do, Where They Are Going.* New York: Harper and Brothers.

Welton, Michael R. 2001. *Little Mosie from the Margaree: A Biography of Moses Michael Coady.* Toronto: Thompson Educational.

Wieting, C. Maurice. 1952. *The Progress of Cooperatives, with Aids for Teachers.* New York: Harper and Brothers.

Woeste, Victoria Saker. 1998. *The Farmers' Benevolent Trust: Law and Agricultural Cooperation in Industrial America, 1865–1945.* Chapel Hill: University of North Carolina Press.

Wood, Louis Aubrey. [1924] 1975. *A History of Farmers' Movements in Canada: The Origins and Development of Agrarian Protest 1872–1924.* Toronto: University of Toronto Press.

3

The Evolution of the Cooperative Model

Kim Zeuli

Pioneer cooperative members and leaders, most notably the founders of the Rochdale Society in nineteenth-century England, are often celebrated for launching the modern cooperative movement (Thompson 1994). The theory of cooperation, or the idea that a group of individuals working together can achieve a common interest essentially unobtainable by the actions of a single person, is in fact indistinguishable from the theory of collective action. Clearly, examples of collective action can be traced back to the earliest ways of mankind (Groves 1985); the concept was not an invention of nineteenth-century British idealists (see Fairbairn, chapter 2 in this volume).

The unique contribution of the Rochdale Pioneers (and other early cooperative organizers) was codifying a guiding set of principles for the creation of a unique business model that embraced cooperative tenets.[1] It can be supposed that the existence of a formal organizational structure and principles, rather than a nebulous theory of cooperation, fostered the subsequent widespread attention given to the cooperative idea in both business and policy (i.e., the cooperative movement).

The distinguishing traits of the cooperative model—the defining characteristics—are, in fact, fairly inclusive. In practice, the cooperative model has always existed in a multitude of forms. As Emelianoff (1942) succinctly stated, "the diversity of the co-ops is kaleidoscopic, and their variability is literally infinite" (13). The cooperative model continues to evolve, reflecting changes in society, agriculture, and, more directly, the interests of its members.

The main objective of this chapter is to present greater insight into the cooperative model and its evolutionary path. Distinction is made between the model, or that which relates to the practical structure of the organization, and cooperative theory, which deals with the more general and abstract questions of cooperation (e.g., when should people cooperate?). The latter is included insofar as it relates to the cooperative form of organiza-tion.[2] For example, cooperative principles, which might be considered part of underlying theory rather than practice, are dealt with rather extensively since they are inextricably linked to the cooperative model.

Structural Evolution: A Property Rights Perspective

The first step in exploring the possible future structure of co-ops, where struc-ture refers to the organizational elements and basic operating rules that com-prise most cooperative firms, requires resolving a more general question: "What determines the organizational structure adopted by a firm?" Answer-ing this question becomes more tractable if an organizational structure is considered as a specific set of property rights, a perspective introduced by Fama (1980) and Jensen and Meckling (1976).[3]

Since its inception in the 1960s, property rights theory has been used to address numerous resource allocation problems. In general, property rights can be defined as the prescribed use or control of a resource (Demsetz 1967). From a firm perspective, property rights are legal restrictions governing how firm resources may be used. More specifically, property rights determine who makes decisions, who bears risk, the validity of the right to use the resource, the transfer of this right, and penalties for violating restrictions. An economic organization can thus be defined as the sum of the property rights for those who contribute resources to the firm (the owners of production factors) and those who purchase its goods and services (customers) (Condon 1987). The most significant property rights in terms of defining organiza-tional structures are those relating to residual claims and the decision pro-cess (Condon 1987; Fama and Jensen 1983). Examples of property rights for co-ops are outlined in Table 3.1.

Very few others have used a property rights perspective to analyze coop-erative structures; four notable exceptions are Condon (1987), Cook (1995), Fulton (1995), and Harris, Stefanson, and Fulton (1996).[4] Condon (1987) lays out a theoretical framework and justification for exploring the connec-tion between property rights and cooperative structure. Cook (1995) and Fulton (1995) use property rights to compare cooperative structures in terms of how well they align member incentives. For instance, Cook argues that co-ops can only achieve their goal (i.e., correct market failures) if they are stable organizations. Stability requires well-defined property rights.

This chapter turns this previous body of work somewhat on its head and examines the incentives that created various structures. Harris et al. (1996), for example, argue that capital acquisition is a problem for traditional co-ops because members have no incentive to invest since ownership per se

Table 3.1

Examples of Cooperative Property Rights

Ownership rights
    Ownership eligibility
    Ownership establishment
    Ownership restrictions per member
    Ownership value
    Ownership liquidity
Decision-making rights
    Decision-making authorities (governing bodies)
    Decision-making process
    Voting rights
    Eligibility for inclusion on governing bodies
Delivery or purchase rights
    Supply or purchasing restrictions
    Supply or purchasing obligations
    Penalties for not fulfilling obligations
Residual claim rights
    Eligibility for receiving firm's net profits
    Distribution of firm's net profits
    Eligibility and process for claiming unallocated equity

provides no benefits. An alternative perspective on this problem, and the one taken here, is to ask why ownership is structured this way.

Internal Cooperative Influences

Property rights specifications ultimately reflect the interests of various agent groups: the firm's owners (members), board of directors, and management (Condon 1987). Under standard economic assumptions, it is logical to conclude that the primary reason members join and create co-ops is to increase their individual welfare. In his classic work on collective action, Olson (1971) notes, "One purpose that is nonetheless characteristic of most organizations, and surely of practically all organizations with an important economic aspect, is the furtherance of the interests of their members" (5).

Cooperative theorists and developers, however, maintain diverse views regarding what member interests might be or, rather, what members primarily want to achieve through their co-op. The most commonly held belief, especially for agricultural co-ops, is that members join to increase their profits and to gain higher prices for their raw commodities and lower prices on their inputs. Members may also ultimately seek the market access cooperative membership provides, the competitive pressure co-ops put on other firms in an industry, or the opportunity co-ops afford in managing some of their personal financial risk. Members may also have nonpecuniary interests and may view cooperative membership as a social responsibility (e.g., when the co-op is a vital part of their local community or increases the welfare of other individuals) or, at the other extreme, as a necessity for maintaining a conveniently located retail outlet (e.g., neighborhood consumer co-ops).

State cooperative statutes typically require that cooperative members or stockholders elect the board of directors.[5] These statutes usually further restrict director eligibility to active cooperative members. Nonmembers may participate in a nonvoting, advisory capacity, although this is not a common practice in most states; therefore, board members theoretically represent the interests of the cooperative membership. The potential for accurate representation of, or aligned interests with, the majority of the membership is strongest when one-member/one-vote policies are in place. Proportional voting can create a board of directors that represents the interests of relatively few members who maintain a disproportionate share of the co-op's patronage. Either way, many state laws strictly preclude directors from entering into any extraordinary contracts with the co-op (Ginder and Deiter 1989). Thus, their incentive to act in a self-fulfilling manner at the expense of the general membership is limited.

Of all three agent groups, cooperative management has the potential to demonstrate the most divergent interests, yet it is critical that they do not: "If the cooperative is to function effectively, these groups [the board and management] must work together on behalf of the entire cooperative membership" (Ginder and Deiter 1989, 318). Management may be more interested in firm-level success factors such as capturing greater market share or revenue growth from nonmember businesses, especially if their compensation depends on firm-level success. Recent case studies of cooperative compensation practices reveal a hesitancy on behalf of boards of directors to link management compensation with firm-level performance goals because of unexpected and undesirable results (Trechter et al. 1997). Even if their compensation is divorced from this type of success, managers may feel that quantified firm-level success is essential currency to trade on future career opportunities.

Diverging member and managerial incentives present a classic principal–agent problem (Sappington 1991). In co-ops, members represent the principals and managers represent the agents. Several studies conclude that such problems are quite extensive in co-ops, citing a lack of motivation on behalf of the members to monitor managers and a difficulty in providing managers with compensation that creates the correct incentives to align member and management interests (Caves and Petersen 1986; Fama 1980; Porter and Scully 1987). In their empirical study of this problem, Richards, Klein, and Walburger (1998) report survey results that voice member dissatisfaction with management objectives.

Clearly, there can be, and often are, conflicting objectives both within and among the agent groups. Torgerson, Reynolds, and Gray (1998) warn, "A challenge for cooperative members is to remain the primary beneficiaries of group action for which they originally organized" (10). Maintaining a member-centered orientation requires strong board governance and representation of member interests. This becomes increasingly difficult as membership becomes more heterogeneous with fewer shared objectives. The Richards et al. (1998) study provides some empirical proof that membership objectives can vary widely and seem to correlate with member age, education, off-farm income, and farm sales. This problem of divergent objectives can be compounded with proportional voting practices. Nonmember business and management control of large unallocated equity reserves can pose further critical challenges to member orientation (Royer 1992). If membership interests lose out to management and a more corporate orientation, management may even press the possibility of converting into an investor-oriented firm. Such conversion has occasionally occurred in the United States and more frequently in Europe, where cooperative structures can be more binding (Torgerson et al. 1998). As will be argued below, however, the conversion rate in the United States will probably increase.

External Influences

Property rights can also be defined by local customs and social norms rather than solely by internal agent groups (Alchian 1977). Businesses certainly exhibit unique corporate cultures that delineate their rules of operation. This is clearly evident when one compares U.S. and Japanese corporations, for example. Co-ops, however, may provide a more striking case of externally defined property rights.

Two distinct American schools of cooperative thought influenced agricultural cooperative development during the early parts of the twentieth century (Torgerson et al. 1998). According to Abrahamsen (1976), "early American cooperative thinkers" were distinguished by their commitment to building cooperative business models rather than theory: "Their thinking led to no finespun theories in the realm of social and political philosophy. Rather, they were concerned with cooperative business efficiency and performance so as best to serve the practical needs of farmers" (76).

European cooperative scholars during that period were more concerned with cooperative philosophy, especially the interpretation of Rochdale principles. As Torgerson et al. (1998) note, "A characteristic of American [cooperative] thought is that it is steeped in pragmatism, contrasted to some European schools that were affected by great social reforms and associated philosophies of the times" (1).

Aaron Sapiro and Edwin G. Nourse remain the most recognized examples of "early American cooperative thinkers."[6] In brief, Sapiro (1920) promoted the organization of large-scale, centralized co-ops along commodity lines to help producer members capture greater market share and thereby influence the terms of trade. As a lawyer, it is perhaps not surprising that he also advocated long-term contracts with growers rather than reliance on member loyalty to ensure timely and sufficient product delivery. Sapiro's influence was greatest in his native state of California and the Pacific Coast, in part because his ideas were better suited to specialty crops (Torgerson et al. 1998).[7]

Creating large co-ops for grain and other staple commodities at the time, which would have involved thousands of farmers in multiple states, would have been incredibly difficult and cumbersome. The failure of national commodity co-ops organized under the Federal Farm Board in 1929 supports this point. Sapiro's efforts and thinking, however, did facilitate the adoption of the Capper–Volstead Act of 1922, the Cooperative Marketing Act of 1926, and the Agricultural Marketing Agreements Act of 1937, all of which have shaped cooperative development and structures in the United States (Torgerson et al. 1998).

Nourse (1944), a Chicago free-market school professor of economics, resolutely opposed monopolies. In stark contrast to Sapiro's vision of aggressive regional co-ops that exerted industrywide market power, Nourse promoted more passive, locally organized and controlled co-ops. Nourse believed that co-ops could capture enough market share to force, solely by virtue of their presence, noncooperative firms into behaving more competitively in specific markets. Producers could thus measure the relative performance of each type of firm—the axiomatic "yardstick hypothesis." To achieve economies of scale and compete with larger firms at the regional level, Nourse advocated the creation of a federated system in which several local co-ops would coordinate their activities (but retain their autonomy) through a larger, regional co-op.

Nourse's (1944) competitive rationale for co-ops created the justification for cooperative development support within broader farm policy programs as well as the specialized tax and antitrust treatment of co-ops (Torgerson et al. 1998). Nourse influenced public policy and cooperative structure through his academic positions and by serving as chairman of the President's Council of Economic Advisors under President Harry S. Truman. Nourse was also an initial cofounder of the American Institute of Cooperation (AIC) in 1925, "created for practical discussion about best cooperative principles and operating practices" (Torgerson et al. 1998, 3).

The same leaders of the AIC formed the National Cooperative Council (NCC) in 1929 to ensure continued advantageous policy treatment of agricultural co-ops. Later, NCC was renamed the National Council of Farmer

Cooperatives (NCFC), which merged with AIC in 1990 and now carries a dual education and policy mission. The NCFC, the Rural Business-Cooperative Service (RBCS) of the U.S. Department of Agriculture (USDA), and several university-based academic centers continue to influence the evolution of the cooperative model. For instance, they provide annual national forums at which academic researchers and cooperative leaders (management, board directors, and cooperative development practitioners) debate various aspects of structural change. They are also called on when new co-ops are being formed to provide advice on how to structure the co-op, how to write the bylaws, and other issues. This group of experts shares approaches and perspectives via joint research projects and participation in the same regional and national conferences. A similar type of influential network, promoting the same corporate culture derived from a unique set of principles, simply does not exist for noncooperative firms.

In part because of the cooperative network's continued influence and in part because the United States has used these principles as a basis for laws governing co-ops (Barton 1989), cooperative principles play an integral role in shaping cooperative structure. Two sets of comprehensive principles are frequently referenced: (1) the original Rochdale principles, and (2) the more contemporary principles recognized by the International Cooperative Alliance (ICA). Abbreviated versions of both are presented in Table 3.2, in which the principles are divided along property rights specifications for ownership, control, and the distribution and derivation of benefits.[8] A final category includes principles not associated with business decisions, such as the duty to educate. Both sets of principles include organization points that manifest social and political concerns.

The thorough nature of the Rochdale principles[9] reflects the situation in which they were created (i.e., early cooperative organizers and scholars were trying to formulate a new and distinct form of organization). The relevance of the principles to today's co-op is a source of continued deliberation among scholars and cooperative leaders. As Barton (1989) observes:

> Each of these Rochdale principles has been subjected to scrutiny by many cooperative observers. Their evaluations differ. Some revere them as canons of cooperative philosophy and action, seeing them all as true principles that are timeless and of universal validity. Others claim that the principles are based on the unique situation in which a pragmatic group of Rochdale pioneers found themselves. One thing is certain. The conditions prevailing in Rochdale, England in the 1840s are far different than those in North America in the 1980s and 1990s. So too are the cooperatives of today far different. (28)

Table 3.2

Cooperative Principles

Property rights	Rochdale	Traditional	20th-Century	ICA
Ownership	Membership is open	Membership is open	Membership is either open or closed	Membership is open and voluntary
	Equity provided by members—equitably	Equity provided by members—equitably	Equity provided by members; may be in proportion to patronage	Equity provided by members—equitably
	Limited equity shares/individual	Limited voting stock/individual		
	Gender equality in membership			
Control	By members—democratic[a]	By members—democratic	By members—either democratic or proportional[b]	By members—democratic
Benefits	Net income distributed to members based on patronage	Net income distributed to members based on patronage	Net income distributed to members based on patronage	Net income distributed to members based on patronage
	Limited equity capital dividends	Limited equity capital dividends	Limited equity capital dividends	Limited or no equity capital dividends

(continued)

Table 3.2 (continued)

Property rights	Rochdale	Traditional	20th-Century	ICA
	Exchange of goods and services at market prices	Business done primarily with member-patrons	Differentiated pricing/service policies among members is an option	
	Cash trading only			
	No unusual risk assumption			
Nonbusiness factors	Duty to educate	Duty to educate		Duty to educate
	Political and religious neutrality			Political neutrality and autonomy
				Duty to work for community development
				Cooperation among cooperatives

Sources: Barton (1989, 27); ICA (1995).
[a]Democratic control = one member/one vote.
[b]Proportional control = votes proportional to equity or patronage.

The ICA is a nongovernmental organization dedicated to promoting cooperative principles worldwide (it comprises over 200 members from 70 countries). According to Hoyt (1996, 1), "Since its creation in 1895, the International Cooperative Alliance (ICA) has been accepted by cooperators throughout the world as the final authority for defining cooperatives and for determining the underlying principles which give motivation to cooperative enterprise."

The ICA (1995) has adopted three formal statements of cooperative principles, first in 1937, and then in 1966 and 1995. In 1995, the ICA adopted seven cooperative principles, all of which have been paraphrased (without loss of intent) for conformity in Table 3.2. The third cooperative principle, member economic participation, was divided into several principles since it encompasses ownership, control, and benefit issues. The ICA has established a broad set of operating guidelines for co-ops that are less concerned with business rules (perhaps in recognition of competitive realities) and more with social issues (thus echoing the Rochdale principles).

Given the ICA's recognized global authority over the determination of cooperative principles, this focus seems appropriate and relevant for many countries struggling to define or redefine cooperative business in much of Eastern Europe and Russia. The voluntary membership principle, for example, is not necessary in the United States or Western Europe, where legal authority demands such practice, but it is an important distinction between former, government-enforced collectives and new co-ops.

Co-ops vary greatly in their adoption and interpretation of these principles. In fact, the degree to which co-ops subscribe to them is occasionally used to classify various forms of co-ops, placing them on a continuum between "quasi" or "hybrids" (when co-ops behave more like investor-owned firms [IOFs] and follow few principles) and "pure" or "true" co-ops (Barton 1989). Cooperative principles are also often interpreted as reflections of the cooperative model's transformation. As the cooperative model adapts to changing business environments, the set of principles most commonly adhered to also evolves, with some principles becoming dominant, others essentially fading from use, and a few new principles being added to the mix. Barton (1989), for instance, proposes four classes of cooperative principles that roughly trace this evolutionary path: (1) Rochdale, (2) traditional, (3) proportional, and (4) contemporary. The traditional and a twentieth-century class of principles are presented in Table 3.2. The twentieth-century principles represent a combination of Barton's proportional and contemporary classes.

The traditional principles, slightly modified versions of the original Rochdale precepts, represent the most commonly adhered to and accepted set of principles in the last century (Abrahamsen 1976). They strictly adhere to the Rochdale values of equality and democracy while dispensing with some of the less relevant points for contemporary businesses. Indeed, some of the excluded Rochdale principles such as religious neutrality and gender equality in membership are now redundant in the United States since they are enforced for businesses by federal law.

The twentieth-century class of principles represents a more startling departure from the Rochdale doctrine and is an attempt to capture the realities of present-day cooperative structures in the United States and parts of Europe (e.g., the Netherlands). The first noticeable difference is a dearth of principles pared down to a few fundamental operational guidelines. The most commonly accepted definition of a cooperative today is derived from its most fundamental principles: a co-op is a user-owned and user-controlled business that distributes benefits on the basis of use (USDA 1995).

Further, each principle contains flexibility, a choice between equitable and proportional practices. Today's increasingly complex cooperative organizations may in fact incorporate both types of practices for different businesses divisions or for different business decisions (e.g., voting may be democratic, but equity may be contributed based on patronage).

Proportional practices signify the greatest divergence from Rochdale principles and remain highly contested. Some cooperative advocates maintain that proportional ownership, control, and/or profit distribution practices destroy the essence of the cooperative model—equitable treatment of members. The adoption of proportional practices is typically justified by the difficulties of doing business with homogenous members (Barton 1989; Emelianoff 1942). If members who provide significant cooperative patronage are not adequately compensated and/or have little influence on business decisions, they may leave the co-op. This is a real fear for agricultural co-ops now competing with IOFs for a limited pool of large farms, which are often the co-ops' primary source of patronage.

It is important to distinguish between the evolution of principles and the evolution of the *adherence* to principles. Barton (1989) and others suggest that the principles themselves have evolved, which is only true in some cases, most notably in the emergence of proportional principles. From a property rights perspective, however, it is more compelling to consider the evolution of the adherence to principles. As argued above, the Rochdale and ICA principles are both espoused as guiding rules for cooperative structure. The influence and incentives of the various agent groups then determine which principles are actually adhered to by the co-op.

Contemporary Cooperative Structures in Agriculture

Given the dramatic changes in agriculture over the past century, it is not surprising that the cooperative model has evolved; as farmers' situations change, so, too, do their incentives as cooperative members. A property rights perspective helps explain the emergence of a new type of cooperative structure, the New Generation Cooperative (NGC), and the continued existence of both centralized and federated structures for traditional co-ops.

For traditional co-ops, one must consider the incentives of the original member-agent group since the structure, or property rights specifications, have changed very little. Indeed, this reluctance to change, even as current membership incentives change, seems to have helped spawn the rise of the NGC. When American farmers first began creating co-ops in the early 1900s, the agricultural landscape consisted of numerous small farmers who were relatively homogenous in terms of farm characteristics. The Rochdale principles that focused on equitable treatment and open membership would thus have made sense for these early co-ops.

As noted above, the "traditional" principles that were largely adopted are closely related to the Rochdale precepts. The farmers had to capture as much supply and capital as possible to compete with the dominant agribusiness firms; this meant trying to attract as many members as possible since few large farms existed. Since all of the farmers would patronize the co-op at similar levels with virtually indistinguishable products, they would have had little incentive to impose proportional policies. Indeed, the promise of equitable treatment and ownership would have helped attract more members.

Most farmers at the time had little capital to invest and few credit institutions that would lend them money for off-farm investment opportunities. Thus, capital for cooperative membership had to be raised through patronage rather than a single up-front investment. Furthermore, the retained equity deepened the farmer's commitment to the co-op every year and helped maintain member loyalty and supplies.

Traditional co-ops have also historically had poor equity redemption policies, often retaining member equity until the member retired from farming, reached a certain age, or passed away. This policy was probably inherited from Northern European co-ops, which still tend to redeem less allocated equity than U.S. co-ops (Van Bekkum and Van Dijk 1997). Equity reserves that were essentially unredeemable in the short term gave these traditional co-ops the financial and supply stability to grow over the years and eventually capture significant market shares (e.g., Land O'Lakes). Since most farmers at the time were not active investors in the stock market, the co-op did not have to compete with the market in terms of offering a comparable return on investment. The 8 percent limit on equity dividends imposed by the Capper-Volstead Act in 1922, therefore, could not have seemed unduly restrictive.

During the past decade, farmers have created a wave of NGC value-added processing operations in the upper Midwest in an attempt to capture a greater share of food chain profits (Egerstrom 1994; Harris, Stefanson, and Fulton 1996). The NGC structure differs from a traditional cooperative structure in four distinct ways, each of which reflects changing member incentives and a changing agricultural structure. First, membership in NGCs is restricted or closed. The optimal operating capacity of the firm typically drives membership numbers. For example, consider the case of a spring wheat processing plant. A feasibility study suggests that annual throughput of 1 million bushels will produce the greatest net profits and best chances for initial success. The NGC would then offer just enough membership shares to cover this requirement. If five members could deliver 1 million bushels, then membership would be limited to these five producers.

NGC members are profit driven and are concerned with building the most viable value-added enterprise. Limiting membership helps ensure that this optimal operating capacity is achieved every year. It also helps decrease business transaction costs; the larger the membership, the greater potential for a heterogeneous membership. Unlike when traditional co-ops were first created, today's agricultural sector is diverse; very small farms coexist with extremely large commercial operations. Today's farmers also have more access to capital, which means NGCs can (and do) require a significant upfront investment from all members.[10]

NGC members typically provide half the capital for the initial cooperative startup. This large infusion of capital translates into a higher percentage of allocated equity returned as cash each year, which is in the members' interest. Instead of having their earnings invested in the co-op, they can diversify their portfolio and potentially earn greater returns investing that money elsewhere.

In contrast to traditional co-ops, NGC membership shares are tradable with value that reflects the worth of the firm. This value is derived from the fact that the shares represent access to the NGC value-added stream of profits. When farmers buy NGC shares, they have the right and obligation to deliver a specified quantity of product. If they are unable to produce this quantity, they are required to fulfill the contract with purchased commodities. Without such contracts, traditional co-ops have suffered from uncertain supplies. Members have been able to sell their commodity to the firm offering the highest price. Supply variation can limit the co-op's growth and marketing opportunities. This would be especially troublesome with processing plants, which need to consistently operate at full capacity in order to achieve profitability. Thus, profit-driven NGC members had the incentive to create stringent supply contracts.

Alongside the NGCs, traditional co-ops continue to exist in both centralized and federated structures.[11] The vast majority of farmer co-ops are centralized, with farmers holding direct membership in the organization. Centralized co-ops range in size and scope. Some have only one business location, while others have multiple branches and main headquarters. In a federated cooperative structure, farmers hold membership in local co-ops, which, in turn, are members of a regional or federated co-op. Within this structure, farmer-member control is indirect. The regionals have traditionally provided centralized buying, manufacturing, and distribution services for their locals (Hogeland 2001). Some large co-ops are a combination of the two structures, with farmers and local co-ops holding direct membership in the regional organization (Cropp and Ingalsbe 1989; Hogeland 2001).

The Continued Evolution

The dynamic agricultural landscape in the United States will continue to induce change in the cooperative structure. Statistics suggest an increasing duality in agriculture: very large farms coexisting with fairly small farms with virtually no medium-sized farms and no average producers. The cooperative sector reflects a similar trend. The past decade has witnessed a dramatic increase in cooperative size due to mergers, joint ventures, and acquisitions (Wadsworth 1999). We can anticipate the growing presence of very large national and international co-ops trying to dominate their industries.

As a consequence, the continued relevance and future viability of the traditional federated structure will be in question. Within the federated structure, both local and regional co-ops have increased in size. A number of local co-ops have grown as large as most regionals were in the late 1950s. This begs the question of whether they need a second-tier regional structure or whether they can capture the same economy of scale benefits on their own. As they have grown, local co-ops have developed increasing independence, shifting their power relationship with the regionals (Hogeland 2001). Locals are now frequently members of more than one regional, while regionals, whose own growth has been accompanied by geographic expansion into other regional territory, now compete with each other for the locals' business (Hogeland 2001).

Cooperative growth will not necessarily parallel increased membership. Such large, highly competitive firms will most likely focus on maintaining a few high-value members. Currently, many of these large co-ops deal with unsustainable "80–20" situations: 80 percent of their sales are derived from 20 percent of their members. As large co-ops continue to compete with investor-oriented firms, their aggressive strategies may not meet the general membership interests. In addition to membership control issues, cooperative laws and traditions can also limit the range of strategies available. Thus, we can expect an increase in cooperative transformations to investor-owned firms, especially for value-added enterprises. Indeed, several successful NGCs have started this process. The benefits of the cooperative model (i.e., favorable tax treatment) in these cases have been outweighed by the costs in terms of constraints on growth. Limiting supply to producers ultimately means more producers and less profit per producer, which is clearly not in the best interest of the current members.

The structure of new farmer-controlled organizations created in the next decade will be diverse. The traditional cooperative model will still be utilized; it has strong support from the cooperative institutions, especially USDA Rural Business-Cooperative Service (RBCS), and continues to be an appropriate vehicle for increasing producers' bargaining power. The downside of open membership and traditional principles is that they are fairly negligible when it comes to marketing and purchasing operations, especially where contracts are employed. The traditional model will, however, be less likely to compete with NGC and Limited Liability Company (LLC) structures in value-added ventures characterized by slim processing margins and large equity requirements. The NGC and LLC models may also be more attractive to groups of producers who were disenfranchised from larger co-ops since these models give them more assurance that they can retain control over their organization so that it continues to serve their interests. The LLC form has the additional advantage of allowing nonproducer investors, thus affording more opportunity to garner sufficient equity for start-up and growth, an attractive feature for small producer groups who may lack capital.

Such detractions to the cooperative model may, however, be overcome with new, more flexible state and federal cooperative laws. The state of Wyoming has led the charge, recently enacting legislation that allows co-ops to have nonproducer investors. The impact this will have on the evolution of the cooperative model could be significant since co-ops, like other businesses, can incorporate in states other than those in which they are located.

Notes

1. Actually, the Rochdale Pioneers did not set forth a list of cooperative principles; however, the rules of conduct and organization that guided their business organization eventually led others to formulate a formal list known as the Rochdale principles (Barton 1989).

2. For a more comprehensive treatment of cooperative theory beyond the scope of this chapter, see works by Axelrod (1984), Emelianoff (1942), and Royer (1987).

3. Fama, Jensen, and Meckling used slightly different terminology, referring to property rights as a nexus of contracts.

4. New institutional economics incorporates property rights theory and transaction costs to justify various forms of organization. This perspective has been employed by several scholars to examine the rationale behind cooperative formation (Staatz 1987). A review of this literature, and indeed addressing their question, is unfortunately beyond the scope of this chapter.

5. There are no federal laws concerning cooperative board of directors' policies.

6. Abrahamsen (1976) also justifiably recognizes the contributions of James Warbasse, Carl Taylor, John Black, E.A. Stokdyk, Joseph Knapp, and Ivan Emelianoff. Given the contemporary fixation with Nourse and Sapiro and the page constraints of this chapter, the discussion will be limited to their contributions and those of Knapp.

7. Since Sapiro's efforts were concentrated in California, his approach is sometimes referred to as the California school of thought (Torgerson et al. 1998).

8. The format of Table 3.2 is a slightly revised version of that presented in Barton (1989).

9. Barton's (1989) list of Rochdale principles is perhaps the most comprehensive, including the more common ten principles proposed by Roy (1981), plus two additional principles derived from rules of conduct in the Rochdale Society 1860 Annual Almanac. Further, Barton has also updated the original language of the principles.

10. A study of NGC startups in North Dakota found that the influx of subsidy payments to area farmers played an important role in NGC development (i.e., farmers had access to more capital than was typical) (Cobia 1997).

11. Co-ops also implement other structural arrangements such as subsidiaries, joint ventures, and holding companies. While a full discussion of these arrangements is beyond the scope of this chapter, it should be noted that these alternative structures have been *used* by cooperative organizations but have not replaced or significantly altered the cooperative model.

References

Abrahamsen, Martin A. 1976. *Cooperative Business Enterprise.* New York: McGraw-Hill.

Alchian, Armen. 1977. *Economic Forces at Work.* Indianapolis, IN: Liberty Press.

Axelrod, Robert. 1984. *The Evolution of Cooperation.* Boulder, CO: Basic Books.

Barton, David G. 1989. "Principles." In *Cooperatives in Agriculture*, ed. David Cobia, 21–34. Englewood Cliffs, NJ: Prentice-Hall.

Caves, Richard E., and Bruce C. Petersen. 1986. "Cooperatives' Shares in Farm Industries: Organizational and Policy Factors." *Agribusiness: An International Journal* 2: 1–19.

Cobia, David. 1997. "New Generation Cooperatives: External Environment and Investor Characteristics." In *Cooperatives: Their Importance in the Future Food and Agricultural System*, ed. Michael Cook, Randall Torgerson, Tom Sporleder, and Dan Padberg, 91–97. Washington, DC: National Council of Farmers Cooperatives.

Condon, Andrew M. 1987. "The Methodology and Requirements of a Theory of Cooperative Enterprise." In *Cooperative Theory: New Approaches* (Agricultural Cooperative Service [ACS] Report #18), ed. Jeffrey S. Royer, 1–32. Washington, DC: USDA.

Cook, Michael L. 1995. "The Future of U.S. Agricultural Cooperatives: A Neo-Institutional Approach." *American Journal of Agricultural Economics* 77: 1153–1159.

Cropp, Robert, and Gene Ingalsbe. 1989. "Structure and Scope of Agricultural Coop-eratives." In *Cooperatives in Agriculture*, ed. David Cobia, 35–67. Englewood Cliffs, NJ: Prentice-Hall.

Demsetz, Harold. 1967. "Toward a Theory of Property Rights." *American Economic Review* 57 (May): 347–359.

Egerstrom, Lee. 1994. *Make No Small Plans: A Cooperative Revival for Rural America.* Rochester, MN: Lone Oak Press.

Emelianoff, Ivan V. 1942. *Economic Theory of Cooperation: Economic Structure of Cooperative Organizations.* Davis: University of California at Davis, Center for Cooperatives.

Enke, Stephen. 1945. "Consumer Co-operatives and Economic Efficiency." *American Economic Review* 35: 148–155.

Fama, Eugene. 1980. "Agency Problems and the Theory of the Firm." *Journal of Political Economy* 88: 288–307.

Fama, Eugene, and Michael Jensen. 1983. "Separation of Ownership and Control." *Journal of Law and Economics* 26: 301–325.

Fulton, Murray. 1995. "The Future of Canadian Agricultural Cooperatives: A Property Rights Approach." *American Journal of Agricultural Economics* 77: 1144–1152.

Ginder, Roger G., and Ron E. Deiter. 1989. "Managerial Skills, Functions and Par-ticipants." In *Cooperatives in Agriculture*, ed. David Cobia, 308–324. Englewood Cliffs, NJ: Prentice-Hall.

Groves, Frank. 1985. *What Is Cooperation? The Philosophy of Cooperation and Its Relationship to Cooperative Structure and Operations* (Occasional paper no. 6). Madison: University Center for Cooperatives, University of Wisconsin–Madison.

Harris, Andrea, Brenda Stefanson, and Murray Fulton. 1996. "New Generation Co-operatives and Cooperative Theory." *Journal of Cooperatives* 11: 15–27.

Hogeland, Julie A. 2001. "The Changing Federated Relationship." Paper presented at the Annual NCR-194 Conference, October 31, Las Vegas.

Hoyt, Ann. 1996. "And Then There Were Seven: Co-op Principles Updated." *Coop-erative Grocer* (January/February):18–22.

International Cooperative Alliance (ICA). 1995. "Statement on the Co-op Identity." *ICA News* 5/6.

Jensen, Michael C., and William H. Meckling. 1976. "Theory of the Firm: Manage-rial Behavior, Agency Costs, and Ownership Structure." *Journal of Financial Eco-nomics* 3: 305–360.

Nourse, Edwin G. 1944. "The Place of the Cooperative in Our National Economy." In *American Cooperation 1942 to 1945*, 33–39. Washington, DC: American Institute of Cooperation.

Olson, Mancur. 1971. *The Logic of Collective Action: Public Goods and the Theory of Groups.* Cambridge, MA: Harvard University Press.

Porter, Philip K., and Gerald W. Scully. 1987. "Economic Efficiency in Coopera-tives." *Journal of Law and Economics* 30: 489–512.

Richards, Timothy J., Kurt K. Klein, and Alan M. Walburger. 1998. "Principal–Agent Relationships in Agricultural Cooperatives: An Empirical Analysis from Rural Alberta." *Journal of Cooperatives* 13: 21–34.

Roy, Ewell Paul. 1981. *Cooperatives: Development, Principles and Management.* Danville, IL: Interstate.

Royer, Jeffrey S., ed. 1987. *Cooperative Theory: New Approaches* (ACS Report #18). Washington, DC: USDA.

———. 1992. "Cooperative Principles and Equity Financing: A Critical Discussion." *Journal of Agricultural Cooperation* 7: 79–98.

Sapiro, Aaron. 1920. *Co-operative Marketing*. Chicago: American Farm Bureau Federation.

Sappington, David E.M. 1991. "Incentives in Principal–Agent Relationships." *Journal of Economic Perspectives* 5: 45–66.

Staatz, John M. 1987. "Farmers' Incentives to Take Collective Action via Cooperatives: A Transaction Cost Approach." In *Cooperative Theory: New Approaches* (ACS report no. 18), ed. Jeffrey S. Royer, 87–107. Washington, DC: USDA.

Thompson, David J. 1994. *Weavers of Dreams: Founders of the Modern Co-operative Movement*. Davis: University of California at Davis, Center for Cooperatives.

Torgerson, Randall E., Bruce J. Reynolds, and Thomas W. Gray. 1998. "Evolution of Cooperative Thought, Theory, and Purpose." *Journal of Cooperatives* 13: 1–20.

Trechter, David D., Robert P. King, David W. Cobia, and Jason G. Hartell. 1997. "Case Studies of Executive Compensation in Agricultural Cooperatives." *Review of Agricultural Economics* 19: 492–503.

U.S. Department of Agriculture (USDA). 1995. *What Is a Cooperative?* (Cooperative information report no. 50). Washington, DC: USDA.

Van Bekkum, Onno-Frank, and Gert Van Dijk, eds. 1997. *Agricultural Co-operatives in the European Union*. Assen, The Netherlands: Van Gorcum.

Wadsworth, James J. 1999. *Cooperative Unification: Highlights from 1989 to Early 1999* (RBS research report no. 174). Washington, DC: USDA, Rural Business-Cooperative Service.

4

Obstacles to Cooperation

Lee Egerstrom

The modern cooperative firm must confront two realms of problems at all times, neither of which is easy to manage through the democratic processes of the cooperative structure. In this chapter, the two realms are identified as "internal obstacles," which are shaped by the structure and strategies of the firm, and "external obstacles," which are the exogenous forces constantly changing the market environment of the firm.

How important is an understanding of these obstacles? Prominent Harvard University faculty who have developed internal obstacles concepts insist that the survival of the firm hinges on how well the firm manages or circumvents these obstacles (Jensen 2001; Porter 1980). Further, certain of these obstacles are common to all firms regardless of governance and ownership structure. Other problems or obstacles are either unique to co-ops or are especially significant within cooperative structures.

This chapter will review these obstacles on the premise that simply "building a better mousetrap" no longer guarantees the success of a firm, if it ever did. The first two sections will review the recognizable internal and external obstacles facing enterprises in general and co-ops in particular, and how these obstacles spill over on governance and management strategies. The final section will identify how co-ops can use their strengths and structures to overcome the consequences of these obstacles.

Internal Obstacles

There are always internal obstacles to leading, governing, and keeping intact all forms of organizations. Most business firms face occasional or constant problems with capital formation, a subject addressed elsewhere in this book. In addition, any firm with multiple stakeholders has frictions between the parties, which academics and business leaders recognize as "agency theory" problems or conflicts (Jensen and Meckling 1976). While that is so, co-ops have specific agency theory conflicts that stem from their ownership structure and democratic governance. Thus, academics have adapted the general concept and tailored a separate set of agency theory conflicts for cooperative firms.[1]

Finally, firms of all ownership structures must develop strategies to deal with competition from within the firm's industry. These challenges usually arise because of external forces; however, the strategy to cope with these forces becomes an internal challenge for a firm when it must unite the stakeholders in a course of action. This latter challenge will be reviewed here as internal obstacles to cooperation because the "agent," or management, must forge strategies for the firm even when doing so raises agency theory problems among stakeholders.

Agency Theory

Jensen and Meckling originally defined agency theory in an article published in 1976. A general and simple definition of the theory by Munshi (2001) shows that it reflects how the agent, or management, must handle situations when selfish motives of different stakeholders may prevent a firm from taking action to gain maximum economic or equity value. Management may be the perpetrator of this shortsightedness, which adds to the "agency costs" for other stakeholders to monitor management's behavior. Often, rival stakeholder groups will want to increase their own wealth at the expense of other stakeholders. With investor-owned firms (IOFs), these pressures may hold a company back from making appropriate long-term investments. In other cases, the interests of the agents may prevent the company from taking steps that might improve shareholder value. The following sections synopsize Jensen and Meckling's (1976) original agency theory's sources of conflict as drawn from Munshi (2001).

Shareholder–Manager Conflict

Managers may act to maximize the wealth or benefits of managers at the expense of owners. Owners incur agency costs in monitoring the managers, and may at times transfer this monitoring responsibility to bondholders.

Shareholder–Bondholder Conflict

The interests of owners (shareholders) and debtholders (bondholders) may be in conflict over the use and payment of debt. For instance, shareholders are more inclined to use debt for risky projects while trying to protect the value of their equity in the firm.

Agency Theory of Cash Dividends

Financing projects with retained operating earnings transfers wealth from shareholders to bondholders if doing so lowers the latter's risks. Shareholders may wish to be paid dividends to reduce the transfer of wealth to other stakeholders such as bondholders or labor.

Dividend Policy

The firm must resolve whose interests are to be served from a dividend policy. Considerations include not only the use of retained earnings, as cited above, but also the tax consequences for stakeholders with payment of dividends, and how dividends may keep managers in securities markets where they are closely monitored. This latter move transfers agency costs of monitoring management to equity analysts and investment bankers.

Capital Structure

Risk and financial/debt leverage increase when a firm takes on debt. At the same time, owners may gain agency cost benefits from debt by forcing debtholders to help manage the managers by imposing discipline on the firm.

In an interview about capital structure, Jensen (2001) said he has not followed how other economists and business professors are adapting agency theory to co-ops: "I grew up in Minneapolis and I have relatives at Minnesota Lake (southern Minnesota). I have not spent much time looking at the impact of agency costs on co-ops, but I always think of those rural grain elevator cooperatives around Minnesota Lake. There are agency costs to resolve with these cooperatives that separate them from other firms."

Key among these issues of agency costs are which enterprises cooperative members should own and which ones they should supply under differing contract relationships. For instance, Jensen (2001) asked whether the firm, or processor, should own the land and raise the crop? He also raised a parallel question, "Should the producers (members) own part or all of the processing stages?"

These, of course, are major issues facing farmers and their cooperative ventures at the start of the twenty-first century (Figure 4.1). Underlying a co-op's strategy is the source and cost of capital. Examples of co-ops wrestling with these questions are found in various roles that co-ops play in livestock

Figure 4.1 **Agency Theory Conflicts**

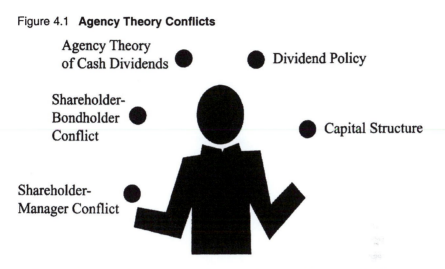

Agency Theory
of Cash Dividends

Dividend Policy

Shareholder-
Bondholder
Conflict

Capital Structure

Shareholder-
Manager Conflict

Source: Jensen and Meckling (1976); graphic by Marisa Egerstrom 2001.

production and processing and in value-added processing and manufacturing of grain-based foods and feeds. "The key becomes which produces the greater efficiency and lowers agency costs," the Harvard Business School professor added (Jensen 2001).

Agency Theory of Cooperatives

By his own account, Jensen (2001) said his agency theory work with Meckling, the late dean emeritus at the University of Rochester Simon School of Business, went largely ignored until the late 1980s. It then found new uses and new popularity, partly inspired by his own continuing work and partly as others applied it to new studies of firms, structures, and finance.

Among the latter, cooperative business scholars adapted the theory to fit inherent problems of cooperative firms. Van Bekkum (2001) credits Jensen with starting this process with work on mutual associations and credit unions, and provides a summary of cooperative agency theory work.[2] This work follows along two paths: the first is the impact on capital and finance that is consistent with the early work of Jensen and Meckling, and the second, newer path focuses more on the behavior of stakeholders within the organization, especially the principals, or owners, versus the agents, or managers. Two economists and cooperative business experts, in particular, deserve mention for encompassing both paths in literature and lectures for cooperative audiences: Michael L. Cook at the University of Missouri at Columbia, and Jerker Nilsson at the Swedish University of Agricultural Sciences (SLU) at Uppsala.[3]

Faber and Egerstrom (2001) cite the cooperative agency theory problems outlined by a German scholar (Horsthemke 1998) that address member behavior within a co-op. This work draws heavily on Cook and Nilsson. Meanwhile, Fulton (2001) stays closer to Jensen and Meckling's (1976) original work and examines cooperative agency theory problems as they apply to finance and capital formation within the cooperative firm. The differences are minor but are noted here for the benefit of students, scholars, or cooperative executives who may want to study agency theory costs and problems in greater depth. The following are brief summaries of the problems.

Free-Rider Problems

This is the lack of incentive for members to invest in co-ops. Fulton (2001) notes that members only invest as much as required, leaving co-ops dependent on debt financing and short of capital. Horsthemke (1998), citing Nilsson (1998), focuses more on the behavior of members, noting that new members with a minimal investment in many cooperative business structures gain access to assets and equities built up by long-time members. Further, he notes that long-time members leaving the co-op have difficulty gaining access to undiluted assets that are used by the firm and its "free-rider" members.

Horizon Problems

This represents the time period a member anticipates before gains are realized from the co-op's investments. Fulton (2001) says members tend to support activities that maximize short-term rather than long-term returns when the co-op compensates member-investors with patronage refunds. Faber and Egerstrom (2001), however, use Horsthemke's (1998) behavioral approach and see a generational division within members. An older member may not want the firm to make investments that would use or put at risk equity that the member has accumulated in the firm, especially if that member wants to retire and redeem the equity in the near future. A newer member may want to use that equity in investments for longer-term objectives and strategies.

Portfolio Problems

This logical problem closely ties the co-op's activities to the special interests of the members, whether viewed from a use of capital or from a behavioral focus. The self-interests of members can make it difficult for the co-op to diversify operations, and it can cause tensions among members based on their need or desire for cooperative services (Figure 4.2).

Figure 4.2 **Cooperative Agency Theory Conflicts**

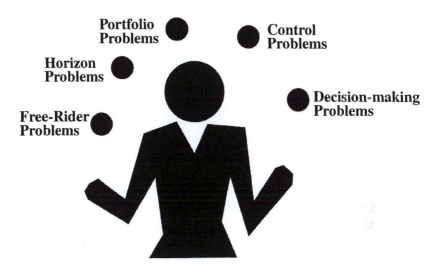

Sources: Faber and Egerstrom (2001) and Fulton (2001); graphic by Marisa Egerstrom 2001.

Control Problems

Especially in large, diversified co-ops, the need for fast, "business-like" action tends to tip the power to management. Further, Fulton (2001) notes that co-ops with shares that are not traded among members and new investors and co-ops with widely dispersed members give the owners little cause to closely monitor management decisions.

Decision-making Problems

Fulton (2001) uses alternative terminology— "Influence Costs Problems"— to describe how members will attempt to use their influence to steer the co-op's decision making. Despite the one-person/one-vote democracy of the cooperative structure, some members often become more influential than others. Furthermore, there are times when management and boards may not easily ascertain their members' wishes given the conflicting signals they receive from influential members advancing their own interests.

Porter's Five Forces

Many of the internal conflicts between stakeholders within an organization, most notably between the principals and the agent, come into play when the organization is considering the use of capital for strategic business planning and investment. When considering business strategy, the external influences that are encouraging or even demanding change within the organization must be weighed. The struggle to make change, however, becomes an internal matter as management and owners (or members) must navigate agency theory problems and agency costs before choosing a course of action.

Michael Porter (1980) provided the most recognized grouping of factors that influence the competitiveness of a firm. Because of his book, *Competitive Advantage*, most managers of firms are familiar with Porter's Five Forces and use them to analyze their own companies' competitive positions within their industries.

Porter (1980) shows that all managers must constantly seek a competitive advantage in at least one area of competition; however, no matter how widely read Porter may be in business and business education, it is reasonable to assume that co-op member-owners are not as acquainted with the forces of competition influencing the business strategies of their firms. This is also true of the typical investor in IOFs. It is this latter assumption that justifies using Porter's external industry forces as an Internal Obstacle for the co-op. Cooperative managers must constantly educate members and communicate reasoning for their firms' strategies. Recognizing this need, Porter's Five Forces are briefly examined here (see Figure 4.3).

Industry Competition

Business firms today face competition from rival firms if the market is relatively open and competition exists. Prices and profits are influenced by the competition in the marketplace, regardless of production or other operating costs. No significant difference exists in industry competition, or rivalry, between co-ops and IOFs.

Market Power of Suppliers

The bargaining power of suppliers changes with the type of firm under study; this can be significant depending on the type of co-op. Fierce competition among suppliers should lower the typical firm's input costs. Applied to co-ops, this should help the consumer-owned or supply co-op; however, it may harm an agricultural, forestry, or other type of producer co-op if it means the firm must lower the payments or returns on the producer's raw materials, for example.

Bargaining Power of Buyers

This power shifts from industry to industry, and there may be key differences between IOFs and cooperative enterprises. Essentially, Porter sees product prices

Figure 4.3 **Porter's Five Forces**

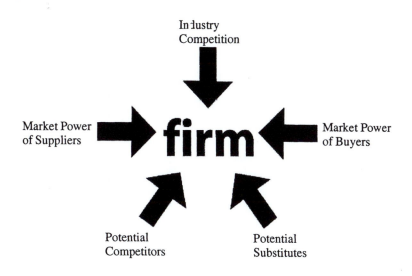

Sources: Adapted from Porter (1980) and Antweiler (2001).

and company profits influenced by the amount of choices with which consumers are provided. Prices and profit margins usually decline when consumers have ample choices. Price may be less important in a consumer co-op if the firm offers special products or product choices sought by the membership.

Potential Competitors

A firm must have a strategy for facing new rivals who are attracted to the industry. The threat of new players is real if the firm and its industry are enjoying wide profit margins. The threat is perceived to be less if profit margins within the industry are generally known to be slim. At the same time, producer co-ops do invest in and enter thin-margin business sectors for various reasons, not the least being when the business activity is a logical extension into value-added processing of co-op members' commodities.

Ocean Spray, the Massachusetts and Wisconsin cranberry growers' co-op, offers a classic example of how agency theory conflicts can lead a new competitor into a market. Its largest member broke from the co-op in the 1990s when profit margins were strong, started Northland Cranberries as an IOF in Wisconsin, and expanded cranberry production and processing at the same time Ocean Spray was expanding. This resulted in surplus cranberry processing production and processing capacity, low operating margins, and a scarcity of profits for both companies.

Potential Substitutes

Any company, IOF or co-op, faces a threat of encountering rival substitute products or services in its core markets. Porter (1980) argues this is predictable business behavior when product prices are perceived by consumers, or industrial buyers, and by rival firms as being high, thus encouraging a search for substitution.

A wider reading of the business literature shows that substitution usually comes from invention such as new technology. The clearest explanation of the motivation to seek substitutes, however, comes from economics literature—especially the Ruttan–Hayami Theory of Induced Technical Innovation (Hayami and Ruttan 1971; Ruttan and Hayami 1995). These authors show the link between comparative farm labor costs and the acceptance of labor-saving farm technology. The same rationale is employed by consumers and firms in comparing costs and selecting substitute products or services.

An example of a co-op diversifying to protect its core business from substitution was the Land O'Lakes' expansion into margarine production, despite being the leading branded butter manufacturer in America. Conversely, a Swedish potato growers' co-op sold its popular brand product, Absolut Vodka, in 1998 when technology changed and vodka was being made from lower-cost grains, not the members' potato crop. Grain-based vodka became the substitute product. Most of the proceeds from the sale were dispersed to members, but a portion was retained for investing in ventures that would add value to their potatoes.

External Obstacles

Porter's (1980) work serves as a transition between the Internal and External Obstacles facing the cooperative firm. His five forces can be viewed collectively as an External Obstacle because they define strategy, especially as it affects use of capital. A strategy assumes that wise managers and stakeholders can anticipate changing forces, however. Ample research studies flatly state that all external changes to an industry cannot be predicted. For instance, consolidation of companies in certain industries leads to plant closings and leaves suppliers without markets (Merriman 2001). The rapidity of change and consolidation, especially in food and agriculture industries, suggests this is a more accurate view of modern markets.

There is no single, agreed-upon list of factors that create external obstacles for all firms. Business libraries are filled with literature dealing with one or more obstacles facing business management, and this literature usually reflects the special expertise of the authors. Bates and Whittington (1997) and, separately, Ward (1992) provide a useful list of external environmental factors gleaned from accounting studies published in the United Kingdom. Their list is noted here as the Strategic Management Accounting (SMA) list. Factors from SMA will be combined with influences from business behavior in the late 1990s and early 2000s to suggest a list of factors more applicable to cooperative businesses.

Strategic Management Accounting

In their SMA approach to analyzing obstacles, Bates and Whittington (1997), along with Ward (1992), see a series of external environmental factors that encircle firms. From their perspectives, SMA analysis should help the firm in establishing organizational objectives and strategies. With that intention in mind, a short reach ties the SMA list to both agency theory and Porter's (1980) forces. Management should make the connection. The challenge of leading an organization through periods of change becomes a balancing act between the internal interests of stakeholders and the right strategies to handle external pressures.

A list of SMA factors includes the following:

- suppliers
- competition
- customers
- market price
- technical developments
- demographics
- social concerns
- legal regulatory factors
- political environment
- economic environment

Differences in some of the above factors may have special meaning to accountants who guide managers and boards of directors. From a broader perspective, however, several of the SMA factors can be combined into fewer, more encompassing categories. For instance, Porter (1980) would see suppliers, competition, market price, and customers as elements of the firm's competitive position in the market. Legal regulatory factors and the political environment are virtually one and the same, and social concerns are integrated into both other factors in the political economy. At the same time, social concerns also hint at cultural issues. These can be found inside the firm, leading to agency theory conflicts, and in the marketplace (Malekzadeh and Nahavandi 1998; Nahavandi and Malekzadeh 1988).

External Cooperative Obstacles

In keeping with most lists used in this chapter, groupings of five factors that encircle the modern cooperative firm on a daily basis have been assembled. These groupings bring together the more individual categories of obstacles defined by SMA studies in the UK, and they emphasize the economic importance of information, as do Bates and Whittington (1997).

In addition, the groupings are an attempt to categorize external obstacles that are likely to cause one or more agency theory conflicts within the cooperative organization (see Figure 4.4). Finally, the groupings draw heavily from business headlines in North America and Europe in the 1990s and 2000s, reflecting attempts by companies to adjust and exploit marketplace opportunities often viewed as obstacles for co-ops.

The external obstacles constantly confronting co-ops include the following:

- *Information.* This includes both access to and quality of information needed by the firm.
- *Resources.* These can range from capital to a plant's access to raw materials, and can include such human elements as the solidarity of members.
- *Political environment.* Includes local, state, and national regulations; tax policy; and international trade regulations that create access or barriers to markets and encourage or discourage competition.
- *Culture.* This is the most unexplored factor determining the viability of the cooperative firm, both internally and externally. Externally, however, cooperative models do allow people to overcome cultural barriers and become entrepreneurs in hostile or competitive environments.
- *Porter's five forces.* These are the factors of business competition that determine the sustainability of the firm regardless of ownership structure.

Positive Aspects of Cooperatives

On the positive side, modern cooperative firms have flexibility in structures and strengths in membership that can overcome both internal and external obstacles. New organization forms, such as New Generation Cooperatives (NGCs), joint ventures, and partnerships, and the reengineering of existing regional and national co-ops to closely resemble holding companies, are but a few examples of how cooperative firms are changing to accommodate both internal and external pressures.

Figure 4.4 **External Cooperative Obstacles**

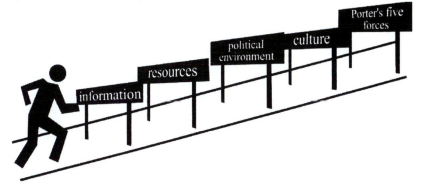

Source: Egerstrom (2001); graphic by Marisa Egerstrom 2001.

Van Dijk (1997) argues that new justifications for cooperation are emerging with modern business trends, combining and modifying the five historic reasons for cooperation. He describes those five historic reasons in the following way:

1. Early cooperators were able to influence markets and market power, especially in competition with private firms that had superior market information.
2. The cooperators were able to overcome barriers to gain access to industrial goods and services.
3. Cooperative auctions and pools gave members economies of scale they could not achieve by themselves.
4. Cooperation, a reason much *en vogue* at the beginning of the twenty-first century, provided members with various tools for risk management.
5. Cooperation sought to improve members' incomes and their community or rural economy through a combination of the previous four historical reasons.

The co-op that has not changed and remains focused on one or more of the above historical purposes may be sliding into oblivion, adds Van Dijk (1997). Thus, he sees a comprehensive sixth reason evolving. It includes the need for the firm to connect ecologically sustainable producers—usually farmers—with sophisticated, global markets; and it means the firm must help members diversify their entrepreneurship. Other elements of this sixth reason include using cooperation to form networks for members to gain access to technologies, to create systems linking producers to consumers, and to lower transaction costs for individual members.

This new sixth reason, as Van Dijk defines it, wraps up and modifies the original or historic reasons for people to form cooperative enterprises to today's business environment. A favorite theme of Van Dijk is that the modern co-op must be entrepreneurial on two levels: (1) the firm itself must be entrepreneurial to survive the forces of competition cited above; and (2) it must, at all times, help members to be individually entrepreneurial. The following is an attempt to describe how co-ops may be doing just that as applied to the five Cooperative External Obstacles cited above.

Information

The historic need to place farmers and other independent producers and consumers on equal footing in the marketplace has not disappeared. Rather, it has shifted. Schuh (2001) notes there have been three "technological revolutions" since World War II. The first involved transportation, affecting the movement of goods, services, and people; a follow-up and related revolution came in the communications sector, linking all but the most remote regions of the world instantly; and the third revolution, the information technology revolution, combines both of the former revolutions.

To date, these revolutions are largely limited to developed countries (Schuh 2001). This means they must still reach the developing countries where 80 percent of the world population lives. The "globalization" pressure of the world economy is, therefore, great; it must continue if there is any hope for global democracy in technology and if markets are to continue growing. It also means that co-ops will face future competition from rivals as yet unknown, and that they must compete each day for access to increasingly complex information about markets and competitors.

I.J. Prins, a former chairman and chief executive officer of the diversified Dutch food and agriculture cooperative Cebeco Handelsraad, explained his firm's international investment strategy in the early 1990s (Egerstrom 1994). According to Prins, the co-op must move beyond its small national borders, which is much like moving past regional boundaries for North American co-ops, if it is to continue seeking economies of scale and scope to contribute to its members' prosperity. One of Cebeco's investments in an unrelated Belgian company had little potential to produce revenue directly to Cebeco's members; however, Prins felt this was a worthwhile investment to gain information about world markets and about operating businesses abroad.

Not many North American cooperative managers would take a similar merger or acquisition proposal to their members for the expressed purpose of gaining market information. Several agency theory tensions would likely arise among members not appreciating the farsighted strategy; however, joint ventures and partnership arrangements with other co-ops and with well-established IOF and private firms do offer access to enormous market and global information. Consider the following arrangements involving North American co-ops.

Farmland Industries and Growmark have joint venture marketing links with Archer Daniels Midland (ADM), the largest IOF agricultural processing firm. The Harvest States food unit of CHS Cooperatives has joint venture flour milling ties with Cargill Inc., the world's largest privately owned agribusiness. Farmland, CHS, and Land O'Lakes have joint ventures in feed and farm supplies. The Saskatchewan Wheat Pool operates export terminals in a joint venture with Cargill. Dairy Farmers of America (DFA), the largest U.S. dairy co-op, has joint venture relations with Land O'Lakes, the second largest, to operate Midwestern dairy processing plants efficiently. DFA, meanwhile, has a joint venture called DairiConcepts with the New Zealand Dairy Board (a dairy pool co-op), which operates cheese processing plants in South Dakota, Minnesota, Wisconsin, and Missouri.

One of the more adventurous efforts to access information was Rooster.com, an "e-commerce" attempt to use modern Internet information technology to link agricultural producers with marketers and consumers. It failed to generate anticipated revenue and closed in 2001. This effort in using new information technology did manage to bring together the largest U.S. agricultural co-ops with their largest IOF and private rivals and partners, including Cargill, ADM, and Dupont.

Such arrangements might be seen as signs of cooperative failures by people who hold to the historic reasons for cooperation as outlined by Van Dijk (1997); however, these arrangements are clearly logical and in step with Van Dijk's description of a sixth reason. They are also especially effective in accessing information for co-ops that are usually smaller than rival IOF and private competitors and at a disadvantage in accessing market information.

Resources

Capital and membership are the most precious resources for co-ops. Members themselves can be extremely important sources of information to guide the firm through periods of change. In order to focus on the external influences on businesses in general, however, two other resources deserve the co-op's attention: (1) production capacity, and (2) what businesspeople call "orphan brands." These resources offer co-ops great opportunities when capital is available and when members are willing to be risk takers for the common good.

Looking at production capacity first, this can mean factories and other assets used in production that become redundant from mergers and acquisitions. These assets can often be acquired and employed by fast-moving co-ops at a fraction of the cost of new construction. With agriculture, it might also mean investing in Brazil, which is rapidly expanding its acreage under cultivation and was expected to surpass the United States as the leading exporter of soybeans by the mid-2000s (U.S. Department of Agriculture, 2001). It is understandable why major European agribusiness companies, Cargill, and ADM are investing in Brazil.

Except for agency theory constraints, it is less understandable why American co-ops are not investing in Brazil. By doing so, co-ops can expand revenue-producing activity for their North American members and correct market prices, as the co-ops did earlier in domestic markets. Any reading of world commodity market trends would note that the world's processing companies, as well as the soybean oil and meal customers, now play soybean supplies from South America off against supplies from North America.

"Orphan brands," meanwhile, are product lines that become available when large, diversified companies restructure their operations or when mergers and acquisitions change the mix of core products for the surviving company. An article in the *Montreal Gazette* ("And Now for the Good News . . ." 2001) reported on Saputo Inc. seeing second-quarter profits soar by 48 percent after integrating its purchase of Dairyworld Foods—an acquisition that made Saputo the largest dairy processor in Canada. The Dairyworld purchase came six months earlier and two years after Saputo's acquisition of Culinar Inc. The increased focus on dairy foods, however, made the snack cakes, cookies, breads, and soups from Culinar expendable, or orphan brands, and they were sold to another Canadian firm, Dare Foods Ltd., in mid-2001.

Mergers and acquisitions constantly change the product mix and market share of major corporations. Peale (2001a, 2001b), the business writer for the *Cincinnati Enquirer*, has chronicled the comings and goings of Procter and Gamble's product lines, the leading household products manufacturer in America. Guy (2001) of the *Chicago Sun-Times*, meanwhile, chronicled how Sara Lee restructured to compete with Procter and Gamble and other food and household goods makers. She noted that Sara Lee had made 25 percent of its product lines orphan brands, selling them to other companies while buying Earthgrains Company for $2.8 billion.

Still, the major reshuffling of products and core businesses by most major corporations was small when compared with General Mills's $10.4 billion acquisition of Pillsbury, also completed in 2001. To satisfy Federal Trade Commission competition concerns, General Mills agreed to sell certain Pillsbury baking mixes and specialty foods to a third food company, International

Multifoods and to keep the Pillsbury Doughboy brand competing with General Mills' Betty Crocker products in several food categories.

Continued merger and acquisition activity means more of such product lines will become available. These are "resources" that fit the product portfolios of co-ops when they add value to member products, make better utilization of cooperative plant assets, or when they serve a risk management strategy for co-ops and members. The DFA provided a new home to a major "orphan" when it acquired the Borden brand and Elsie the Cow icon. Harvest States Foods at CHS Cooperatives is consolidating ethnic foods and tortilla manufacturing companies to expand value-added production for its grains and flours. In fact, Land O'Lakes did the same thing when it acquired the Alpine Lace deli cheese line of products.

Political Environment

The World Trade Organization, created at the conclusion of the 1994 Uruguay Round of Trade talks, had taken shape over two decades of negotiations with new countries seeking full status in international trade channels ("China and Taiwan WTO Talks Continue" 2001). While that evolutionary work continued, a prospective Doha Round of talks in Qatar was agreed to in general terms by major trading countries. This new round was expected to occupy trade negotiators' time for most of the 2000s.

While international rules of the game are constantly changing, local, state, and national regulations are also undergoing change. The international spread of diseases, such as bovine spongiform encephalopathy (BSE) or mad cow disease, and such acts of terror as the spreading of anthrax, are encouraging far more regulatory controls and precautions than at any time in history (Egerstrom 1997, 2001; Lee and Hesman 2001). Hence, two paradoxical forces are constantly at work governing the market behavior of companies—a general quest for more liberalized trade and open borders, and more regulation on how companies can do business regardless of liberalized market access. These external forces are not likely to go away and will likely nudge co-ops and other firms into more alliances, joint ventures, and partnerships to lower transaction costs and reduce market risks.

Culture

Co-ops are still a market-correcting tool used by would-be entrepreneurs to overcome barriers to entry or intense management requirements in a variety of industry sectors; however, cooperative models remain underutilized for these purposes in most countries, and perhaps in the United States as well.

This becomes apparent when new cooperative starts are reviewed in Finland (Lukkarinen 2000). Merger and acquisition (M&A) activities are shrinking the number of co-ops in most industrialized countries as existing cooperative firms mimic their IOF and private competitors in seeking greater market strength and greater economies of scale. Even while several older, established co-ops converted to joint stock companies in Finland, Lukkarinen notes that the number of cooperative ventures actually increased during the 1990s.

More than 700 new co-ops were established between 1993 and 1997—a remarkable feat in that Finland has a population similar to that of Wisconsin. The biggest growth came from workers taking business matters into their own hands and starting worker-production co-ops, and from self-employed, often professional people forming creative business ventures to jointly market their skills and share business overhead services and costs.

Two points must be made about Finland: (1) it shares a historic Northern European culture that has had people turning to cooperative solutions to economic and business problems for the past 200 years, and (2) new people from within that culture—especially women—are retooling the cooperative models and emerging as organizers and leaders of the new co-ops. According to Lukkarinen (2000), women as "cooperative entrepreneurs" are bringing new energy and new fields of enterprise to the cooperative movement in Finland, especially in social services, health care, marketing of handicrafts, cultural activities, and media.

In contrast, two socioeconomic studies in the United States at the start of the twenty-first century suggest that co-ops have great potential for encouraging and promoting entrepreneurship. A study for the National Foundation for Women Business Owners projected that women of color would own 1.2 million businesses by 2002, generating sales of $100.6 billion and employing 822,000 people (Center for Women's Business Research 2001). Meanwhile, McGuckin (2001) found that M&A activity led to about a 10 percent job loss at acquired firms while at the same time it led to an overall increase in jobs, higher worker wages, and productivity gains in U.S. manufacturing. The two studies should be reviewed against the potential for creating new co-ops.

The Center for Women's Business Research (2001) study finds that minority women now own about 28 percent of all U.S. businesses. Of these businesses, 58 percent are in the service sector, which also had the greatest growth (33 percent) between 1997 and 2002. Agriculture represents 7 percent of these firms. A final point to note: The fastest growing states for minority women-owned enterprises are, in descending order, Montana, North Dakota, Maine, Oklahoma, South Dakota, Vermont, West Virginia, Idaho, New Hampshire, and Alaska. Of that list, six states are in the heart of "cooperative country," where there is a strong history of cooperative culture. Even so, until such time as Finland-style new co-ops are formed to aid these minority entrepreneurs, most will need to operate as individual owner-operators in businesses started with their own capital.

McGuckin's (2001) study, meanwhile, finds conflicting effects on workers from the constant M&A and restructuring activities of large corporations. On the one hand, M&A increases total jobs and wages, improves survival prospects for the acquired firm, and brings greater efficiency to the total economy; however, about 20 percent of ownership changes lead to significant job losses and slow growth in wages, and because these firms tend to be the largest, about two-thirds of affected workers either experience job loss or slower wage growth.

Anecdotal information gleaned from business news accounts show considerable discounting in value of plants and assets by companies wishing to unload these assets to complete M&A deals. Just as "orphan brands" open opportunities for co-ops wishing to expand and diversify, the buying, selling, and closing of plants opens doors for producer co-ops to acquire production assets, and opens opportunities for new worker co-ops to buy, own, and operate their own production plants. The business climate is primed for a cooperative revival in North America similar to what is occurring in Finland.

Globalization of the economy is not a new force adding to the factors Porter sees as keeping business enterprises under constant stress; however, there is strong evidence that the pressure from globalization is mounting (Batterson and Weidenbaum 2001), and that this pressure is most likely speeding the impact of Porter's Five Forces on the firms.

Conclusion

Opportunities emerge almost on a daily basis for cooperative firms, given the constant changes occurring in both domestic and international markets. Whether or not co-ops can seize the opportunities, however, depends on how well the principals, agents, and other stakeholders can overcome agency theory tensions regarding use of capital, how well-informed the members are in understanding external forces descending on their firm or industry sector, and how flexible the firm's stakeholders are in adapting new business forms and structures. This latter element is important if the firm is to protect existing member equity and still have the capacity to adapt, expand, and change core businesses as opportunities and challenges arise.

Is this just more business jargon or platitudes to toss at cooperative managers and members? It is not if managers and members take a historical look at their industries, use modern business analytical tools to gauge their own market position and competitiveness—like the Danish business professor Strandskov (1996)—then apply deductive reasoning in shaping business strategy.

A quick trip through this process would show that the speed of change is increasing, but that the process is not new. Using agriculture as an example, economic historians note that successful European agricultural systems were adjusting to globalization of markets while the United States was still in its infancy (Bieleman 1996, 1999), and that such change has profound socioeconomic impacts on people (Mak 2000). Moreover, these changes are occurring in the United States and North America as well (Levy 2000), and may be more profound than people in agriculture and rural communities are comfortable in acknowledging. The U.S. Department of Agriculture (2001) boldly comments on these changes in its *Food and Agriculture Policy: Taking Stock for the New Century* by noting that farming "no longer anchors most rural economies" and that at the beginning of the twenty-first century seven of eight rural counties are dominated by a mix of manufacturing and service sector enterprises.

If this change has occurred, then a process of rationalizing a local or regional economy must include spatial analysis to determine what and where people may take collaborative action (Box 2000). It must also employ the tools used by other sophisticated business managements (Fulton 2000; Jensen and Meckling 1976; Porter 1980) and adapt the process to cooperative enterprises (Lukkarinen 2000; Ruttan and Hayami 1995; Van Dijk 1997).

Can this be done? It can and must be done if cooperative enterprise is to survive in competitive markets (Strandskov 1996). What's more, studies on transnational merger and acquisition activity show that enterprises can and do gain economic benefits from cultural diversity and market knowledge by expanding into new markets and territories (Malekzadeh and Nahavandi 1998). What this means is that modern multinational corporations gain strength by decentralizing authority and emulating cooperative firms by integrating stakeholder cultures with greater information. All too often, co-ops see such diversity as a cause of agency theory obstacles rather than a source of strength. It is strength; it is the basis of cooperation.

Notes

1. Among stakeholders in any firm are workers, a group also influenced by agency theory conflicts. The workers are not specifically studied in this chapter, but they will be a necessary part of future research. For instance, the term "synergy" has great appeal to investors and managers considering merger and acquisition activity. For workers, the term "synergy" can more often than not be translated as "redundancy," bringing a loss of jobs. McGuckin (2001) notes that such changes in the firm can bring mixed results to employees.

2. Van Bekkum (2001) has achieved the almost contradictory goals of being both thorough and concise in describing agency theory and its application to co-ops (see pages 23–34 of his doctoral dissertation cited in the References). Further, Van Bekkum offers a pertinent summary of scholarly work that has advanced the theory over the past two decades.

3. Nilsson is not certain how cooperative scholars settled on the five *agency theory* problems that are now widely used. In an exchange of Internet e-mail messages during 2001, Nilsson said the first references he can find were from Peter Vitaliano's 1983 article, "Cooperative Enterprise: An Alternative Conceptual Basis for Analyzing a Complex Institution," published in the *American Journal of Agricultural Economics* 65: 1078–1083, and from John Staatz, in his 1984 doctoral dissertation, "A Theoretical Perspective on the Behavior of Farmers' Cooperatives," published at Michigan State University, East Lansing. Neither of those works, however, listed the five recognized agency theory problems in use today. The first reference to the five problems Nilsson recalls seeing was in a 1990 Swedish-language book that did not attribute credit to the source or sources.

References

"And Now for the Good News: Say Cheese—Saputo All Smiles." 2001. *Montreal Gazette*, November 8, 1C.

Antweiler, Werner. 2001. *COMM 498 Lecture Notes, University of British Columbia.* Available at http://pacific.commerce.ubc.ca/antweiler/comm498/notes25.html (December 2001).

Bates, Ken, and Mark Whittington. 1997. "Intense Competition, Revised Strategies and Financial Performance in the U.K. Food Retailing Sector." In *Strategies and Structures in the Agro-Food Industries*, ed. Jerker Nilsson and Gert Van Dijk, 207–224. Assen, The Netherlands: Van Gorcum.

Batterson, Robert, and Murray Weidenbaum. 2001. *The Pros and Cons of Globalization.* St. Louis: Center for the Study of American Business, Washington University.

Bieleman, Jan. 1996. "Dutch Agriculture 1850–1925: Responding to Changing Markets" [English translation of *Wirtschafts Geschichte: Nahrungsmittel und ihre Market im 19. und 20. Jahrhundert*). Berlin, Germany: Akademie Verlag.

———. 1999. "The Dutch Golden Age and Dutch Agriculture." In *Agrarian Systems in Early Modern Europe*, ed. Britt Liljewall, 159–185. Stockholm: Nordiska Museet for the Royal Swedish Academy of Forestry and Agriculture and the Swedish University of Agricultural Science.

Box, Sarah. 2000. "Economic Geography—Key Concepts." Wellington, New Zealand: The Treasury. Available at www.treasury.govt.nz/workingpapers/2000/00–12.asp (December 2001).

Center for Women's Business Research. 2001. *Minority Women-Owned Businesses in the United States, 2002.* Washington, DC: National Foundation for Women Business Owners, Sponsored by the Kauffman Center for Entrepreneurial Leadership.

"China and Taiwan WTO Talks Continue." 2001. *The Asia Insider* (Washington, DC), September/October: 2–3.

Egerstrom, Lee. 1994. *Make No Small Plans: A Cooperative Revival for Rural America.* Rochester, MN: Lone Oak Press.

———. 1997. "Officials Try to Quell 'Mad Cow' Fears in Wake of Rattled Markets." *Saint Paul Pioneer Press* (St. Paul, MN), April 18, 1D.

———. 2001. "Mad Cow Disease Task Force to Form." *Saint Paul Pioneer Press*, March 30, 1D.

Faber, Doeke, and Lee Egerstrom. 2001. "New Generation Cooperatives in the New Millennium." In *A Cooperative Approach to Local Economic Development*, ed. Christopher D. Merrett and Norman Walzer, 167–185. Westport, CT: Quorum Books.

Fulton, Murray. 2001. "Traditional Versus New Generation Cooperatives." In *A Cooperative Approach to Local Economic Development*, ed. Christopher D. Merrett and Norman Walzer, 11–24. Westport, CT: Quorum Books.

Guy, Sandra. 2001. "Sara Lee Plans to Boost Place in Home Products." *Chicago Sun-Times*, October 5, 1C.

Hayami, Yujiro, and Vernon W. Ruttan. 1971. *Agricultural Development: An International Perspective*. Baltimore: Johns Hopkins University Press.

Hoover's Online Company Capsule. 2001. Available at www.hoovers.com/co/capsule/2/0,2163,40272,00.html.

Horsthemke, Ansgar. 1998. *Die Genossenschaften in den USA unter besonderer Berücksichtigung der New Generation Cooperatives*. Stuttgart, Germany: University of Hohenheim at Stuttgart.

Jensen, Michael C. 2001. Personal interview.

Jensen, Michael C., and William H. Meckling. 1976. "Theory of the Firm: Management Behavior, Agency Costs and Ownership Structure." *Journal of Financial Economics* 3, no. 4: 305–360.

Lee, Thomas, and Tina Hesman. 2001. "Officials Focus on Terrorism Danger for Food Supply." *Post-Dispatch* (St. Louis), September 27, 1A.

Levy, Melissa. 2000. "Counting on the Rural Vote." *Economic Development Digest* 12, no. 1: 1A.

Lukkarinen, Margita. 2000. *New Co-operatives Creating Jobs*. Geneva: International Cooperative Alliance. Available at www.coop.org/europe/rareports698.html (December 2001).

McGuckin, Robert H., ed. 2001. *Why All the Uncertainty, Fear, and Doubt? Are Mergers and Acquisitions Bad for Workers?* (Research report 1295–01–RR). New York: The Conference Board.

Mak, Geert. 2000. *Jorwerd: The Death of the Village in Late C20th Europe* (English translation). London: Harvill Press.

Malekzadeh, Ali R., and Afsaneh Nahavandi. 1998. "Leadership and Culture in Transnational Strategic Alliances." In *Cultural Dimensions of International Mergers and Acquisitions*, ed. Martine C. Gertsen, Anne-Marie Soderberg, and Jens Erik Torp, 11–27. New York: Walter de Gruyter.

Merriman, Ed. 2001. "Dean Foods Says Goodbye to Oregon Cabbage Growers." *Capital Press* (Salem, OR), April 20, A1, 4.

Munshi, Jamal. 2001. Personal interview and published 1994 lecture notes. Available at http://munshi.sonoma.edu/working/agencyTheory.html (December 2001).

Nahavandi, Afsaneh, and Ali R. Malekzadeh. 1988. "Acculturation in Mergers and Acquisitions." *The Academy of Management Review* 13, no. 1: 79–90.

Nilsson, Jerker. 1998. "Agency Theoretical Problems in Co-operatives." In *The Reader: Marketing and Governance in the European Co-operative Food and Agribusiness*. Uppsala: Department of Economics, Swedish University of Agricultural Sciences.

Peale, Cliff. 2001a. "Justice OKs Clairol purchase. P&G Won't Have to Divest Any Products, Review Says." *The Cincinnati Enquirer*, November 8, 1D.

———. 2001b. "P&G Scrubs Comet to Brighten Earnings Outlook." *The Cincinnati Enquirer* October 3, 1D.

Porter, Michael. 1980. *Competitive Strategy.* New York: Free Press.

Ruttan, Vernon W., and Yujiro Hayami. 1995. "Induced Innovation Theory and Agricultural Development: A Personal Account." In *Induced Innovation Theory and International Agricultural Development: A Reassessment,* ed. Bruce M. Koppel, 22–36. Baltimore: Johns Hopkins University Press.

Schuh, G. Edward. 2001. *Globalization and Local Economic Development: The Demand for Reform of Local Governmental Institutions.* Paper presented at "The Times They Are A-Changing: Working Partnerships for Viable Communities," an international summit on community and rural development, July 22, Duluth, MN.

Strandskov, Jersper. 1996. "First Merge Nationally (Regionally), Then Penetrate the Entire Production–Marketing Chain." In *Seizing Control: The International Market Power of Cooperatives,* ed. Lee Egerstrom, Pieter Bos, and Gert Van Dijk, 83–98. Rochester, MN: Lone Oak Press.

U.S. Department of Agriculture (USDA). 2001. *Food and Agriculture Policy: Taking Stock for the New Century.* Washington, DC: USDA. Available at www.usda.gov (December 2001).

Van Bekkum, Onno-Frank. 2001. "Cooperatives: A New Institutional Economic Approach." In *Cooperative Models and Farm Policy Reform,* 10–38. Assen, The Netherlands: Van Gorcum.

Van Dijk, Gert. 1997. "Implementing the Sixth Reason for Co-operation: New Generation Co-operatives in Agribusiness." In *Strategies and Structures in the Agrofood Industries,* ed. Jerker Nilsson and Gert Van Dijk. Assen, the Netherlands: Van Gorcum.

Ward, K. 1992. *Strategic Management Accounting.* London: Butterworth-Heineman.

PART II

PUBLIC POLICY ISSUES

5

Legal Framework of Cooperative Development

Mark J. Hanson

Cooperatives—Legal Structure Built on Principles

"Cooperation is not dead! The legal structure is tired, worn out, and needs to be buried," announced a frustrated partner of mine. The law practice of working with producer-owned businesses, cooperative and otherwise, throughout the country seems to focus on the unreasonable restrictions of co-ops and the flexibility of limited liability companies (LLCs). The advance of business and economics has always outpaced the law. Producers and cooperators desiring social and economic change in the 1920s decried legal impediments to cooperation and the law changed.

In the past twenty years, producers have successfully formed hundreds of New Generation Cooperatives (NGCs), which are based on producer investment and proportional patronage returns; however, the financially successful co-ops are running into structural roadblocks resulting in conversion to LLC or taxable corporations, or the contribution of assets to joint venture entities that can operate profitably for the benefit of their owners. Now, many NGCs are starting the expensive conversion to LLCs because taxation issues have convinced their leaders that "all the co-ops are facing the same thing" and "everyone is making the change to an LLC" (Uecker and Talley 2002).

Successful NGCs do not fit well with many of the social and political principles developed and legislated 80 to 150 years ago that have remained part of American co-ops. These principles for member-financed cooperative stores simply do not work with the capital-intensive, value-added processing co-op of the twenty-first century. The economics of agriculture have changed from gaining efficiencies through direct marketing of raw agricultural products to users to further processing of unique or higher-quality agricultural products into higher-valued consumer products. The new business model is capital intensive and necessarily so in order to derive competitive market presence and economies of scale.

A new cooperative model has been developed called a "Wyoming Processing Cooperative," which is essentially a co-op that operates in an LLC structure on the Rochdale cooperator's business principle of returning profits to the patrons of the co-op (Hanson 2001b). Wyoming's cooperative law allows outside investment and eliminates the restrictions imposed by federal corporate cooperative tax law while requiring profits returned to patrons based on patronage and allowing returns to investors based on capital investment. This structure has been praised by producers and cooperators as allowing the co-ops the flexibility to adapt their structures to changing business conditions, but it has also been criticized by traditional cooperators as not being a true cooperative law (Frederick 2002; Torgerson 2002, 2).

This chapter reviews the formation of cooperative legal principles codified through the development of state statutes to organize co-ops. The provisions of typical state cooperative statutes and modern corporate cooperative statutes are analyzed, and the formation of a value-added agribusiness is compared under corporate cooperative statutes versus LLC or Wyoming Processing Cooperative structures. The federal control of corporate cooperative legal structure through federal tax law and other statutes is then examined.

For those who believe that cooperation is not dead and needs to be given the opportunity to further develop, a number of state and federal objectives and legislative changes are identified that will foster cooperative development.

Formation of Cooperative Legal Principles

Farmers in the United States have organized companies to find markets for their products for 200 years (Goldberg 1928, 270). The development of legal principles to structure marketing companies as co-ops began with the Order of Patrons of Industry, commonly known as the Grange, which spread concepts for collective action to farmers in order for them to organize as Rochdale co-ops (Evans and Stokdyk 1937, 20; Goldberg 1928, 272).

Rochdale Cooperation

Workers in England formed a cooperative store in 1844 called the Rochdale Society of Equitable Pioneers. Their plan emphasized participation in profits according to business conducted with the co-op rather than participation in profits based on invested capital (Holyoake 1908, 277; Woeste 1998, 20). This principle defined and differentiated Rochdale cooperation. The society published twelve principles, four of which became the legal foundation for American co-ops and are referred to as the "Rochdale Principles": (1) business at cost with net returns paid to members based on patronage, (2) democratic control—one person/one vote, (3) limited dividends on invested capital, and (4) ownership (or beneficial membership) limited to patrons (Woeste 1998, 20). The Rochdale store was not capital intensive and, in fact, limited the capital of its members (Holyoake 1908, 277).

The national Grange endorsed the "Rochdale Principles" to be adopted as rules by local organizations of farmers for any commercial organization (Nourse 1927, 35). The rules included organization as stock companies with the purchase of at least one share of stock required for membership, required purchases each year, interest on capital limited to 8 percent, and profits distributed in proportion to purchases (36). One vote per member was also a Grange principle (Goldberg 1928, 272).

The Grange Fails, But Cooperative Principles Succeed

The explosive growth of the Grange movement relied in part on cooperative strategy to overcome failed or unprofitable marketing conditions. The Rochdale Principles were appropriately developed for purchasing co-ops, and the Grange rules were developed for cooperative stores, with the legal structure fitting the business. These same rules were applied to Grange elevators and shipping associations with minor changes to the purchasing or store requirements (Nourse 1927, 37). The Grange's attempt to use a collective purchasing or cooperative store model for marketing ventures failed. Rochdale Principles restrict business volume to a level supported by the members' pooled capital, generally from operations. Marketing activities, especially those of storing, grading, or processing products, requires significant outlays of capital, and the Rochdale cooperative business model had limited capital per member (Woeste 1998, 24).

The meaningful operations of the Grange were short, rising rapidly and generally collapsing in the 1870s (Hanna 1931, 6; Nourse 1927, 34). Even so, the impacts of organizing farmers and promoting the Rochdale Principles as cooperative legal requirements have carried forward to co-ops today (Fite 1978, 8; Woeste 1998, 22).

Development of State Organizational Statutes

Farmers Allowed to Form Cooperatives Under General Statutes

In many states, the formation of corporations in the mid-1800s was by special legislative act. As states developed general business incorporation acts by industry, union movements and the Grange farmer protest movements led farmers to appeal to their state legislatures for general statutes to form local co-ops (Hanna 1931, 5–7; Nourse 1927, 39–50).

Michigan authorized the formation of cooperative stores in 1865 (*Michigan Laws* 1865; Nourse 1927, 39). Massachusetts passed a cooperative law in 1866 (*Massachusetts Laws* 1866) governing cooperative procedures that were a pattern for the statutes of Pennsylvania (1868), Minnesota (1870), Connecticut (1875), and Ohio (1884) (Nourse 1927, 40). The Massachusetts statute generally allowed co-ops to be formed as a corporation to conduct lawful pursuits, including agricultural businesses, with capital stock limiting a member's interest in the co-op to $1,000, voting power of not more than one vote per member, and limited liability of members. The statute also authorized a distribution of the profits to the purchasers and stockholders as described in the bylaws, provided that 10 percent of the net profits were deposited in a sinking fund until the amount of the sinking fund balance was a sum equal to 30 percent in excess of the capital stock (*Massachusetts Laws* 1866).

In 1877, Kansas, Wisconsin, and Pennsylvania enacted cooperative laws (Nourse 1927, 42–43). The Kansas law was brief, requiring "one man, one vote" (42). The Wisconsin law was similar to the Massachusetts law but limited debts to two-thirds of the paid-up capital and prescribed voting: "members and not shares of stock shall vote in electing officers and transacting any business of the association of whatsoever nature, but no proxies shall be allowed" (42).

The Pennsylvania law was longer and more detailed, covering limited voting, patronage dividends, trade for cash, and so forth; it also included a unique base capital provision characterized as "permanent" and "ordinary" stock. "Ordinary" stock could be bought and sold, but each member held permanent stock allowing one vote and patronage dividends that were applied to payment for the stock until the $1,000 maximum was attained (Nourse 1927, 43).

The First Model Statutes. In 1911, Wisconsin and Nebraska enacted cooperative laws that prescribed by statute the distribution of profits by patronage dividends to members. Prior laws had allowed co-ops to distribute dividends as provided in the bylaws (Nourse 1927, 46). The Wisconsin law required earnings to be apportioned first to pay dividends on stock not to exceed 6 percent; then, of the remainder, not less than 10 percent for a reserve fund until it was equal to 30 percent of capital stock; 5 percent for education to teach cooperative development; then, of the remainder, one-half according to purchases of shareholders and upon wages of employees, and the other half according to the purchases of shareholders and nonshareholders, provided that for processing co-ops the dividend would be on raw products delivered instead of purchases (*Wisconsin Laws* 1911). The Wisconsin law was generally adopted in sixteen other states in the following eight years (Nourse 1927, 46). The cooperative laws based on the Wisconsin model generally required capital stock co-ops to operate on the Rochdale Principles of limited capital holdings, democratic voting, and distribution of profits based on patronage (48).

Nonstock Cooperative Alternative

An alternative to capital stock co-ops was developed concurrently with the Wisconsin and Nebraska state statutes primarily to avoid the corporate attributes associated with capital stock. Critics alleged that capital stock co-ops were merely a modified form of for-profit corporations and that an alternative organization should (1) avoid capital stock by putting all invested capital on a "loan" basis, (2) eliminate the competitive-price relationship with the member (transfer price for product) and substitute a net returns settlement, and (3) restrict cooperative transactions to members only (Nourse 1927, 52–58).

In 1909, California enacted a nonstock cooperative law (Statues of California 1909), providing for a membership association on a nonprofit basis that allowed equal or unequal voting and property interests as provided in the articles of incorporation. Capital contribution from members was authorized as "membership" fees. Six states adopted nonstock cooperative laws based on the California model from 1909 to 1921 (Nourse 1927, 65).

Nonstock cooperative laws were further modified by provisions of a U.S. Department of Agriculture (USDA) model nonstock cooperative act under the title "Suggestions for a State Co-operative Law Designed to Conform to Section 6 of the Clayton Act" (Nourse 1927, 73–92). The USDA model act required co-ops to only conduct business with members. Seven states enacted statutes based on the USDA model nonstock cooperative act (Hanna 1931, 42).

The Capper–Volstead Cooperative Definition

The initial period of cooperative statutes allowed the farmer businesses considerable flexibility to form and adapt co-ops to business conditions. As co-ops formed to exert market power, the principles were litigated in the context of antitrust violations (Guth 1982; Sapiro 1923).

The Clayton Act provided certain exemptions for co-ops organized without stock. In 1922, the Capper–Volstead Act was enacted by Congress to provide an exemption from antitrust enforcement for narrowly defined farmer co-ops organized as stock or nonstock co-ops whose membership was limited to agricultural producers, restrict voting to one vote per member or limit dividends on equity to 8 percent per year, and handle products for members whose value exceeded that of products handled for nonmembers (Lauck 1999, 491–493).

The Capper–Volstead Act definition of co-ops continued to be the federal definition of co-ops for purposes of federal regulatory relief and financial assistance. The impact of federal financial assistance institutionalized the cooperative business structure. The federal government loaned $330 million to co-ops from 1929 to 1932, an additional $68 million by 1934, and more than $400 million on an annual credit basis by the end of World War II (Lauck and Adams 2000, 67–68).

By 1970, one-third of the capital used by co-ops (subject to the Capper–Volstead definition with some modification) stemmed from debt, and the federally chartered banks for co-ops provided nearly all of the remaining debt financing (Lauck and Adams 2000, 68). The restriction of outside capital and limited capital returns did not impede cooperative development when favorable federal debt financing was available.

Commodity Marketing Acts

The most pervasive development in cooperative law occurred from 1921 through 1926, with more than forty states enacting a commodity marketing act to incorporate co-ops (Sapiro 1927, 8).

Sapiro's Plan. The movement was started by Aaron Sapiro based on his California commodity cooperative marketing experiences (Larsen 1967, 446–454). Sapiro's plan consisted of (1) organization of the association on a commodity basis; (2) limitation of membership to and democratic control by actual growers; (3) control of the deliveries by means of a long-term, legally binding contract signed by every member; (4) pooling of product according to grade, basing returns to each member on the average annual price received for the pool to which they contributed, and providing orderly marketing of the product throughout the productive period; and (5) control of a sufficient portion of the entire crop to be a dominant factor in the market and to make possible an economic distribution of overhead expenses (Knapp 1973, 9; Sapiro 1923, 200–201).

According to Sapiro (1927), the fruit growers in California experimented with cooperation to suit their needs and federated local associations of growers for marketing all of the growers' fruit:

[T]his was an organization by the commodity in contrast to organization by locality. . . . This adjustment could not be made by a single farmer; nor by a local association or even a small group of locals. But it could be made by farmers who could control and be certain of the control of a large percentage of the commodity and could help guide the flow of that commodity into the markets of the world. . . . The inevitable happened. Law began to conform slowly to the economic advance. The farmers had found a definite trend; and law put flesh on its dry bones and grew again in the same measure. (Sapiro 1927, 2–3)

A National Model: The Bingham Act. Sapiro, whose national stature with farm organizations allowed him to participate in preparing drafts of the Capper–Volstead Act, prepared a draft commodity marketing law based on the cooperative requirements of the Capper–Volstead Act and the California marketing principles. The first commodity marketing act was adopted in Texas in 1921, but the best form and most widely adopted model was the Bingham Cooperative Marketing Act (Bingham Act) enacted by Kentucky in 1922 (Sapiro 1927, 7).

The Bingham Act was uniquely conformed to the Capper–Volstead Act. It thwarted unwarranted judicial intervention of competitors by legislatively announcing public policy issues requiring farmers to cooperate while providing a legal framework for cooperative organization and operations. The key features of the Bingham Act are as follows:

- public policy statements of the producers' right to conduct cooperative marketing;
- provisions for a preliminary investigation of the marketing conditions to ensure success of the co-op;
- statutory authority to conduct the commodity marketing for the members of the co-op;
- restriction of members to agricultural producers, including share crop landlords and tenants;
- authorization of district voting for directors, directors and officers elected from the membership other than by appointment, or election of directors to represent the interests of the general public;
- statutory authorization of a marketing contract with members, including remedies of liquidated damages and injunction as a penalty for breach of the contract;
- criminal penalty for inducement of breach of the contract or spreading false reports about the finances or management of the co-op;
- penalties against warehousemen for soliciting or persuading members to breach marketing contracts;

- a declaration that commodity marketing or the marketing contracts shall not be deemed to be a conspiracy or combination in restraint of trade, an attempt to lessen competition, or an attempt to fix prices arbitrarily in violation of any law of the state (Acts of Kentucky 1922, 1922).

A substantial amount of litigation ensued in many jurisdictions following the enactment of the commodity marketing acts, but the acts were held to be constitutional (Sapiro 1927, 10–11; Meyer 1927, 90–93; Tobriner 1928, 19–34). The general adoption of the Bingham Act started the uniform acceptance of legal principles for marketing co-ops and was referred to as the "Standard Act" (Evans and Stokdyk 1937, 298). Many legislatures modified the Standard Act with local concerns over operations; however, the main provisions of the Bingham Act were enacted.

A Ten-year Effort for National Uniformity Fails. The push for uniformity of the commodity marketing acts was undertaken by the National Conference of Commissioners on Uniform State Laws in 1925. After consideration of five consecutive drafts over ten years, the Conference and the American Bar Association approved the draft for submission to state legislatures. A national uniform cooperative law was referred to as an "epochal development in the field of marketing law" (Evans and Stokdyk 1937, 300), but the uniform law was not widely included. Only two states had adopted the Uniform Act with modifications by 1945 (Jensen 1950, 12). Even so, with the Uniform Act and substantial case law supporting the principles and language of the Bingham Act, the co-op as an organizational structure had reached legal maturity by 1950 (Ela 1950, 524).

Modern Corporate Cooperative Statutes

In the late 1980s and 1990s, Minnesota, Colorado, and Ohio redrafted their cooperative statutes. While commodity marketing acts were restricted to agricultural producers marketing their products, many states had modified these statutes to allow nonagricultural producers to form co-ops for other purposes. The modern corporate cooperative statutes are general cooperative statutes with certain provisions to accommodate agricultural producer co-ops. In Minnesota, five different stock and nonstock cooperative statutes were recodified and revised into one corporate cooperative statute (Hanson 1993; *Minnesota Laws* 1989).

Colorado repealed and reenacted one of its corporate cooperative statutes (Colorado Session Laws 1996, 1996; The New Colorado Cooperative Act 1996), and Ohio adopted a corporate cooperative statute in 1998 (*Ohio Laws*

1998). The impetus for revision was the increased interest in and formation of a new generation of value-added co-ops (Hanson 2001a, 41–42). Most of the NGCs are processing co-ops with a different focus from commodity marketing co-ops.

A Comparison of Modern Corporate Cooperative Acts to a Commodity Marketing Act. The modern corporate cooperative acts generally differ from commodity marketing acts in facilitating modern corporate functions. The Rochdale Principles embodied in the commodity marketing acts are largely unchanged. Table 5.1 compares the major distinctions.

Cooperative Organization Under Noncooperative Statutes. State cooperative statutes provide a framework for organization and incorporation (Baarda 1982). Co-ops can also be organized under general business corporation statutes to meet federal cooperative tax criteria, and under LLC statutes to operate on a cooperative basis and be taxed on a pass-through or partnership tax basis. Organization and incorporation under noncooperative statutes require substantial modification of articles, bylaws, and operating agreements to achieve operation on a cooperative basis.

A New Model Under Old Statutes: New Generation Cooperatives

Starting in the 1970s and 1980s and rapidly developing in the 1990s, a new form of co-op—the "value-added" or "new generation" co-op—was being organized throughout the Midwest by agricultural producers to further process agricultural products (Hanson 2000b; Patrie 1998).

The New Generation Cooperatives (NGCs) were formed under existing cooperative statutes but were capitalized and operated differently from supply and marketing co-ops. NGCs acquired or constructed processing facilities through 40 to 50 percent member equity and 50 to 60 percent debt financing. The member equity is obtained from each member subscribing to stock in proportion to the amount of crops or livestock committed to be delivered to the co-op.

Through stock subscriptions, the member producers essentially purchase the processing and marketing capacity of the co-op to process and market the agricultural products committed for delivery under marketing contracts. Products delivered are in proportion to stock purchased, and patronage is paid to the producers based on product delivered. The different variations of this model utilize common stock for the voting membership stock, and preferred stock is divided into delivery shares. In both cases, the amount of product committed to be delivered under uniform delivery and marketing agreements are proportional to delivery share ownership (Hanson 2000a).

Table 5.1

Comparison of Modern Corporate Cooperative Statute with Commodity Marketing Act

Modern cooperative statutes	Commodity marketing act
Organization	
Statutory policy declarations	Policy declaration—orderly marketing stabilizes marketing of agricultural products
Purpose—any lawful purpose	Marketing, processing, handling agricultural products of members; or manufacturing, selling, or supplying members with machinery, equipment, or supplies
Incorporators—one or more persons	Requires 10 to 20 persons; a majority must be residents of state
Stock and nonstock organization—with same power and authority	Grants powers to both stock and nonstock co-ops
No similar provisions	Preliminary investigation of marketing conditions by university
No similar provisions	Statement that cooperative marketing is in public interest
Articles of incorporation	
Required provisions	
Board Authority to designate classification of shares if not designated in articles	No similar provision
General statement of rights and obligations of shares	Similar
Statement of governance rights (voting)—description of voting allocations	One vote per member; no variance
Statement of restrictions on share transfer (approval of board) and whether bylaws and board may further restrict transfer	Bylaws required to only allow transfer to producers
Limitations on dividends on stock (typically 8 percent)	No similar provision
Allocations and distributions of income in excess of dividend based on patronage	No similar provision

Amendment—by board majority and majority of members voting; board may amend articles until co-op has members or stockholders with voting rights; board authority to adopt specified amendments or without shareholder approval	Approval by two-thirds of board and majority of all members; no authority for board amendments
Bylaws—co-op may have but need not have bylaws. Initial adoption by board; subsequent adoption by members unless bylaw authorizing board:	Must have bylaws adopted by members
Admission, withdrawal, and suspension of members	Note mandatory redemption upon withdrawal
Voting rights; privileges of members	One vote per member
Reports and financial statements to members	No similar provision

Powers

Generally, all acts necessary and proper to conduct co-op's business or to accomplish purposes of co-op	Generally similar; may be more restrictive
Accept deposits from co-op members	No similar provision
Acquire and dispose of stock or ownership interests in other entities	Restricted to co-ops with similar producer membership
Establish, pay, and operate pension share bonus and option plans and benefit plans for directors, employees, and agents	No similar provision
Indemnify directors, officers, and employees	No similar provision
Create subsidiary corporations, co-ops, LLCs, and other business entities	Similar but related to tax; no authority for LLCs

Agricultural marketing contracts

Contracts authorized for delivery of products; default remedies include specific performance, liquidated damages; criminal penalties for contract interference	Generally same except no penalty for contract interference, and restrictions on warehousemen

Board of directors

Board governance of cooperative— all authority of co-op exercised by board unless otherwise provided by articles or bylaws	Board governance; authority to exercise powers not explicit

(continued)

Table 5.1 (continued)

Modern cooperative statutes	Commodity marketing act
Limitation of directors' liability	No similar provision
Encumber all assets without shareholder approval	No similar provision
Sale or disposition of all property without shareholder approval—to subsidiary, in ordinary course of business	No similar provision

Members

Districts—authorized in bylaws implemented by board	Authorized in bylaws
Member violations of bylaws—surrender or conversion of equity; cancellation of membership; redemption authorized not mandated	Similar; however, appraisal of interests and redemption within one year of withdrawal or expulsion required
Required reports to members	No similar provision
Access to records by members	No similar provision
Voting—who may vote, mail and absentee voting, proportional patronage voting	One vote per member
Limits of liability for corporate debts	Similar
Approval required for certain transfers of all or substantially all of the assets	No similar provision

Stock

No similar provision	No member may own more then 1/20 of stock of co-op; common stock may only be owned by producers
Authority and rights for preferred stock	With or without right vote; purchase of property, value
Perfected lien of co-op for debts and obligations to co-op	No similar provision

Allocations and distributions

Reserves authorized; net income in excess of dividends distributed at least annually on basis of patronage; form of distribution prescribed	No similar provision; distributions of income referenced in marketing contract

Mergers and consolidations

Generally authorized with other co-ops and in certain cases with corporations	No similar provision

Nonuniform State Cooperative Laws Impede New Generation Cooperative Organization

The nonuniform development of agricultural co-ops and cooperative law has resulted in significant variations in state cooperative statutes—many of which were enacted from 1910 to 1925. In fact, few states have the same cooperative statute. This author and his partners have formed NGCs under stock and nonstock cooperative laws of many of the agrarian states, and although some state cooperative statutes have impediments, these can be generally overcome by shareholder agreements, article or bylaw provisions, or financing provisions.

Organization Under Commodity Marketing Acts: Indiana. Indiana enacted a commodity marketing act in 1925, which has had few amendments, to incorporate stock and nonstock, nonprofit co-ops whose members must be agricultural producers (*West's Annotated Indiana Code* 1998). Forty other states have similar commodity marketing acts. The statute requires all members to be individuals or political subdivisions of Indiana engaged in the production of agricultural products, with the redemption of expelled or retired members' interests to be as provided in the bylaws. The co-op may restrict voting to one vote per member regardless of the number of shares owned or capital invested. Distributions after restoration of deficits, payments of stock dividends, and allocations to reserves are as provided in bylaws to members, nonmembers, and patrons, but only on the basis of patronage. The limitations of a commodity marketing act require skillful lawyering to organize NGCs.

Organization Alternatives Under Separate Stock and Nonstock Cooperative Statutes: Missouri. Missouri enacted stock and nonstock cooperative statutes in 1923 and 1925. In these statutes, twelve persons may incorporate a stock co-op to produce or furnish goods or services; to conduct an agricultural or mercantile business on a cooperative plan; or to sell to or buy from all stockholders, groceries, or other merchandisers (Missouri Statutes 2001, § 357.010). Stock may only be owned by natural persons (as opposed to juridical persons such as corporations), and co-ops must be organized in Missouri on a cooperative plan. As enacted until 1945, the directors were elected on a basis of one vote for each share of stock owned, but now the legislation requires one vote per shareholder and states that the policies of the co-op, including declaration of dividends, setting aside reserve funds, and method of distributing profits are reserved and conferred upon the shareholders (§§ 357.090, 357.100). Profits are distributed to shareholders or, if authorized, to nonstockholders on a patronage basis after first setting aside 10 percent for a reserve fund until the fund equals 50 percent of the paid-up capital stock (§357.130). Dividends on stock may be declared not to exceed 10 percent.

Missouri also enacted a commodity marketing act that requires eleven or more persons, a majority of whom are residents of Missouri, to incorporate a nonstock, nonprofit co-op (Missouri Statutes 2002, §§ 274.010–274.300). Membership is restricted to agricultural producers. The nonstock co-op is governed by the board of directors, who must be members; however, one-third of the directors may refer any question to the membership (§ 274.150). In the case of the death, withdrawal, or expulsion of a member, the directors, when authorized by the membership, must appraise the value of the former member's property rights and pay the amount to the former member or the member's heirs or representatives as if the member had continued member-ship (§ 274.090). This requirement can be burdensome or cause the dissolu-tion of an NGC in that the statute shifts the burden of the member to the co-op to find replacement equity for a member who leaves.

The Missouri stock cooperative restrictions on stockholders to natural persons or Missouri co-ops, and the high statutory reserve in excess of paid-up capital stock (50 percent), significantly impair the formation of NGCs or other contemporary cooperative businesses. As a result, most new co-ops are organized on a nonstock basis with stock-like equity participation units es-tablished in the organizational documents.

Organization Under Unique For-profit and Nonprofit Distinctions: Michi-gan. Michigan generally organizes its corporate law into for-profit and non-profit corporations. Each division has provisions for incorporating a co-op, while for both the operation is on a cooperative basis similar to other stat-utes. Other than the differences in the operational provisions between a for-profit and nonprofit co-op, a primary consideration is that the shares or equity of a for-profit co-op offered to members is subject to the Michigan securities registration requirements, while the shares or equity offered to members of a nonprofit co-op are generally not required to be registered.

NGCs that organize in Michigan typically organize initially under the non-profit corporation cooperative laws but are operationally better suited to the provisions of the for-profit cooperative corporation laws. The nonprofit and for-profit distinctions for corporations do not appropriately apply to co-ops.

A New Era: Unincorporated Cooperative Associations

As more NGCs were organized, farmers voiced their complaints about state law restrictions and impediments of federal law. Midwestern states with anti-corporate farming laws (*Iowa Code* 2001, Ch. 9H; Minnesota Statutes 2001,

§ 500.24) did not allow co-ops to participate in confined hog feeding, dairy, and egg-laying operations. In these cases, corn farmers desired to process corn into feed to be fed to the poultry or livestock owned by the co-op and to realize profits from marketing pork, milk, or eggs. Iowa and Minnesota both modified their anticorporate farming laws to allow restricted farmer entities, including co-ops, to engage in these ventures.

Iowa Chapter 501 Statute. Iowa enacted a cooperative statute in 1996 "to provide an opportunity for producers of agricultural commodities to contribute a portion of their production for a single enterprise for purposes of enhancing the value of that production and to restrict control of these enterprises to agricultural producers" (*Iowa Laws* 1996, Ch. 1010, §1). This corporate cooperative statute required "farming entities" (*Iowa Code* 2001, §§ 501.101, 9H.4) to have at least 60 percent of the voting control and financial rights, and required "authorized persons" to have 75 percent of the voting control and financial rights (§§ 501.101[2][6]), with the profits distributed on a patronage basis and interests in the co-op not to exceed 8 percent of the total. In some cases, profits may be allocated to reserves or retained savings (§ 501.503).

The statute also requires redemption of a member's interest over a period not to exceed seven years upon withdrawal or expulsion. Some ventures had incorporated and attempted to obtain a § 521 certification as a farmer's co-op from the Internal Revenue Service. The process resulted in questions as to whether such a co-op operated on a cooperative basis (Brown 1998). In 1998, the Iowa legislature substantially amended the corporate cooperative statute to eliminate the terms of "incorporation," "incorporators," "stock," "shareholders," and similar corporate terms and replace them with "association," "organizers," "members," "interests," and similar LLC terms (*Iowa Laws* 1999).

With these changes, promoters claimed that a co-op organized under the statute would be considered an unincorporated association and qualify for partnership type pass-through taxation similar to an LLC (Brown 1998). A revenue ruling confirming this approach has not been obtained.

Wyoming Processing Cooperative Law. In 1999, lamb producers in Wyoming and its surrounding states desired to acquire lamb meat, wool, and pelt processing and marketing businesses to make lamb production more profitable. The lamb producers realized that more capital would be needed than could be supplied by producers on a per lamb basis. They wanted to organize their business on a cooperative basis, but the existing models did not fit their business plan (Hanson 2001b, 8–9).

The Wyoming legislature adopted changes in the existing cooperative statute, and a new processing cooperative statute was enacted to be effective on July 1, 2001 (*Wyoming Laws* 2001). A ruling request submitted to the Internal Revenue Service confirmed that a co-op organized under the Wyoming processing cooperative statute would be considered an "unincorporated association" and subject to partnership taxation or corporate taxation by election similar to an LLC (PLR 2001).

A Wyoming processing co-op can be formed and organized on a cooperative plan as provided in the Wyoming Processing Cooperative Statute to market, process, or otherwise change the form or marketability of crops, livestock, and other agricultural products and purposes necessary or convenient to facilitate the production or marketing of agricultural products by patron members.

A Wyoming processing co-op has flexibility in two important areas that are not available to corporate co-ops. The nature of the patronage relationship with its members can be determined by the organizational documents, and the co-op can enter what would otherwise be considered nonpatronage source business without tax at the co-op thereby passing income, losses, and tax credits through to the members; the co-op can also attract capital through outside investments (Hanson 2001b, 6–8).

The co-op's owners are its members divided into two classes. Patron members have rights and obligations to deliver the product to the co-op, while nonpatron members do not have product delivery obligations and are primarily "investment" members. Patron members may also participate as investment members. The patron members have preference in both governance and financial rights.

The voting rights of the members are differentiated between patron and investment members. Patron members vote on a democratic basis of one vote per member subject to certain exceptions. The patron member vote, however, is counted collectively based on a majority of the patron members voting on an issue. Investment members have voting rights proportional to their investment or as otherwise provided in the bylaws. The collective nature of the patron member's vote ensures patron members maximum representation in cooperative voting.

The co-op is governed by a board of at least three directors. At least one director must be elected by the patron members. Directors elected by patron members have at least 50 percent of the voting power of the board or voting power on an equal governance basis.

The financial rights are distinguished between patron members and investment members. The patron members are allocated financial rights (i.e., profits, losses, and distributions) based on patronage or business done by the patron member for or with the co-op. Investment members are allocated financial rights based on capital contributions. Financial rights are allocated between patron members collectively and investment members based on capital contributions, provided, however, that the patron members collectively receive at least 15 percent of the profit allocations and distributions.

Restrictions on member control, contributions, governance rights, and financial rights must be stated in the bylaws or within separate member control agreements. Investment members have redemption rights if bylaw amendments alter governance or financial rights that affect their investment. To protect both patron and investment members upon their entrance to the co-op, the co-op must disclose to any person or entity acquiring membership interests in the co-op the capital structure, business prospects, and risks of the co-op, including the nature of governance and financial rights of the membership interests being acquired and of other classes of membership and membership interests (Hanson 2001b, 6–8).

Variations in Statutes Will Ultimately Lead to Organizational Forum Shopping

The modern corporate cooperative acts retain the cooperative principles of the 1920s but typically do not restrict the purposes for which a co-op may be formed. The Iowa Chapter 501 cooperative statute, while restrictive, made the first step in allowing co-ops to form without the restrictions of federal corporate cooperative taxation and allows up to 25 percent nonproducer ownership and control. The Wyoming cooperative processing law provides the most flexible format for organizing a business organization on the cooperative business principle of distribution of earnings to patrons on the basis of patronage with or without federal corporate cooperative taxation.

The large variation in cooperative laws among states invariably leads to shopping for the best state statute when a new co-op is to be organized. The business principles of operating successfully drive new co-ops, especially NGCs, to seek an organizational statute that accommodates their business plan and structure. Forum shopping has been in practice for many years, with many corporations throughout the country incorporating under Delaware corporate statutes.

Impact of Federal Law on Cooperative Structure

A co-op is organized or incorporated under state law and must abide by the requirements of the organizational statute to maintain its charter to operate as a separate legal entity. While some state statutes under which a co-op may be organized offer more flexibility than others, federal laws require a co-op to have a certain legal structure (required by its articles and bylaws) in order to receive the corresponding benefit of the federal law.

Corporate Cooperatives Structured to Meet Tax Law

Virtually all corporate co-ops must be structured and operate on a cooperative basis as determined by the cooperative taxation provisions ("Subchapter T") of the federal Internal Revenue Code (the "Tax Code") in order to not be taxed as a corporation. The combined state and federal marginal tax rate is 35 to 40 percent of taxable income in many states. Co-ops that operate on a cooperative basis under Subchapter T of the Tax Code are allowed to deduct patronage-sourced income that is allocated on a patronage basis. Simply stated, a corporate co-op organized under state law may avoid a combined state and federal 35 to 40 percent tax at the co-op level by operating on a cooperative basis prescribed by Subchapter T of the Tax Code and properly allocating its patronage-sourced income to its members. Two types of co-ops qualify to deduct income allocated to patrons: (1) an "exempt" or § 521 co-op, and (2) a nonexempt co-op that operates on a cooperative basis for the purposes of Subchapter T.

Operation on a Cooperative Basis. The U.S. Tax Court has determined three guiding principles for operating on a cooperative basis: (1) subordination of capital; (2) democratic control by members; and (3) proportional allocation of income on the basis of patronage (*Puget Sound Plywood* 1965). In the 1990s, the IRS added four additional factors in considering whether a corporate co-op is operating on a cooperative basis: (1) existence of a joint effort on behalf of members; (2) a minimum number of patrons; (3) member business should not exceed nonmembers' business; and (4) upon liquidation, present and future patrons must share in the distribution of any remaining assets in proportion to the business each did with the co-op during some reasonable period of years (Frederick and Reilly 2001, 26–27).

An exempt § 521 co-op has two additional deductions from gross income that are not available to a nonexempt co-op: (1) amounts paid as dividends on capital stock, and (2) amounts allocated to patrons with respect to income that is not patronage-sourced. To qualify for these two additional exemptions, an exempt co-op generally must (1) have substantially all (85 percent) agricultural producer members; (2) return profits in excess of expenses and permitted reserves to all patrons (members and nonmembers) on the basis of patronage with the co-op; (3) restrict dividends on capital stock not to exceed the legal rate of interest in the state of incorporation or 8 percent, whichever is greater; and (4) restrict nonmember marketing business not to exceed member business, and restrict nonmember nonproducer purchasers not to exceed 15 percent of all purchases (Frederick 1996; *Internal Revenue Code* 1992, § 521).

Deduction Only Applies to Patronage-sourced Business. Co-ops that qualify for the ability to deduct income allocated to patrons are further restricted in that the deduction applies to patronage-sourced business for nonexempt co-ops and for patronage- and nonpatronage-sourced business approved within the exempt co-op's scope of business certified by the IRS (*Internal Revenue Code* 1992, §§ 521, 1381–1388). The limitations of both of these restrictions are beyond the scope of this article but have been discussed extensively by Frederick and Reilly (2001). In general, a deduction qualifying for patronage-sourced business income requires that the income must be related to the patronage business and not be derived from other products, ingredients, or further processing by others. In limited cases, the income from investments in joint ventures that further process and market a co-op's products may qualify as patronage-sourced business.

Many of the Tax Code regulations were promulgated in the 1950s through the 1970s prior to the advent of NGCs and LLCs. At that time, virtually all companies were organized as corporations and all income was taxed at the entity level. Deductions such as those for income generated from patronage-sourced businesses or for exempt co-ops, the scope of business for which the patronage-sourced business deductions were derived, have been narrowly construed and restrictively regulated by the IRS.

Antitrust: Capper–Volstead Protection

The Capper–Volstead Act (*U.S. Laws 1922* 1992) has been hailed as the "Magna Carta of Cooperative Law." This acknowledgment was appropriate because marketing co-ops and, especially, stock co-ops, were being successfully challenged under state and federal antitrust laws as illegal combinations that restrained trade in the early part of the 1900s (Guth 1982). The Capper–Volstead Act provided a limited antitrust exemption for co-ops that (1) limit membership to agricultural producers; (2) operate for the benefit of members as producers; (3) restrict voting to one vote per member or limit dividends on equity to 8 percent per year; and (4) handle products for members that have a value exceeding the value of products handled for nonmembers. Subsequently, the Cooperative Marketing Act of 1926 was enacted, which allowing co-ops that meet these requirements to share marketing information (Cooperative Marketing Act of 1926, 1992).

The criteria for a co-op qualifying for protection under the Capper–Volstead Act were developed primarily from the U.S. Department of Agriculture (USDA), but it is important that these same criteria formed the basis of the commodity marketing acts adopted throughout the country (Guth 1982).

Agricultural Marketing Act of 1929

This act defines co-ops to include the requirements of the Capper–Volstead Act (Agricultural Marketing Act of 1929, 1992). The act was originally intended to define which co-ops were eligible for cooperative bank financing but has subsequently been used as the test for (1) the protection against handler coercion and discrimination in the Agricultural Fair Practices Act; (2) the cooperative exemption from the registration requirements of the Securities Act of 1934; (3) the cooperative exemption from the trust provisions of the Perishable Agricultural Commodity Act; and (4) the cooperative trucking exemption from trucking regulations under the Interstate Transportation Act (Frederick 2002).

Entity Selection: Corporate Cooperative vs. LLC or the Wyoming Cooperative

Co-ops are organizations that have been developed on social and policy principles, primarily the Rochdale Principles and business principles of the patronage relationship. When producers are organizing an agricultural business that requires delivery and processing of products, an evaluation of the types of entity to organize focuses on corporate co-ops versus LLCs and now the Wyoming Processing Cooperatives (Wyoming Cooperatives).

Pass-Through Taxation and Limitations of LLCs

Limited liability companies (LLCs) offer pass-through taxation—that is, no tax at the entity level and a pass-through of gains, losses, and tax credits to members. An LLC can be organized to separate governance and financial rights (i.e., voting can be proportional or disproportional to the investment). Allocations and distributions can, but need not, be proportional to the investment. LLCs require operating agreements signed by all members and are cumbersome to amend. Unlike bylaws as organizational rules, operating agreements are viewed as member contractual rights.

The flexibility of an LLC requires a careful crafting of organizational documents to effect business provisions and a careful analysis of the tax ramifications. The federal partnership tax law was developed for partnerships and has not been revised to accommodate LLCs. If the business will require member delivery of the product to be processed by the LLC, the issue of transfer price and allocation of income based on the product delivered versus investment must be addressed. An LLC structure can be adopted to allocate or distribute income based on product delivered but the documentation and agreements are cumbersome and complicated.

Corporate Cooperative Restrictions and LLC Alternatives

The Business Principle: Income Allocated Based on Patronage. The most important business principle of a co-op is allocation and distribution of income based on patronage (i.e., business done for or with the co-op) rather than investment. In other corporations, the investor need not do any business or purchase or use any of the corporation's products or services to receive stock dividends representing profits allocated through share ownership of profits of the corporation. A co-op is organized to benefit members who deliver or acquire product to or from the co-op. Noncooperative businesses can acquire and market products of their investors; however, the product procurement and marketing is done on a contractual basis typically based on the transfer price of the product.

A co-op is organized to allocate income to members based on business done for or with the co-op. In NGCs, members invest money to purchase stock or equity proportional to the amount of product to be delivered. In essence, the processing facility can be considered to be divided and allocated into processing and marketing units with each member purchasing a block of processing and marketing units through his/her equity ownership. This collective action on behalf of the members' units results in the income attributable to those units being allocated and eventually distributed to each member. The cooperative organizational statutes of the various states facilitate and, in many cases, mandate this principle.

If producers, with or without others, intend to form an agricultural business that does not utilize their products or is intended to reward producers solely on investment, the business should not be organized as a co-op.

Subordination of Capital. Organization on this business principle as a co-op carries several nonbusiness principles, especially with corporate co-ops. State and federal statutes have legislated that subordination of capital means outside investment should receive no more than an 8 percent dividend on equity. During most of the last twenty-five years, 8 percent would not have paid for the use of capital and, in fact, would pay less than a commercial bank debt. LLCs and Wyoming Cooperatives can have outside investors and pay returns at market rates to attract that outside investment.

Dealing Primarily with the Products of Members. Exempt corporate co-ops are to deal only with the products of producers, and the value of member products must exceed nonmember products. While nonexempt corporate co-ops may deal with a greater amount of nonmember products, this principle is embodied primarily in federal corporate cooperative tax law. Most processing and marketing businesses need a variety of grades and pricing of products to be successful marketers. Certain nonmember producers may offer to sell products at harvest at a substantial discount. A corporate cooperative processing entity would be at a competitive disadvantage if it could not acquire products from nonmember producers at the same discount as its competitors. If a corporate co-op is authorized to conduct business with nonmembers on a noncooperative basis, the income is not deductible as patronage-sourced business and, therefore, will be subject to state and federal tax at the co-op level. LLCs and Wyoming Cooperatives can acquire products from members or nonmembers at the most competitive price.

Limitation of Patronage-sourced Income. Although a corporate co-op is based on a single-level tax theory—income is either taxed at the entity or at the member level—the deduction at the co-op level is only available for patronage-sourced business, which, through years of IRS challenges is restrictively interpreted to mean that level closely associated with the members' products. For example, if a farmer's corporate co-op produced a pharmaceutical drug from a plant that was extracted in the co-op's processing facility, combining that drug with other drugs in a capsule to be labeled and marketed to consumers, the drug extracted from the farmer's plants would likely have a small value relative to the overall capsule; therefore, the income from the sale of the capsules would not be patronage-sourced and would be taxed at the state and federal marginal rate of approximately 35 to 40 percent at the cooperative level. LLCs and Wyoming Cooperatives can pass this income through to their members.

Tax Credits and Losses. Corporate co-ops that are taxed under Subchapter T have a number of corporate tax attributes under Subchapter C of the Tax Code, including the inability to pass losses or tax credits through to members. For ethanol production co-ops, start-up operational losses are retained at the co-op level, and tax credits, which may exceed $2 to $3 million, generally remain unused by corporate co-ops. LLCs and Wyoming Cooperatives can pass these losses and credits through to their members.

Operation at Cost with All Profits Returned Based on Patronage. This is a principle embodied in federal corporate cooperative tax and case law and in some state statutes. Nonpatronage-sourced investment venture partners and other participation in profits are precluded, which limits outside capital and management who desire profit participation as part of their compensation, similar to corporate management. An LLC or Wyoming Cooperative can allow outside investment and management participation in profits as part of their compensation.

Governance: Board of Directors Elected by One Member/One Vote. Corporate co-ops are governed by a board elected from members and membership voting on the basis of one member/one vote. This principle has two facets: (1) how the members vote, and (2) who they can vote for to govern the co-op. The Rochdale Principle of one member/one vote was an alternative to voting based on investment and paralleled the Rochdale Principle of subordination of capital with no voice in management. Co-ops in some states have recognized that in the case of a federated co-op (i.e., a co-op with one or more co-ops as members), a fair method of member voting is on a basis proportional to patronage (Barton 1989, 26–33).

In addition, board governance frequently has directors selected from districts based on geographical areas, products, patronage, or other distinctions. The general principle of one member/one vote, while an alternative to voting based upon investment, does not vest voting authority with the patrons who have the most at risk with the success or failure of the co-op. Consequently, member governance tends to be less effective than it should be and board elections can be political and based on popularity.

Corporate co-ops usually require that directors elected from the membership be patrons and, in many cases, that they be producers. Representation of patron members on the board is important, but equally important is board representation to facilitate strategic planning; capitalization; and hiring, retention, and termination of management on appropriate terms. The producer board members of a capital-intensive processing and marketing co-op may not possess the same skills and knowledge as a diverse board with outside directors who are familiar with the processing and marketing industry or of capital availability.

LLCs and Wyoming Cooperatives can allocate voting based on patronage and investment. The directors elected by members need not be members, which allows the hiring of outside directors for their expertise.

State and Federal Opportunities to Assist Cooperative Development

State and federal assistance should recognize five factors in making changes to assist cooperative development: (1) the cooperative business model must compete favorably with other business models or it will not be used; (2) many if not most cooperative opportunities require capital beyond the means of producer members; (3) the cooperative business model must grow with the success of the co-op; (4) co-ops need more flexibility today to succeed than at any previous time; and (5) cooperative development can represent sustainable rural development and have exponential benefits beyond the cooperative business.

Legislative Changes to Remove Legal Impediments

Legal principles originally developed to support cooperation have become statutory legal impediments. The statutory changes and cooperative requirements of the 1910s and 1920s do not fit today. Cooperative development is best served when the ingenuity of the cooperator is allowed to apply cooperation competitively to the business plan. Today's cooperators who try to develop value-added processing businesses are hamstrung by restrictions applicable to cooperative stores of the mid-1800s and business conditions of the early 1900s.

Business organizations have evolved since 1960 to Delaware-style corporations and LLCs. Until the Wyoming Processing Cooperative Law, the cooperative legal principles essentially had matured by 1925. Simply stated, the corporate cooperative form of business offers few advantages and a number of significant business disadvantages over other forms of business for today's processing businesses; however, only the cooperative form of business rewards the users of the business, which is why state and federal governments should support its continued development.

Tax Laws. Federal tax law has one of the most chilling effects on cooperative development. Much of the regulations and tax law theory were developed before the advent of LLCs and are only compared to the differences of a corporation. While corporate cooperative taxation provides some advantages over corporations, in most areas cooperative organization competes with LLCs:

- *Certification of cooperatives under § 521.* The certification criteria for producer co-ops under § 521 should be changed to certify co-ops in which 50 percent or more of the ownership or control is held by producers; dividends on capital do not exceed three times the prime rate on a preferred basis or the collective return on patron investment on an equity basis; and patron voting is not based on the amount of investment but on patronage or marketing rights. Certification should be allowed as a corporate co-op qualifying for Subchapter T taxation or a co-op on an Iowa or Wyoming plan qualifying for Subchapter K partnership taxation.

- *Patronage-sourced business.* The restrictions on the deduction for patronage-sourced business should be revised to allow producer co-ops to prepare and effectively market their product in the marketplace. A pasta co-op should not be taxed on the income attributable to a prepackaged spaghetti dinner just because the beef and tomato ingredients cost more than the spaghetti noodles.
- *Tax free or tax deferred reorganization of corporate cooperative to an Iowa or Wyoming cooperative.* The reorganization of a corporate co-op to an Iowa or Wyoming co-op is taxed as a liquidation of the corporate co-op. The tax law should allow a corporate co-op to complete a tax reorganization from a corporate co-op to an Iowa or Wyoming co-op or, as an alternative, allow the deemed liquidation to be deferred until actual liquidation of the Iowa or Wyoming co-op after conversion.

Securities Laws. When producer co-ops start businesses, capital is needed from producers and others. The federal and most state securities laws are not well-suited for producer entities raising capital. Co-ops should not be treated as public companies in raising funds under the registration and public company reporting requirements. The securities laws should allow co-ops with proper disclosure to raise $50 million or less from patrons, accredited investors, and nonaccredited investors within an influence radius (e.g., local rural investors) as certified by the securities division of any state without registration or reporting requirements. This would allow local and rural investors to participate in co-ops.

Cooperative Laws. States should facilitate Wyoming-type cooperative laws to allow co-ops to organize without federal corporate cooperative tax restrictions. Federal laws such as the Capper–Volstead Act and the Marketing Acts of 1926 and 1929 should be held to a twenty-first-century definition of a co-op to meet their original intent of being effective tools to help cooperating farmers (Lauck 1999, 491–493).

Financial Assistance

Producers have limited financial resources to start up and develop co-ops. Much of the financial assistance available is in the form of grants and loan guarantees.

Equity. Financial assistance programs should be expanded to include subordinated debt and an equity investment to match producer equity plus an exit strategy should be included.

Incentives Tied to Market Power. Government assistance programs should be targeted to enhancing producer market power. For example, more than eight farmer cooperative ethanol production facilities were built in Minnesota with state financing incentives. Some attempts were made to market the ethanol collectively on a cooperative basis, but it was never achieved. Today, these same plants market with four or more different marketers, and the corn farmers who organized cooperatively are competing against each other for ethanol markets.

References

Acts of Kentucky 1922. *Kentucky Laws* (Chapter 1).
Agricultural Marketing Act of 1929. 1992. *U.S. Laws 1929.* § 1, 12 U.S.C.S. § 1141. Rochester, NY: Lawyers Cooperative Publishing.
Baarda, James R. 1982. *State Cooperative Incorporation Statutes for Farmers' Cooperatives* (ACS cooperative information report no. 30). Washington, DC: USDA.
Barton, David C. 1989. "Principles." In *Cooperatives in Agriculture,* ed. David Cobia, 21–34. Englewood Cliffs, NJ: Prentice-Hall.
Brown, Donald. 1998. *What Came First, the Chicken or the Egg? IRS Tax Treatment of Value-added Cooperatives.* Presentation at LTA General Session NCFC Annual Meeting, January 19–20, Orlando, FL.
Colorado Session Laws 1996 (codified as Colo. Rev. Stat. 7–56–101 et seq.). 1996. *Colorado Laws.*
Cooperative Marketing Act of 1926. 1992. *U.S. Laws 1926.* §§ 1–7, 7 U.S.C.S. §§ 451–457. Rochester, NY: Lawyers Cooperative Publishing.
Ela, Emerson. 1950. "Cooperatives Under the Law." In *Cooperative Corporate Association Law—1950,* ed. A. Ladru Jensen, A 517–525. Washington, DC: American Institute of Cooperation.
Evans, Frank., and E.A. Stokdyk. 1937. *The Law of Agricultural Co-operative Marketing.* Rochester, NY: Lawyers Cooperative Publishing.
Fite, Gilbert C. 1978. *Beyond the Fence Rows.* Columbia: University of Missouri Press.
Frederick, Donald A. 1996. *Income Tax Treatment of Cooperatives: Internal Revenue Code Section 521.* Washington, DC: USDA, Rural Business-Cooperative Service.
———. 2002. "Is This Really a 'Cooperative' Law? *The Cooperative Accountant* 55, no. 2 (Summer): 36–39.
Frederick, Donald A., and John D. Reilly. 2001. *Income Tax Treatment of Cooperatives: Background.* Washington, DC: USDA, Rural Business-Cooperative Service.
Goldberg, Charles L. 1928. "Co-operative Marketing and Restraint of Trade." *Marquette Law Review* 12: 270–292.
Guth, James L. 1982. "Farmer Monopolies, Cooperatives, and the Intent of Congress: Origins of the Capper–Volstead Act." *Agricultural History* 56, no. 1 (January): 67–82.
Hanna, John. 1931. *The Law of Cooperative Marketing Associations.* New York: Ronald Press.
Hanson, Mark J. 1993. *Minnesota Cooperative Law—Chapter 308A.* Privately published.

———. 2000a. *Starting a Value-added Agribusiness: The Legal Perspective*. Macomb: Illinois Institute for Rural Affairs, Western Illinois University.

———. 2000b. "Seeking Outside Capital: The Time Has Come to Change How Cooperatives Are Financed." *NCFC Cooperator* (publication of the National Council of Farmer Cooperatives) (August/September): 10–12.

———. 2001a. "Cooperative Organization for Value-added Agribusiness." In *A Cooperative Approach to Local Economic Development*, ed. Christopher D. Merrett and Norman Walzer, 41–54. Westport, CT: Quorum Books.

———. 2001b. "A New Cooperative Structure for the 21st Century: The Wyoming Processing Cooperative Law." *The Cooperative Accountant* (publication of National Society of Accountants for Cooperatives) (Fall): 3–9.

Holyoake, George Jacob. 1908. *The History of Co-operation*. London: Unwin.

Internal Revenue Code of 1986 as Amended. 1992. 26 U.S.C.S. §§ 521, 1381–1388. Rochester, NY: Lawyers Cooperative Publishing.

Iowa Laws. 1996. Chapter 1010, codified as Iowa Code Chapter 501.

———. 1999. Chapter 1152.

Iowa Code. 2001. §§ 501.101, 501.101(2)(6), Ch. 9H, Ch. 9H.4, 501.103. St. Paul, MN: West Group.

Jensen, A. Ladru. 1950. "The Bill of Rights of U.S. Cooperative Agriculture." In *Cooperative Corporate Association Law—1950*, ed. A. Ladru Jensen, 3–16. Washington, DC: American Institute of Cooperation.

Knapp, Joseph G. 1973. *The Advance of American Cooperative Enterprise: 1920–1945*. Danville, IL: Interstate.

Larsen, Grace H. 1967. "Aaron Sapiro." In *Great American Cooperatives*, ed. Joseph G. Knapp and Associates, 446–454. Washington, DC: American Institute of Cooperation.

Lauck, Jon K. 1999. "Toward an Agrarian Antitrust: New Direction for Agricultural Law." *North Dakota Law Review* 75, no. 3.

Lauck, Jon K., and Edward S. Adams. 2000. "Farmer Cooperatives and the Federal Securities Laws: The Case for Non-application." *South Dakota Law Review* 45, no. 1.

Massachusetts Laws. 1866. Chapter 290.

Meyer, Theodore R. 1927. "The Law of Co-operative Marketing." *California Law Review* 15, no. 2.

Michigan Laws. 1865. Chapter 288.

Minnesota Laws. 1989. Chapter 144. Codified as Minnesota Statutes (Chapter 308A).

Minnesota Statutes. 2001. *Minnesota Statutes Annotated*. § 500.24.

Missouri Statutes. 2001. *Missouri Revised Statutes*. § 357.010, 357.090, 357.100, 357.130.

Missouri Statutes. 2002. *Missouri Revised Statutes*. § 274.010–300. (1993, 2002).

"The New Colorado Cooperative Act: A Setting for a Business Structure." 1996. *Colorado Law Review* 3.

Nourse, Edwin G. 1927. *The Legal Status of Agricultural Co-operation*. New York: Macmillan.

Ohio Laws. 1998. Ohio Revised Code (Title 17, Chapter 29).

Patrie, William. 1998. *Creating "Co-op Fever": A Rural Development Guide to Forming Co-operatives* (RBS service report 54). Washington, DC: USDA, Rural Business-Cooperative Service.

Private Letter Ruling (PLR). 2001. Internal Revenue Service Private Letter Ruling No.125369–01.

Puget Sound Plywood Inc. v. Commissioner. 1965. 44 T.C. 305.

Sapiro, Aaron. 1923. "Cooperative Marketing." *Iowa Law Bulletin* 8, no. 4 (May): 193–210.

———. 1927. "The Law of Cooperative Marketing Associations." *Kentucky Law Journal* 15, no. 1 (November): 1–21.

Statutes of California, 1909. 1909. *California Laws* (Chapter 26).

Tobriner, Matthew O. 1928. "The Constitutionality of Cooperative Marketing Statutes." *California Law Review* 17: 19–34.

Torgerson, Randall E. 2002. "Commentary: States Need to Carefully Consider New 'Cooperative' Laws." *Rural Cooperatives* 69, no. 3: 2–36.

Uecker, Toby, and Aisha A. Talley. 2002. "Ethanol Investors Consider Switch to LLC." *Madison Daily Leader*, August 19.

U.S. Laws 1922. 1992. 42 Statute 388. Codified at 7 U.S.C.S. §§ 291–292 (1922). Rochester, NY: Lawyers Cooperative Publishing.

West's Annotated Indiana Code. 1998. §§ 15–7–1–1 to 15–7–1–33. St. Paul, MN: West Group.

Wisconsin Laws. 1911. Chapter 368.

Woeste, Victoria Saker. 1998. *The Farmer's Benevolent Trust*. Chapel Hill: University of North Carolina Press.

Wyoming Laws. 2001. 2001 General Session, Enrolled Act No. 83. Codified as Wyoming Statutes §§ 17–10–201 to 17–10–253.

6

Finance and Taxation

Jeffrey S. Royer

Economists have used theoretical models to analyze many of the problems of cooperative finance and taxation. These models include those constructed to analyze the choices a co-op must make in developing an optimal financial structure or determining the best combination of cash and noncash patronage refunds to distribute to patrons, to assess the ability of co-ops to redeem or service member equity, or to help co-ops choose plans for the acquisition and retirement of equity. Other models have been built to study how corporate taxation of cooperative earnings would be expected to affect the market behavior of co-ops and to predict whether taxation of co-ops would have a positive effect on economic welfare. Models also have been developed to analyze the comparative financial performance of co-ops and to study nontraditional organizational forms designed to allay problems stemming from the structure of property rights within co-ops.

Analyses of the problems of cooperative finance and taxation require unique models because the standard theories of finance and investment used to analyze for-profit businesses do not generally apply to co-ops due to the fact that the pecuniary benefits that patrons receive from membership in a co-op are usually distributed based on patronage rather than stock ownership. In addition, these benefits usually take the form of patronage refunds or favorable prices instead of dividends on stock or capital appreciation. Because co-ops typically lack a secondary market for trading equity, members cannot rely on the market value of stock to measure the performance of a co-op or its investment decisions.

Furthermore, the evaluation of a potential investment or the performance of an existing investment requires more than simply calculating the present value of the stream of cash flows to the co-op produced by the investment. The flow of patron benefits through product markets also must be considered.

As Cotterill (1987) has demonstrated, assessing these benefits can be quite complex and depends on numerous factors, including market structure and the membership policies of the co-op.

The standard concepts of finance theory also do not apply to the methods co-ops use to raise equity capital. Most co-ops that systematically plan for the accumulation and retirement of patron equity use the first-in/first-out revolving fund method of financing. Under this plan, a co-op retains a proportion of the patronage refunds it issues to patrons each year. These retained patronage refunds are added to the revolving fund to provide equity capital and to be eventually redeemed in turn. The oldest equities are redeemed first, usually at the discretion of the board of directors and according to the current financial needs of the co-op. Although a co-op's bylaws frequently include general rules for allocating patronage refunds and redeeming equity, the organization usually has considerable flexibility in determining the operation of the revolving fund and in setting the proportion of patronage refunds it pays in cash.

It is this method for raising and redeeming equity capital that makes co-ops unique and creates the need for special analyses of cooperative finance and taxation problems. Because of the complexities associated with the operation of the revolving fund or alternative systems for the acquisition and redemption of equity,[1] many of the problems of cooperative finance resist pure theoretical analysis. For instance, the method of comparative statics frequently used in neoclassical economic models to logically derive testable hypotheses about the financial behavior of firms is of limited use in cooperative finance models due to the discontinuities and nonlinearities associated with the revolving fund.

Consequently, by necessity, most analyses of cooperative finance problems and comparisons of alternative cooperative financing strategies have been conducted using empirical methods based on optimization and simulation models. The conceptual basis for such models is generally restricted to the choice of an appropriate objective for the co-op, and the results of analyses based on these models represent prescriptions for optimal behavior given the stated objective rather than testable hypotheses subject to econometric validation.

This chapter reviews the theoretical concepts that provide the foundation for analyses of the problems of cooperative finance and taxation; however, given the nature of these analyses, considerably more attention will be paid to empirical models than might be the case in other theoretical reviews. Nonetheless, an attempt will be made to focus on concepts and methods rather than the results of such analyses.[2]

Determining the Optimal Portfolio of Alternative Debt and Equity Instruments

Some of the earliest analyses in the area of cooperative finance focused on recognizing the cost of the equity capital provided by cooperative members. Snider and Koller (1971) observed that some co-ops placed no cost on revolving fund capital, thereby underestimating their overall cost of capital. Consequently, co-ops were expected to rely too heavily on equity capital relative to debt capital and to overinvest in facilities while incurring unnecessarily high capital costs.

Tubbs and West (1971) added that farmers who provided capital contributions to co-ops frequently made substantial but unrecognized financial sacrifices. Indeed, Tubbs and West argued that farmers in higher tax brackets could actually lose money by accepting patronage refunds because the immediate tax obligation on a patronage refund paid partially in cash could exceed the present value of the refund if the co-op's revolving period was long enough.

Discussion of the relative costs of debt and equity capital eventually spurred the development of several models to determine the optimal portfolio of alternative debt and equity instruments needed to finance a co-op, and to evaluate the effects of changes in the co-op's capital structure. Typical of these models is a recursive linear programming model constructed by Dahl and Dobson (1976). In this model, the co-op seeks to minimize its total cost of capital by selecting the optimal mix of financial instruments available to it while satisfying a set of operational constraints. Financial instruments include common and preferred stock, seasonal and term loans, certificates of indebtedness, and revolving fund capital. Constraints are used to represent the co-op's annual capital needs, requirements on the repayment of term debt, and limits on the sales of certain instruments based on historical sales data and bylaw authorizations.[3]

Dahl and Dobson (1976) used this model to determine the optimal financial structure for a representative local farm supply co-op over several years under alternative financing plans, including five- and ten-year revolving plans; various proportions of patronage refunds paid in cash; and redemption of equity held by members who leave the co-op's service area, retire, or die. They also computed the cost of capital and examined the co-op's liquidity and solvency under each plan.

Beierlein and Schrader (1978) and VanSickle and Ladd (1983) developed similar models. Beierlein and Schrader analyzed the effects that changes in a co-op's financial structure had on the financial value of the co-op to its members, using a simulation model that focused on the present value to members of the cash flows from the co-op. VanSickle and Ladd used a complex non-linear programming model based on maximization of the after-tax profits of cooperative members.

An important limitation of these models is that they do not account for the tradeoffs between the level of cash patronage refunds and the length of the revolving period. Both cash patronage refunds and the revolving period are determined outside the models and taken as given. Although these studies include comparisons of various financial strategies, no direct comparisons of the level of cash patronage refunds and the length of the revolving period are possible because changes in these parameters are accompanied by changes in other variables.[4]

Determining Optimal Equity Acquisition and Retirement Practices

Descriptive and Statistical Studies of Equity Redemption

Increasing patron frustration with the equity redemption practices of co-ops made equity redemption and the tax treatment of patronage refunds important issues in the late 1960s and 1970s. This was reflected in the original bill for the U.S. Tax Reform Act of 1969 that would have required co-ops to pay 50 percent of patronage refunds in cash and to redeem the noncash portions within fifteen years. In 1979, the U.S. General Accounting Office recommended that unless co-ops voluntarily adopted more equitable programs of equity redemption, the Secretary of Agriculture should propose mandatory equity retirement programs and/or interest payment on retained equity. Similar measures were considered by several state legislatures.

In response to these issues, several studies were conducted to survey the equity redemption practices of co-ops and to assess the efficacy of their equity redemption programs. These studies were mainly descriptive and employed only rudimentary statistical techniques to analyze the differences among various groups of co-ops. They are important in the context of this discussion because of their inherent conceptual problems.

In the first national study of equity redemption, Brown and Volkin (1977) surveyed the 1974–75 equity redemption practices of marketing co-ops in thirteen commodity groups as well as farm supply and related service co-ops. Their sample included both local co-ops, with memberships consisting of individual producers, and federated co-ops, with memberships consisting of other co-ops.

Brown and Volkin (1977) compared the financial condition, debt service obligations, and cash patronage refund practices of co-ops that operated equity redemption programs ("program" co-ops) with those that did not operate redemption programs ("no-program" co-ops) and determined that only size, as measured by total assets, was related to the existence of an equity redemption program. Based on these comparisons, they concluded that almost all co-ops could adopt some type of equity redemption program and that the usual reasons for not operating an equity redemption program, including poor financial condition, had little merit (1977, 30). Similar methods have been used to study the equity redemption practices of Illinois grain marketing co-ops (Conley and Lewis 1980) and Kansas grain marketing and farm supply co-ops (Newman 1983).

The analyses contained in Brown and Volkin (1977) and related studies suffer from serious conceptual flaws. These studies seemingly disregard the fundamental relationships among the various sources and applications of funds within a business organization and the effects of changes in the use of funds on financial structure. It should go without saying that uses such as cash patronage refunds and equity redemption compete with one another for available funds. For a given level of funds, increasing the proportion of patronage refunds paid in cash will decrease the amount of equity that can be redeemed, everything else being equal. Increasing both cash patronage refunds and equity redemption will indeed affect a co-op's financial structure by lowering its stock of allocated equity and requiring a liquidation of assets or the acquisition of additional debt.

The primary problem with these studies is that they seem to confuse the *ex ante* and *ex post* states of the co-ops. The authors appear to suggest that because there are no statistical differences between the financial strength of program and no-program co-ops, a no-program co-op should be able to adopt an equity redemption program without weakening its financial structure. By making this suggestion, the authors fail to distinguish between the financial condition of a no-program co-op before and after adopting a program. Certainly, adoption of an equity redemption program would be expected to have an impact on the financial condition of a no-program co-op.

Another conceptual weakness of these studies is that they group under "program" co-ops all of those co-ops that maintain equity redemption programs, regardless of whether they systematically redeem large amounts of allocated equities or redeem small amounts on an irregular basis. In financial terms, co-ops that redeem equity on an irregular basis actually may be more closely related to no-program co-ops. By reducing the differences between program and no-program co-ops, this classification scheme increases the probability of accepting the hypothesis that there is no difference in the financial strength of the two groups.

In short, the methods used in these studies do not elucidate the relationship between the financial strength of a co-op and its ability to redeem equity or the effectiveness of a specific equity redemption plan. It would be more meaningful to compare the financial status of the same co-op, or group of co-ops, before and after implementation of a specific equity redemption plan.

Another approach, one taken in more recent studies, is to analyze equity redemption from a continuous rather than discrete perspective—that is, to focus on the amount of equity redeemed by co-ops instead of whether or not they maintain an equity redemption plan. To its credit, an updated study of the equity allocation and redemption practices of co-ops by Rathbone and Wissman (1993) abandoned the methods of the Brown and Volkin (1977) study and avoided its spurious conclusions.[5]

Simulation Models

Several simulation models have focused on evaluating the comparative performance of alternative equity retirement plans. Royer and Cobia (1984) modeled the operation of various first-in/first-out revolving funds, percentage-of-all-equities, and special plans under several scenarios constructed to represent different patterns of patronage throughout a patron's farming career. Performance of the equity retirement plans was measured using a "disparity index," defined as the difference between actual equity financing and financing in proportion to use. The index can assume values from zero to one—the higher the value, the greater the disparity between actual financing and financing according to use. In effect, the index measures the percentage of equity not held in proportion to patronage.

Barton and Schmidt (1988) extended the approach taken by Royer and Cobia to also include comparisons of base capital plans, special plans based on a patron's age, and special plans for the settlement of estates. They based their simulations on a profile of patronage over the life of a patron estimated from cross-sectional data on the annual sales of Kansas farm operators. Performance of the equity retirement plans was evaluated according to the range of capital targets that could be met by each plan and the present value to patrons of the cash flow from redemption, as well as proportionality as measured by the disparity index. A similar model was developed by Corman and Fulton (1990) and used to assess the effects of equity retirement plans on cooperative growth and member returns. Corman and Fulton also employed their model to examine the effects of alternative assumptions about net margins, nonmember business, tax treatment, and membership.

Although these models have been useful in analyzing the operation and expected effects of alternative equity retirement plans, their general usefulness in analyzing problems of cooperative finance is limited by the simplistic and unrealistic assumptions upon which they are based. For example, neither the Royer and Cobia (1984) model nor the Barton and Schmidt (1988) model assumes any growth in the size of the co-op during the period over which performance of the equity retirement plans is simulated. Corman and Fulton do incorporate growth into their model; however, in order to do so, they must assume that members maintain a constant level of patronage through-out their association with the co-op.[6]

Growth Models

A growth model, first presented by Cobia et al. (1982, 210) and later documented and described by Royer (1993), can be used to analyze the choices a co-op must make regarding cash patronage refunds, growth, and the revolving period. In this model, the percentage of patronage refunds the co-op pays in cash, the rate of growth in the co-op's stock of equity capital, and the length of the co-op's revolving period are related to one another and to the rate of return to equity earned by the co-op.[7] The model differs from programming models in that the length of the revolving period can be endogenized—that is, it can be treated as a variable, the value of which can be solved given stated values of other variables. Earlier models based on linear and nonlinear programming methods do not determine the length of the revolving period. Instead, the revolving period is treated as a parameter, the value of which is taken as given.

The Royer (1993) model can be used by a co-op to determine the combinations of cash patronage refunds, equity growth, and revolving periods that are feasible given its rate of return to allocated equity, as demonstrated in Table 6.1. According to the table, if a co-op chooses to increase the proportion of patronage refunds it pays in cash, it also must increase the length of its revolving cycle or lower the planned rate of growth in its stock of equity to accommodate the change. For example, consider a co-op that wishes to maintain a 10 percent rate of growth while earning a 30 percent rate of return to equity. If the co-op decides to increase cash patronage refunds from 40 percent to 50 percent, it must increase its revolving period from 8.5 years to 11.5 years.

This model has been used by Royer (1983) to assess the ability of representative co-ops to comply with proposed equity servicing requirements, such as the mandatory equity retirement and interest payment programs proposed in 1979 by the U.S. General Accounting Office. Royer and Shihipar (1997) used a simulation model linked to this model to predict which patronage refund and equity revolvement practices should dominate given selected

Table 6.1

Length of Revolving Period (years) **for Selected Percentages of Cash Patronage Refunds and Rates of Growth in Equity** (given 30 percent rate of return to equity)[a]

Cash patronage refunds	Rate of growth					
	0	5	10	15	20	25
20	4.2	4.8	5.7	7.0	9.8	
30	4.8	5.6	6.8	9.0	16.7	
40	5.6	6.7	8.5	12.8		
50	6.7	8.3	11.5			
60	8.3	11.0	18.8			
70	11.1	16.6				
80	16.7	36.7				
90	33.3					
100						

Source: Royer (1993).

[a]An empty cell indicates that equity revolvement is infeasible given the level of cash patronage and rate of growth.

patron and cooperative characteristics, including patron age. That analysis also employed a patron age distribution estimated from data from Barton and Schmidt (1988) and a collective choice model based on the preferences of the median patron.[8] Caves and Petersen (1986) used a growth model mathematically equivalent to the Royer model to determine the sustainability of growth in large co-ops.

Analyses of Cooperative Tax Strategies and Policy

The net earnings of co-ops generally are taxed according to the single-tax principle. This principle, recognized by state and federal income tax law, usually ensures that cooperative earnings are taxed at either the cooperative level or the patron level, but not at both. The principle is based on the concept that co-ops are nonprofit extensions of the business enterprises of the patrons who own them. The federal taxation of agricultural co-ops, as well as that of any corporation operating on a cooperative basis, is defined in Subchapter T of the Internal Revenue Service Code.[9]

Opponents of the tax treatment of co-ops contend that Subchapter T should be eliminated. They point out that the income of most corporations is taxed twice—once at the corporate level as corporate income and once when distributed to shareholders as dividends. They also argue that because corporations must pay tax on dividends on capital stock and retained earnings, Subchapter

T deductions give co-ops an unfair advantage in raising capital and competing against other firms.

Proponents of current cooperative tax treatment suggest that single-tax treatment is not unique to co-ops but is applied to other business forms, including partnerships and Subchapter S corporations. They also point out that Subchapter T treatment is not restricted to agricultural co-ops. Almost any business that chooses to distribute income to patrons on the basis of patronage can exclude that income from its taxable income. Supporters of cooperative tax treatment also argue that opponents overlook the tax benefits other corporations receive. Special deductions and credits allow many corporations to reduce their effective tax rates below what co-ops pay.

Economists have conducted two types of analyses relating to cooperative tax treatment. In the first, models such as those discussed in the previous section have been used to determine optimal cooperative financial strategies under current tax treatment. In the second, theoretical models have been used to study how the corporate taxation of cooperative earnings would be expected to affect the market behavior of co-ops, and to predict whether taxation of co-ops would have a salutary effect on economic welfare.

Junge and Ginder (1986) used a simulation model to demonstrate that patronage refund distributions subject to federal self-employment tax could result in negative cash flows for patrons facing relatively low income tax rates; they concluded that co-ops may need to consider paying a higher proportion of patronage refunds in cash, shortening their revolving cycles, or distributing patronage refunds in nonqualified form.[10] In related studies, the growth model described in Royer (1993) has been used to compare alternative methods of distributing cooperative earnings to members, including qualified and nonqualified patronage refunds (Royer 1987) and a combination of cash patronage refunds and unallocated retained earnings (Royer 1982).

Taylor (1971) investigated the effects of imposing a corporate income tax on a farm supply co-op that maximizes the total returns to its members, including its own earnings, which are returned to members as patronage refunds. Taylor concluded that an income tax would encourage the co-op to distribute more of its returns as nontaxable consumer surplus instead of patronage refunds by lowering the price it charges members. As a consequence, the co-op's output would increase, moving it away from the social optimum at which total economic welfare, or the sum of consumer and producer surplus, is maximized. Taylor argued against taxation of cooperative earnings because of the concomitant misallocation of resources and because the loss in member returns would exceed tax revenues. Although Taylor did not analyze a corporate tax on marketing co-ops, similar conclusions would apply.

Royer (2001) examined the effects of corporate income taxation on the output decisions of a marketing co-op under a wider range of assumptions about the behavior of the co-op and its members. Although the results of that analysis are consistent with Taylor's conclusions, they are more general, and they demonstrate that an income tax could be used to move cooperative output closer to the social optimum under some circumstances.

Generally speaking, the imposition of an income tax motivates a co-op that maximizes total member returns to relax its restriction of output. The level of output relative to the social optimum depends on the tax rate and the slopes of the raw product supply and processed product demand curves. Indeed, the corporate tax rate could be adjusted to motivate the co-op to operate closer to the optimum given the raw product and processed product curves.

Taylor's (1971) conclusions are seen as applying to the special case of a co-op that maximizes total member returns and is a price taker in the processed product market. In that case, the co-op will operate at the social optimum in the absence of an income tax, and output after imposition of a tax will be greater than the welfare-maximizing level; however, if the co-op is a price setter in the processed product market—that is, if it faces a downward-sloping demand curve—it will maximize member returns by restricting output to a level below the social optimum. Then, an income tax could be used to counteract the restriction of output due to market power in the processed product market and to move the co-op toward the social optimum.

The Royer study also analyzed the case in which the co-op does not or cannot set the quantity of raw product it processes in an effort to maximize member returns. Instead, it processes whatever quantity of raw product its members choose to deliver. In that case, the imposition of an income tax will have a neutral effect on the co-op's output. The co-op's earnings will be reduced proportionately by the tax, however, and the organization can be expected to shift all of its earnings to its members by increasing the raw product price in an effort to avoid tax.

Comparative Financial Performance of Cooperatives and Profit-Maximizing Firms

The comparative financial strength of co-ops began to receive attention in the early 1980s when there were growing concerns about the negative impacts of high interest rates and the high level of borrowed capital held by co-ops relative to other firms. The first comparisons of the financial condition of co-ops to other firms generally were descriptive and did not involve formal statistical analyses or hypothesis testing. Most recent comparisons of cooperative financial ratios have focused on testing hypotheses about cooperative performance based on differences in organizational objectives. These studies are closely related to other studies that have concentrated on testing hypotheses about the comparative economic efficiency of co-ops based on how cooperative property rights are structured.

The dairy industry has been the subject of many empirical studies of the comparative financial performance or economic efficiency of co-ops because of the relative availability of data. Studies centering on the dairy industry include Porter and Scully (1987), Parliament, Lerman, and Fulton (1990), and Ferrier and Porter (1991). Several other studies, including additional studies of the dairy industry, have also been conducted.[11] These include a study by Royer (1991) that compares the financial ratios of thirteen groups of marketing, farm supply, and service co-ops to industry standards.

Parliament et al. (1990) tested several hypotheses concerning comparative cooperative financial performance using median and quartile data on nine regional dairy co-ops from 1971 to 1987. Although co-ops were hypothesized to have less liquidity and greater leverage than an industry sample of dairy product manufacturers, actual cooperative liquidity was found to be greater and cooperative leverage was found to be less than the industry sample. The hypothesis that co-ops could be expected to have greater leverage ratios was based in part on the idea that they are "equity bound"—that is, it is more difficult for them to generate funds internally because of the lack of a secondary market for equity.

The Parliament et al. (1990) study is representative of several others in that it uses nonparametric statistical methods to compare median financial ratios from a cooperative sample to the median and quartile ratios from published industry standards. Nonparametric methods include a variety of statistical procedures for analyzing data that do not satisfy all of the requirements of classical statistical methods. They frequently employ ordinal or nominal measurements, such as rank, position, and frequency, instead of continuous measurements, and are based on medians and interquartile ranges rather than means and variances. Nonparametric methods are often necessary because industry standard data, such as those published by services like Robert Morris Associates and Dun & Bradstreet, include only median and quartile information.[12]

The findings of the Parliament et al. (1990) study stand in contrast to the studies by Porter and Scully (1987) and by Ferrier and Porter (1991), which test hypotheses about the comparative economic efficiency of co-ops. According to Porter and Scully, the structure of property rights within co-ops leads to technical, allocative, and scale inefficiencies in these organizations.[13]

Porter and Scully (1987) argue that co-ops are economically inefficient because of the transferability problem that stems from the structure of cooperative property rights. In a co-op, the residual claims to the organization's cash flow usually are distributed to members in the form of patronage refunds or favorable prices. In addition, restrictions are generally placed on the transfer of the rights to these claims. In particular, equity ownership is limited to members, who must be producers and active patrons of the co-op. Consequently, the flow of future residual claims cannot be capitalized into stock values and transferred to investors through a secondary equity market, the absence of which leads to horizon, portfolio, and control problems. These problems were identified by Jensen and Meckling (1979) in the context of the labor-managed firm, but are also applicable to co-ops.

The horizon problem arises when an investor's claim on the cash flow generated by an asset is expected to terminate before the end of the asset's useful life. Consequently, the investor is likely to underinvest in the asset because the return to the investor is less than the return generated by the asset. The horizon problem occurs in co-ops because residual claims are distributed to members as current payments. Consequently, the benefits a member receives from an investment are limited to the time horizon over which he or she expects to patronize the co-op. Because of the horizon problem, co-ops will tend to underinvest in assets with long-term payoffs, particularly research and development, marketing, and other intangible assets. The horizon problem also encourages managers and boards of directors to increase current payments to members instead of investing in additional assets, and to accelerate equity retirement rather than building the level of equity in the organization.

The portfolio problem occurs because cooperative members invest in the co-op in proportion to use, and equity shares in the co-op generally cannot be freely purchased or sold. Members are, therefore, unable to diversify their individual investment portfolios according to their personal wealth and preferences for risk taking. Moreover, because outside investors, who could diversify the risks of the co-op, usually are excluded from investing in a co-op, members alone must shoulder these risks. Consequently, members are expected to require higher returns on cooperative investments and to be more reluctant to invest in new assets than corporate shareholders.

The control problem stems from the inability of co-op members to trade equity shares, thus precluding the concentration of equity among members and diluting the incentive for individual members and boards of directors to make difficult or costly decisions such as those concerning product innovation and management discipline. The absence of a secondary equity market also denies members an external means for monitoring the organization's value and assessing management's performance. In addition, because of restrictions on equity ownership, co-ops usually lack equity-based management incentive mechanisms such as equity ownership or purchase options that can be used to attract or motivate managers.

According to Porter and Scully (1987), the horizon problem and the concomitant tendency of co-ops to underinvest in long-term investments prevents them from choosing the optimal mix of inputs, resulting in allocative inefficiency. Co-ops are hypothesized to be technically inefficient because of the control problem, which makes managers more likely to shirk and pursue objectives other than cost minimization. The control problem also may result in scale inefficiency because of the agency costs associated with the large membership necessary for achieving scale economies.

Applying a statistical frontier production function to 1972 data on the inputs and outputs of cooperative and noncooperative fluid milk processing plants, Porter and Scully (1987) concluded that the co-ops were less efficient than the non-co-ops and that the relative inefficiency of the co-ops could be attributed to intrinsic weaknesses in the structure of property rights in co-ops instead of the pursuit of alternative objective functions. Using a linear programming approach and the same data, Ferrier and Porter (1991) reached similar conclusions.

Porter and Scully (1987) argue that co-ops survive, despite their relative inefficiency, because of favorable tax treatment, advantageous credit terms, and free services from the government. They acknowledge that co-ops provide member services not offered by other processors and may enhance market performance by mitigating monopsonistic exploitation by processors. They also recognize that the vertical relationships between co-ops and their members may lower transaction costs. Nevertheless, they contend that a redistribution of resources from co-ops to other dairy processors would increase output and benefit society.

Sexton and Iskow (1993) review several of the studies on comparative financial performance and economic efficiency and conclude that there is no consensus as to whether co-ops are less efficient than other firms. They expose several biases in the studies by Porter and Scully (1987) and by Ferrier and Porter (1991) that tend to underestimate the efficiency of cooperative organizations. They also note that the Parliament et al. (1990) study of the dairy industry avoids the problems of geographic and product mix heterogeneity that flaw the other studies.

Sexton and Iskow (1993) do argue in favor of the formal efficiency concepts and the statistical and programming models used by Porter, Scully, and Ferrier over the simpler statistical methods used by Parliament et al. (1990). They also criticize the ratio analysis used by Parliament et al. on the basis that financial ratios generally lack a rigorous foundation in economic theory and are difficult to interpret precisely. They argue that the ratio values may be influenced by the favorable treatment co-ops receive from the government.

In addition, Sexton and Iskow (1993) contend that examining data for only one part of the vertically integrated relationships between co-ops and their members can lead to misleading results. They conclude their comparison of these studies with a call for additional research in the area and suggest that it should combine the rigorous measures of efficiency employed by Porter, Scully, and Ferrier and the careful sample selection procedures used by Parliament et al.

Nontraditional Forms of Cooperative Financial Organization

Some economists have argued that the existence of problems intrinsic to the cooperative organizational form, such as the horizon, portfolio, and control problems, threaten the long-term survivability of co-ops. These authors state that, although co-ops may initially serve some economic purpose within a market, they eventually will be forced to exit or reorganize as the market evolves because of inherent weaknesses attributable to the structure of their property rights. Two authors, Cook (1995) and Harte (1997), have formalized these ideas in cooperative life-cycle models, which seek to explain the formation, growth, and eventual decline of a co-op.

Cook (1995) also outlines various organizational alternatives available to co-ops. He argues that a co-op that continues to operate throughout the life cycle will eventually tend toward undercapitalization. He describes several strategies for generating additional internal and external capital, including restructuring the co-op so that governance and financial contributions are maintained in proportion to individual patronage.

One means for achieving this objective would be the formation of a "patron-owned corporation" (POC), as defined and described by Royer (1992). A POC is an organization in which control is held in proportion to common stock holdings, earnings are distributed in proportion to stock holdings, retained earnings are not allocated to individual owners, and owners share in equity appreciation through a secondary market for equity. If it is assumed that equity is held in proportion to patronage, there is no difference in the distribution of earnings or voting rights between a POC and a co-op.

Another alternative to the traditional cooperative organizational form is the New Generation Cooperative (NGC) or "value-added" co-op, as described by Harris, Stefanson, and Fulton (1996). An NGC is typically involved in value-added processing activities and characterized by a link between producer capital contributions and product delivery rights. Equity shares and the associated delivery rights can be traded, and share prices can appreciate, reflecting the returns members expect to receive over time based on the revenue the co-op receives from processing and marketing the product. These co-ops, which share some characteristics with POCs, represent an attempt to allay the problems stemming from the structure of property rights in traditional co-ops while preserving the essential elements of a co-op. An attractive feature of these organizations is that they are financed in proportion to use.

A distinguishing characteristic of NGCs is the direct link between producer capital contributions and product delivery rights. Each member of an NGC contracts with the co-op to deliver a particular quantity of product annually and must purchase equity shares in proportion to this quantity. The member must meet this contract requirement either by delivering his or her own product or by purchasing product from other producers for delivery to the co-op, except under unusual occurrences such as crop failure. The contract also provides the member a guaranteed market for his or her product because the co-op is obligated to purchase the quantity specified in the contract, subject only to quality restrictions.

Economists have argued that the linkage of capital contributions and delivery rights and the existence of appreciable, tradable equity shares have eliminated the free-rider and horizon problems in NGCs. The free-rider problem may exist in a traditional co-op because ownership by itself carries no benefits. The co-op's earnings are distributed to members on the basis of patronage, and individual members do not have an incentive to invest in it although investment is fundamental to the organization's success. In an NGC, the distribution of earnings is tied to ownership because of the link between member equity shares and delivery rights. The horizon problem is avoided in NGCs because future earnings are reflected in the value of tradable equity shares.

The NGC organizational form is not without drawbacks, however. Appreciation in the value of the co-op's equity capital can reward initial investors on the basis of share holdings instead of use. The need for significant upfront capital contributions tied to delivery rights establishes financial barriers to new membership, and substantial appreciation in the value of equity shares has created barriers to exit, preventing retiring members from liquidating their equity shares. These problems have stimulated the creation of leasing arrangements by which newer members lease delivery rights from older ones. Some NGCs also facilitate membership by allowing new members to purchase shares over several years.

Recent theoretical work on co-ops has rejected the concept of the co-op as a homogeneous organizational form and has recognized a variety of cooperative models that differ in function and in the ownership, control, and benefit functions they employ. Despite the increased understanding and additional realism these models offer, Kyriakopoulos (2000) asserts that they are based on weak theoretical models and limited empirical evidence. He suggests that empirical validation of these models would require a stronger theoretical basis and systematic data.

Conclusions

During the past thirty years, the rigor and sophistication of the economic models used to analyze problems of cooperative finance and taxation have increased substantially. Economically sound models currently exist for analyzing the choices a co-op must make in developing an optimal financial structure, determining the best combination of cash and noncash patronage refunds to distribute to patrons, and evaluating alternative plans for acquiring and redeeming equity. Appropriate models also exist for assessing the ability of co-ops to redeem or service member equity and to analyze alternative cooperative tax strategies and the expected effects of corporate taxation of cooperative earnings.

Although many of the problems of cooperative finance resist pure theoretical analysis because of the complexities associated with the operation of the revolving fund or alternative systems for the acquisition and redemption of equity, it still is important for the models used to analyze these problems to have a sound conceptual basis. Unfortunately, some of the models discussed in this chapter exhibit serious conceptual flaws. As a consequence, the empirical conclusions based on them are spurious and of little value. Indeed, recommendations based on these models have potential for inflicting financial harm on those co-ops that use them to make financial decisions. Although one might expect the early models used to analyze problems of cooperative finance and taxation to be simpler and less sophisticated than more recent models, it has always been important for researchers to be careful to avoid fundamental conceptual errors and to refrain from adopting models without seriously examining their conceptual underpinnings.

Given the state of the models and methods now available for analyzing problems of cooperative finance and taxation, there are at least three areas in which further analysis could be very productive. First, following Cotterill's (1987) lead, it still would be important for additional work to be directed toward integrating the financial decisions of co-ops with the pricing and output decisions they must make. Despite the fundamental importance of patronage refunds to co-ops, theorists have given little attention to explaining how they are taken into consideration by patrons when making marketing and purchasing decisions and by managers in establishing pricing strategies. The recent emergence of NGCs, with their emphasis on the linkage of product delivery rights to producer capital contributions, reinforces the importance of the integration of marketing or production decisions with financial structure.

NGCs and other nontraditional forms of cooperative organization represent a second area in which additional analysis would be useful. Certainly, leasing arrangements and other mechanisms for attenuating the entry and exit problems associated with NGC membership deserve more attention. In addition, as Kyriakopoulos (2000) observes, much of the recent analysis of alternative cooperative organizational forms is based on weak theoretical foundations and limited empirical evidence, and additional theoretical analysis and empirical validation of these forms would be valuable.

Closely related are the conceptual concerns surrounding recent studies of cooperative financial performance and economic efficiency, which suggest a third important area for further analysis. Sexton and Iskow's (1993) call for new research that would combine rigorous measures of performance or efficiency with careful sample selection procedures is well taken given the potential contributions additional work in this area could make.

Notes

1. In addition to first-in/first-out revolving fund plans, co-ops may use percentage-of-all-equities or base capital plans to systematically redeem patron equities. Under a percentage-of-all-equities plan, a co-op redeems a percentage of all patron equities on an annual basis. Each patron receives redemption of the same percentage regardless of when the equities were allocated. With a base capital plan, each patron's equity requirement is readjusted annually according to the co-op's capital needs and the proportion of the co-op's total patronage attributable to the patron during a moving base period. Patrons who are underinvested continue to provide equity investments while overinvested patrons generally are not required to continue contributing equity and may begin to receive at least partial redemption of excess investments. Co-ops also may employ special plans for redeeming equities held by estates or by patrons who are over a certain age, are no longer farming, are no longer in the co-op's service area, claim hardship, or request redemption on an "on call" basis. These special plans can be used alone or in conjunction with a systematic plan.

2. The unique methods co-ops use to raise equity capital and associated issues such as equity retirement and cooperative taxation have received the most attention in the literature. An important exception is Cotterill (1987), which seeks to develop a unified theory of agricultural cooperation that integrates pricing, investment, and financing decisions. Because of the scope, length, and complexity of that paper, no attempt is made to summarize it here. It is noted, however, that Cotterill presents a one-period model that is inadequate for analyzing decisions involving specific plans, such as the revolving fund plan, for the acquisition and retirement of member equity.

3. Models of this type can be formally stated as follows. The co-op seeks to minimize the total cost of capital, represented by C:

$$\text{Minimize } C = \sum_{j=1}^{n} c_j x_j$$

$$\text{subject to } \sum_{j=1}^{n} a_{i_j} x_j \le b_i \quad \text{for } i = 1, 2, \dots, m$$

$$\text{and } x_j \ge 0 \quad \text{for } j = 1, 2, \dots, n$$

where the x_j ($j = 1, 2, \ldots, n$) represent the levels of the various financial instruments available to the co-op and the c_j represent the annual cost coefficients associated with those instruments. The relationships of the form $\sum a_{ij} x_j \leq b_i$ ($i = 1, 2, \ldots, m$) represent various constraints imposed upon the co-op.

4. For instance, in the Dahl and Dobson (1976) model, several combinations of cash patronage refunds and revolving periods are analyzed, but the debt/equity and current ratios are allowed to vary. In the VanSickle and Ladd (1983) model, the length of the revolving period is initially treated as a variable dependent upon parameterized values of the level of cash patronage refunds (279, Table 3); however, practical considerations lead to the inclusion of constraints on the length of the revolving period that effectively reduces it to a parameter (279, Table 4).

5. Although Newman (1983) utilized methods similar to those of Brown and Volkin (1977), he separated program co-ops into three groups based on specific equity redemption plans. Co-ops operating revolving fund plans were financially stronger than the others, but he drew no conclusions about causality. Newman also supported the findings of Dahl and Dobson (1976) that suggest some co-ops would be adversely affected by the implementation of a mandatory equity redemption program. These findings were acknowledged by Conley and Lewis (1980), but they concluded that "the financial strength of no-program cooperatives was not significantly different than that of program cooperatives. Thus, concern about financial strength should not be an obstacle to an equity redemption program" (58).

6. In addition, Barton and Schmidt (1988) commit a subtle but important error by using the present value to patrons of the cash flow from redemption in evaluating the relative performance of equity retirement plans. Under assumptions of zero growth and a constant rate of return to the co-op's assets, the total cash flow to patrons will be identical regardless of whether it comes in the form of cash patronage refunds or equity redemption. An increase in the funds used for equity redemption would require an equivalent and compensating decrease in the funds used to pay cash patronage refunds. Although a particular equity retirement plan might appear attractive from the perspective of the present value of the cash flow from redemption, adoption of the plan would require adjustments in current patronage refund and equity redemption practices. Accordingly, some patrons would benefit and others would be harmed, but total cash flow, and the subsequent present value, would be invariant. See Royer (1993, 52) for a detailed explanation.

7. The length of a co-op's revolving period can be related to the percentage patronage refunds it pays in cash, the rate of growth in its stock of equity capital, and its rate of return to equity as follows. Net margins in year t (NM_t) are a function of the stock of equity capital at the end of the previous year (E_{t-1}):

$$NM_t = rE_{t-1}$$

where r is the co-op's rate of return to equity. Retained patronage refunds in year t (RPR_t) are determined by the percentage of patronage refunds the co-op pays in cash (c):

$$RPR_t = (1 - c) NM_t$$
$$= (1 - c) rE_{t-1}.$$

The equity available for retirement in year $t(ER_t)$ is equal to retained patronage refunds less the growth in the co-op's equity stock during the year:

$$ER_t = RPR_t - g\, E_{t-1}$$
$$= [(1-c)\, r - g]\, E_{t-1} \qquad \text{for } g \geq 0$$

where g represents the rate of growth in equity. In a first-in/first-out revolving fund plan, equity retired in year t is equal to retained patronage refunds T years before:

$$ER_t = RPR_{t-T} = (1-c) r\, E_{t-T-1}.$$

If the rate of growth is positive,

$$E_{t-T-1} = (1+g)^{-T}\, E_{t-1}.$$

After appropriate substitutions, the length of the revolving period (T) can be expressed as a function of the percentage cash patronage refunds paid in cash, the rate of growth in the co-op's equity stock, and its rate of return to equity:

$$T = -\frac{\log\left[1 - \dfrac{g}{(1-c)r}\right]}{\log(1+g)} \qquad \text{for } (1-c)r > g, g > 0$$

For a more complete derivation and description of this model, including the case in which the rate of growth is zero, see Royer (1993).

8. Knoeber and Baumer (1983) had earlier modeled the proportion of patronage refunds retained by a co-op as arising from a portfolio decision of its median member who seeks to maximize expected utility by allocating wealth between investments in farming assets and co-op equity.

9. For a complete description of cooperative tax treatment, see Royer (1989).

10. Nonqualified patronage refunds are noncash allocations that patrons do not agree to accept as current ordinary income; therefore, they do not qualify for exclusion from the co-op's taxable income. A co-op deducts the cash it pays to redeem nonqualified allocations, however, and a patron who receives cash in redemption of a nonqualified allocation includes it in taxable income. See Royer (1989) for additional information.

11. For a list of some of these other studies, see Royer (1999, 59).

12. Consequently, studies that rely on nonparametric statistical methods are unable to utilize additional information about the distribution of the cooperative sample. Nonetheless, there may be considerable justification for preferring the comparison of median ratios instead of means. The median may be a better measure of central location than the mean because it may be closer to the bulk of the distribution and, therefore, is more typical of possible observed values in asymmetric distributions. In addition, the sample median is less sensitive to outliers or extreme values, which

occur relatively often in heavy-tailed distributions and can result from errors in recording data.

13. Technical, allocative, and scale efficiency are separable components of overall economic efficiency. Technical efficiency pertains to the firm's ability to produce the maximum output from a given set of inputs and is measured relative to a production frontier. Allocative efficiency concerns the firm's ability to minimize the cost of producing a particular level of output by selecting the optimal mix of inputs given input prices. Scale efficiency refers to the firm's ability to select the optimal scale of production. See Porter and Scully (1987, 492, 499–504) for additional information.

References

Barton, David G., and Royce L. Schmidt. 1988. "An Evaluation of Equity Redemption Alternatives in Centralized Cooperatives." *Journal of Agricultural Cooperation* 3: 39–58.

Beierlein, James G., and Lee F. Schrader. 1978. "Patron Valuation of a Farmer Cooperative Under Alternative Finance Policies." *American Journal of Agricultural Economics* 60: 636–641.

Brown, Phillip F., and David Volkin. 1977. *Equity Redemption Practices of Agricultural Cooperatives* (FCS research report 41). Washington, DC: USDA, Farmer Cooperative Service.

Caves, Richard E., and Bruce C. Petersen. 1986. "Cooperatives' Tax 'Advantages': Growth, Retained Earnings, and Equity Rotation." *American Journal of Agricultural Economics* 68: 7–13.

Cobia, David W., Jeffrey S. Royer, Roger A. Wissman, Dennis Paul Smith, Donald R. Davidson, Stephen D. Lurya, J. Warren Mather, Phillip F. Brown, and Kenneth P. Krueger. 1982. *Equity Redemption: Issues and Alternatives for Farmer Cooperatives* (ACS research report 23). Washington, DC: USDA, Agricultural Cooperative Service.

Conley, Dennis M., and Kevin B. Lewis. 1980. "Evaluating Financial Obstacles to Equity Redemption in Cooperatives: Program Compared to No-program Cooperatives." *Agricultural Finance Review* 40: 51–60.

Cook, Michael L. 1995. "The Future of U.S. Agricultural Cooperatives: A Neo-institutional Approach." *American Journal of Agricultural Economics* 77: 1153–1159.

Corman, Jeff, and Murray Fulton. 1990. "Patronage Allocation, Growth and Member Well-being in Co-operatives." *Canadian Journal of Agricultural Economics* 38: 45–66.

Cotterill, Ronald W. 1987. "Agricultural Cooperatives: A Unified Theory of Pricing, Finance, and Investment." In *Cooperative Theory: New Approaches* (ACS service report 18), ed. Jeffrey S. Royer. Washington, DC: USDA, Agricultural Cooperative Service.

Dahl, Wilmer A., and W.D. Dobson. 1976. "An Analysis of Alternative Financing Strategies and Equity Retirement Plans for Farm Supply Cooperatives." *American Journal of Agricultural Economics* 58: 198–208.

Ferrier, G.D., and Phillip K. Porter. 1991. "The Productive Efficiency of U.S. Milk Processing Co-operatives." *Journal of Agricultural Economics* 42: 161–173.

Harris, Andrea, Brenda Stefanson, and Murray Fulton. 1996. "New Generation Cooperatives and Cooperative Theory." *Journal of Cooperatives* 11: 15–28.

Harte, Laurence N. 1997. "Creeping Privatisation of Irish Co-operatives: A Transaction Cost Explanation." In *Strategies and Structures in the Agro-food Industries,* ed. Jerker Nilsson and Gert Van Dijk, 31–53. Assen, The Netherlands: Van Gorcum.

Jensen, Michael C., and William H. Meckling. 1979. "Rights and Production Functions: An Application to Labor-managed Firms and Codetermination." *Journal of Business* 52: 469–506.

Junge, Katie A., and Roger G. Ginder. 1986. "Effects of Federal Taxes on Member Cash Flows from Patronage Refunds." *Journal of Agricultural Cooperation* 1: 22–37.

Knoeber, Charles R., and David L. Baumer. 1983. "Understanding Retained Patronage Refunds in Agricultural Cooperatives." *American Journal of Agricultural Economics* 65: 30–37.

Kyriakopoulos, Kyriakos. 2000. *The Market Orientation of Cooperative Organizations: Learning Strategies and Structures for Integrating Firm and Members.* Assen, The Netherlands: Van Gorcum.

Newman, Mark D. 1983. "Cooperative Equity Redemption Plans and Financial Strength: New Empirical Evidence." *Agricultural Finance Review* 43: 41–49.

Parliament, Claudia, Zvi Lerman, and Joan Fulton. 1990. "Performance of Cooperatives and Investor-owned Firms in the Dairy Industry." *Journal of Agricultural Cooperation* 5: 1–16.

Porter, Phillip K., and Gerald W. Scully. 1987. "Economic Efficiency in Cooperatives." *Journal of Law and Economics* 30: 489–512.

Rathbone, Robert C., and Roger A. Wissman. 1993. *Equity Redemption and Member Allocation Practices of Agricultural Cooperatives* (ACS Research Report 124). Washington, DC: USDA, Agricultural Cooperative Service.

Royer, Jeffrey S. 1982. "Distributing Cooperative Benefits to Patrons." *Cooperative Accountant* 35, no. 2: 17–27.

———. 1983. "Financial Impact of Mandatory Equity Programs on Farmer Cooperatives." *Agricultural Finance Review* 43: 30–40.

———. 1987. "Cash Flow Comparisons of Qualified and Nonqualified Allocations of Cooperative Patronage Refunds." *Agricultural Finance Review* 47: 1–13.

———. 1989. "Taxation." In *Cooperatives in Agriculture,* ed. David Cobia, 287–307. Englewood Cliffs, NJ: Prentice-Hall.

———. 1991. "A Comparative Financial Ratio Analysis of U.S. Farmer Cooperatives Using Nonparametric Statistics." *Journal of Agricultural Cooperation* 6: 22–44.

———. 1992. "Cooperative Principles and Equity Financing: A Critical Discussion." *Journal of Agricultural Cooperation* 7: 79–98.

———. 1993. "Patronage Refunds, Equity Retirement, and Growth in Farmer Cooperatives." *Agricultural Finance Review* 53: 43–55.

———. 1999. "Cooperative Organizational Strategies: A Neo-institutional Digest." *Journal of Cooperatives* 14: 44–67.

———. 2001. "Agricultural Marketing Cooperatives, Allocative Efficiency, and Corporate Taxation." *Journal of Cooperatives* 16: 1–13.

Royer, Jeffrey S., and David W. Cobia. 1984. "Measuring the Equity Redemption Performance of Farmer Cooperatives." *North Central Journal of Agricultural Economics* 6: 105–112.

Royer, Jeffrey S., and M.L. Mohamad Shihipar. 1997. "Individual Patron Preferences, Collective Choice, and Cooperative Equity Revolvement Practices." *Journal of Cooperatives* 12: 47–61.

Sexton, Richard J., and Julie Iskow. 1993. "What Do We Know About the Economic Efficiency of Cooperatives: An Evaluative Survey." *Journal of Agricultural Cooperatives* 8: 15–27.

Snider, Thomas A., and E. Fred Koller. 1971. *The Cost of Capital in Minnesota Dairy Cooperatives* (Agricultural Experiment Station Bulletin 503). St. Paul: University of Minnesota, Minnesota Agricultural Experiment Station.

Taylor, Ryland A. 1971. "The Taxation of Cooperatives: Some Economic Implications." *Canadian Journal of Agricultural Economics* 19: 13–24.

Tubbs, Alan R., and Richard R. West. 1971. *The Use of Debt in the Cooperative Capital Structure* (Agricultural Economics Research 336). Ithaca, NY: Department of Agricultural Economics, Cornell University.

VanSickle, John J., and George W. Ladd. 1983. "A Model of Cooperative Finance." *American Journal of Agricultural Economics* 65: 273–281.

_____ PART III

MANAGEMENT ISSUES

7

Understanding Cooperative Behavior: The Prisoners' Dilemma Approach

Joan Fulton

Member commitment has been a longstanding issue for cooperatives as was documented by Jesness (1923). For example, in Rockwell, Iowa, a local grain marketing co-op realized that it had to directly address the issue of member commitment if it was to overcome the problem of members initially patronizing the co-op and then being lured to a competitor in response to price incentives. Naturally, with members defecting to competitors, the co-op was unable to remain viable; and once the co-op ceased business, the competitors no longer offered such attractive prices. The Rockwell, Iowa, co-op incorporated a penalty clause into its original structure for farmer members that delivered grain to a competitor, but this did not deter defectors (Fowke 1957; Knapp 1979). In less developed countries, co-ops that are organized in a bottom-up structure, compared to a top-down structure, are more likely to have strong member commitment and be successful (Fulton, Bhargava, and Daily 1993).

The problem of member commitment stems from two characteristics of co-ops. First, for most co-ops, patronage is voluntary, with members having no obligation to do business with the co-op. Second, co-ops often provide a good or service that is characterized as a public good. A public good is a good or service for which use by any one individual does not preclude any other individual from using the good or service. Furthermore, it is difficult and often impossible to exclude people from consuming the public good or service. Co-ops provide a public good when they serve the role of competitive yardstick and ensure that investor-oriented firms (IOFs) charge a fair market price.

The challenge faced by co-op management is how to keep cooperative members from free riding and patronizing another firm while enjoying the competitive pricing that exists because of the co-op's presence in the market. Free riding occurs when individuals use a good or service without actually paying for it. Cooperative researchers have examined this free ridership problem (Fulton et al. 1993; Fulton, Popp, and Gray 1996; Staatz 1987). Specifically, they have used the Prisoners' Dilemma game form to understand the factors contributing to the free rider problem as well as the factors that contribute to member loyalty to the co-op.

Many cooperative member education programs have been targeted at communicating to members the importance of the co-op in order to secure long-term commitments. In recent years, the New Generation Cooperatives (NGCs) have been able to overcome the free rider problem by employing a closed cooperative format combined with long-term delivery contracts and large up-front financial investments by the producer members.

Recent changes in the business environment have created a situation in which commitment and free ridership are once again important challenges, however. The business environment has been characterized by increased consolidation and concentration as illustrated by Daniels (1999) and Fulton (2001). Two highly published examples are the Cargill and Continental Grain merger in 1999 and the Tyson and Smithfield merger in 2001.

Agricultural co-ops find that they must get larger to remain competitive. The result has been extensive reorganization activity through mergers/acquisitions and joint ventures/strategic alliances. The merger of Cenex and Harvest States Cooperatives in 1998, resulting in CHS Cooperatives, is an example of two co-ops merging to become a farm to market agribusiness and remain competitive (Porter 2001). An example of a co-op merging with an IOF is the merger of Minnesota Corn Processors and ADM (Reuters 2002). An important question that the firms now face is, "How do we ensure that the reorganized business functions effectively?" Just as there is an incentive for individual members to free ride and not patronize the co-op in traditional co-ops, there is often an incentive for one of the partners in the business reorganization to renege on the agreement.

Game theory is a useful tool for analyzing these business reorganizations since it provides insight on economic situations in which the interactions of the players and the reactions of the players to specific actions by other players are of interest. Three game forms useful for evaluating business reorganizations are the Prisoners' Dilemma, the Assurance Problem, and the Chicken Game.

In this chapter, the results of game theory analysis are compared with an empirical analysis of cooperative restructuring. The results are consistent with the conclusions of game theory. The following section describes the three game forms: (1) the Prisoners' Dilemma, (2) the Assurance Problem, and (3) the Chicken Game. For each game form, a generic description is provided along with an explanation of the application of this game form for business organizations.

Because business decisions are made in a dynamic or multi-period environment, rather than a static environment, it is important to consider multi-period effects. The insights from the game theory on the multi-period Prisoners' Dilemma game are then presented. For reference purposes, related cooperative research is described, with special attention paid to the results of applied research.

Game Theory

As noted previously, game theory is a useful tool for analyzing cooperative business reorganizations. The Prisoners' Dilemma, the Assurance Problem, and the Chicken Game (Taylor 1987) are three game forms that have been identified as being useful for evaluating players' interactions and reactions.

It is helpful to present the game theory material in a systematic format. First, the overall assumptions and layout of the game form will be described. Next, the game forms are considered with the Prisoners' Dilemma first, then the Assurance Problem, followed by the Chicken Game. In the presentation of each game form, the original application of the game form is described first, followed by a discussion of how it provides insight for business organizations. Following the presentation of the single-period examples, the multi-period Prisoners' Dilemma game form is presented.

Each game form considered in this chapter assumes that the game can be adequately described with two players—Player 1 and Player 2—each facing two decisions, A and B. A payoff matrix is used to describe the outcomes for each possible scenario. Player 1's outcomes are represented in the rows of the matrix while Player 2's outcomes are represented in the columns of the matrix. Each entry in the matrix has two numbers. The first number is the payoff for Player 1 while the second number is the payoff for Player 2.

Prisoners' Dilemma

In the Prisoners' Dilemma game, the two players are prisoners that the police have taken in for questioning. Both of the prisoners are guilty of a major crime, but the police do not have enough evidence to convict them of the crimes and must rely on the testimony of the prisoners to get a conviction. The prisoners are put in separate rooms for interrogation. Each prisoner is shown the payoff matrix that is displayed in Table 7.1.

In this example, the payoff represents the time that each prisoner or player will spend in jail. Since the two prisoners are in separate rooms and are

Table 7.1

Prisoners' Dilemma

		Player 2	
		Action A (Confess)	Action B (Deny)
Player 1	Action A (Confess)	−15, −15	0, −20
	Action B (Deny)	−20, 0	−2, −2

unable to communicate with each other, they must each separately evaluate the possible jail sentences they could encounter. It is useful to work through an example. Player 1 will first consider his or her best move if Player 2 selects Action A (confess). If Player 2 confesses, then Player 1 could experience an outcome of 15 years in jail (if Player 1 confesses as well) or 20 years in jail (if Player 1 denies). The best strategy for Player 1 is to confess (Action A) and get the outcome of 15 rather than 20 years in jail.

Alternatively, Player 2 might select Action B (deny). If Player 2 selects Action B, then Player 1 will experience an outcome of 2 years in jail or no jail time. In this situation, the best strategy for Player 1 is to confess (Action A) and get the outcome of no jail time rather than 2 years in jail.

The dominant strategy for Player 1 is to confess (Action A) because it is the best action for Player 1 no matter what action Player 2 selects. Player 2 would work through a similar analysis and discover that the dominant strategy for him or her is to select Action A (confess). Since the dominant strategy for both players is to select Action A, the top left cell (confess, confess) is identified as the dominant strategy equilibrium. With both players selecting their dominant strategy of confessing (Action A), they both end up with a payoff of 15 years in jail. It is interesting to note that if they had both denied the crime (Action B), they would have both been much better off, ending up with only 2 years in jail.

As illustrated above, the dominant strategy equilibrium in the Prisoners' Dilemma game is not Pareto optimal[1] even though it is the dominant strategy. The conclusion is that the players, each acting in his/her own best interests, will make choices that result in an outcome that makes them both worse off than they could be. The use of the word "dilemma" in the title for this game form is, thus, very appropriate. The players each have a dominant strategy, but if they select their dominant strategy, they will end up worse off than if they had selected Action B. The generic game form for the Prisoners' Di-

Table 7.2

Generic Prisoners' Dilemma Game

		Player 2	
		Action A (Confess)	Action B (Deny)
Player 1	Action A (Confess)	x, x	z, y
	Action B (Deny)	y, z	w, w

Table 7.3

Prisoners' Dilemma Game as Applied to Cooperative Business Patronage

		Player 2	
		Action A (Defect)	Action B (Cooperate)
Player 1	Action A (Defect)	10, 10	30, 5
	Action B (Cooperate)	5, 30	25, 25

lemma game is described in Table 7.2 with $y < x < w < z$. The important illustration from this game form is that of situations in which all players acting in their best interests result in an outcome that is Pareto inferior.

There are two important problems here. One is that the two prisoners cannot communicate with each other to even attempt to form some sort of a deal to each select the "deny" action. Even if they could communicate with each other, there is little reason to believe that they would move to the Pareto optimal outcome. Both of the players have an incentive to select the "confess" action. Thus, this game form presents a dilemma.

It is useful to identify examples of how the Prisoners' Dilemma game form applies in cooperative businesses. Staatz (1987) discusses how participation in a cooperative business by the members is a Prisoners' Dilemma game. Each player has two possible actions: (1) to cooperate and patronize the co-op, or (2) to defect and patronize the competition (Table 7.3). The Prisoners' Dilemma game form is useful to describe those cooperative situations in which the competitive firm offers a better price than the co-op.

One example is the situation wherein the co-op serves as a competitive yardstick in the marketplace. So long as the co-op is an active player in the

Table 7.4

Assurance Problem (Battle of the Sexes)

		Player 2	
		Action A (Ballet)	Action B (Dog races)
Player 1	Action A (Ballet)	50, 40	10, 10
	Action B (Dog races)	0, 0	40, 50

industry, the competitive firm offers a good price. If the co-op were not an active player in the industry, the other firm would not offer prices in the same competitive manner. So the member customers of the co-op have an incentive to patronize the competitive firm and receive a better price in the short run. In Table 7.3, this occurs if player 1 cooperates and player 2 defects (5, 30), or if player 1 defects and player 2 cooperates (30, 5). In each case, the defector gets the higher price for his/her commodity. However, if all of the members patronized the competitive firm, the cooperative would not be able to stay in business and everyone would be worse off with the remaining firm pricing in a noncompetitive manner (10, 10). The optimal situation occurs when players 1 and 2 both patronize their co-op. They may not get the best price in the short term (each receives a value of 25 instead of 30), but in the long term, the cooperative survives. If all of the members patronized the competitive firm, however, the co-op would not be able to stay in business; everyone would be worse off with the remaining firm pricing in a noncompetitive manner.

Assurance Problem

The Assurance Problem game form is also referred to as the Battle of the Sexes game (Runge 1981, 1984). In this situation, two players, a man and a woman, are going on a date. The woman would prefer to go to the ballet, while the man would prefer to go to the dog races. This is a date, however, so both players want to do something together. The values in the payoff matrix illustrate this (Table 7.4). If both players decide to go to the ballet, Player 1 will receive a payoff of 50 while Player 2 will receive a payoff of 40. On the other hand, if they decide to go to the dog races, Player 2 will receive the higher payoff of 50 while Player 1 will receive a payoff of 40. If the players each decide to select their first choice of entertainment, with the woman

Table 7.5

Generic Assurance Problem (Battle of the Sexes) **Game**

		Player 2	
		Action A (Ballet)	Action B (Dog Races)
Player 1	Action A (Ballet)	t, s	u, v
	Action B (Dog races)	w, x	y, z

going to the ballet and the man going to the dog races, they would both end up with a payoff of 10. This much lower payoff results from the fact that, although they have selected their first choice of entertainment, they had another objective of going on the date together. Notice that both players end up with a payoff of 0 if Player 1 selects the dog races and Player 2 selects the ballet. In this situation, the players are not going on the date together and neither of the players has selected the entertainment choice that he or she would prefer.

The generic Assurance Problem, or Battle of the Sexes, game form is presented in Table 7.5. One interesting outcome of this game form is that there is no dominant strategy for either player. It is always the case that a player's best strategy depends on what the other player decides to do. For example, if the woman decides to go to the ballet, then the best strategy for the man is to also go to the ballet. It follows, then, that in the generic Assurance Problem $t > w$, $t > u$, $s > v$, $s > x$, and $y > u$, $y > w$, $z > v$, $z > x$. The payoff values in the diagonal cells are greater than those in the off-diagonal cells, illustrating the fact that the players prefer to do the same thing.

In the Assurance Problem game form, there is no dominant strategy equilibrium. Two outcomes are Pareto optimal and those are the outcomes on the diagonals where the two players undertake the same action. Two factors are important in determining whether the players move to one of the Pareto optimal outcomes. First, the players must communicate with each other so that they both know which action the other one will select. Second, once they have communicated their intentions, the players must both have a strong sense of commitment to follow through and actually select the action they indicated. When there is open communication and the players are committed to their actions, the probability that one of the Pareto optimal outcomes will result is high.

An example of a co-op or business application of the Assurance Problem

Table 7.6

Assurance Problem Game Applied to Cooperatives

		Player 2	
		Action A (Work together)	Action B (Work independently)
Player 1	Action A (Work together)	20, 20	12, 10
	Action B (Work independently)	10, 12	15, 15

Table 7.7

Chicken Game

		Player 2	
		Action A (Go straight)	Action B (Swerve)
Player 1	Action A (Go straight)	−5, −5	5, 3
	Action B (Swerve)	3, 5	0, 0

game form is when producers face the choice of purchasing their inputs jointly, and working together, or purchasing their inputs independently (Table 7.6). If the producers work together and purchase their inputs jointly, the supplier gives them a significant discount and the producers receive their inputs for less; however, if the producers have not effectively communicated with each other and one of them acts as though he or she is going to work together and the other one acts as though he or she is working independently, they both end up paying more for inputs and, thus, end up with a lower payoff. In this situation, it could be that the supplier is willing to provide a significant discount on a joint purchase, given that the players submit one order and the supplier is able to ship one large order. When the players do not act in a consistent manner, the supplier charges them more and they are worse off.

Chicken Game

The Chicken Game is illustrated in Table 7.7. The players in the Chicken Game are two people who have been challenged to a bet with a maximum payoff of 5, but also with the potential to lose a value of 5. They are to drive

Table 7.8

Generic Chicken Game

		Player 2	
		Action A (Go straight)	Action B (Swerve)
Player 1	Action A (Go straight)	*w, w*	*x, y*
	Action B (Swerve)	*y, x*	*z, z*

down a one-lane road toward each other. Since it is a one-lane road, there is no room for the two cars to pass as they meet. If one of the players does not swerve off the road, they will crash. Each of the players has been instructed that he or she will win if the other player swerves and he or she goes straight. Of course, if neither of the players swerves, the two cars crash and they both lose (–5, –5). If both of the players swerve, they do not crash but both players have to face the humiliation of having swerved (0, 0). Player 1, therefore, would prefer it if Player 2 swerved (5, 3), and in a similar manner, Player 2 would prefer it if Player 1 swerved (3, 5).

The generic Chicken Game is illustrated in Table 7.8 with $z > x > w$ and $z > y > w$. The Pareto optimal outcomes are the off-diagonal outcomes. In this situation, one player is willing to provide the public good only if the other player is not willing to provide the public good. Fulton et al. (1996) argue, in a footnote, that while this is an interesting game form to consider when evaluating the provision of public goods, there is no reason to expect that it is especially appropriate for cooperative businesses; however, recent examples of producers facing the departure of a processing facility, such as the sugarbeet growers in Renville, Minnesota, or turkey producers in Iowa, may have characteristics of the Chicken Game. The resulting NGCs were established because producers realized that the outside investors were no longer willing to provide the processing operation and that they would have to do it themselves.

Multi-Period Prisoners' Dilemma

As noted above, the dominant strategy equilibrium for the single-period Prisoners' Dilemma game is that both players will confess. This results in a Pareto inferior outcome. Both players are worse off (each spending 15 years in jail) than if they had selected the strategy to cooperate (by agreeing to deny they only spend two years in jail); however, both players were following the dominant strategy and acting in a manner that was in their own best interest. While the Prisoners' Dilemma game form is a useful tool to explain the provision of public goods and other business phenomena, the Pareto inferior outcome as dominant strategy equilibrium is sometimes not consistent with real-world observation.

If the Prisoners' Dilemma game form fully described the provision of public goods, then we would find that public goods would never be provided. Since there are many real-world examples, both business examples as well as examples in the public sector, of public goods that are provided, we have to conclude that the Prisoners' Dilemma game form is not a complete description of the provision of public goods. One possible explanation is that the payoff is not characterized by the Prisoners' Dilemma, but, rather, by some other payoff structure such as the Assurance Problem. As discussed earlier, the probability of reaching a cooperate/cooperate outcome is high when the payoff is that of an Assurance Problem, when the players communicate with each other, and when there is a high level of commitment.

Another useful model to explain the provision of public goods is the Prisoners' Dilemma model, but in a multi-period rather than a single-period form. When players realize that the game will be repeated, rather than a single event, the outcome of the game can differ. In fact, there are conditions that will more likely result in the players moving to the cooperate/cooperate outcome. In particular, players realize the value of what they are giving up by not selecting the cooperate/cooperate outcome. If certain conditions or factors are in place, there is a greater chance that the cooperate/cooperate outcome will occur. Five factors influence the outcome. The multi-period Prisoners' Dilemma game is more likely to result in the cooperate/cooperate outcome when the following occur:

- the length of the game is infinite, or at least unknown to the players;
- players react by imposing some sort of penalty when one of the players defects;
- the rate of time preference, or discount rate, of the players is low;
- the payoff for cooperation is sufficiently larger than the payoff for defection;
- there are a small number of players who are relatively homogeneous.

In essence, when the Prisoners' Dilemma is played over an infinite time period, the players perceive a different payoff structure. The additional return that each player can experience by selecting the cooperate/cooperate outcome is available to each player over multiple time periods. There is an incentive for the players to find a way to each select the cooperate/cooperate outcome and reap the higher returns; however, while there is an incentive for the players to select the cooperate/cooperate outcome, there are also incentives for individual players to "cheat" and select the defect/defect outcome. The factors that influence the players' tendency to "cheat" are noted above and explained further below.

Length of Game

It is essential that the length of the game be infinite or at least of unknown duration to the players. There are more incentives for the players to figure out how to achieve the cooperate/cooperate solution when the game is infinite in duration. With a multi-period game, the players evaluate the stream of benefits over the infinite number of periods. Since all players are better off when they determine a way to move to the Pareto optimal outcome, and this increased payoff will be experienced every period for an infinite number of periods, the players have an incentive to find a way to select the cooperate/cooperate solution and work together.

The incentive for the players to work together exists because the players see the long-term, multi-period, benefits of selecting the cooperate/cooperate outcome. When there is an end point in sight for the players, then the incentive for at least one of the players to be enticed by the additional returns from "cheating" is greater, and the chance of not achieving the cooperate/cooperate outcome increases.

Reaction to Defection

As noted above, the tendency for the players to move to the cooperate/cooperate outcome relies on whether or not the players view the long-term benefit of the stream of income over the multiple periods. It is also important to note that the tendency for a player to cheat also exists. If a player were to cheat in one period of the game, and there was no reaction by the other players (in other words, the other players continued to select the cooperate choice), then the first player would have the incentive to cheat all of the time. Eventually, all of the players would realize that it was in their best interests to behave in a selfish manner and the game would move to the defect/defect outcome as a long-term equilibrium that is not Pareto optimal.

If, on the other hand, the players do react (i.e., retaliate) when one player defects, then long-term stability of the cooperate/cooperate solution is possible. The players simply send the message to the cheating player that such behavior is not acceptable and if the first player responds by then cooperating in subsequent time periods, a stable (i.e., Pareto optimal) solution can result.

Players' Discount Rate

A third factor that is important in determining whether the cooperate/ cooperate solution will be achieved is the discount rate, or rate of time preference of money, of each player. As noted above, in the multi-period game, the players evaluate the present value of the flow of returns from all of the time periods that the game will be played. Present value calculations involve discounting future payments to determine the value in today's dollars, since a dollar today is worth more than a dollar in the future. The rate at which returns are discounted is the individual's discount rate, or rate of time preference of money. Since different people have different financial situations, they necessarily have different discount rates. Individuals who have a great need for cash immediately have a high discount rate, while individuals who have more flexibility in their cash requirements tend to have a low discount rate.

A multi-period Prisoners' Dilemma is less likely to result in the cooperate/ cooperate solution when one or more of the players has a high discount rate, since in that situation the players have a need for cash today and will find the immediate benefit from defecting more attractive than the longer-term payoff from selecting the cooperate outcome.

Payoff Differential for Cooperation

The likelihood of achieving the cooperate/cooperate solution is greater the larger the difference between the payoff the players receive from the cooperate/cooperate and defect/defect outcomes. If the differential is large, there is more incentive for the players to find a way to agree to selecting the cooperate/cooperate solution and to maintaining the cooperate/cooperate solution over time; however, if the differential is small, then players will not invest the time and energy to figure out how to work together.

Number and Homogeneity of the Players

The final factor affecting whether the cooperate/cooperate solution is achieved is related to the nature of the players themselves. There is a greater chance of achieving the cooperate/cooperate solution with a smaller number of players and when the players are more homogeneous. The smaller the number of players, the easier it is for them to coordinate and achieve the cooperate/ cooperate outcome. The more homogeneous the players, the more likely they are to have similar goals and the easier it is for them to agree and achieve the cooperate/cooperate outcome.

Cooperative Research and Game Theory Applications

A series of articles appeared in the 1980s that utilized game theory to advance the theory of cooperative business organizations (Sexton 1984, 1986; Sexton and Sexton 1987; Staatz 1983, 1987; Zusman 1982). The impetus for this research was a realization that the existing models fell short. In particular, the importance of bringing member behavior into the models was realized (Sexton 1984; Zusman 1982). Previous models had utilized neoclassical economic tools of optimization based on profit-maximizing or cost-minimizing decisions. Game theory is appropriate when the interaction and reaction of players' behavior is important.

Zusman (1982) presents a model to analyze the group choice processes in a co-op. He then explores implications of allocative efficiency for a marketing co-op, with specific attention paid to the allocation of the costs of production among the members and the resulting distribution of income. His results indicate that when members are heterogeneous and market different quantities of output, conflict over the cost allocation rule can result.

Staatz (1983) uses cooperative game theory to explain decisions involving the allocation of costs and benefits within co-ops. He notes that cooperative game theory is useful because of the different groups (e.g., farmer members, board of directors, management, labor) that make up cooperative decision makers. He identifies six conclusions. First, in some circumstances it will be necessary for the co-op to charge different prices to different members or else some members will take their business to the competition. Second, in situations where average cost is U-shaped, it may not be possible for the co-op to provide incentives for all members to continue to patronize the co-op. In other words, it may not be possible for the co-op to serve all of its members in a cost-effective manner.

Third, there may be more than one feasible allocation of costs for the co-op that satisfies the objectives and falls within the firm's constraints. In this situation, it is the responsibility of management and the board of directors to select the allocation used by the co-op. Fourth, if cooperative decision makers select an allocation that does not meet all constraints, members are likely to exit the co-op. Fifth, bargaining by members over the allocation of costs and benefits can be intense if dissatisfied members do not leave the co-op. Finally, Staatz notes that when the co-op's decision makers can convert apparent zero-sum games to non-zero-sum games and expand the potential core of the game, all members are better off and cooperative commitment will be easier to attain. Staatz uses the example of how a long-term marketing pool that has the commitment of its members will lead to increased market opportunities, thus expanding the core for all members.

By using formal mathematical models, Sexton (1986) explores cooperative formation through cooperative game theory and the theory of coalition formation. An emphasis is placed on individual decision makers and their incentives to undertake joint action. The main idea is that the decision by a member as to whether or not to enter the co-op is critical to whether or not a co-op will even be formed and should be modeled as endogenous. Following up on this, Sexton and Sexton (1987) utilize a cooperative game theory model to explore a consumer coalition or consumer co-op.

In their research, Fulton and Vercammen (1995) examine nonuniform pricing schemes for co-ops wherein different members would pay (or receive) different prices. They show that nonuniform pricing can solve economic inefficiencies that result when uniform pricing is in effect.

Staatz (1987) provides a useful overview of game theory as applied to co-ops. He begins with the modeling of cooperative behavior as a cooperative game. He then presents the Prisoners' Dilemma game as applied to farmer co-ops. After describing the Prisoners' Dilemma game in the single-period format, he moves to the multi-period Prisoners' Dilemma game. Referencing Taylor (1976), Schotter (1981), and Axelrod and Hamilton (1981), he notes the five elements (presented earlier) that are critical in obtaining the cooperate/cooperate outcome in the multi-period Prisoners' Dilemma game. Staatz then goes further, identifying the following conditions that affect farmer loyalty to an agricultural co-op:

- Cooperative loyalty will be greater among those who will be farming for an infinite period.
- Cooperative loyalty increases as the penalties for disloyalty are increased.
- A farmer's loyalty decreases as he or she becomes more leveraged (has a higher discount rate).
- Cooperative loyalty is greater in small co-ops than in larger co-ops. (131)

In empirical applications of the Prisoners' Dilemma and Assurance Problem games, Fulton et al. (1996) and Fulton (1998b)[2] examine the factors that contribute to the success of local cooperative business restructuring. Based on the theory of the Prisoners' Dilemma and Assurance Problem, they hypothesize that joint venture and strategic alliance agreements would be more effective when the following seven conditions occur:

1. The cooperatives are committed to working together in the long term.
2. Managers who defect from an arrangement are punished according to guidelines in a contract or through the negative image they receive in the business community.

3. All of the cooperative businesses involved are financially sound.
4. The benefits/costs of *cooperating/not cooperating* are well known to all participants, and the payoff for cooperation is larger than the payoff for not cooperating.
5. The number of co-ops involved is limited, and the co-ops are homogeneous.
6. The managers remain informed about the operations of the business arrangement and have an open line of communication with each other.
7. The managers of the co-ops have a sense of mutual respect and trust for each other. (5)

These hypotheses were confirmed following an analysis of the information collected from interviews with managers of local co-ops in Colorado. In particular, Fulton et al. (1996) asked managers to identify the factors that were critical to the success of the joint venture and strategic alliance agreements. In follow-up research in Colorado and Indiana five years later, Vandeburg, Fulton, Hine, and McNamara (2000, 2001)[3] obtained numerical ratings from managers on the importance of each of the different factors in the success of joint venture and strategic alliance agreements. With the numerical ratings, they conducted a statistical analysis and in that way confirmed the previously noted hypotheses using statistical tests.

Additional research, as reported by Fulton and Keenan (1997) and Fulton (1998a)[4], also confirms the importance of commitment and communication when it comes to the provision of public goods. This latter research examined the factors that lead to the satisfaction and degree of involvement that managers of local co-ops have with their state cooperative councils.

Conclusions

Game theory is a useful tool for explaining the behavior of members within a cooperative business, as well as the behavior of cooperative business organizations as they work together in joint ventures and strategic alliances. In the application of game theory, it is important to determine which game form is most closely represented by the situation being considered. In particular, it is important to distinguish between those situations where the payoff matrix is most closely represented by the Prisoners' Dilemma game and those cases where the payoff is most closely represented by the Assurance Problem game. In the former case, in the single-period game, there is a dominant strategy equilibrium that is not the Pareto optimal outcome.

In the case of the Assurance Problem game, there is no dominant strategy equilibrium and players can be expected to move to a Pareto optimal outcome if they can communicate with each other and if a high level of trust exists among the players. If the payoff is a Prisoners' Dilemma game that is multi-period in nature, then the outcome depends on the length of the game, the players' discount rates, the relative payoffs for defecting or cooperating, the penalty for defecting, and the number and degree of homogeneity of the players. An important area for future empirical research is to examine different situations in cooperative businesses to evaluate whether the payoff matrices would best be described as a Prisoners' Dilemma or an Assurance Problem.

Notes

1. A Pareto optimal situation is one in which it is not possible to make one player better off without making another player worse off. When an outcome is not Pareto optimal, or is Pareto inferior, it is possible to move to a different outcome and make at least one player better off without making the other players any worse off. In the Prisoners' Dilemma game, a movement from the confess/confess outcome to the deny/deny outcome makes both prisoners better off.

2. These two publications report the same research. Fulton et al. (1996) is presented in a more academic format, while Fulton (1998b) was written to be of interest to managers and directors of local co-ops and is more applied in nature.

3. These two publications report the same research. Vandeburg et al. (2000) is presented in a more academic format, while Vandeburg et al. (2001) was written to be of interest to managers and directors of local co-ops and is more applied in nature.

4. These two publications report the same research. Fulton and Keenan (1997) is presented in a more academic format, while Fulton (1998a) was written to be of interest to managers and directors of local co-ops and is more applied in nature.

References

Axelrod, Robert, and William Hamilton. 1981. "The Evolution of Cooperation." *Science* (March 27): 1390–1396.

Daniels, J. Grayson. 1999. "Consolidation and Collaboration in Agribusiness." Unpublished master's thesis, Purdue University.

Fowke, Vernon. 1957. *The National Policy and the Wheat Economy.* Toronto: University of Toronto Press.

French, Charles, John Moore, Charles Kraenzle, and Kenneth Harling. 1980. *Survival Strategies for Agricultural Cooperatives.* Ames: Iowa State University Press.

Fulton, Joan. 1998a. "State Cooperative Councils Serve Vital Cooperative Education Purpose." In *American Cooperation*, ed. National Council of Farmer Cooperatives, 169–175. Available at www.americancooporation.org/yb1998–c07.a03.pdf (January 2003).

———. 1998b. "A Local Solution: As Agriculture Industrialized, Local Supply and Grain Co-ops in Colorado Remain Profitable Through Joint Ventures and Alliances." *Rural Cooperatives* (May/June): 19–21.

————. 2001. *Value-added and New Generation Cooperatives*. Presentation to ANR In-Service, Purdue University, November. Available at www.agecon.purdue.edu/ext/pubs/NewGenerationCooperatives/Slide1_PNG.html (September 23, 2002).

Fulton, Joan, Mukesh Bhargava, and Sally Daily. 1993. "Bottom-up Versus Top-down Organization of Cooperatives in Development: The Case of Dairy Cooperatives in India." In *Cooperative Values in a Changing World*, ed. Donald W. Attwood and Jill Hanley, 101–115. Saskatoon: Centre for the Study of Co-operatives, University of Saskatchewan.

Fulton, Joan, and Michael Keenan. 1997. "State Cooperative Councils: What Are the Local Member Cooperatives Looking For?" *Journal of Cooperatives* 12: 35–46.

Fulton, Murray, and James Vercammen. 1995. "The Distributional Impacts of Non-uniform Pricing Schemes for Cooperatives." *Journal of Cooperatives* 10: 18–32.

Fulton, Joan, John Foltz, and Susan Hine. 2002. "Driving Forces and Success Factors Associated with Business Restructuring." *Feed and Grain* (June/July): 11–12.

Fulton, Joan, Michael P. Popp, and Carolyn Gray. 1996. "Strategic Alliance and Joint Venture Agreements in Grain Marketing Cooperatives." *Journal of Cooperatives* 11: 1–14.

Jesness, O.B. 1923. *The Cooperative Marketing of Farm Products*. Philadelphia: J.B. Lippincott.

Knapp, Joseph. 1979. *Edwin G. Nourse: Economist for the People*. Danville, IL: Interstate.

Porter, Andrew. 2001. "Driving Forces and Success Factors for Agribusiness Reorganization: A Case Study of Cenex Harvest States Merger." Unpublished master's thesis, Purdue University.

Reuters. 2002. "Minnesota Corn Processors to Merge with ADM Unit." *Forbes.com*. Available at www.forbes.com/newswire/2002/07/11/rtr659300.html (September 23, 2002).

Runge, C. Ford. 1981. "Common Property Externalities: Isolation, Assurance, and Resource Depletion in a Traditional Grazing Context." *American Journal of Agricultural Economics* 63(4): 595–606.

————. 1984. "The Assurance Problem in Collective Action." *Journal of Politics* 46: 154–181.

Schotter, Andrew. 1981. *The Economic Theory of Social Institutions*. New York: Cambridge University Press.

Sexton, Richard. 1984. "Perspectives on the Development of the Economic Theory of Cooperatives." *Canadian Journal of Agricultural Economics* 32: 423–436.

————. 1986. "The Formation of Cooperatives: A Game-Theoretic Approach with Implications for Cooperative Finance, Decision Making, and Stability." *American Journal of Agricultural Economics* 68: 214–225.

Sexton, Richard, and Terri Sexton. 1987. "Cooperatives as Entrants." *RAND Journal of Economics* 18: 581–595.

Staatz, John. 1983. "The Cooperative as a Coalition: A Game-theoretic Approach." *American Journal of Agricultural Economics* 65: 1084–1089.

————. 1987. "A Game-theoretic Analysis of Decision Making in Farmer Cooperatives." In *Cooperative Theory: New Approaches* (Service report 18), ed. Jeffrey S. Royer, 117–147. Washington, DC: USDA, Agricultural Cooperative Service.

Taylor, Michael. 1976. *Anarchy and Cooperation*. New York: John Wiley.

————. 1987. *The Possibility of Cooperation*. Cambridge, UK: Cambridge University Press.

Vandeburg, Jennifer, Joan Fulton, Susan Hine, and Kevin McNamara. 2000. *Driving Forces and Success Factors for Mergers, Acquisitions, Joint Ventures, and Strategic Alliances Among Local Cooperatives*. Paper presented at the NCR 194 Annual Meeting, December 13, Las Vegas. Available at www.agecon.ksu.edu/accc/ncr194/Events/2000meeting/VandeburgFulton.pdf (September 23, 2002).

———. 2001. "Local Cooperative Restructuring." *Purdue Agricultural Economics Report* (May): 4–8.

Zusman, Pinhas. 1982. "Group Choice in an Agricultural Marketing Cooperative." *Canadian Journal of Economics* 15: 220–234.

8

Creating Value in a Knowledge-based Agriculture: A Theory of New Generation Cooperatives

Peter Goldsmith

Cooperative Enterprises in the Economy

Cooperative firms play a significant role in many sectors of the U.S. economy. Revenues of farmer co-ops surpassed $100 billion in 1996. Using cooperative cost of goods sold, marketing co-ops handled 28 percent of U.S. commodity output in 1996 (USDA/RBS 1998). Traditionally, co-ops served an economic role by adding discipline to the marketplace. For example, farmers who are integrating their product upstream or downstream work together to protect themselves from monopoly market conditions (Sexton 1986b). In such instances, overall social surplus is reduced as monopoly prices diverge from competitive prices. The quantity transacted is also suboptimal. By joining together in a co-op, agents counter the monopolist "holdup" by forcing prices down. This increases quantities transacted and better allocates resources in the economy. Co-ops are, therefore, valuable entities for economies faced with poorly performing markets.

Theoretical Constraints

There are several preconditions that a cooperative theorist must address in order to understand these complex institutions and their ability to compete with other business forms. These issues are endemic to the "cooperative's problem." Any discussion cannot "assume away" the following issues:

(1) nonstationarity, (2) dynamics, (3) conditionality, and (4) the objective function.

Nonstationarity

Stationarity of model variables and assumptions is a beneficial characteristic in economics. It is a necessary condition for global and nontrivial equilibria. For example, if key parameters drift, an additional level of dimensionality occurs in the problem. Cooperative theory has a long tradition of modeling aspects of organizational behavior. Accordingly, cooperative theorists assume key model parameters too are stationary. This is okay when studying industrial organization and its traditional theories about the "firm." Economists assume that price discovery, organizational structure, risk parameters, and objective functions are fixed.

In cooperative theory, nonstationarity is important when defining the diversity of a co-op's membership. Helmberger and Hoos (1962) may be correct to assume that the n members of the co-op are, at $t = 1$, a homogeneous set. Agents defining the co-op's objective function can reach consensus—a traditional assumption applied in cooperative theory.

What happens, though, when the members at $t = (2 \ldots n)$ become more heterogeneous? This will affect the equilibrium location for the process. Since the n individuals are bound by idiosyncratic "producer problems," it is incorrect to assume that homogeneity will persist over time. A co-op model that denies this characteristic (assumes stationarity) is simple but not robust. Because co-ops are comprised of idiosyncratically optimizing agents, it is wrong to assume that structural elements of the cooperative problem will not change over time.

Dynamics

All business firms face changing market conditions to which they must adapt. The co-op also has some characteristics of typical investor-owned firms (IOFs) (Emilianov 1942; Helmberger and Hoos 1962; Ladd 1974; Savage 1954; Zusman 1982). For example, profit maximization may be the IOF's objective function. The investor/owners concur with these ends. Thus, over time, the number of variables that affect the IOF's mission changes very little. The overall focus of the firm changes little due to the profit motive. There is a temporal consensus about the basic values of the firm and its direction.

With respect to dynamics, the co-op's objective function contains some very different elements. There is the powerful force of n dynamic, growing and evolving unconstrained, independent co-op members. Each member firm grows at its own rate and direction. In terms of services needed from or expectations of the co-op, this evolution affects the firm in a multidimensional manner. The simultaneity of the firm, optimizing concurrently with n members who are individually optimizing, increases the dimensionality of the problem compared to the typical IOF. The co-op has greater and more challenging dynamic properties, therefore, than those faced by the IOF. While the IOF faces a dynamic external environment, the firm's "problem" is straightforward and constant. For the co-op, the business environment is dynamic while at the same time the co-op members operate on individual planes with separate dynamic properties.

Conditionality

Conditionality is the third precondition to the co-op member's problem. As will be shown later, the co-op's price and quantity decisions are not directly responsive to market signals. Not only is there a derived demand, but prices are also neither exogenous nor objective. There is strategic price setting. The behavior of the co-op is fully conditional on member behavior. In this sense, the co-op is comparable to a sole proprietorship, whereby the fluctuations in utility or wealth of the owner are synonymous with the firm. Phillips (1953), in his classic article on vertical integration, produced such a conceptualization. For him, the co-op was simply an extension of the individual proprietor's optimization.

Objective Function

The final precondition is the role of the individual utility function. Sexton (1986a, 1986b) and Staatz (1983) have advanced cooperative theory by identifying a factor driving the co-op: member utility maximization. It is a constant valuation procedure by which members critically assess the value and purpose of membership. Though the process occurs with every member and co-op, it is not a homogeneous process. The intensity of assessment or level of commitment varies by co-op and by individual member. Cooperative theories should model this behavior on two different levels.

The first level is the relationship of a member's cooperative patronage to his or her overall income,[1] called patronage elasticity (see Appendix, Equation 1). It describes the role the co-op plays in the member's overall optimization and welfare. Does the co-op matter to the survivability of the farmer-member? If patronage is critical to farmer profit, then elasticity is high and producer commitment is greater. If patronage is minimal, say the producer has multiple marketing outlets, then elasticity and commitment are low.

The second level is the risk behavior that carries over from the individual member to the co-op. Due to significant member–cooperative firm linkages, identifying the farm firm's economic behavior becomes integral to solving the co-op's problem. Helmberger and Hoos (1962), LeVay (1983), Phillips (1953), Sexton (1986a), and Staatz (1987) assume the farm firm to be risk neutral. Model tractability is enhanced when aggregation occurs over a homogeneous set of individuals with linear objective functions. Realism and robustness are sacrificed, however.

Sexton (1986b) and Staatz (1983) allow for risk-averse behavior. In the co-op's problem, aggregation occurs over a heterogeneous set of individuals with nonlinear utility functions. The second moment becomes significant— thus, the importance of risk. Lin (1974, 497) writes, "[E]mpirical studies explicitly implying the profit maximization hypothesis have generally provided results inconsistent with observed or plausible behavior. . . . [I]t is hypothesized that farmers' operational decisions are more consistent with utility maximization than with profit maximization." Thus, a comprehensive cooperative theory has to confront the objective function aggregation issue.

Models of the Cooperative's Problem

This section continues the theory-building process by formalizing the fundamental behavioral relationship between members and their co-op. This is accomplished by means of three cooperative firm models and incentives for their formation. Existence and incentives for co-op formation distinguish the co-op's problem from that of the IOF. These models, combined with the concepts introduced above, provide a means for extending models of cooperative firm behavior.

The first model is a neoclassical model of cooperative existence. The cooperative–membership relationship is shown using standard technology, efficiency conditions, and marginal analysis. The other two models employ a game-theoretic approach. Game theory uses a cost-minimizing assumption as well, but it also expands the understanding of why individuals join co-ops. The "gaming" models were the first to address the plural optimization occurring in a co-op (see Chapter 7 in this volume for more on game theory).

This multiperspective approach (three variant models) fully accounts for the complex cooperative–member problem. This section uses the conclusions of Sexton (1986a) and Staatz (1983), along with a neoclassical model, to develop an understanding of the co-op's problem and to identify how the co-op organizational form needs to be adjusted to survive under dynamic conditions.

Cooperative Existence

The theory of the firm begins with the firm as a predetermined institution. Both the technology and the profit-maximizing objective function are exogenous. In standard economic texts (see Kreps 1990; Varian 1984), existence is assumed when the supply side of the economy is discussed. There is no discussion about genesis. The firm is synonymous with its production function. Microeconomic theory begins with coverage of the supply function, profit function, technology, and cost function. Though these are some of the most vital topics in economics, they are *ex post* behavioral issues when the study of foundation or existence is important.

The topic of cooperative existence is the study of why cooperative organizations originate. This area of study can be characterized in the following manner: In a temporal context, at $t = 0$, n independent agents produce a similar commodity under purely competitive market conditions. At $t = 1$, some event (exogenous or endogenous) occurs. Agents have increased expected utility by uniting in the co-op rather than competing alone. The higher expected utility could be in the form of higher profits, lower costs, reduced risks, or simply increased utility. Some market integration (vertical or horizontal) then occurs. A part of the transaction is internalized through ownership control.

By exploring from three different perspectives why farmers leave the spot market, the theoretical assumptions in co-op modeling are emphasized and the co-op's problem is illuminated. By understanding the causal conditions and initial environment, the underlying relationships of co-ops are better understood. This understanding of co-op formation is then applied to the current phenomenon of New Generation Cooperative (NGC) formation in the next section. The theoretical constructs discussed in the first two sections provide the framework for understanding how producers can create value through group action as agriculture becomes a knowledge-based industry.

The Model

The Farmer's Problem

There are N farms selling output Y in a competitive market. There are two inputs in the production process: X_d and Z_i. X_d and Z_i are perfect substitutes. The only difference is their origination. The market for X_d can be monopolistic, whereby $Z_i = 0$. As the supply and number of suppliers of Z_i increase, the market becomes more competitive. The production function on the farm is $Y = f(X_d + Z_i)$ (Figure 8.1). It has the standard properties of concavity and

Figure 8.1 **The Farmer's Problem**

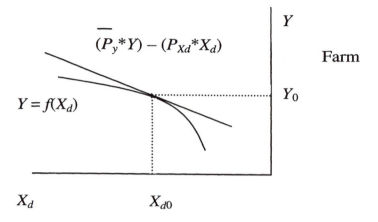

$$\overline{(P_y*Y) - (P_{Xd}*X_d)}$$

$Y = f(X_d)$

Y

Farm

Y_0

X_d

X_{d0}

continuity. For simplicity, the objective function assumes a standard linear profit maximization and is described further in the Appendix, Equation 2.

P_y, the output price, is exogenous due to the competitive output market conditions. In the standard competitive market firm's problem P_{xd}, the price of the input good is exogenous. Input supplies normally would be purchased in the spot market; however, in this model, there is a different linkage between marketing stages. Through common ownership and commitment, P_{xd} is not determined in the spot market but is now an *endogenous* variable solved by the joint problems of the producer farmers and the supplier co-op. The farmer's problem is solved through an individual decision-making process, while the co-op's problem is solved using a group process. The decision variables are X_d, the quantity of cooperative-supplied input, and Z_i, the quantity of the spot-market-supplied input. P_{zi}, the price of the spot-market-purchased input, is exogenous due to the competitive market assumption.

The Co-op's Problem

The N farmers are members of a co-op as well. The supply co-op operates in markets ranging from competitive to imperfectly competitive. Using Helmberger and Hoos's (1962) "surplus (S)" and setting it equal to zero (see Appendix, Equations 3 and 4), profits are zero because the co-op returns all surpluses to the membership. This now *cannot* be solved directly because in addition to technology constraints, there are also output supply constraints. The only choice (group) variable is P_{xs} (Figure 8.2). X_s and, thus, Z_j (from

Figure 8.2 **Comparative Statics and the Cooperative's Problem**

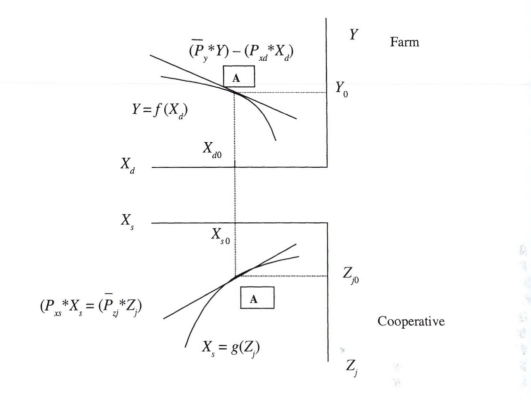

the technology constraint) are endogenous variables, as X_s depends on member patronage and Z_j depends on the derived demand. P_{zj}, the price of the co-op's input, is exogenous because it is purchased in the spot market.

Simultaneous Equation System

The co-op, which operates at the discretion of the member–customer, is part of an important linkage between optimization problems in both the farm and the supply markets. Thus, there is distinct *simultaneity* occurring in the model. This simultaneous optimization is not trivial considering the owner–patron structure of the co-op. Instead of two distinct optimizations, a system of equations is needed to determine the equilibrium. By assumption, $X_s = X_d$ and $P_{xs} = P_{xd}$. Member farmers use all of the co-op's output. X_s and Z_j are substitutes (see Appendix, Equations 5 to 11). X_s is a cooperative purchased input, and Z_i is a spot-market-purchased input.

Figure 8.3 **Capacity Challenges**

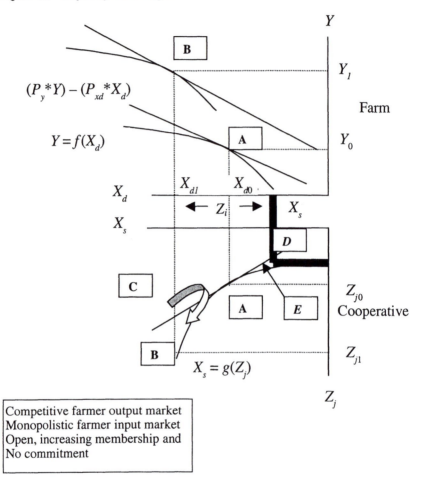

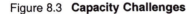

Comparative Statics

In a monopolistic market for X_d, it is theoretically possible to be at Point A, which not only maximizes profits in the farm market but also is optimum with respect to capacity in the co-op market. At this point all inputs are supplied by the cooperative, $Z_i=0$. This will be difficult to maintain in an open co-op, however. This is Helmberger and Hoos's (1962) "inimicability" between new and original members. Point B (Figure 8.3), for example, arises due to increased memberships with no technical change on the farm or in the co-op. If X_{d0} increases to X_{djg}, the farm market can only be kept in equilibrium if P_{xd} remains constant. If the co-op were an independent agent, it would raise P_{xs} to maintain the tangency with its now lower marginal physical product. Since it is not, a wedge is driven between the marginal physical product and the co-op's budget line. This can be seen as Area C.

With P_{zj} as a constant, equilibrium is only maintained if P_{xs} is allowed to move. Open membership forces the co-op to keep pace in terms of output. Competition in the farm output market forces cooperative directors to keep input price P_{xs} constant. The co-op firm, in turn, incurs economic losses. The co-op could recapitalize, obligating its newest members to achieve a more appropriate scale. This is unlikely as historically traditional co-ops prefer to generate capital through debt or by slowly building capital through retained patronage.[2]

The co-op is sustained in the short run by three strategies. The first is to tap its reserves of the good will that come from the common ownership position. This could occur, for example, by adjusting the quality characteristics of X_s. The second strategy, alluded to by Helmberger and Hoos (1962), is to allow the erosion of the firm's equity position.

The third solution is to take advantage of its monopolistic position and move P_{xs} upward. None of these solutions produces long-run equilibria. Equilibrium could be attained if the single service restriction (diversification) is relaxed. Through economies of scope, or cross-subsidization, cooperative viability is possible. For example, a "natural" monopoly position in one market could sustain the suboptimal return in another that was more competitive.

The more realistic industry scenario involves some form of competition at the supply level and a co-op without commitment.[3] There are ample substitute suppliers willing to supply and indirectly create an overcapacity situation for the co-op. Assuming the Noursean tradition that a co-op's purpose is to improve disadvantageous markets, the co-op may solidify the market enough to attract market players. For example, once the co-op has broken the monopoly supplier situation by attracting rivals into the market, the function of the co-op may be complete. Member agents implicitly signal this by distributing their patronage, which results in underutilizing the co-op's fixed investments.

Since X_d and Z_i are substitutes, farmer members do not differentiate between the sources. Being first and foremost optimizers at the farm level, they choose the minimum of P_{xd} and P_{zi}. This forces the co-op to engage in strategies such as product differentiation to maintain market share. This increases the value of X_s and reduces the substitutability between X_d and Z_i. Depending on the technology and the contestability of the market, the co-op may have to engage in predatory tactics to forestall competitors (see Appendix, Equation 12).

If the co-op does not counter the threat of a more competitive market, the

Figure 8.4 **Strategic Repositioning**

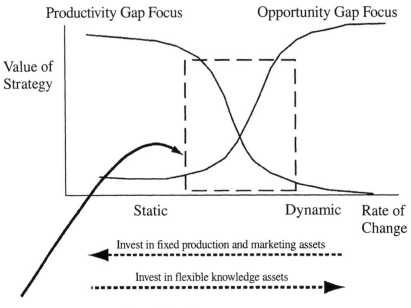

Region of Strategic Repositioning

co-op indefinitely remains in a suboptimum capacity situation. This would occur at Point D, overcapacity, where economic losses result (Area E). This makes empirical sense as single-service open co-ops are quite rare in markets where there exists even the slightest competition.

Conclusion

The neoclassical model shows the tenuous relationship between the open co-op and its members. The model demonstrates two dominant characteristics of the co-op's problem: (1) conditionality, and (2) divergence in objective functions. The member in an open and/or no commitment scenario freely substitutes X_d and Z_i. Patrons optimally allocate resources efficiently. The co-op is prohibited from similar business behavior, however. Thus, it is an imbalanced relationship, whereby the members are not committed to the co-op but at the same time the co-op is obligated to its membership. The cooperative enterprise cannot respond to these *internal* market signals in the same manner as its proprietary counterpart might respond to external market signals. Therefore, its responses are not the traditional reallocation of inputs in response to exogenously changing prices.

Game-Theoretic Models

Another perspective on cooperative existence originates from the efforts of Sexton (1986a, 1986b) and Staatz (1983) in the mid-1980s. They used game theory to demonstrate group dynamics occurring in the co-op's "game." Game theory addresses the issue of group choice when the preferences of a group partially conflict (Staatz 1983). Their models were the first to consider heterogeneous membership. By doing so, they exposed the predicaments of the stationarity and multiobjective functions as aspects of co-ops.

Sexton's Model

Several assumptions help define the core of the co-op's problem. The first is that membership in the organization is voluntary. There is free entry and exit. This is a reasonable assumption as it is consistent not only with how many co-ops behave but also with the Rochdale principles of cooperative associations.

Second, members are *fully* rational. They understand not only their own utility functions but also can evaluate the benefits of groups. Their utility functions are well-behaved and, by definition, adhere to the axioms of preference.[4] Output prices and all but one of the set of input prices are established in competitive markets ($P_i^c = \{ p_1 \cdots p_{n-1} \}$). It is this exception in the input market that gives incentive for the cooperative (supply) formation. For Z, the noncompetitive market input, its price is defined as P_z^m. The production function then is $Y_i = f_i (X_i, Z_i)$. Finally, the farmer's problem is similar to that of the neoclassical model. Profits are maximized subject to the technology and pricing constraints.

The Model

The co-op forms to circumvent monopoly pricing by the supplier of Z. Z_s is defined as the output purchased by subgroup or coalition S. S is defined as a subset of the N total number of farmers, $S \subseteq N$. P_{zs}^* is the price necessary to get coalition S together. Sexton then defines the *existence* condition (see Appendix, Equation 13). Existence is related to two comparable input prices, P_{zs}^* and P_z^m. Existence only occurs if profits within the coalition are greater than those under monopoly pricing.

This idea of positive returns from the coalition S purchasing good Z can be expressed using the value function (see Appendix, Equation 14). The value function is defined as the payoff received by subgroup S from its commitment to the purchase of Z: $V [S (P_{zs}^*)]$. The following condition must exist for any coalition to endure (Sexton 1986a). There is superadditivity across all coalitions. Members must gain by uniting. Because of voluntary entry and exit, as well as complete rationality, the core of the game only exists, ergo the co-op only exists, if the subgroup is stable. Stability is a function of member or individual satisfaction with the returns from membership.

The cooperative core is defined by the following three conditions (see Appendix, Equation 15 to 17) (Sexton 1986a), with X_i as the payoff received by the individual member within the coalition. The first condition of the co-op's game's core is that patron benefits must be as great as if farmers operated in isolation: $V(i)$. Sexton's second condition is one of Pareto optimality. The sum of the individual payoffs equals that attainable if all players acted jointly. Finally, there is the condition of subgroup rationality. Individuals cannot do worse in the group than if they were on their own. Under such adverse conditions, the member would leave the coalition rather than suffer the lower returns from group membership.

Conclusion

Under the above assumptions, three interesting conclusions about cooperative behavior are revealed. First, if member heterogeneity exists, the cooperative core does not exist under conditions of uniform pricing. Under purely theoretical limit conditions, the subgroup rationality condition (3) fails when each coalition member does not pass a benefits/costs test. Marginal benefits (supply co-op) among members will differ. A uniform pricing policy, which does not attempt to discriminate, runs the risk of reducing the benefits of membership to the larger members and inducing coalition disintegration.

Second, under conditions of cost function subadditivity, expansion of the coalition not only benefits entering members (individual rationality) but benefits the original members, too. Their costs are being reduced. More important is the converse. If there are no increasing returns to scale, open membership places a hardship on the original members. Thus, there is a divergence in interests between existing and new members. This was shown above in the neoclassical model.

Finally, Sexton (1986a) addresses the issue of explicit and implicit decision-making power in the co-op. Explicitly, co-ops are democratic organizations. Each member receives one vote. The above description of the core implies a unanimity criterion (Staatz 1983). If members can exit at will and if contributions to the success of the co-op are not uniform, then power within the co-op is not divided uniformly among patrons. The balance of power, therefore, is skewed by credible exit threats.

Staatz's Model

Co-ops face many decisions in which member preferences cannot be assumed to be homogeneous (Staatz 1983). Under such conditions, game theory allows for solutions whereby strategy, bargaining, *ex ante* commitments, and *ex post* repercussions actively affect the coalition. If all members were homogeneous, the median member's preferences could be used as a proxy for the group. On the other hand, with some heterogeneity, group decision solutions can expand exponentially as new members enter the organization.

In Staatz's (1983) model, he assumes that individual rationality occurs over an individual's utility function, not over the profit function, as in Sexton. Even though Staatz avoids the issue of risk aversion among the membership (he does assume neutrality), he does introduce coalitions responding to individual preferences.

The Model

There are N potential cooperative members. They are not assumed to be homogeneous, and empirically, they are likely to be heterogeneous. They now have free will to form any number of coalitions. A coalition can vary in size from 1 to N. These coalitions are formed in order to produce a service used by its members. The cost function of this enterprise is *subadditive*, $C(q^{S+T}) \leq C(q^S) + C(q^T)$. S and T are separate coalitions, and they are also subsets of N, $\{S,T \subset N, S \cap T = 0\}$.

The characteristic function of the model is $V(q^S)$. It embodies not only the cost to the individual member of obtaining the good while in the coalition, $A[C(q^S)]$, but also the acquisition price outside the coalition. It is the minimum cost of obtaining q, whether occurring within or outside the coalition (Staatz 1983).

In addition to the subadditivity condition, there are two conditions for the game's core that ensure the co-op exists. The first is the rationality constraint, $A[C(q^S)] \leq V(q^S)$, where $A[C(q^S)]$ is the cost allocation to group S. A group S member is rational only if coalition cost allocation is less than all other alternatives. Patrons not only know their own preferences but can also discriminate between membership benefits and other alternatives. Thus, there is an assumption of perfect information. The second condition for the co-op's core is the zero surplus condition, $\sum^{S \in N} A(q^S) = C(q^N)$. The sum of the cost allocations accruing from the coalition is equal to the cost of producing the service.

A final component of the Staatz game-theoretical model is the harm function. This idea is quite useful (see Appendix, Equations 18 and 19). It describes an important strategic element affecting the balance of power in the co-op. For example, there is the harm a member can impose on the rest of the coalition, h_o. There is also the harm patrons cause themselves by leaving the coalition, h_s. The harm to the coalition, h_o, is defined as the average cost without the member minus the average cost with the member times the quantity lost. The harm to the patron, h_s, is the minimum cost of obtaining the necessary quantity, q, minus the co-op's average cost without the member times the amount required by the individual (Staatz 1983, 1987).

The harm to the membership, h_o, is a function of the cost increase due to a member departing the group. Thus, the assumption of subadditivity of costs and some form of economies of scale allocates *differential* power among the membership. This harm function is scalar in value if the membership is homogeneous. It would be zero for constant returns to scale technology. Constant returns to scale, though, break the first requirement for a coalition—subadditivity.

H_s depends on several factors. The first factor is the quality of outside opportunities for substitute supplies available to the departed member. The second is the contractual *ex ante* provisions by the co-op to punish those who leave. The third relates to information quality. Is the individual's threat to leave credible? There may be asymmetric information as to the alternatives for the departed member and how well he or she will take advantage of them.

By understanding the harm functions that are involved in coalition maintenance, heterogeneity is *not* a sufficient condition for unequal distribution of power. A necessary condition is a less-than-monopolistic supply market environment, so it may not necessarily matter how much one firm dominates the patronage of the co-op. Because of the democratic voting assumption, if trading alternatives do not exist, then core condition (1), the rationality constraint, will not bind. The disgruntled member has to remain.

This is an important concept because it reveals two aspects about the relationship between members and their co-op: (1) exogenous market conditions affect the behavior of the co-op, and (2) a potential "holdup" occurs between the membership and the cooperative firm. A holdup is defined as quasi-rent extraction across the bilateral exchange interface due to the unequal possession of market power by one of the agents (Tirole 1988).

Open membership changes the core and has some interesting dynamic implications as well. If entry and exit are voluntary and heterogeneous, individuals make rational comparative decisions about the quality of life within the coalition. At this point, subgroup jointness of cost functions exists. This is simply the idea of membership theoretically never being in equilibrium, but, rather, forming, disbanding, and then regrouping. The coalition is not only a function of its own cost function, but of the relationship of that cost function to exogenous alternatives. This adds a measure of uncertainty to the co-op's existence and will affect its behavior.

Conclusion

Staatz's (1983) model, therefore, shows how co-ops arise from the joint decisions of individuals searching for a cost-minimizing alternative. There are several conditions and characterizations of this union. First, the cost function must be subadditive under some relevant range. Second, there are two core conditions: (1) individuals are rational and can compare alternative allocations, and (2) all costs are allocated. The harm functions then provide a value ranking of the coalition members. These characteristics of the coalition combined with the other formative conditions—heterogeneous membership, democratic voting structure, and open membership—all contribute to a unique form of business uncertainty and behavior.

A definite linkage between the farmer member and the co-op emerges from these three models. Thus, a model depicting the co-op's problem has to involve the characteristics of those primary optimizers. Their utility, risk preferences, and overall behavior are fundamental to the model. Also, due to voluntary entry and exit, noncommitment, and Staatz's harm function, exogenous market conditions are integral as well. Finally, there is the conceptualization of the co-op's problem and a long-run equilibrium involving a dynamic game.

Assuming a dynamic business environment, all three models portend problems maintaining commitment. As the group becomes heterogeneous over time and as market conditions change, schizophrenic conditions emerge as the needs of the owner-patrons compete with those of the co-op—challenging its existence. The cooperative form must be adapted to mitigate the agency problems described above and to ensure that group action provides economic value in the supply chain. The following describes an alternative model, the NGC, which addresses many of the agency problems described so far.

Cooperatives in a Knowledge Industry

Structural change is a disruptive process. Whether you were in the steel industry in the 1970s or production agriculture in the 1990s, the effects were unsettling (CP 2000; Rose and Thomas 2000). Producers must either exit the industry or adopt new business models, but to accomplish this they are faced with the difficult task of strategically repositioning themselves. In Illinois alone, there were forty value-added processing business plans in development during 2000 (Saputo 2000). These "long jump ventures" into processing are risky, though, and raise fundamental questions about how producers select appropriate strategies.

Specifically, three aspects of the strategy process are of interest. The first is whether long jump–type ventures such as hog slaughter or ethanol production are strategically sound. The second aspect is a discussion of how firms develop sound strategy. Finally, using this understanding of strategy, relationship management and service innovation are offered as an alternative to long jump brick- and-mortar investments for creating value. To support this, a case study of the Atkins Ranch Meat Company (ARMC), a farmer-owned integrated meat company from New Zealand, will demonstrate how relationship management represents an evolutionary step in the cooperative form.

The effects of structural change in North America are acute for grain farmers and hog producers, especially in the prairies of Canada and the American Midwest. A recent article stated that 6,000 Canadian farmers were forced out of business in 2000, and 6,000 more will be forced out in 2001 (CP 2000)— a 7 percent annualized attrition rate (Statistics Canada 2000). In the United States, the number of hog operations fell at a similar rate, 6.7 percent, since 1989 (NASS 2000a, 2000b, 2000c). Other than a brief respite in 1997, hog prices have fallen over the last ten years (NASS 2000d). This is due, in part, to the rapid increase in production capacity by integrated swine systems. Consequently, returns to outdated organizational forms decline and capital leaves to search out superior opportunities. For example, capital continues to flow to integrated systems, such as Smithfield Foods, whose market capitalization has risen almost $1 billion or 148 percent, since 1996 (Morningstar 2000).

One of the most common strategic choices for producer groups are producer-built processing plants (e.g., hog slaughter and ethanol). Producers pursuing vertical integration often give three rationales. The first is for them to take control of their own crop (Producers Alliance 1999; Smith 1998). Harold Tilstra—a farmer from Luverne, Minnesota, who is senior vice chair of Cornerstone Cooperative and chair and chief executive officer of a producer-owned ethanol company called Agri-Energy LLC—commented that "such a concept [producer-owned value-added production] is critical to farmers seeking to survive in the future. Agriculture margins are increasingly narrow . . . and . . . retaining commodity ownership until additional value has been built into their crops means more returns for producers as well as economic growth for their communities" (cited in Smith 1998).

A second rationale is that integration allows producers to capture the higher returns and lower price volatility downstream (Ball 2000; Forster 1996; Siebert, Jones, and Sporleder 1997; Smith 1998, 2000). Gary Ball, salesman for Ursa Farmer Co-op in Illinois, shared the following: "As a rule, selling pork makes money and when it doesn't, it loses a whole lot less than selling hogs. It is clear the independent pork producer needs to capture a larger portion of the farm to market share. Owning and operating your own packing plant is the most profitable and efficient way to secure a larger slice of the farm to market share" (Ball 2000, 10).

This is analogous to a story about the famous nineteenth-century American bank robber Jesse James. When finally apprehended, James was asked why he robbed banks. He supposedly replied, "because that is where the money is." Just because greater returns reside downstream is not a sufficient condition to justify direct investment. Producers recognize that an ever-increasing proportion of a food product's final value is produced and captured by enterprises beyond the farm gate (Fabi 2000). A key question of strategy remains: "How can producers best capture a greater proportion of the value in the downstream supply chain?"

Finally, a practical rationale for integrating downstream is to replace markets lost due to industry consolidation (Ball 2000; Illinois Farm Bureau 1999). Consider American Premium Foods (APF), a recently established Illinois NGC whose objective is to build a producer-owned hog slaughter plant. APF funds itself through producer equity (30 percent), government grants (11 percent), and debt capital (14 percent capital leasing and 45 percent bank financing). The average APF member has invested $23,400 (Smith 2000). When asked why they thought a new packing plant was a good idea, members felt they had to do something because traditional marketing channels had disappeared (American Heritage Farms, Inc. 1999; Baumgartner 2000).

While these rationales are common justifications provided for forming an NGC (see American Family Farms Co-op 1999; American Heritage Farms, Inc. 1999; Illinois Farm Bureau 1999; Merrett, Holmes, and Waner 1999; Producers Alliance 1999; Smith 2000; Waner 1999), there is no discussion of the fundamental value created by the new organization nor the uniqueness the venture brings to the supply chain. Schumpeter (1951, 1997), a leading theorist of innovation and entrepreneurship, outlines an important linkage between uniqueness, dynamics, and a firm's ability to command a premium price. The reward for organizing new combinations of resources valued in the market is entrepreneurial profits. These rents provide the incentive for innovation and are the catalyst for economic development (Schumpeter 1997); therefore, the premiums that producers seek will materialize not only by reorganizing into new organizational forms, but, more importantly, by creating unique value not found elsewhere in the marketplace. Assuming a dynamic innovation process, innovation rents and unique market positions for a new venture are not perpetual but dissipate over time through competition and substitution (Schumpeter 1951).

Strategic Positioning

For producers, the forces of structural change are strong and the need for strategies to participate in downstream markets is critical. Strategic positioning is an adaptive strategy for value creation in response to acute changes in a firm's competitive environment (D'Aveni and Ilinitch 1992; Itami 1987; Mintzberg 1994; Mintzberg, Ahlstrand, and Lampel 1998; Prahalad 1993; Prahalad and Hamel 1990; Quinn, Doorley, and Paquette 1990; Rumelt 1982). Two of the most compelling concepts from the strategic positioning literature are core competency (Prahalad and Hamel 1990; Quinn et al. 1990) and tacit knowledge (Itami 1987; Nonaka and Takeuchi as cited in Mintzberg et al. 1998). These concepts help explain why some firms succeed in creating value in dynamic environments while others languish.

First, successful adaptors understand their capabilities as bundles of competencies, not products or functions (Mintzberg and Quinn 1996). This is especially critical in dynamic industries or during periods of structural change when products become outdated and adaptation is required. Competencies are the human capital in the firms, the shared knowledge, the corporate history, communication networks and traditions, organizational structure, and collective learning (Prahalad 1993). It is all that remains if you were to remove the products. Itami (1987) identifies core competencies as invisible assets, stating that even though they are difficult to measure, these are the essence of a firm's value: "Invisible assets are the real source of competitive power and the key factor in corporate adaptability for three reasons: they are hard to accumulate, they are capable of simultaneous multiple uses, and they are both inputs and outputs of business activities" (14). When applied to producer ventures, if all producers are attempting to do is vertically integrate through physical asset accumulation, they can at best be no better than anyone else in the market with the same bundle of physical assets.

Key components of core competency are information and knowledge. Managing the flow of information and productivity of these knowledge assets is complex yet critical for strategic repositioning. A firm that has little experience in an industry has little access to critical information flows or experiences to build the intangible assets necessary for competitive success (Prahalad and Bettis 1986). External information flows originate in the firm and flow to clients and suppliers. Internal flows pass to the firm from clients and suppliers, and intrafirm flows occur across functions and divisions within the firm (Itami 1987). These information flows and management are critical to the learning organization (Senge 1990) and are the buildup of, and production from, the stock of invisible assets and the firm's core competencies.

Without these experiences, the firm cannot create the intangible asset base necessary for competitive success and value creation. Firms can purchase hard assets, but as they are not inimitable, they do not generate value by themselves but, rather, rely on the intangible assets as the source of value (Itami 1987).

This understanding of the significance of the core competencies is consistent with Nonaka and Takeuchi's (1995) discussion of tacit knowledge and effective decision making. Knowledge is explicit when it is articulated and codified in writing, and verbalized or coded in drawings, computer programs, or other products. Tacit knowledge, however, is uncoded and nonverbalized. It reflects the difference between what we know and what we can tell (Polyani 1966). Thus, tacit knowledge may never be able to be verbalized or articulated. It can be acquired largely through personal experience and is often embedded in the routines of organizations or individuals and, therefore, difficult to copy and convey. Much of the knowledge needed for successful decision making in a complex world is not explicit. It is made up of unique experiences generated over time and through interactions that cannot be replicated by formal rules (Mintzberg 1987):

> Managers . . . need to get out of the old mode of thinking that knowledge can be acquired, taught, and trained through manuals, books, or lectures. Instead, they need to pay more attention to the less formal and systematic side of knowledge and start focusing on highly subjective insights, intuitions, and hunches that are gained through the use of metaphors, pictures, and experiences. (Nonaka and Takeuchi as cited in Mintzberg et al. 1998)

Decisions are made on instinct and common sense; they then become explicit and are finally judged within the organizational context. Once judged either favorably or unfavorably, they are interpreted and become part of the tacit knowledge base. This occurs in a spiraling process from tacit to explicit and back again through an important confirmation step (Nonaka and Takeuchi as cited in Mintzberg et al. 1998).

Strategy emerges from this incremental process of building experiences and expertise that are brought to bear on the next set of challenges (Quinn 1977). A firm wishing to engage in a long jump venture—say from production to processing—must access this tacit knowledge that produces value, in addition to gaining access to physical assets. A structurally inconsistent situation arises from this, however. To be successful, tacit knowledge is essential as it is fundamental to value creation and competitiveness. Yet, by definition, a firm undertaking a long jump venture possesses little tacit knowledge overlap.

Strategic Positioning: The Opportunity Gap

Understanding one's own core competencies and having access to or possessing tacit knowledge are fundamental to strategic repositioning. Prahalad (1993) captures the significance of these concepts in his model of the productivity and opportunity gap (Figure 8.4; see p. 174). A firm has two basic strategic choices: (1) to focus on productivity, or (2) to focus on opportunity. Each strategy has its place. A productivity gap orientation focuses on present routines, processes, products, and markets. Decisions in such firms involve improving the productivity of known systems and routines. This strategy is important for success when markets are static, mature, or fully competitive. If preferences remain unchanged or markets are mature, firms are able to invest in assets that correspond to long production runs and lower marginal costs (Ng and Goldsmith 1998). In fully competitive markets, the price is fixed and profitability is driven by improving production efficiency and minimizing costs.

Historically, commercial agriculture has focused on the productivity gap. The fields of farm management and agricultural economics, based on the neoclassical traditions of Walras (1954, cited in Varian 1984) and others, have historically focused on optimizing the input mix and minimizing costs. Example methodologies are the production function approach, linear programming, and the measurement of productive efficiency. These have been appropriate methodologies because agricultural markets historically have been competitive, have been dominated by commodities, have employed broad and relatively static standards and grades, and have involved market prices exogenous to the farm's problem.

The difficulty arises when markets are dynamic, when firms enter a period of structural change, or when markets become less competitive and characterized more by rivalry. Product- or production-based strategies are lost because the markets are lost. The comfortable fit between production process, product, and market is altered. In terms of strategic positioning, a continued focus on the productivity gap is simpler because it attempts to make known processes better, serves known markets more effectively, and produces known products more efficiently. It must be noted, however, that globalization and the structural change that results seriously challenge the traditional business model of being the world's low-cost producer of commodities. Technology is packaged in ever more usable formats adaptable by almost any producer in the world (Goldsmith, Ramos, and Steiger 2002). Falling farmer incomes in North America reflect decreasing commodity prices that are outpacing producers' abilities to increase productivity. The productivity gap strategy is a failed strategy as costs become harder to reduce, foreign

Figure 8.5 **Region of Strategic Repositioning***

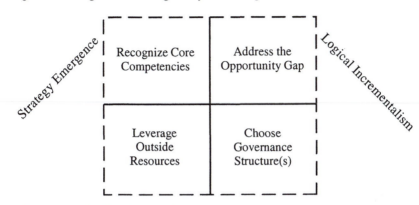

*During periods of market turbulence

producers are willing to accept lower prices, and a commodity's share of total food value declines. This requires U.S. producers to shift away from the productivity gap and focus on the other half of the value creation equation, which is defined by Prahalad (1993) as the opportunity gap.

To accomplish such a strategic repositioning, a firm assesses itself not on its current or historical production plan (i.e., the products that it produces), but on its core competencies. During times of increasing turbulence and instability, firms need to refocus on investment in, and leveraging of, knowledge assets that are inimitable and that provide them with a competitive advantage in markets where direct competition between firms (rivalry) is the norm. The concept of core competency shifts the strategy process away from the obvious to the yet unexploited. Farmers looking to create more value from their competencies shift their managerial focus from the production side of the business to the marketing side. The marketing knowledge gained then feeds back into changes and adaptations to the production plan and asset mix. Combining a firm's understanding of its core competencies with a demand or market perspective allows firms to create value by more directly addressing client needs and opportunities. New opportunities in agriculture arise from the uniqueness of the farm as a resource base when matched with the needs of downstream clients or consumers.

Strategic repositioning during periods of market turbulence involves a four-part process that Prahalad (1993) calls the strategic architecture (Figure 8.5). The first step is to recognize a firm's core competencies. What are the firm's inimitable resources? In the case of an agricultural co-op, what intangible assets does it bring to the supply chain? The second step is to move beyond the productivity gap and a cost focus and give attention, instead, to

Figure 8.6 **Value Creation Triad**

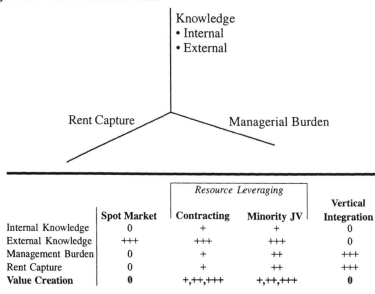

	Spot Market	Resource Leveraging		Vertical Integration
		Contracting	Minority JV	
Internal Knowledge	0	+	+	0
External Knowledge	+++	+++	+++	0
Management Burden	0	+	++	+++
Rent Capture	0	+	++	+++
Value Creation	**0**	**+,++,+++**	**+,++,+++**	**0**

the opportunity gap and a value focus. Rackam and Devincentis (1999) call this *value chain mapping*—a creative process that is used to look for new opportunities involving suppliers and clients. Part of this process involves understanding broad trends and indicators from secondary sources. More importantly, this process involves a mutual understanding by the supplier and the client of each other's business practices. Farmers will be hard-pressed to create value without an understanding of what clients value. The third step leverages resources. Firms need to access resources outside their own firm in order to acquire the necessary tacit knowledge and to avoid the managerial burdens of vertical integration.

Finally, during the fourth step, the firm determines the appropriate governance structure to leverage knowledge and capture value. Contracting, or the use of a minority joint venture as opposed to integration may better balance the knowledge requirements, managerial burden, and rent capture (Figure 8.6). The Value Creation Triad relates governance structure and value creation. By itself, governance does not create value; however, it can be conducive to creating value. The triad models a tradeoff problem between the need for knowledge that can be sourced either internally or externally, the management burden, and the ability to capture rents. There are numerous governance options open for producers to participate in the supply chain (Adams and Goldsmith 1999). On one end of the governance continuum resides the spot market strategy option through which producers operate decoupled selling commodities. At the other extreme resides the long jump option of full integration wherein the producers own both sides of the transaction.

Interestingly, neither extreme strategy on its own contributes the necessary tacit knowledge. In the spot market case, producers' value in the supply chain is captured in the commodities they sell. External knowledge may be high, but none of that information flows back to producers, as the marketing stages are decoupled between production and processing. With vertical integration, producers own both sides of the transaction. The ability to capture rents from the new supply chain arrangement is highest because of complete ownership. Correspondingly, the managerial burden is high. What limits the value creation in this scenario is the inability to source knowledge because producers' internal knowledge base is rooted in production, and vertical integration constrains information partnering. Producers, realizing the inconsistency between available knowledge and management responsibility, might try to access knowledge outside the firm (Figure 8.7). As stated above, however, tacit knowledge is the source of value and innovation rents. Consequently, contributors of knowledge will require a premium for the knowledge and innovation they are contributing to the chain. It is, therefore, imperative that both parties in the relationship view these exchanges to be mutually beneficial. Producers are forced away from a pure vertical integration strategy to quasi-integration, such as contracting and joint ventures, where managerial burdens are less and knowledge leveraging can occur.

We have argued that long jump producer-owned ventures are flawed attempts at strategic repositioning. Structural change causes economic duress for producers, prompting them to look for alternatives to the commodity model. The next section introduces Relationship Management (RM) as an alternative. An RM strategy, relying on an assessment of core competencies, focuses on the opportunity gap. It addresses the knowledge and managerial constraints described above; it involves quasi-integration, not vertical integration; it allows superior risk diversification; and it provides access to higher returns and lower volatility of downstream markets.

Relationship Management

Relationship management (RM), also known as one-to-one marketing and relationship marketing, may be a better strategic fit for agricultural producers. RM is a fairly new field. It arose out of the quality movement in the 1980s and was formalized by Leonard L. Berry (1983, 1995). In RM, upstream supplying firms change their strategic position from an arm's length relationship with clients, focused on product exchange, to one of partnering.

Figure 8.7 Innovation Adoption Under Familiarity Constraint

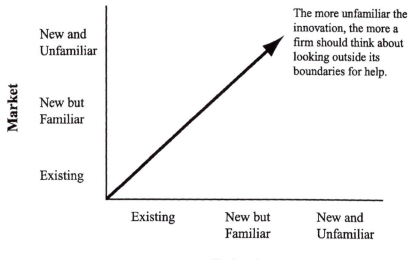

The more unfamiliar the innovation, the more a firm should think about looking outside its boundaries for help.

Technology

Source: Adapted from Afuah (1998).

Client share, the percentage of client needs being met by an individual supplier, dominates the traditional strategy of market share (Moon 2000; Peppers and Rogers 1993). The upstream firm is not simply selling a product; rather, it is selling a bundle of attributes and services. The quality may be unobservable *ex ante* but critical to the downstream client *ex post*. The ability to increase client share is wholly dependent on building a relationship and exchanging knowledge with the downstream firm. Value and its associated innovation rents are created through the sharing of knowledge and joint learning (Pine, Peppers, and Rogers 1995; Slater and Narver 1995).

RM is also about market deference. When greater value is produced downstream in the chain while at the same time many industrial firms are aggressively rationalizing their supplier base, supplying firms create value by customizing their offerings, servicing needs, and adapting their production systems, more effectively matching the downstream firm's needs. While in agriculture there has been much talk about "rights" to a certain portion of the food value pie (Fabi 2000), an RM strategy focuses on increasing supplier's value capture by mutually increasing the size of the value pie. By assisting the downstream firm to respond more quickly and uniquely to their clients' needs, greater total chain value is created, providing the possibility for additional rents to flow upstream along the chain to the supplier. This type of strategy requires a willingness by firms to collaborate and not compete across stages in the supply chain.

As a strategy, it moves the supplying firm's focus from transactions (products) to relationships and is consistent with the shift from the productivity gap to the opportunity gap. In RM, the supplying firm crosses the boundary of the transaction to engage in a partnering relationship with the client (Table 8.1). The nexus between upstream supplier and downstream client is no longer simply a product but, more importantly, a knowledge exchange. This knowledge transaction serves as a resource for both firms, helps bind the supplier to the client, and serves as a value center. RM is a dynamic concept because of joint learning and feedback. As both firms evolve within their respective competitive spaces and with each other, new knowledge flows across the relationship membrane and is integrated into the value creation process. The boundary between the two firms becomes blurred as incentives become aligned, knowledge ownership becomes fuzzy,[5] and joint satisfaction becomes fundamental.

The upstream firm captures value because the relationship is inimitable and important to the downstream client. If the supplier delivered a commodity product or service, it would receive commodity-level prices and encounter commodity-level competition. If, however, the supplying firm's relationship creates a unique offering for its client that is differentiated, then it is less likely to be copied, it can command a premium price, it will inhibit rivalry, and it can promote income stability. Instead of the zero-sum game of transaction-based relationships, risk, cost, and value sharing become fundamental components of the relationship.

Traditionally, the production process of the upstream farm firm does not reflect the needs of the downstream client. The focus of the transaction is the product (e.g., corn or hogs), and producers are defined as such. Since the product is a commodity, the characteristics of the end product are commonly known and, thus, are not unique to a particular supplier. The price signal, which normally occurs *ex post* (at harvest), provides sufficient, though limited, information for the producer to adjust the production plan. The transaction is completely at arm's length.

In RM, the process is the opposite. The supplier first understands the needs of the client and then goes about producing the good by leveraging its own core competencies combined with knowledge partners. Information is present *ex ante* not *ex post*, is not limited to price, and may involve numerous product and service attributes. Suppliers have a greater opportunity to market their core competencies through a relationship, which is much broader and more dynamic, than simply through a product-based transaction. In commodity agriculture, firms within marketing segments historically focused on

Table 8.1

Key Differences Between the Concepts of Relationship Marketing and Transactional Marketing

Criterion	Relationship marketing	Transactional marketing
1. Primary objective	Relationship	Single transaction
2. General approach	Interaction-related	Action-related
3. Perspective	Evolutionary-dynamic	Static
4. Basic orientation	Implementation-oriented	Decision-oriented
5. Long-term vs. short-term	Generally long-term	Generally short-term
6. Fundamental strategy	Maintain existing relationships	Acquisition of new customers
7. Focus in decision process	Post-sale	Pre-sale
8. Intensity of contact	High	Low
9. Degree of mutual dependence	High	Low
10. Measuring customer satisfaction	Direct	Indirect (market share)
11. Dominant quality dimension	Quality of interaction	Quality of output
12. Production of quality	Concern of all	Primary concern of production
13. Role of Internal marketing	Substantial strategic importance	Limited importance
14. Importance of employees	High	Low
15. Production focus	Mass customization	Mass production

Source: Hennig-Thurau and Hansen (2000).

their immediate markets, isolated in their own supply chain "silos." Alternatively, the trend in the economy at large has supply chain players crossing antiquated supply chain boundaries to leverage resources from their partners in order to address increasingly complex production problems (Quinn et al. 1990; Rackam, Friedman, and Ruff 1996).

In agriculture, the lack of coordination in the supply chain creates huge impediments to value creation (Zell 2000). There are numerous opportunities in agriculture for quality control, identity preservation, and property rights protection for producer–client relationships to create value. Producers bring the following core competencies to the supply chain:

- *Land:* Crop production is extensive, and producer control and care are not easily replaced by integrated supply chain systems.
- *Production flexibility:* While during the last twenty years crop production has become more specialized in response to a commodity production system, potential exists for producers to adapt to a new agricultural model dominated by dynamic niche markets that employ more flexible production systems.
- *Lack of organizational bureaucracy:* Producers directly control their production and, thus, are able to respond to the market's demand for identity preservation and other quality control needs.
- *Production risk mitigation:* Producers could play an important role in decreasing supply risk if, for example, they were aligned in a regionally diversified fashion.
- *Logistics:* With on-farm storage capabilities and transport, producers could address many of the material flow needs of downstream procuring firms.

Furthermore, the vast knowledge base of food and ingredient manufacturers and retailers would benefit producers and producer organizations. This downstream knowledge would enable farmers to better leverage their core competencies to create new products and services for the supply chain. RM addresses the predicament faced by farmers who want to reduce volatility and risk by conducting business in more stable portions of the supply chain. Through a supply chain relationship, producers would be integrating themselves into the supply chain without the managerial burden of vertical integration discussed earlier. The relationship itself is a form of capital—social capital—that generates rents and binds firms together. The supplier, by creating a unique offering, creates relationship specificity. This specificity raises the cost of exit for the client, which adds stability to the relationship. This should be especially appealing for those agricultural producers who wish to reduce volatility.

The process used to implement an RM strategy involves (1) client identification, (2) differentiation, (3) interaction, and (4) customization (Peppers
and Rogers 1993). To these four steps we add a fifth: bidirectional double-
loop learning (feedback). Client identification is similar to market segmenta-
tion, except that it is conducted at the firm level. Using secondary data and
referrals, target firms and their business characteristics are amassed. The second step involves client differentiation. Clients will differ in terms of their
value to the supplier and their needs. A system like Curry and Curry's (2000),
which involves a client pyramid, is a good way to differentiate customers by
value to the supplier. Clients can be differentiated in many ways such as by
product, sales, purchase practices, and location. The third phase of implementing an RM strategy is interacting with the firm. This is a critical step not
only because of its importance in terms of knowledge management but because of its complexity and expense. The success or failure of RM is how
well the supplier understands its clients' needs and can establish a learning
relationship. The challenge is for the supplier to shift its focus from its own
production system in order to learn about the downstream business. Only by
understanding the needs and pressures that face the downstream firm can the
supplier adapt its production and marketing processes. The needs assessment, the process of learning about a client's needs, is normally conducted
with the employee responsible for input buying and with senior managers of
the client firm. Both provide valuable information on client needs. The buyer
provides the technical information and immediate concerns about the purchase, while senior management provides a broader and more dynamic vision of how the product affects the rest of the company as well as the needs
of the client's client (Wood 2000). (See Anderson and Narus 1998, Curry
and Curry 2000, and S4 Consulting 2000 for some semi-structured interview
instruments designed to elicit client needs.)

The fourth stage, customization, is the introduction of client needs into
the product and service offering of the supplying firm. The secret to competitive advantage lies in the ability to customize products and services. In
this area, farmer-producers may have an advantage because bureaucracies
struggle to produce lot sizes of one. While large firms may be able to access
and process large quantities of data, smaller, more nimble organizations are
better able to implement knowledge. Speed not only in service but also in
research and development (R&D) and production are becoming more and
more critical. Bureaucracies are again at a disadvantage because of their
preference for long production runs and routines. Turbulent environments
favor organizational forms that are more flexible and which have fungible
capital (Ng and Goldsmith 1998).

Bidirectional double-loop learning, the fifth stage, closes the relationship process, feeding information back to help the supplier improve its product and service offerings. Client interaction is not simply an initiating event but an ongoing dialogue. This makes RM a dynamic strategy wherein if a client needs change, the supplier must continually adapt its offerings.

Where do co-ops and group action fit into this business strategy? While individual entrepreneurs may be very successful in direct marketing efforts to independent retail outlets (Duffy 2000), the greater trend in supply chain management is supplier rationalization (Rackam et al. 1996). More and more input supplies are originating from fewer and fewer suppliers. Also, concentration and supply chain coordination is occurring downstream, so scale and scope have become critical to providing good service:

> In the last few years, customers have been rejecting traditional transaction-based vendor relationships at a dizzying pace. They've been downsizing their supply base, and replacing their myriad vendors with a small number of long-term relationships offered to only a select few. There's a widely quoted figure that customers are working today with a third fewer suppliers than they did ten years ago. (Rackam et al. 1996, 3)

Therefore, the ability to deliver quantity, provide speed, and yet serve a broad range of needs requires a large organization. Group action in the form of NGCs or limited liability companies (LLCs) afford the scale to have dedicated or sourced expertise bridging the gap between production competencies and supplier needs. Scale would also help the organization raise capital to invest in service-related assets like storage, transportation, and product research. These assets, if assembled strategically into a sizable organization, would lose their traditional specificity due to location. Interregional or international producer organizations could reduce tangible asset specificity and production risk through geographic and political diversification. While such organizations are more complex, they benefit from greater product and service flexibility, access to critical resources, and greater market access. Brick and mortar producer-owned processing ventures, on the other hand, create dedicated vertical facilities that are highly specific. As one venture capitalist put it,

> I keep trying to convince my partners and our client companies that we don't want to invest in hard assets. They are too short lived and risky. We certainly don't want to invest in bureaucracies. We want to invest in people who . . . can manage outside contracts with the best sources in the world, and who can concentrate their energies on that small core of activities that create the real uniqueness and value-added for the company, but it's a tough sell against traditional thinking. (Quinn et al. 1990)

Finally, RM addresses a continual problem for co-ops—sourcing capital. As a strategy, RM leverages resources through mutually beneficial supply chain relationships. The challenge for producer groups is how best to invest limited resources. Not only are there specificity risks to hard assets as described above, but investment in tacit knowledge acquisition is also critical. This would indicate, then, that producers would be better served if they invested in soft rather than hard assets. The following case study provides an excellent example of producers leveraging limited resources and selecting soft over hard assets.

Atkins Ranch

An interesting empirical observation of RM in action is from an ad hoc case in New Zealand. Following the wide-ranging economic reforms in the mid-1980s of the New Zealand economy, including the agricultural sector, a small group of Wairarapa[6] sheep farmers recognized that they had to develop an alternative marketing channel for their core product, lamb, because traditional channels where not providing sufficient economic returns.

After some initial research in 1988, the group discerned that there was a market opportunity in the Bay Area of California for providing a high-quality chilled lamb product to both the hotel and restaurant trade as well as to supermarkets that were servicing either ethnic communities of traditional lamb consumers or high-disposable-income consumers. They faced two basic questions: (1) how to develop the market in the Bay Area? and (2) how to establish a supply chain flexible enough to ensure a sufficient supply of the specified premium product?

A closed membership co-op of 106 producers was established to provide the initial financing for the development and establishment of these marketing opportunities. The cooperative members each had to provide an initial investment of approximately NZD 10,000 (1 NZD = US$0.68). This was later increased through two additional funding drives to approximately NZD 40,000. For this equity investment, members received the first right of supply for the new marketing channel. The co-op developed a flexible market-driven supply chain that began with information collection and knowledge acquisition from the customer and client in the marketplace and then flowed directly back to the individual chain participants, including producers. This allowed chain members to adjust their operations to deliver the combination of product and service attributes that maximized their residual claims. The co-op initially made minimal investments in hard physical assets; all of the financing was effectively used for market development and supply chain relationship development. Bank financing was engaged only after markets were established and product was being produced. This financing was used to support the organization's working capital requirements with the inventory provided as collateral.

Two key tactics demonstrate Atkins Ranch's (ARMC) focus on the opportunity gap. They began their strategic repositioning downstream in the areas of distribution and marketing. This exemplifies a proper demand-pull strategy as opposed to one of supply-push. First, to assist with the U.S. market development, they hired an expatriate international food-marketing consultant based in Berkeley, California. This individual possessed numerous years of international food industry experience as a past executive of a California-based international supermarket company. The consultant provided ARMC with substantial explicit and tacit knowledge, which helped the co-op understand the dynamics of the market, how supermarkets within the region purchased meat products, and who managed the in-store product marketing and promotion, and how. This tacit knowledge was critical to the success of the operation as the market in California differed substantially from the New Zealand market. Second, an ARMC farmer-director relocated to the Bay Area so that he could not only understand the market better and establish the U.S. head office, but also be located closer to their consultant. This facilitated the tacit knowledge transfer and learning process.

In order to gain access into the supermarket industry, they not only required the consent of the regional purchasing managers; they also needed to develop individual relationships with the meat department managers in each individual store to obtain preferential meat counter space. This type of relationship development was imperative in the hotel and restaurant industry as well, where the head chefs make all of the purchasing decisions. As a consequence, relationship development and management became a strategic initiative of the organization. The relationships were mutually beneficial for both parties. The co-op received superior market information, which allowed it to better meet its clients' requirements, and product was customized daily to each individual store's requirements. This reduced the meat manager's labor costs and in-store promotional activities, and, in return, ARMC received preferential meat counter positioning and better market information, both of which translated into increased sales.

Active RM has been critical to ARMC's success. Direct client feedback was quickly transformed into value either by altering the product mix for the next delivery to better match clients' needs or, if substantial market changes were observed, information was passed back to New Zealand. The local processor-partner could then alter the product mix or processing schedule and producers could adjust their animal specifications or production practices. Given the twelve–week delay between initial slaughter and delivery into the

North American market, it is important that members at the top of the chain receive information about changes in demand requirements and specifications as soon as possible.

ARMC developed a successful cold chain through a series of mutually beneficial relationships with the chain members. They rented cooling, fabrication, and processing space; utilized labor from a local cool store; and accessed knowledge and services from a local meat processor, all in the San Francisco area. A solid relationship with the fabrication facility and their butchers was important so that product could be customized on a daily basis to customer needs. This increased the value of the product and services provided to meat managers, who soon recognized that very little additional in-store skilled labor was necessary.

Similarly, in New Zealand, all the animals were processed into primary cuts; packaged in Captec, a specialized vacuum-sealed seven-layer foil bag filled with nitrogen; and chilled through a local meat processor. The Captec technology allowed for the lamb to age without quality deterioration due to oxidation. In actual fact, the meat improved during shipping, becoming more tender and minimizing adverse aromas.

The prevailing market dynamics often resulted in quick and unexpected changes in product requirements, so it was necessary for producers to be flexible. As a result, many of the members were required to make changes, often substantial ones, to their production processes and practices. Lambs could no longer be sold when it suited farmers; instead, they were sold to the co-op when it best suited the market. The increased managerial complexity was more than made up for by the returns generated from the overall operation.

Conclusion

As described here, agricultural structural change is a powerful force, and producers must adapt to remain competitive. There are numerous strategies available to producer organizations as they attempt to find their place in the supply chain. Strategic management theory and empirical evidence suggest that long jump or radical strategic shifts are unlikely to be successful. The logic is that sustained competitive advantage is derived from the ability of firms to produce value. In order to produce this value, firms require access to knowledge. The type of knowledge that generates innovation rents is knowledge that is inimitable, tacit knowledge. By understanding their core competencies, firms come to understand their own uniqueness in the marketplace as well as their inadequacies. In an attempt to add value to their offerings, firms that are resource constrained are led to avoid long jump ventures and, instead, to move incrementally, remaining close to their competencies.

Through the NGC form and RM, producer-owned supply firms assess knowledge and participate in value creation without the knowledge and managerial burden of vertical integration. ARMC is an excellent case of producers foregoing a brick and mortar investment even though doing so would have given them direct control over their product. Instead, they invested their limited funds in soft knowledge assets such as market reconnaissance and marketing expertise. These investments served them well by not only generating value at the initial stages, but, also, by giving them flexibility as market conditions changed over time.

Appendix

$$\left(\frac{\partial Y_i}{\partial P_j}\right) * \left(\frac{P_j}{Y_i}\right)$$

[1]

where Y_i is the income proxy for utility for the ith individual and P_j is the patronage in the jth cooperative.

$$\underset{X_d, Z_i}{\text{Max}} \quad \Pi = \left(\bar{P}_y * Y\right) - \left(\left(P_{x_d} * X_d\right) + \left(\bar{P}_{z_i} * Z_i\right)\right)$$

S.T.

[2]

$$Y = f\left(X_d + Z_i\right)$$

$$\underset{P_{x_s}}{\text{Max}} \, S = \left(P_{x_s} * X_s\right) - \left(\bar{P}_{x_j} * Z_j\right)$$

S.T.

$$X_s = q\,(Z_j)$$

[3]

$$\underset{P_{x_s}}{\text{Optimize}} \left(P_{x_s} * X_s\right) = \left(\bar{P}_{x_j} * Z\right)$$

S.T.

$$X_s = g\,(Z_j)$$

[4]

$$\text{MAX } \Pi_{xd} \left(P_y * Y\right) - \left(\left(P_{x_d} * X_d\right) + \left(P_{z_i} * Z_i\right)\right)$$

S.T.

$$Y = f\left(X_d + Z_i\right)$$

[5]

$$\text{Optimize}_{P_{x_s}} \left(P_{x_s} * X_s \right) = \left(\bar{P}x_j * Z \right)$$

S.T.

$$X_s = g \ (Z_j)$$ [6]

$$X_d = X_s$$ [7]

$$PX_s = PX_d$$ [8]

Setting $Z_i = 0$ and solving 5 for the reduced form yields $X_d{}^*$ in Equation 11.

In Equation 5, X_s is a function of P_{xs}, P_{zj}, and Z_j. $X_s = (P_{zj}{}^*Z_j)/P_{xs}$. Equating X_s and X_d leaves two equations with two unknown variables, P_x and X, and two known, P_{zj} and P_y.

$$\text{Max}_{X_d, \ Z_i} \quad \Pi = \left(\bar{P}y * Y \right) - \left(\left(P_{x_d} * X_d \right) + \left(\bar{P}z_i * Z_i \right) \right)$$

S.T.

[9]

$$Y = f\left(X_d + Z_i \right)$$

$$\frac{\partial \Pi}{\partial X_d} = \bar{P}_y * f' \left(X_d + Z_i \right) - P_{x_d} = 0$$ [10]

The cooperative's surplus equilibrium equation is rewritten as:

$$X_d^* = \left(\frac{P_{x_d}}{\bar{P}_y} \right) * \frac{1}{f' \left(X_d + Z_i \right)}$$

$$X_s = \frac{\bar{P}_{z_j} * Z_j}{P_{x_s}}$$

[11]

$$\therefore \text{ The Slope} = \frac{\bar{P}_{z_j}}{P_{x_s}}$$

$$\Phi_s = \Pi_s \left(P_{zs}^* \right) - \Pi_s \left(P_z^m \right) > 0 \qquad [12]$$

where:

$$\Pi_s = \Sigma_{i \in s} \Pi_i \left(P^j \right) \qquad [13]$$

$V(r \cup s) > V(r) + V(s), r \cap s = 0$

where:

$$V(r \cup s) = V(S) \qquad [14]$$

$$X_i \geq V(\_i\_) \quad i = 1,\dots,n \qquad [15]$$

$$\Sigma_{i \varepsilon N} X_i = V(N) \qquad [16]$$

$$\Sigma_{i \varepsilon S} X \geq V(S) \quad \text{for all } S \subset N \qquad [17]$$

$$h_0 = [C(q^{n-s})/q^{n-s} - C(q^n)/q^n] \times [q^{n-s}] \qquad [18]$$

$$h_s = v(q^s) - [C(q^n)/q^n] \times [q^s] \qquad [19]$$

Notes

Parts of this chapter appeared previously in Goldsmith (1995) and Goldsmith and Gow (2002). Special thanks to Mr. Jungik Kim for help in preparation of parts of this manuscript.

1. Income serves as a proxy for utility.

2. This is a differentiating feature of the New Generation Cooperatives, which generally require up-front member equity contributions either in cash or in the form of delivery commitments.

3. Commitment is a formal agreement of patronage between a co-op and a member.

4. The axioms of preference are completeness, reflexivity, transitivity, continuity, strong monotinicity, local nonsatiation, and strict convexity (Varian 1984, 111–113).

5. Sporleder (1993) introduced the idea of "fuzzy prerogatives" with respect to the blurred boundary between firms involved in strategic alliances. Adams and Goldsmith (1999) extend this concept with respect to interorganizational trust.

6. From the Wairarapa Valley region of the North Island of New Zealand.

References

Adams, Claire-Louise, and Peter Goldsmith. 1999. "Managerial Decision-making: Strategic Alliances as a Governance Choice." *International Food and Agribusiness Management Review* 2, no. 2: 221–248.

Afuah, Allan. 1998. *Innovation Management: Strategies, Implementation, and Profits*. New York: Oxford University Press.

American Family Farms Co-op. 1999. *Business Overview and By-laws*, December 17.

American Heritage Farms, Inc. 1999. *Business Plan* (September).

Anderson, James C., and James A. Narus. 1998. "Business Marketing: Understanding What Customers Value." *Harvard Business Review* (November–December): 53–65.

Ball, Gary. 2000. "Time to Step Up to the Plate." *Illinois Park Press* 32, no. 2: 10.

Baumgartner, M. 2000. Personal communication with the director, American Premium Foods.

Berry, Leonard L. 1983. "Relationship Marketing." In *Emerging Perspectives on Services Marketing*, ed. Leonard L. Berry, G. Lynn Shostack, and Gregory Upah, 25–28. Chicago: American Marketing Association.

———. 1995. "Relationship Marketing of Services—Growing Interest, Emerging Perspectives." *Journal of the Academy of Marketing Science* 23 (Fall): 236–245.

Canadian Press. 2000. "Day Meets with Farmers, Says They Need Aid, Not Internet Connections," November 1.

Curry, Jay, and Adam Curry. 2000. *The Customer Marketing Method: How to Implement and Profit from Customer Relationship Managements*. New York: Free Press.

D'Aveni, R., and A. Ilinitch. 1992. "Complex Patterns of Vertical Integration in the Forest Products Industry: Systematic and Bankruptcy Risks." *Academy of Management Journal* 35, no. 3: 596–625.

Duffy, Patrick. 2000. "Generating Rural Progress." *Rural Cooperatives* 67, no. 4: 16–24.

Emelianov, Ivan. 1942. *Economic Theory of Cooperation*. Ann Arbor, MI: Edward Brothers.

Fabi, Randy. 2000. "U.S. Farm Income Biggest Problem Facing Farmers-USDA." *Reuters*, April 11.

Forster, D. Lynn. 1996. "Capital Structure, Business Risk, and Investor Returns for Agribusiness." *Agribusiness: An International Journal* 12, no. 5: 429–442.

Goldsmith, Peter. 1995. Business Behavior as a Function of Business Structure: A Transaction Theory of Cooperatives. Unpublished Ph.D. dissertation, Ohio State University.

Goldsmith, Peter, and Hamish Gow. 2002. "Strategic Positioning Under Agricultural Structural Change: A Critique of Long Jump Co-operative Ventures." *International Food and Agribusiness Management Review* (October).

Goldsmith, Peter D., Gabriel Ramos, and Carlos Steiger. 2002. "Intellectual Property Protection and the International Marketing of Agricultural Biotechnology: Firm and Host Country Impacts." In *Economic and Social Issues in Agricultural Biotechnology*, ed. R.E. Evenson, V. Santaniello, and D. Ziberman, chap. 17. Oxen, UK: CABI Publishing.

Helmberger, Peter, and Stanley Hoos. 1962. "Cooperative Enterprise and Organizational Theory." *Journal of Farm Economics* 44, no. 2: 275–290.

Hennig-Thurau, Thoraten, and Ursula Hansen, eds. 2000. *Relationship Marketing: Gaining Competitive Advantage Through Customer Satisfaction and Customer Retention*. Berlin: Springer.

Illinois Farm Bureau. 1999. "New 'Producers Alliance' Launched by IFB Board." Press release, April 19, Bloomington: Illinois Farm Bureau.

Itami, Hiroyuki. 1987. *Mobilizing Invisible Assets*. Cambridge, MA: Harvard University Press.

Kreps, David. 1990. *A Course in Microeconomic Theory*. Princeton, NJ: Princeton University Press.

Ladd, George. 1974. "A Model of a Bargaining Cooperative." *American Journal of Agricultural Economics* 56: 509–519.

LeVay, Clare. 1983. "Agricultural Co-operative Theory: A Review." *Journal of Agricultural Economics* 34, no. 1: 1–44.

Lin, William, G.W. Dean, and C.V. Moore. 1974. "An Empirical Test of Utility vs. Maximization in Agricultural Production." *American Journal of Agricultural Economics* 56: 497–508.

Merrett, Christopher D., Mary Holmes, and Jennifer Waner. 1999. *Directory of New Generation Cooperatives*. Macomb: Illinois Institute for Rural Affairs, Western Illinois University.

Mintzberg, Henry. 1987. "Crafting Strategy." *Harvard Business Review* (July–August): 67–75.

———. 1994. *The Rise and Fall of Strategic Planning*. New York: Free Press.

Mintzberg, Henry, and James Brian Quinn. 1996. *The Strategy Process*. Upper Saddle River, NJ: Prentice-Hall.

Mintzberg, Henry, Bruce W. Ahlstrand, and Joseph Lampel. 1998. *Strategy Safari*. New York: Free Press.

Moon, Youngme. 2000. *Interactive Technologies and Relationship Marketing Strategies*. Harvard Business School Note # 9–599–101. Cambridge, MA: Harvard University.

Morningstar. 2000. Available at www.morningstar.com.

National Agricultural Statistics Service (NASS). 2000a. *Hogs and Pigs Report*. Available at usda.mannlib.cornell.edu/reports/nassr/livestock/php_bb/ (August 2001).

———. 2000b. *Hogs and Pigs Report: Final Estimates* (NASS report no. 951). Available at usda.mannlib.cornell.edu/usda/reports/general/sb/b9511298.txt.

———. 2000c. *Hogs and Pigs Report* (NASS report #904). Available at http://usda.mannlib.cornell.edu/data_sets/livestock/94904/.

———. 2000d. *Livestock: Marketing Year Average Prices (Hogs-ALL) Received by Farmers: United States* (Agricultural Prices Annual Summary 07.14.95 through 07.24.00). Available at usda.mannlib.cornell.edu/usda/.

Ng, Desmond, and Peter Goldsmith. 1998. *Micro Economic Evolution of an Organization: A Dynamic Programming Model of Organizational Evolution*. Proceedings of the WCC-72 Research Symposium, Las Vegas, June.

Nonaka, Ikujiro, and Hirotaka Takeuchi. 1995. *The Knowledge-Creating Company: How Japanese Companies Create the Dynamics of Innovation*. New York: Oxford University Press.

Peppers, Don, and Martha Rogers. 1993. *The One to One Future: Building Relationships One Customer at a Time*. New York: Doubleday.

Peppers, Don, Martha Rogers, and Bob Dorf. 1999. "Is Your Company Ready for One-to-One Marketing?" *Harvard Business Review* (January–February): 151–160.

Phillips, Richard. 1953. "Economic Nature of the Cooperative Association." *Journal of Farm Economics* 35, no. 1: 74–87.

Pine, B. Joseph, Don Peppers, and Martha Rogers. 1995. "Do You Want to Keep Your Customers Forever?" *Harvard Business Review* (March–April): 103–114.

Polyani, Michael. 1966. *The Tacit Dimension*. New York: Doubleday.

Prahalad, C.K. 1993. "The Role of Core Competencies in the Corporation." *Research and Technology Management* 36: 40–47.

Prahalad, C.K., and Richard Bettis. 1986. "The Dominant Logic: A New Linkage Between Diversity and Performance." *Strategic Management Journal* 7, no. 6: 485–501.

Prahalad, C.K., and Gary Hamel. 1990. "The Core Competence of the Corporation." *Harvard Business Review* (May–June): 79–91.

Producers Alliance. 1999. *Producers Alliance Business Plan*. Bloomington: Illinois Farm Bureau.

Quinn, James Brian. 1977. "Strategic Goals: Process and Politics." *Sloan Management Review* 19: 21–37.

Quinn, James Brian, T. Doorley, and P. Paquette. 1990. "Technology in Services: Rethinking Strategic Focus." *Sloan Management Review* 31, no. 2: 79–87.

Rackam, Neil, and John R. Devincentis. 1999. *Rethinking the Sales Force: Redefining Selling to Create and Capture Customer Value*. New York: McGraw-Hill.

Rackham, Neil, Thomas L. Friedman, and Richard Ruff. 1996. *Getting Partnering Right*. New York: McGraw-Hill.

Rose, Judd, and Karen A. Thomas. 2000. "Hard Economic Times Bring Depression, Shame for Struggling Farmers." Available at www.cnn.com/2000/HEALTH/05/25/farm.psych/ (November 12, 2002).

Rumelt, Richard. 1982. "Diversification Strategy and Profitability." *Strategic Management Journal* 3, no. 4: 359–370.

S4 Consulting. 2000. *Customer Interview Guide*. Powell, OH: S4 Consulting.

Saputo, Joe (Director of Development, Illinois Department of Agriculture). 2000. Presentation to Advisory Committee of Illinois Ag Entrepreneur Development Initiative, Peoria, IL.

Savage, J. 1954. Comments on "The Economic Nature of Cooperative Organizations." *Journal of Farm Economics* 36: 529–534.

Schumpeter, Joseph. 1951. *Essays of J.A. Schumpeter*, ed. Richard V. Clemence. Cambridge, MA: Addison-Wesley.

———. 1997. *The Theory of Economic Development*. New Brunswick, NJ: Transaction.

Senge, Peter. 1990. *The Fifth Discipline*. New York: Doubleday.

Sexton, Richard. 1986a. "The Formation of Cooperatives: A Game Theoretic Approach with Implications for Cooperative Finance, Decision Making and Stability." *American Journal of Agricultural Economics* 68: 214–225.

———. 1986b. "Cooperatives and the Forces Shaping Agricultural Marketing." *American Journal of Agricultural Economics* 68: 1167–1172.

Siebert, John W., Robert Jones, and Thomas L. Sporleder. 1997. "The VEST Model: An Alternative Approach to Value Added." *Agribusiness* 13, no. 6: 561–567.

Slater, Stanley, and John C. Narver. 1995. "Market Orientation and the Learning Organization." *Journal of Marketing* 59, no. 3: 63–74.

Smith, R. 1998. "Minnesota Ups Ethanol Leadership." *Feedstuffs*, August 31; available at www.Feedstuffs.com.

————. 2000. "Illinois Producers Plan Cooperative to Capture Higher Returns off the Hoof." *Feedstuffs*, June 26; available at www.Feedstuffs.com.

Sporleder, Thomas L. 1993. *Strategic Alliances as a Tactic for Enhancing Vertical Coordination in Agricultural Marketing Channels.* Presented at the International Agribusiness Management Association Symposium III, San Francisco, June.

Staatz, John. 1983. "The Cooperative as a Coalition: A Game Theoretic Approach." *American Journal of Agricultural Economics* 65: 1083–1089.

————. 1987. "A Game Theoretic Analysis of Decision-Making in Farmer Cooperatives." In *Cooperative Theory: New Approaches* (USDA/ACS report no. 18), 117–147. Washington, DC: USDA, Agricultural Cooperative Service.

Statistics Canada. 2000. Available at www.statcan.ca/english/Pgdb/Economy/Primary/prim14b.htm (July 2001).

Tirole, Jean. 1988. *The Theory of Industrial Organization.* Cambridge: MIT Press.

U.S. Department of Agriculture (USDA). 1993. *Farmer Cooperative Statistics, 1992* (Report no. 39). Washington, DC: USDA, Agricultural Cooperative Service.

USDA, Rural Business-Cooperative Service. 1998. *Cooperative Historical Statistics* (Report no. 1, Section 26). Washington, DC: USDA, RBS.

Varian, Hal. 1984. *Microeconomic Analysis.* 2d ed. New York: W.W. Norton.

Waner, Jennifer. 1999. *New Generation Cooperatives: Case Study.* Macomb: Illinois Institute for Rural Affairs, Western Illinois University.

Wood, U. (Principal, S4 Consulting). 2000. Personal communication.

Zell, Sam (Chairman of the Board, Equity Group Investments, LLC, USA). 2000. *Factors That Investors Use to Evaluate Investment Opportunities.* Keynote address, World Congress, International Food and Agribusiness Management Association, Chicago.

Zusman, Pinhas. 1982. "Group Choice in an Agricultural Marketing Cooperative." *Canadian Journal of Economics* 15: 220–234.

PART IV

COOPERATIVES IN ECONOMIC DEVELOPMENT

9

The Challenges Facing Cooperative Marketers and Bargaining Cooperatives in Today's Food System

David J. Schaffner

Marketing Cooperatives—Evolving Challenges

U.S. cooperatives controlled 27 percent of the total farm market, including crop, livestock, and poultry, in 1999, providing a marketing dollar volume of $72 billion (Kraenzle 2001). Down $4 billion from 1998, when the market share was 30 percent, the market share has regressed to its 1992 level. Although commodity prices in general declined, even sectors such as grain first-handlers and cotton marketers, areas where co-ops have traditionally been major players, have seen an erosion of market share. Changes in the marketplace are challenging co-ops that seek to regain their once-vibrant role in the agribusiness complex (Cotterill 1997). Although the cooperative form of business organization allows members to expand their control over the marketing and processing of their products and, thus, to capture value, at issue is their ability to overcome organizational flaws and to respond to the fast-moving external environment. This chapter provides an overview of the place of co-ops in the marketing and bargaining arenas and explores rationales for their future existence as a form of business organization.

Internationally, U.S. co-ops do not show up as major players either in agricultural commodity processing or in further upstream value-added activities. In many commodity sectors—flour milling, soybean processing, corn milling, and beef and pork slaughtering—many of the same firms, such as ConAgra, Cargill, and Archer Daniels Midland (ADM), rank among the top four.

A few large regional co-ops compete at the national level: Atlanta-based Gold Kist is the second largest producer of broilers and Ag Processing (AGP) is the fourth largest U.S. soybean processor. Although grain co-ops assemble much of the grain at the farm level, when this same grain is exported, it enters markets dominated by large investor-owned firms (IOFs). With the acquisition of Louis Dreyfus by ADM and of Continental Grain by Cargill in the late 1990s, only three major players remain in the world grain and grain products market—Cargill, ADM, and Bunge Corporation.

These transnational corporations (TNCs), as they are sometimes called, roam the world seeking production and processing sites that offer the most favorable combination of labor, inputs, transportation, and government regulations to which they can apply their advantages in capital and technology and be low-cost producers. Since capital and technology can be transferred to almost any country of the world, the main issue that TNCs face is how to combine the other factors of production, mentioned above, most effectively. This "global sourcing" by TNCs presents a formidable challenge to co-ops trying to compete in the global food system.

In addition to facing the juggernaut of the TNCs, co-ops often suffer conflicting objectives when attempting international involvement. Enhancement of services to members competes with the need to ensure survival through growth and earnings. The fundamental strategy of an IOF is to shift capital among enterprises and nations with the objective of improving rates of return. On the other hand, a co-op, presumably founded with the purpose of providing markets or enhancing services, aims to improve returns to a group of members within a specific region and nation (Seipel and Heffernan 1997).

Several points may explain the reluctance of agricultural marketing co-ops' members and boards to think globally. In regional, multicommodity co-ops, the diverse interests of members may constrain investment in overseas assets. Likewise, the importation of commodities for domestic processing or marketing may tend to provide greater benefit to some producers than to others.

A related problem occurs due to the rigidity of physical assets owned by a co-op in its country of origin, for which the members hold the co-op responsible. Any proposed international activity by a co-op that is perceived as possibly decreasing the value of member assets is likely to meet membership resistance, even though the activity may enhance the survival of the co-op as a going concern. Given that the owners of a co-op (farmer-members) typically have a greater voice in the decision-making process than the owners (shareholders) of an IOF, co-ops will have a narrower set of strategic options to consider. Unfortunately, for the most part, farmers from a given nation, as a group, see producers from other nations as direct competition for a share of the finite pie of international commodity markets (Seipel and Heffernan 1997).

Agricultural Producers' Motives for Engaging in
Cooperative Marketing Activities

Much of the literature addressing cooperative marketing questions farmers' motives for joining together in cooperative marketing activities or examines cooperative performance in differentiated (branded product) marketing vis-à-vis the performance of IOFs (Cotterill 1997; Dahl 1991; Goldberg 1972). Producers joining a co-op typically have in mind one or more of the following objectives (Rhodes 1983):

- to improve net economic returns (which often involves one or more of the points made below);
- to ensure a market for their commodities, often stated as "to have a home for production";
- to achieve channel leadership or countervailing power, which is often a function of the degree to which farmers feel they have been "exploited" by IOFs;
- to expand demand for the producer's product through promotion and/or other market development activities domestically and internationally.

By focusing on providing a home for production—an immediate user benefit—co-ops have often neglected strategic planning and the need for a longer-term perspective. In one survey of the chief financial officers of several major co-ops, they reported difficulty in getting boards to deal with strategic planning (Hardesty 1992). Often, boards stray into operational issues and tend to have a very short-term perspective. Management cannot totally overcome this problem by adopting a longer-term perspective due to the fact that boards of directors are the chief policymakers of firms. Caswell's (1989) research, however, shows that cooperative boards, for the most part, do not include individuals with a broad range of management experience and an understanding of strategic planning and financial management.

A major thesis of cooperative marketing, set forth by Helmberger and Hoos in a 1962 *Journal of Farm Economics* article, is that a co-op with open membership, rather than limiting member deliveries to the volume where long-run marginal costs equal the price received, will welcome new members and accept increased quantity to market. In this mode, the co-op provides the competitive yardstick effect on the market first described by Nourse in his 1922 paper, *The Economic Philosophy of Cooperation*. The effect of the competitive yardstick is that the total market's finished output increases, and consumer prices decrease.

While such open-membership policies benefit potential new members, they are contrary to the interests of existing members. Many co-ops have recognized the trap that open membership presents and have moved to closed systems where delivery rights to the co-op are then capitalized and tradable among existing or new members (Welch's in its grape products and Sunsweet in prunes are two examples). One of the distinguishing features of New Generation Cooperatives, discussed in the next section, is their policy of closed membership.

To achieve the demand expansion objective, co-ops must have a market orientation. Co-ops are often criticized for not accepting the idea of being consumer-driven firms (Caswell 1989; Hardesty 1992). In many respects, the objective of providing a home for production is in direct conflict with the philosophy that marketing success is grounded in a consumer orientation. The co-op's ability to be market oriented may also be hampered by the narrow scope of its product lines. When a co-op is a single-commodity marketer, its members and board may be reluctant to add new commodities to its membership base. Members are very protective of management's attention to their commodities and are wary of investing in nonpatronage products. Taking this short-term view reduces the co-op's ability to meet customers' needs by broadening its product line and, thus, strengthening its marketing program (Hardesty 1992).

New Generation (Closed-Membership) Cooperatives

Many New Generation Cooperatives (NGCs) appeared in the 1990s, especially in the Northern Great Plains states. While most of these co-ops share the characteristic that they are involved in value-added types of activities (e.g., pasta manufacturing, frozen dough, ethanol production), a major distinguishing feature of NGCs is that they are closed-membership co-ops. This means that the total quantity of delivery right shares that the NGC sells to producers depends on the capacity of the NGC to efficiently process and market. If, for example, an NGC operates a frozen dough facility that uses a quantity of flour equivalent to 60 million bushels of wheat, then the NGC will sell 60 million shares that require the owners to deliver to the NGC one bushel of wheat per share.

Because of this closed-membership approach, the price of the 60 million shares will fluctuate depending on the performance and earning potential of the NGC. Examples of NGCs that have defined successful marketing strategies are Thumb Oilseed Producers Cooperative in Michigan and Dakota Growers Pasta (DGP), headquartered in Carrington, North Dakota (see Box 9.1, "Dakota Growers Pasta—Finding a Niche"). If the NGC performs well and the earning potential of the shares improves, then

Box 9.1

Dakota Growers Pasta—Finding a Niche

Dakota Growers Pasta (DGP), a defined (closed) membership cooperative organized in 1991 as a vertically integrated operation, assembles its members' durum wheat, mills durum wheat into semolina, produces pasta from semolina, and markets the pasta. One of the nation's more noteworthy New Generation Cooperatives, by adding value to its members' durum wheat DGP is succeeding in a highly competitive industry characterized by wide swings in price and availability. After distribution of the processing net margins, member gain has been substantially higher than the durum market price.

Using grower agreements, DGP initially offered stock at $3.85 per bushel. Owning stock obligates a member to deliver a set amount of high-quality durum wheat per share to the NGC. If members cannot supply the desired quality, the DGP will purchase the wheat on their behalf and charge them the purchase or current market price, plus a service fee. In 1999 and 2000, poor durum crops forced DGP to purchase from outside its membership, which increased costs and reduced final returns to members.

While undergoing many changes since 1994, DGP has maintained the same basic approach. The company uses the semolina in its vertically integrated facility, consisting of a grain elevator, mill, four pasta production lines, and a warehouse, to store the finished goods.

The cost savings from integration provide a competitive advantage relative to other firms. DGP has become the third largest U.S. pasta manufacturer, and members have received patronage refunds every year since 1996. The company has remained profitable by increasing the value that members received for their durum relative to nonmembers.

As a marketing strategy, from the beginning, DGP has focused on the private-label business, the quickest way to enter this industry. Approximately 60 percent of DGP's sales are in retail, followed by 20 percent in food service and 20 percent in the ingredient market. The majority of sales are under private labels, although DGP also has its own labels: Dakota Growers, Pasta Sanita, and Zia Briosa. DGP began a certified organic pasta product line in 2000, and has entered into an agreement with the second largest Italian pasta manufacturer, Gruppo Euricom, to serve as its exclusive distributor of private label and brand label retail products and food service products in North America.

In 2001, DGP signed an agreement with Semolina Specialties, a Crosby, North Dakota, producer-owned co-op that produces hard-to-make specialty and flavored pasta products. DGP will supply 35 million pounds of semolina flour and market Semolina Specialties' pasta products. Also, DGP has revamped the image of its main brand, Dakota Growers, and is penetrating more markets outside North Dakota and Minnesota. Although higher costs and the inability to pass along price increases due to industry excess capacity made 2001 a difficult year for DGP, the NGC returned to profitability by the third quarter of 2002 with net earnings of $2.2 million (Dakota Growers 2002). Despite the positive balance sheet, Dakota Growers converted from a cooperative to a corporation in 2002—a possibility hinted at in chapter 3 of this volume. While Dakota Growers is now structured as a corporation, it still reserves delivery rights for farmer-investors who own Series D Delivery preferred stock (Dakota Growers 2002).

Source: Boland and Barton (2001, 4–8).

the share price will increase as members transfer their delivery rights to other members or to other producers who wish to become members. Conversely, if the earnings potential of the shares is perceived to be weaker than when first offered, market share prices will decrease.

The closed-membership approach addresses a common lament of cooperative management: that members often do not consider themselves to be their co-op's owners/investors. Not understanding the financial requirements of their co-ops and not accepting their responsibilities under the user-financed principle of co-ops, many members consider equity retains to be a necessary, or perhaps even unnecessary, evil, and see them as deductions from their earnings rather than investments.

In an open-membership co-op, members derive benefits from their membership only as long as they are patrons of the co-op. This problem also contributes to member reluctance to invest in the co-op. In contrast, when IOFs invest in product and market development activities, the expected future stream of revenue and, hence, profits is capitalized into the price of the company's stock (in essence, this makes up for the current returns that stockholders are foregoing). Open-membership co-ops are unable to "pay" current patrons for investments that will accrue benefits far in the future and, consequently, suffer from what has been termed "the horizon problem" (Hardesty 1992).

In summary, the closed-membership co-op addresses two of the major shortcomings of traditional open co-ops: (1) the tendency of the successful co-op to keep accepting additional members and product, thus driving down profitability, and (2) the disincentive for co-op members to invest in a co-op when the only benefit derived from membership is a home for the product. In the long run, both shortcomings contribute to a co-op's competitive yardstick effect on the market by exerting downward pressure on price–cost margins (Rogers and Petraglia 1994).

Branded Product Marketing

Co-ops have a long history of product differentiation through branding and promotion (Rogers 1994). In the early 1900s, the threat of overproduction clouded the future of the California orange industry. To the president of the California Fruit Growers Exchange, F.Q. Story, the solution to the problem was easy—an advertising program "to get people to eat more oranges" (Knapp 1969, 249). Members were reluctant to undertake an advertising program because the benefits would also accrue to nonmembers. Finally, in 1905, a funding contribution of $250 to advertise Exchange fruit in England and Continental Europe was approved.

Box 9.2

Citrus World—A Success Story in Branded Product Marketing

Florida's Citrus World, a federated co-op with thirteen members, ten of which are packing houses, successfully developed a value-added branded product to provide greater returns for its members. Altogether, the co-op represents 1,000 growers, who control 60,000 acres of citrus groves across Florida. In 1998, Citrus World's sales of $450 million represented 6 percent of all Florida orange juice and some 15 percent of the state's grapefruit.

In 1987, Citrus World moved to develop its own label, Florida's Natural, a not-from-concentrate (NFC) product. According to grower Bill Raley, the decision was difficult and controversial for the board of directors, who "wondered whether we could afford the investment of many millions of dollars." Citrus World's popular advertising uses real employees and growers, not actors, and they make sure viewers know its product is different, coming from a co-op of Florida growers whose only business is making juice. Florida's Natural now holds an 18 percent share of the NFC orange juice market.

While spending a fraction of what their major competitors—Coke's Minute Maid and Pepsi's Tropicana—do on advertising, Citrus World has very successfully squeezed its folksy image for all its worth. One ad shows growers with boxes of oranges on their laps, holding a "stockholders' meeting" in the back of a truck. Other workers cut "overhead" by chopping a branch from an orange tree.

Based on sales of $450 million, Citrus World paid members $71.9 million in patronage returns in 1998, the second highest in its history. Citrus World's CEO, Steve Caruso, advises co-ops that it is never too late: "Citrus World was 55-years-old when we decided to go into value-added processing. In hindsight, it certainly has been shown to have paid off."

Source: Merlo (1998, 24–26).

With Story persisting in his efforts, the Exchange approved a major advertising campaign, which was launched in Iowa in 1908 at a cost of $7,000 and resulted in a 50 percent increase in orange sales. Convinced by this success that advertising worked, the Exchange increased its ad budget to $25,000 and its advertising agency, Lord and Thomas, coined the name "Sunkist" as a trademark for its highest-quality oranges. In 1952, the California Fruit Growers Exchange officially changed its name to Sunkist Growers (Sunkist n.d.).

Along with Sunkist's long history of branding, advertising, and successful product differentiation, there are several highly visible and successful branding efforts by co-ops, including Ocean Spray in cranberries and juices, Welch's in grape products, Land O'Lakes in dairy, Sunmaid in raisins, Citrus World in processed citrus products, and numerous others covering regional markets (see Box 9.2, "Citrus World—A Success Story in Branded Product Marketing").

Research during the past twenty years shows that co-ops hold small market shares in the more concentrated, more processed, more differentiated, higher-margin markets. Using 1982 Bureau of the Census data, Rogers and Marion (1990) found that the 100 largest co-ops accounted for 6.9 percent of the total value-of-shipments in food and tobacco manufacturing; in fact, the 20 largest co-ops accounted for most of this 6.9 percent. By contrast, the 100 largest IOF food manufacturers account for 92 percent of all measured media advertising of food and tobacco products. According to another study from the mid-1980s, co-ops occupied the number one spot in 15 of 145 products (Wills 1985). Some of these 15 are the names mentioned in the preceding paragraph.

To what extent are co-ops "aggressive" in advertising? Combs and Marion (1984) and Gruber, Rogers, and Sexton (2000) explored this question in two different time periods. Advertising is considered the primary vehicle for processed food product marketers to achieve product differentiation. The generally accepted proposition is that with greater levels of advertising intensity, market share and profitability improvement will follow. The earlier analysis by Marion and Combs concluded that cooperative advertising per brand was about 40 percent of IOF brand advertising, and co-ops achieved less price enhancement for their brands than for comparable IOF brands.

Agreeing that on the macro level co-ops advertise less than IOFs, Gruber et al. (2000) went on to examine forty-nine food product markets that each contained at least one co-op. In this sample set, two-thirds of the observations involved manufacturers who conducted no advertising; however, in markets where the participants advertised, it was found that co-ops' advertising-to-sales ratio is about one percentage point higher than a comparable IOF's. Why, then, do co-ops lag behind IOFs in value-added marketing? The following points explain why co-ops do not appear to be as successful:

- Co-ops have traditionally participated in food manufacturing during the early stages of processing, this being a logical vertical extension of the farmer-members' agricultural production operations. Historically, at their roots, most IOFs provide a consumer product—Kellogg's cereal, Pillsbury flour, Heinz pickles, and so on. Their strategic decisions to ensure a supply and quality of raw material through vertical integration and contracts came at a later date.

- The influence of governing boards may play an important role in a co-op's reluctance to move into the advertised brand segment of markets. Most cooperative boards are fairly homogeneous, made up of farmer-members, thus they are very user-oriented and tend to be product driven. In contrast, IOF boards are not raw product or user oriented, but are very much oriented toward the marketplace and what is necessary to achieve goals, such as increasing market share, with resultant improvements in profit margins and return on investment (Caswell 1989). Caswell found that co-ops generally do not have outside directors and that it is rare for a member-patron to sit on the board of more than one co-op. The result of this low level of interfirm contact is that cooperative boards are nearly completely isolated. In contrast, IOF directors often serve on multiple boards and offer varying expertise for participation in firm decision making. If this interaction of board members is an important source of information and expertise, then the structure of cooperative boards may inhibit the quality of their decision making.

• Although differentiated product marketing in general is more profitable than first-stage processing activities or private label markets, there are significant barriers to entering many food product markets—ready-to-eat cereal, malt beverages, tomato products, to name a few—where existing market concentration and existing brand equity preclude any significant head-to-head competition by a new entrant.

The Role of Bargaining Cooperatives in the U.S. Food System

During the past half-century, the food-processing industries have become increasingly concentrated, giving buyers of agricultural products ever-greater market power. In an attempt to achieve countervailing power, farmers have organized agricultural bargaining co-ops. A bargaining co-op's basic purpose is to join producers in a cohesive economic unit that has greater market power when negotiating price and other terms of trade with processors than individual producers have in the purely competitive economic model (see Box 9.3, "CherrCo Helps Bring Market Stability to Tart Cherry Industry").

Bargaining co-ops, in contrast with the marketing co-ops discussed earlier, do not become involved in handling the raw product—they do not have bricks-and-mortar processing facilities. Rather, the bargaining co-op, while generally taking title to the producer's product in order to achieve some power when negotiating with buyers, is a neutral force in the actual marketing of the final product. Bargaining co-ops' products usually end up as differentiated, value-added products.

One rationale for bargaining co-ops is their ability to provide agricultural producers "countervailing power." In John Kenneth Galbraith's (1956) *American Capitalism: The Concept of Countervailing Power*, the argument is made that an overreliance on the pure laissez-faire model will result in the economic exploitation of the weaker party. Galbraith believes that an important activity of the state is to nurture countervailing power, for in its absence more governmental control or planning is sought, and the economy's capacity for autonomous self-regulation is reduced.

Box 9.3

CherrCo Helps Bring Market Stability to Tart Cherry Industry

The tart cherry industry, facing surplus supplies, fluctuating production, and weak pricing arrangements during the late 1980s and early 1990s, was at a crisis point in 1997. The industry responded by coming together to form CherrCo, a bargaining co-op with an innovative approach. Rather than processing value-added products, this "supercooperative" bargains on behalf of its members.

In early 1997, CherrCo organizers held discussions around the country, resulting in 78 percent of the cherry industry buying into the idea. Two goals were communicated: (1) to stabilize prices of the industry's commodity products, and (2) to achieve price levels that help keep growers and processors in business. As a federated co-op, CherrCo now has twenty-eight member co-ops in the United States and Canada, representing 75–80 percent of Michigan's tart cherry production and significant portions of the production in New York, Utah, Washington, Wisconsin, and Ontario. Member co-ops' production ranges from about 600,000 pounds to more than 10 million pounds, annually.

As a bargaining co-op, CherrCo's primary directive is to establish minimum prices for various grades and packs of frozen and hot pack tart cherries. Once a minimum price is set, individual members select cooperative-licensed sales agents, who can represent many members. Sales information, including who is selling to whom and at what price, is treated as proprietary and is not shared with other members. By licensing the agents, CherrCo can ensure that they follow procedures as well as abide by the established price.

CherrCo also tracks the nation's tart cherry inventory. When and where possible, CherrCo and the licensed agents pool production to meet customer demands. Before processing, cherries are sent to storage facilities and consigned to CherrCo; however, the bargaining co-op never has the cherries in its physical possession. CherrCo does not own any processing plants; its members decide what they will do with their cherries and to whom they will sell.

A major side benefit of CherrCo is better communication throughout the industry. As CherrCo's president, James Jensen, says, "We're all at the table together and, while we are not all holding hands, we are at least not throwing things at each other." Each of CherrCo's twenty-eight members holds a seat on the board, and those directors meet quarterly in addition to serving on committees dealing with marketing, quality, grower relations, and strategic planning.

Despite the advent of CherrCo and passage of a new federal tart cherry marketing order, the industry still faces plenty of challenges. Cherry producers need to expand exports and could do more to fine-tune supply management mechanisms. For this specialty fruit industry, dwarfed by other segments of U.S. agriculture, working through these challenges is critical.

Source: Karg (2000, 4–6).

It is interesting to note Galbraith's caveat regarding the shortcomings of many farmer bargaining efforts:

The co-operative is a loose association of individuals. It rarely includes all producers of a product. It cannot control the production of its members, and in practice, has less than absolute control over the decision to sell. A strong bargaining position requires the ability to wait—to hold some or all of the product. The co-operative cannot make the non-members wait; they are at liberty to sell when they please and, unlike the members, they have the advantage of selling all they please. In practice, the co-operative cannot fully control even its own members. They are under the constant temptation to break away and sell their full production. (1956, 161)

Bargaining Benefits

While producer price improvement is the commonly stated objective of commodity bargaining, a number of other ancillary but important nonprice issues can also be resolved. In the United States, fruit and vegetable bargaining co-ops negotiate on a wide range of items in addition to price. The most commonly negotiated nonprice terms of trade are time, method of payment, and quality standards. Other frequently negotiated terms of trade include methods of grading, duration of contracts, and responsibilities and rights during production. Despite the presence of bargaining, growers commonly complain that they often end up "financing the processors" by not receiving payments for crops until well after delivery (Iskow and Sexton 1992).

In many collective bargaining situations, the responsibility for a cost item is shifted from producer to processor, who is in a better position to minimize joint costs. As an example, in the 1970s, pea growers in Washington State were being docked for split and damaged peas, although the processor owned and operated the combine. Through bargaining, rather than penalizing the grower, who had no control, the incentive to control damage was placed on the processor (Lang 1980).

Some processing crop growers argue that certain production practices or conditions of obtaining a contract, such as buying seed or other inputs from the processor, are either costly, ineffective, or unnecessary. During the bargaining process, information on these issues can be gathered and brought to the table, resulting in a more reasoned decision as to whether such joint costs are necessary. Deciding many nonprice factors that influence producer income, such as uniform and fair quality standards, time of payment, and harvest coordination, can be a bargaining goal.

Iskow and Sexton's (1992) survey revealed that fewer than 25 percent of bargaining co-ops negotiate on quantity. For many crops, the quantities to be produced and exchanged are decided between individual growers and their processors, rather than through a negotiation process involving the co-op. In other cases, processors purchase all member production each year, or growers and processors enter into long-term contracts spanning several years.

As for the ability to improve prices, the evidence is sketchy but leads to the conclusion that over the long run, producer group bargaining achieves only slight gains at best. This is especially true if no production control mechanism is in place. In the United States, most bargained commodities are not subject to production controls. Also, the section of the Capper–Volstead Act prohibiting co-ops from carrying out activities that result in "undue price enhancement," while vague in its potential application, keeps bargaining cooperative market power in check.

Requirements for Effective Agricultural Bargaining Cooperatives

First and foremost, the bargaining co-op must be recognized by processors as the exclusive bargaining agent and source of supply for the product. Recognition can come either voluntarily or by government mandate. In the case of voluntary recognition, the bargaining organization must do more than control the majority of production. Most bargaining co-ops have more than a 50 percent market in the geographical area in which they operate. The Iskow and Sexton (1992) study found that two-thirds of the bargaining co-ops surveyed held a market share of greater than 50 percent, and the average percentage of production negotiated through all thirty-six co-ops interviewed was 60.3 percent.

In addition to controlling at least the majority of production in its geographical market area, the co-op must also exercise member discipline. Producers must deliver on their end of the contract to legitimize the bargaining agent in the processor's eyes. Nothing will destroy a bargaining co-op faster than having members not perform on their delivery contracts. While such contracts may be enforceable in court, such enforcement becomes a moot point if, in the meantime, the bargaining co-op's credibility is destroyed.

The only U.S. attempt to develop a law that mandated agricultural bargaining was the Michigan Agricultural Marketing and Bargaining Act passed in 1972. This law set up a system whereby grower co-ops, once certified by the state, were to act as exclusive bargaining and marketing agents for all producers in a bargaining unit. The law read much like industrial relations laws governing collective bargaining between labor and employers. The Michigan Act required bargaining in good faith, and although growers did not have to join the bargaining co-op, they were bound by the terms of the contract negotiated and had to pay fees to the co-op for services rendered. The law prevented handlers from directly negotiating with growers, whether they were members of the unit or not, and it also provided for mediation of issues and, as a last resort, binding arbitration of unsettled issues (Bunje 1980).

Processors and individual producers, disgruntled with the restrictions the Michigan Act placed on their individual actions, almost immediately challenged the act in the courts on constitutional grounds. The court test ultimately ended up in the U.S. Supreme Court, which, in 1984, struck down the sections of the Michigan Act that required producer participation in a certified association. The Court held that the law conflicted with federal law permitting farmers to organize, but prohibiting coercion of any farmer to join.

Other states—Maine, California, and Washington—passed similar laws in the 1970s, requiring processors and farmer bargaining co-ops to engage in "good faith bargaining." While producer groups feel that these laws helped gain recognition and credibility, they question the usefulness of such laws. Problems arise with respect to enforcement of such laws, given the difficulty of actually proving that a processor has not bargained in good faith (Iskow and Sexton 1992).

Market intelligence and a well-formulated strategy are prerequisites for success at the bargaining table. Data on product supply, including costs of production, comparative costs in various regions, imports/exports, and processors' alternatives for sourcing raw material, must be obtained. Likewise, on the demand side, consumption trends, factors affecting consumption, and processor profit margins are a few examples of the types of information needed.

To negotiate from a position of power, the bargaining co-op must know more about its product than anyone else. All of this information is used to develop a bargaining strategy; bargaining for a price increase must be justified in the context of both the short- and long-run economic situation.

To achieve market power and stability of operations, most bargaining co-ops establish marketing contracts with their members. Through the contracts, producers have a legal obligation to deliver production to the co-op; however, as discussed earlier, grower contracts do not guarantee the ability of bargaining co-ops to hold membership. An effective communication and education program can best nurture member loyalty and trust. In fact, most co-ops have field representatives whose major responsibilities are not only to bring nonmembers into the fold, but to keep members informed on market developments and bargaining activities, so that they are not informed via "surprise" announcements in the media.

In evaluating a bargaining co-op's performance, producers must view its long-term performance record, rather than the results in one specific year (see Box 9.4, "Raisin Bargaining Association—A Season of Discontent"). In any given year, the bargained price may not be the most attractive at harvest. The nonjoiner "freeloader" poses a persistent problem for bargaining co-ops. In the absence of legislation that establishes legal recognition of bargaining entities, and where nonmembers as well as members are bound by the terms of the contract (as in the voided Michigan Act), there are always incentives for producers not to join. These incentives exist because non-members can frequently share in the bargaining benefits without sharing the costs, and processors may write sweetheart contracts with nonmembers to weaken the bargaining co-op's position.

The Economics of Agricultural Bargaining

How much bargaining can improve the producer price situation is, for the most part, determined by the degree of competition among buyers and by elasticity of demand. Producers are limited to bargaining with those to whom they sell (first handlers). Thus, if the "fat" in the system is further up the channel of distribution, and, presuming in this case that the first handler sector is competitive, the amount producers can expect to gain is limited by the first handlers' ability to obtain "fat" from others (Moore 1968).

An end product with inelastic demand characteristics would find processors in a favorable position to pass on cost increases. Also, wherever large value is added to the product and raw material costs are a small proportion of the processor's selling price, the processor can more easily absorb increased raw material costs. For example, in a product where raw material cost of final product is 10 percent of final price, a 20 percent increase in raw material cost will result in only a 2 percent price increase.

For the long-run viability of a bargaining effort, however, supply control is the issue. As producer returns are improved, output will tend to expand. At this point, co-ops must grapple with surpluses that can only be controlled through industrywide government or quasi-government programs such as marketing orders. In about 20 percent of the industries with bargaining co-ops, a state or federal marketing order also exists to control the commodity's quality or volume (Iskow and Sexton 1992). Co-ops' inability to achieve some level of supply control has long been the downfall of cooperative marketing efforts. In the 1920s, Aaron Sapiro's highly propagandized organizational efforts rarely survived for more than a year or two due to this inability. The efforts of the Raisin Bargaining Association to combat the difficulties facing the raisin industry, described in Box 9.4, illustrate this same struggle in the twenty-first century.

In summary, the extent of prevailing monopsonistic or collusive oligopolistic behavior will determine the benefits that accrue from bargaining. If prebargaining prices have been kept substantially below levels that would be expected with purely competitive behavior, it is possible for price determination in a bargaining environment to result in an outcome through which (1) all

Box 9.4

Raisin Bargaining Association—A Season of Discontent

The Fresno, California-based Raisin Bargaining Association (RBA) was formed in 1966 to negotiate an annual field price for San Joaquin Valley members' raisins with packers. That negotiated price becomes the pricing standard for the industry. Today, the RBA represents 2,000 members—40 percent of the industry's volume; another 30 percent of growers belong to Sun-Maid Growers, the well-known raisin-processing co-op; and the rest are independents.

Before the RBA, president Vaughn Koligian says, "Packers were able to play large growers against small growers and even take advantage of the operator who wasn't a good negotiator." The twenty or so packers often paid a range of prices for raisins of the same quality. First offered in 1967, the RBA contract has been modified over the years, but its foundation remains intact. "The strength of the contract comes from the fact that the grower passes title of his product to RBA in consideration for the marketing of that product," Koligian says. "Taking title gives us control over the raisins and separates RBA from a number of other bargaining associations. It also places a greater burden on us to ensure our members have a home for their products."

Unfortunately, the 2000–2001 year has been a season of turmoil, dissent, and financial hardship. Shaken by bearish supply-demand forces and a protracted price dispute, the industry is reeling. With the 2000 raisin crop at a record 440,000 tons, up nearly 47 percent over the previous year, prices plummeted. From a high of $1,300–1,400 per ton in 1998–99, after months of acrimonious wrangling, the price of the 2000 crop was finally set by arbitration at $877.50 per ton.

A small group of growers, unhappy with the arbitration outcome and RBA, have formed a rival bargaining association, the California Raisin Reform Association. Many growers and packers alike believe the industry can support only one bargaining association, however. Koligian, in defending the RBA, says, "It's shortsighted of people to judge this association by the 2000–2001 season. We've worked hard for our members and carried the water for a lot of independent growers who don't belong to RBA or Sun Maid." Other industry leaders endorse the RBA's effectiveness over the past 34 years and state that they would rue the day if the RBA were lost.

Source: Merlo (2001, 14–19).

sellers receive a higher price, (2) sellers are able to sell more product, and (3) buyers make at least normal profits (Helmberger and Hoos 1963).

References

Boland, Michael, and David Barton. 2001. "Finding a Niche—How Dakota Pasta Co-op Found Success in a Highly Competitive Market." *Rural Cooperatives* (July/August): 4–8.

Bunje, Ralph B. 1980. *Cooperative Farm Bargaining and Price Negotiations* (Cooperative information report no. 26). Washington, DC: USDA.

Caswell, Julie A. 1989. "The Cooperative–Corporate Interface: Interfirm Contact Through Membership on Boards of Directors." *Journal of Agricultural Cooperation* 4: 20–28.

Combs, Robert P., and Bruce W. Marion. 1984. *Food Manufacturing Activities of 100 Large Agricultural Marketing Cooperatives* (Working paper no. 73). Madison, WI: North Central Project 117.

Cotterill, Ronald. 1997. "The Performance of Agricultural Marketing Cooperatives in Differentiated Product Markets." *Journal of Cooperatives* 12: 23–33.

Dahl, Reynold P. 1991. "Structural Change and Performance of Grain Marketing Cooperatives." *Journal of Agricultural Cooperation* 6: 66–81.

Dakota Growers. 2002a. News Archive: Dakota Growers Pasta Company Completes Conversion, July 2, 2002. Available at www.dakotagrowers.com/news/conversion.shtml (August 2003).

Dakota Growers. 2002b. News Archive: Third Quarter Profits Rise Sharply. Available at www.dakotagrowers.com/news/conversion.shtml, (August 2003).

Galbraith, John Kenneth. 1956. *American Capitalism: The Concept of Countervailing Power*. 2d ed. Boston: Houghton Mifflin.

Goldberg, Ray A. 1972. "Profitable Partnerships: Industry and Farm Co-ops." *Harvard Business Review* (March/April): 108–121.

Gruber, Jennifer, Richard T. Rogers, and Richard J. Sexton. 2000. "Do Agricultural Marketing Cooperatives Advertise Less Intensively than Investor-owned Food-processing Firms?" *Journal of Cooperatives* 15: 31–46.

Hardesty, Shermain. 1992. *Cooperative Principles and Regulations: Aiding or Hampering Cooperatives' Efforts at Value-added Marketing?* Davis: University of California at Davis, Center for Cooperatives.

Helmberger, Peter G., and Sidney Hoos. 1962. "Cooperative Enterprise and Organization Theory." *Journal of Farm Economics* 44: 275–290.

———. 1963. "Economic Theory of Bargaining in Agriculture." *Journal of Farm Economics* 45: 1272–1280.

Iskow, Julie, and Richard Sexton. 1992. *Bargaining Associations in Grower-processor Markets for Fruits and Vegetables*. ACS research report no. 104. Washington, DC: USDA, Agricultural Cooperative Service.

Karg, Pamela J. 2000. "CherrCo Helps Bring Market Stability to Tart Cherry Industry." *Rural Cooperatives* (November/December): 4–6.

Knapp, Joseph G. 1969. *The Rise of American Cooperative Enterprise*. Danville, IL: Interstate.

Kraenzle, Charles A. 2001. "Co-op's Share of Farm Market, Major Cash Expenditures down in '99." *Rural Cooperatives Magazine* (January/February): 4–10.

Lang, Mahlon G. 1980. "Marketing Alternatives and Resource Allocation: Case Studies of Collective Bargaining." *American Journal of Agricultural Economics* 62: 760–765.

Merlo, Catherine. 1998. "A Star Is Born." *Rural Cooperatives* (July): 24–26.

———. 2001. "Season of Turmoil." *Rural Cooperatives* (September/October): 14–19.

Moore, John R. 1968. "Bargaining Power Potential in Agriculture." *American Journal of Agricultural Economics* 50: 1051–1053.

Nourse, E.G. 1922. "The Economic Philosophy of Cooperation." *American Economic Review* 12: 577–597.

Rhodes, James V. 1983. "The Large Agricultural Cooperative as a Competitor." *American Journal of Agricultural Economics* 65: 1090–1098.

Rogers, Richard T. 1994. "Advertising Strategies by Agricultural Cooperatives in Branded Food Products, 1967–1987." In *Competitive Strategy Analysis for Agri-*

cultural Marketing Cooperatives, ed. Ronald W. Cotterill, 58–97. Boulder, CO: Westview Press.

Rogers, Richard T., and Bruce W. Marion. 1990. "Food Manufacturing Activities of the Largest Agricultural Cooperatives: Market Power and Strategic Behavior Implications." *Journal of Agricultural Cooperation* 5: 59–73.

Rogers, Richard T., and Lisa M. Petraglia. 1994. "Agricultural Cooperatives and Market Performance in Food Manufacturing." *Journal of Agricultural Cooperatives* 9: 1–10.

Seipel, Michael F., and William D. Heffernan. 1997. *Cooperatives in a Changing Global Food System* (Research report 157). Washington, DC: USDA, Rural Business-Cooperative Service.

Sunkist. n.d. "About Sunkist Web site." Available at www.sunkist.com/about/history-sunkist.asp.

Wills, Robert L. 1985. "Evaluating Price Enhancement by Processing Cooperatives." *American Journal of Agricultural Economics* 67: 183–192.

10

Producer Marketing Through Cooperatives

Randall E. Torgerson

The fundamental rationale for group action among farmers with regard to the marketing of their products is their disparity in size and scope of activity as individual sellers compared with the buyers they face. Farmers are many in number yet relatively small in size compared to crop and livestock dealers, processors, and food and fiber distributors. Farmers have historically sought to overcome their deficiency in marketing power by organizing cooperative bargaining associations and marketing cooperatives to assemble greater volumes of graded products to meet buyers' specifications and to deal with them on more equal terms. They have also organized because marketing services were not available in their communities, or marketing opportunities and services were offered at higher costs than what co-ops could accomplish.

Farmers have certain goals and objectives when embracing group action strategies for marketing. Chief among these goals is income enhancement from their farm enterprises as well as a possible increase in the value of the farm itself as an operating business.

Second, farmers seek more control over marketing conditions for their products rather than being faced with a take-it-or-leave-it proposition. They seek improved prices and other terms of trade for raw products marketed through their cooperative marketing businesses that will enable them to take their products further through the value-added chain to the ultimate consumers or buyers. Finally, producers enjoy their independence as autonomous business units and can maintain their structure as independent businesses by cooperating with other similar production units using effective forms of group action.

Theory of Pressure Groups

In his seminal treatment of the economics of collective action, John R. Commons (1950) presented the concept of studying the structure of social action and analyzing the economic system as a system of human relations. He argued that pressure groups such as farm organizations, co-ops, and labor unions were among the most vital institutions in society and the lifeblood of democracy. The basis for this theory is that competitive market mechanisms do not of themselves bring about fair results to different groups in society due to the existence of private power. This unfairness is due to disparities in the bargaining power between these different groups and corporate interests. Since machine politicians and persons of wealth tend to control legislatures, Commons argued that individuals have to attach themselves to pressure groups that will pursue their long-run interests in the marketplace and in public policy debates.

These pressure groups are not only the most representative and beneficial forces influencing American economic policy, but, Commons (1950; 1957) suggests at one point, they are, in fact, an occupational parliament that is more representative of the people than the legislatures based on territorial representation. Olson (1965) carried forth many parts of Commons's theory but introduced the influence of size on organizational behavior and performance. He introduced the problems of incentives for individuals to take collective action and contended that the costs of organization are an increasing function of the number of individuals in the group placing constraints on large groups from furthering their own interests.

The Commons–Olson theory of collective action is especially useful in analyzing organizational developments in agriculture and how types of collective action utilized by farmers determine market outcomes and policy changes. It was a forerunner of John Kenneth Galbraith's (1957) theory of countervailing power by which farmers can offset their individual weaknesses in the market by (1) seeking to build countervailing power in the market, (2) dissolving the power of those with whom the farmer deals, or (3) achieving advantages of enhanced market power associated with changes in demand. It is also a forerunner of more recent attempts to develop a theory of social capital.

This approach to analysis is important in understanding members' use of organizations and the development of institutional mechanisms to represent interest groups. More importantly, it provides useful insights into the functional and structural relationships among various types of group action used in representing the economic and social interests of farmers and other rural residents. Key marketing and market policy outcomes can frequently be best understood having analyzed the interactions of farmers' professional organizations and co-ops as pressure groups representing members' interests. A coordinated "cooperative systems" approach (Torgerson 1968) has not only the potential for maximizing producer returns from the marketplace, but also for maximizing influence in the policy arena.

Taxonomy of Group Action in Agriculture

Various types and patterns of group action are clearly discernable in countries throughout the world where farmers have had the right to freely organize among themselves. Initial steps are found in agricultural societies that focused on improved production practices. Some of these organizations and periodic farmer movements (Benedict 1953; Muhm 2000; Shannon 1957) evolved into general farm organizations that took on a wider array of activities representing the economic and social interests of farmers and their communities (Knapp 1969). These are professional associations representing farmers on issues associated with the business of farming. Due to inherent marketing problems and chaotic conditions associated with the commercialization of agriculture emerging from subsistence farm production units, these professional associations of farmers embraced the idea of utilizing marketing co-ops to penetrate markets and to provide more coordination and services. They actively promoted and fostered the development of cooperatively owned businesses for acquiring needed inputs as well as for product marketing.

As more specialization in farming occurred in the post–World War II era, farmers also affiliated along commodity lines in another type of professional association. Two basic forms of group action, representing the economic interests of farm operators and their farm firms, emerged: (1) farmers' professional associations, and (2) co-ops (Emelianoff 1942; Hibbard 1921; Knapp 1969) (Figure 10.1).

Approaches to cooperative marketing evolved in two distinct forms: horizontal and vertical. Horizontal approaches involved the assembly, transport, and grading of raw commodities and livestock to shipping points where they were sold to buyers or processors (Breimyer 1965). Capital requirements of these commodity marketing co-ops were relatively low, but served an important role in market coordination and in the development of critical mass for negotiating price terms and supplying greater volumes to the market on an orderly basis.

Instances of vertical cooperative marketing also became widely practiced in processing raw commodities into value-added products such as making butter or cheese from milk, milling feed or flour from grain, and slaughtering livestock. Requirements for processing, storage, and distribution of

Figure 10. 1 **Structure of Farmer Organizations**

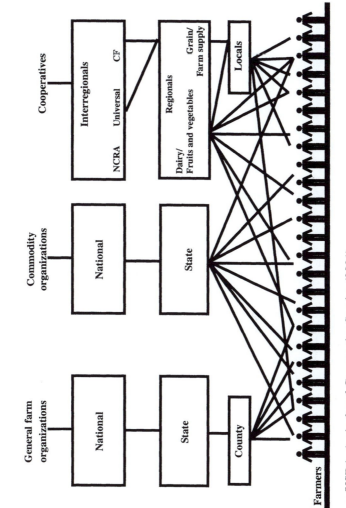

Source: USDA, Agricultural Cooperative Service (2001).

products in vertically coordinated systems commanded much higher levels of capitalization and management structure than were required under horizontal marketing arrangements.

For the most part, marketing efforts, both horizontal and vertical, initially took place in locally organized co-ops. It soon became apparent that local co-ops exhibited a deficiency in purchasing strength and/or marketing capabilities that was not too different from those encountered by the farmers themselves as individual marketers. Linkages among local co-ops were, therefore, formed at the regional level through a federated structure as a means of overcoming this deficiency. Regional co-ops were able to aggregate volumes from local creameries, elevators, and shipping associations, thereby providing access for farmers to distant markets and also offering greater strength in pricing larger quantities of products assembled for sale (Nourse 1922, 1928). They also could offer purchasing and merchandising services to locally owned co-ops and to farmer members. A farmer-owned cooperative system emerged, therefore, in several commodity sectors and regions, extending in some countries to the national level. This structure was subsequently replicated in other farmer-owned service organizations such as rural electric, farm credit, and other forms of cooperative enterprise.

In order for farmers to sustain the orientation and operation of cooperatively owned businesses, a unique interrelationship of professional organizations in agriculture, organized on both a cross-commodity (general farm) and commodity basis, and the cooperative businesses themselves had to be developed. Together, they represent a bundle of collective action utilized by farm operators that meets their specific functional and structural needs, and these actions must be understood in their totality as an interrelated system over time. Each basic organizational type has a unique structure and functional role performed on behalf of the farm operators and the farm firm.

Interrelations of Group Action Forms in the Marketing Process

Several examples illustrate the close interrelationship and operations of these forms of group action in marketing farm products. For purposes of illustration, brief descriptions of this "model" of collective marketing will be drawn from California, the Midwest, and from European settings.

The California Model

One of the best examples of an organizational interrelationship that maximizes producer influence in marketing is in the California specialty crops industry. The establishment and growth of many co-ops in the region was influenced by Aaron Sapiro, a California attorney who worked in the State Division of Agricultural Marketing and became a nationally recognized organizer and cooperative advocate in both the United States and Canada (Larsen and Erdman 1962). He argued for organizing farmers in direct-membership regional commodity co-ops that became dominant in their respective sectors (Sapiro 1920). These co-ops engaged in orderly commodity marketing and hired professional management to run them.

The outcome of these organizational efforts has been the establishment of dominant regional co-ops in each sector such as Sun Maid in raisins (Woeste 1998), Blue Diamond in almonds, Diamond Growers in walnuts, Sunsweet in dried plums, and Sunkist in citrus fruit. These are marketing co-ops that have succeeded in establishing brand-name products and developed markets worldwide for fresh and value-added products.

Not anticipated by Sapiro was that two closely interconnected forms of collective action in pricing and marketing of crops would emerge in the region, comprising what I refer to here as the California Model. Growers not only organized successful commodity marketing co-ops but they also organized cooperative bargaining associations that negotiate farm gate contract terms with investor-owned processors and marketing co-ops purchasing non-member tonnage on the open market. Growers have often maintained dual membership in both types of organizations (Figure 10.2). The reason is that they highly value the presence of a professional commodity association negotiating the best possible farm gate prices under the supply and demand conditions facing the industry (Bunje 1980).

At least twenty-nine cooperative bargaining associations have been identified, including those operating in California such as the Apricot Producers of California, the California Canning Peach Association, the California Pear Association, the California Tomato Growers Association, the Olive Growers Council, the Prune Bargaining Association, and the Raisin Bargaining Association (Iskow and Sexton 1990).

The negotiated price for moving a product to processors effectively becomes a benchmark or reference value of farm gate prices for the entire industry. On the one hand, assuming effective organizational strength and negotiating prowess by the bargaining association, growers selling to corporate processors have the benefit of receiving the best prices possible. On the other hand, growers who are members of marketing co-ops also have a better gauge to measure the performance of their value-added cooperative marketing endeavors by knowing the industrywide farm gate prices established through collective bargaining.

During periods of industry restructuring, cooperative bargaining associations have also been instrumental in encouraging members to organize

Figure 10.2 **A Systems Perspective of Alternative Forms of Economic Organization in Agriculture**

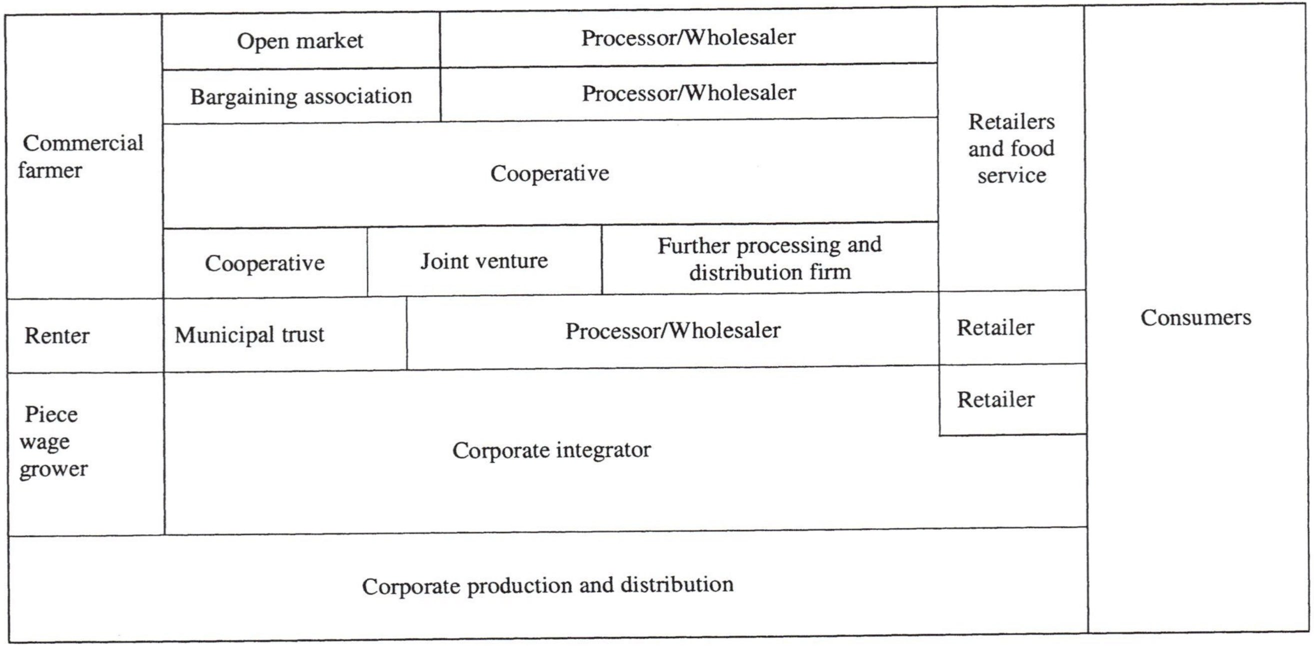

				Consumers
Commercial farmer	Open market	Processor/Wholesaler	Retailers and food service	
	Bargaining association	Processor/Wholesaler		
	Cooperative			
	Cooperative	Joint venture	Further processing and distribution firm	Retailer
Renter	Municipal trust	Processor/Wholesaler	Retailer	
Piece wage grower	Corporate integrator			
	Corporate production and distribution			

marketing co-ops, as was the case when the California Pear Association helped foster Pacific Coast Producers in 1971 when U.S. Products decided to terminate its tree fruit packing plant. Growers provided a home for their raw products by assuming cooperative ownership. As another example, leaders in the California Canning Peach Association raised serious questions about management practices in the failing Tri Valley Growers cooperative in the late 1990s. The combination of representation in both cooperative bargaining associations and marketing co-ops has increased the marketing power and organizational effectiveness of California farmers.

The Midwest Experience

Broad farm organizations, dating from the early organizational activities of the National Grange, National Farmers' Union, and American Farm Bureau Federation and their state affiliates, have each been key in advocating and fostering the development of local and regional marketing co-ops throughout the Midwestern and Plains states (Knapp 1969, 1973). Some, such as Agway, CHS Cooperatives, Growmark, and livestock marketing co-ops, can directly trace their origins to the catalytic roles of these or other professional associations (Keillor 2000; Muhm 1998). Evidence that this interrelationship continues can be found in the representation of farm organization nominees on the board of directors of regional co-ops like Growmark and Southern States, the active role of the Farmers' Union in promoting organization of new co-ops, and the scrutiny that these organizations provide to both local and regional cooperative operations.

Professional associations represent an outside forum for debate and guidance to practices utilized by co-ops. At the state level, both the Farm Bureau and Farmers' Union have actively questioned the practices of some co-ops engaging in business activities that are perceived by members as directly competing with their farm operations. Recent practices raised as an issue include engagement in hog production and custom farming services ("Co-op resolution . . ." 2001).

Similarly, commodity associations such as those representing corn, wheat, and pork growers have been among the most active forms of professional associations at the state and national levels in fostering New Generation Cooperatives in the 1990s. Many new businesses in the ethanol, bakery, pasta, and meat industries can attribute their presence as co-ops to the proactive role of commodity associations (Torgerson, Reynolds, and Gray 1998).

In Michigan, Public Law 344 provides for an accreditation process through which the state Department of Agriculture certifies a bargaining agent for producer groups that apply to operate under the law (Shaffer 1979; Stuckman

1976). The Michigan Agricultural Cooperative Marketing Association (MACMA), bargaining affiliate of the Michigan Farm Bureau, is the negotiating agent for processing apples and asparagus. In the past, it also negotiated for tart cherries and cabbage. The farm gate prices it negotiates apply to investor-owned as well as cooperative marketers.

Sequel in European Countries

Europe has a long history of encouraging cooperative marketing and interconnected working relationships that extend to the European Union (EU) level. Before the Common Agricultural Policy was implemented, national general farm organizations—especially in Northern Europe—engaged in formal price negotiations with sanctioned governmental boards that effectively established price levels for various commodity sectors (Torgerson 1971). Marketing co-ops, which in a number of cases handled up to 100 percent of given commodities, carried out their value-added processing and distribution functions through strongly developed federated systems. As in the United States, however, a clear trend in the past thirty years has been for farmers to hold direct membership in regional or national marketing co-ops rather than rely on federated marketing systems (Bekkum and Van Dijk 1997; Utterstrom 1980).

Marketing co-ops have recently merged across national borders in a few instances. The complementary and synergistic roles of professional farm associations and marketing co-ops represent a formidable market power position on behalf of members. Europe's development of effective elected farm leadership to serve as spokespersons for these organized systems has surpassed that of other countries throughout the world.

An understanding of the interrelations of basic organizational forms in the marketing process is key to a more holistic approach to agricultural marketing and achieving benefits for members. The parallels in these forms of group action across continents are striking. Practitioners and researchers of collective action in agriculture must further document how the interface of these forms occurs, how conflicts are resolved, and how strategies for providing maximum effectiveness in representing the economic interests of the farm firm are achieved. This area of inquiry promises to yield important insights for the development of new marketing mechanisms while further strengthening the legal foundations for group action in agriculture (Bunje 1980).

Pooling as a Basic Cooperative Practice

A basic but often not understood concept of cooperative marketing is the practice of pooling products sold (Bakken and Schaars 1937). The theory, as advocated by Sapiro, is the assembly of large quantities of graded products that are sold under the direction of a pool manager to the collective benefit of all pool participants. This practice overcomes the typical situation of farmers individually dumping products on the market all at one time during peak harvest periods.

Producers benefit from the clout associated with the development of critical mass as an influence in the marketplace, and the benefit of professional management selling the products into the market at intervals that maximize returns. Pool returns are an average of the sales from the pool over a discrete time period and typically result in a higher payment to participating members than if they had sold their crops or livestock independently.

A fundamental requirement of effective pool management is the maintenance of strict quality standards within defined pools, thereby offsetting the tendency of some farmers to sell their premium output independently and only sell lower-grade products through a pool. Pooled marketing requires constant producer education to understand the benefits of collective marketing and the intricacies of pool management. It is clearly a form of risk management by sharing collectively the risks and rewards of marketing.

Cooperative Marketing as a Dimension of Farm Policy

Cooperative marketing is a dimension of farm policy with strong support in law and from Congress and the Executive. The degree of public support can vary over time depending upon the well-being of the farm community, philosophical orientation toward individual versus collective action in the body politic, and on the performance of various types of group action over time.

Public Goods Aspects

A basic rationale for policy support is the public goods aspects of cooperative marketing. The public good aspects appear in several forms, including competition enhancement, countervailing power, improvement in quality measures, and market orientation that translates into less reliance upon governmental programs. Competition enhancement is often associated with the competitive yardstick school of cooperative thought introduced by Nourse (Knapp 1979). Since farmers make production decisions individually and co-ops generally do not control those decisions, co-ops bring more to the market and pay more to farmers than would otherwise be true in their absence (Helmberger 1964).

Empirical testing of the competitive yardstick theory by Rogers and Petraglia (1994) has shown that agricultural co-ops were associated with improved market performance in the food-manufacturing sector. Mueller, Helmberger, and Paterson (1987) provide further analysis in evaluating a Federal Trade Commission case against Sunkist Growers. Findings that co-ops as a dimension of market structure are a pro-competitive force add credence to farmers' continued use of their limited antitrust exemption as a part of marketing policy under the Capper–Volstead Act. Co-ops enable members to help correct market imperfections while improving their returns and improving consumer welfare by keeping the market system honest.

Co-ops also provide members with a countervailing force in the marketplace to monopolistic purchasing power by processors and food distributors that tend to dominate the marketing channel. Cooperative bargaining associations allow farmers to negotiate with these buyers on a collective basis and improve price and terms of trade as a result. The California Model described earlier provides important advances when supported by good-faith bargaining, dispute resolution, and enforcement provisions under state law that are perceived as a forerunner of national improvements in farm bargaining legislation (Marcus 1994).

Marketing co-ops enable farmers to jointly match buyer needs in the supply chain and, in some cases, to partner with them. Co-ops have led the industry in establishing grades and standards in virtually all industries. This fact has brought improved product recognition for items produced due to adherence to quality standards, raising industry performance and consumer acceptance as a whole while at the same time remunerating more to producers.

Finally, market orientation by co-ops has built capacity for farmers to access markets and deal with marketing problems in a pragmatic fashion. Marketing instruments such as federal marketing orders and agreements have been used decisively for industry self-regulation in bringing more orderly marketing conditions to various sectors (Breimyer 1965). As the cooperative marketing wherewithal has strengthened, farmers benefit by receiving more from the marketplace rather than from relying on federal programs to enhance income.

Public Policy Instruments

Several policies established at the national level have augmented the practice of cooperation among farmers throughout the country. These include anti-trust statutes, tax policies, the federal marketing order program, cooperative technical services, the Agricultural Fair Practices Act of 1967, and loan and grant programs.

Section 6 of the Clayton Act of 1914, the Capper–Volstead Act of 1922, and the Cooperative Marketing Act of 1926 each provides protection from prosecution under the anti-trust laws to farmers who are organized for marketing purposes through co-ops. Safeguards against abuse include that they do not use predatory or coercive practices and that the Secretary of Agriculture is authorized to determine that they do not unduly enhance prices. To qualify for these protections, the farmers must be organized for the mutual benefit of members as producers and conform to one or both of the following requirements: (1) that no member is allowed more than one vote because of the amount of stock or membership capital owned, or (2) the association does not pay dividends on stock or membership capital in excess of 8 percent per year. Furthermore, the association may not deal in products of nonmembers in an amount greater in value than those it handles for members.

While the Clayton Act only refers to nonstock associations, the Capper–Volstead Act covers both stock and nonstock co-ops. The Cooperative Marketing Act of 1926 further provides that price and other information can be exchanged between farmers and different levels in federated farmer cooperative systems, such as between local co-ops that are member-owners of regional co-ops.

The Cooperative Marketing Act of 1926 also provides for a unit in the USDA to conduct research, collect statistics, provide technical assistance, develop educational materials, and assist producers interested in organizing new co-ops—all aimed at helping to improve farm income through collective action (Rasmussen 1991). This group of services is unique throughout the world because it emphasizes farmers helping themselves as a matter of national policy through cooperative action. The agency carries out no regulatory functions, as do governmental bodies known as "cooperative registrars" in other countries. Assistance to co-ops has also been provided historically through the cooperative extension service at the county, state, and national levels.

The Agricultural Marketing Agreements Act of 1937 sanctions increased industry self-regulation by farmers organized through cooperative associations and the government to market on an orderly basis. In many respects, it codifies the marketing approach advocated by Sapiro. It enables commodity co-ops to promulgate regulations through marketing orders, providing the force of law for such things as uniform pricing of milk according to use to all handlers in the dairy industry, and for managing reserve pools, research, and promotion programs to regulate movement of products into the marketplace in a more orderly fashion. The authorization for farmers to initiate or vote out such orders and agreements clearly sanctions group action in marketing perishable farm-produced crops, livestock products, and selected commodities.

Another landmark piece of legislation is the Agricultural Fair Practices Act of 1967 (Torgerson 1970). It recognizes the need to allow farmers to join together voluntarily in cooperative organizations and declares that interference with this right is contrary to the public interest. It establishes six standards of fair practices required of handlers in their dealings in agricultural products. Besides being the first reaffirmation by Congress in many years of the policy support of group action by farmers, the law also represents step one in providing sanctions for negotiated pricing by producers through their associations.

The Internal Revenue Code provides that earnings generated from cooperative businesses are taxed once either at the co-op or the patron level (Frederick 1993). This single tax treatment means that cooperative margins on business done with or for patrons are not taxable to the co-op if they are distributed or allocated to patrons, based on a written obligation to do so, on the basis of business done with the co-op.

At the foundation of these rules is a recognition of the cooperative operating principle of providing service at cost as a user-owned and-controlled business. This places co-ops on a similar tax basis as partnerships and limited liability companies. Section 521 of the Internal Revenue Code provides for a certification process, often utilized by farmers organized into value-added marketing co-ops, that requires that all of the members of the co-op be producers, and that the co-op work with all producer customers on a patronage basis. The co-op is obligated to pay patronage to those few nonmember producers it may deal with in the same amount it pays to member-producers. This certification, and the subsequent maintenance of this status, allows a co-op to eliminate the risk of having the IRS determine some of its business activities to not be patronage-sourced activities and, thus, subject to state and federal tax at the entity level, which can run as high as 40 percent for net income exceeding $300,000.

Further encouragement for group action comes from loan guarantee and grant programs encouraging the development of value-added initiatives by producers. The 1996 Federal Agriculture Improvement and Reform (FAIR) Act includes an extension of the USDA Business and Industry loan guarantee program to producers purchasing stock in new value-added co-ops. A provision in the Risk Management Protection Act of 2000 provides value-added market development grants to agricultural producers, many organized through co-ops, to help defray the costs of feasibility studies and business plans as well as to provide working capital for start-up needs.

These dimensions of farm policy toward co-ops represent a significant authorization for farmers and ranchers to use collective action in marketing to further their economic interests. A continuing challenge is for them to take full advantage of the opportunities provided.

The Farm Program vs. Cooperative Marketing Dilemma

Farm programs initiated following the Great Depression of the 1930s have for more than 70 years sought to offer farmers more stability in incomes from farming through direct government payments, placing excess production in government-held stocks and making Section 32 food purchases of commodities in surplus for use in school lunch and other food programs. Given the propensity of production agriculture to out-produce its markets, low returns in markets for basic food and feed grains have been perpetually used to justify continuation of these programs as a way to maintain "family farms."

In the process, however, farm program payments have increasingly gone to approximately 150,000 production units throughout the United States, representing more than seventy percent of the total U.S. farm output. Many of these production units bear no resemblance to "family" operations. Mid-sized and small farms have received a disproportionately smaller amount of this public payment support. The Bush administration pointed out this disconnect in its recent report to Congress on farm policy principles as part of the debate over provisions of a 2002 farm bill, and has asked the rhetorical question of whether this continued level of direct payments to commercial-sized producers can continue to be justified as a matter of public policy (USDA 2001).

The critical issue is that the direct payments have historically served as an incentive to increase farm size and as a disincentive for producers to organize and generate income increasingly from the marketplace. Instead, they have relied on governmental price support programs as a major source of income, in some years representing one-third to one-half of the income generated in 2000, for example. This cushion of federal support has insulated producers from market forces to a degree and, therefore, made them less prone to use their collective tools of action in the marketplace.

The Price of Becoming Subservient to Governmental Programs

Becoming overly dependent upon governmental subsidies—often referred to as "farming the government"—without building markets for products can be a self-defeating strategy, as recently learned in several commodity sectors. Tobacco growers, for instance, relied upon quotas, auction markets, and storage of lower-quality leaf through farm program "cooperatives" rather than developing markets and end-product uses for their leaf through co-ops.

When major tobacco manufacturers recently decided to contract directly with growers rather than procuring through the auction warehouse system, many growers interpreted this as a direct assault on the tobacco program. They felt powerless in dealing with the powerful tobacco companies that offered contracts. The tobacco auction markets suddenly became obsolete, excess baggage, leaving some growers without a home for their product. Peanut growers, and growers of other traditional program crops face similar challenges because they did not develop an effective producer-owned marketing structure to protect their economic interests.

New Generation Cooperatives as a New Marketing Strategy

In an effort to gain more earnings from downstream marketing margins between the farm gate and consumers' ultimate purchases, farmers and ranchers have aggressively organized value-added marketing co-ops during the past three decades. This renewed interest in new marketing initiatives has often been popularized as "cooperative fever" and has resulted in the creation of New Generation Cooperatives (Patrie 1998).

A major influence in the development of marketing initiatives has been the catalytic work of commodity associations such as the National Pork Producers Council, the National Wheat Growers, the National Corn Growers, the Durum Growers Association, and sugar beet associations. Each represents a prime example of a professional association's role in promoting and fostering new cooperative development.

What distinguishes the new cooperative initiatives from the myriad of existing marketing co-ops are several features in organizational design and followed practices. The fervor, hard work, and excitement surrounding the creation of this new marketing structure has stimulated interest from other parts of the United States and from abroad. The ultimate test for this "model" of cooperative marketing is member benefits through performance results of the co-ops established and the sustainability of the organizational model over time. Recent evidence suggests that the advantages and limitations are all part of a learning experience in the creation of new dimensions of cooperative marketing.

Organizational Characteristics of New Generation and Open Membership Cooperatives

New Generation Cooperatives (NGCs) are distinguished from other co-ops in that equity investment is a prerequisite to establishing delivery rights to the NGC. These delivery rights are part of a producer marketing agreement (contract) that pools the delivery of products and links them to equity units purchased. If a member is unable to deliver the agreed-upon raw products, purchase of commodities is authorized by the NGC for undelivered contract obligations.

Delivery rights are allocated according to plant processing capacity. This fixes or closes membership at a level related to plant capacity. Delivery rights are in the form of equity shares that can be sold to other eligible producers at prices agreed to by the buyer and seller. The NGC's board of directors approves all stock transfers to ensure that they are held by eligible producers. The value of delivery rights (shares) may appreciate or depreciate in value depending upon the NGC's performance.

High levels of cash patronage refunds are issued annually to producers since they have substantial risk capital invested in the organization. Control of the organization is vested with members, usually on a one-person/one-vote basis. In some states, cooperative law permits voting on a proportional basis according to the number of shares held. Consideration for expansion of the number of delivery rights is often given to existing members before offering nonmembers an opportunity to buy into the organization.

These characteristics are often contrasted with those of traditional open membership co-ops. Up-front equity investment in many "open" membership co-ops has been less, with greater reliance placed upon the accumulation of equity through retention of a part of the annual earnings invested in the member's allocated account. Due to this method of accumulation, equity in open membership co-ops can tend to become out of balance between former and current member-users. To correct this situation, several marketing co-ops have adopted base capital plans to maintain equity in the hands of current users (Rathbone 1997).

While member marketing agreements are often used in open membership co-ops, they are not viewed as delivery rights. Members have usually been free to deliver all that they produce to the co-op. No active internal market for trading equity typically exists. According to state law, control has generally been on a one-person/one-vote basis.

Advantages of the New Generation Approach

A key advantage of the New Generation Cooperative Model (Torgerson 1999; 2001) is that substantial equity capital is raised at the outset of the new business. This obligation to capitalize is distributed equitably in proportion to future use of the marketing organization. This commitment of capital by members means that they have a keen interest in seeing that the business succeeds. Assuming the business is performing adequately, exiting members can sell their delivery rights to other producers at a value reflecting the NGC's performance. The existence of this internal market provides liquidity often not found in open membership co-ops. Moreover, the ability to sell appreciable delivery rights better meets a specific goal of farm operators, namely, the enhancement of the value of their farm enterprises in contrast to open membership co-ops that typically hold share values at par.

The allocation of delivery rights according to plant capacity places the NGC in a very market-oriented position in knowing that it is dealing with a discrete volume of product. As the market for the value-added product grows, more deliveries of raw product can be authorized through the issuance of additional delivery rights.

New value-added marketing initiatives make producers aware of market characteristics and what it takes to succeed. This education process is brought about through first studying the prospectus and, after investing, by participating in organizational deliberations, informational meetings, and leadership positions. The downstream market literacy of producers is, therefore, enhanced measurably by this type of collective action.

Cooperative value-added processing activity brings vitality to rural areas. The existence of a processing plant—in addition to providing producer members higher returns—creates jobs, helps build local community infrastructure, and provides for a multiplier effect in terms of local economic development (Trechter and King 2001). These combined benefits make NGCs, like open membership co-ops, an institutional development tool for revitalizing local communities and rural areas.

Limitations of the New Generation Cooperative Approach

While the idea of local ownership and control is one of the attributes leading to the formation of many NGCs, a limitation is that they may result in fragmented marketing in a food and agricultural distribution system that is becoming increasingly dominated by a few global firms. Many NGCs were started with the "small is beautiful" philosophy and have not met the test of sustainability as economic entities over time. This begs the question of whether the phenomenon of creating locally owned processing capacity is not running counter to the trend in purchasing behavior of many food distributors that actually want fewer, rather than more, suppliers.

Further, a potential exists that the NGCs will fall into the trap faced by the farmers themselves as individual marketers, namely, the presence of many isolated units making independent production decisions. Two unintended results can be (1) creating a buyer's market by virtue of fragmented selling by many NGCs, and (2) adding to unwanted industry production capacity by virtue of making production decisions in isolation that lead to overproducing the market.

Another factor concerns exclusivity, which can be both a strength and a weakness. To the extent that NGCs are only open to those who can afford high up-front capitalization investments, they are viewed as being more restrictive and not providing market access for all farm operators in the rural community. It is often argued that successful NGCs bid up land rents, prohibiting nonmember farmers from successfully renting land. The concept of a rising tide lifting all boats, as in open membership co-ops, does not exist. Closed membership co-ops, therefore, start from an organizational strategy that sociologists and those embracing a strong social philosophy of cooperation find objectionable from a community development perspective (Torgerson 2002).

The need for deep pockets in value-added processing businesses is another limitation. Even though NGCs are started by design with substantial up-front equity subscription, the launching of a new business is risky and can potentially implode before the business becomes solid. This is especially true when competing in an industry characterized by oligopsony, or relatively few dominant suppliers. New startups need the wherewithal to withstand the squeezing of margins by large firms that do not want entry into the marketplace by potential competitors—as experienced by ProGold's entry into the high fructose corn syrup industry. Similarly, the creation of a market for new products can be much costlier than first anticipated.

Finally, NGCs often find they must proceed beyond primary into further processing in order to achieve returns justified from investments in value-added activity. The ability and willingness of members to provide additional capital in each of these circumstances is required. Generally, co-ops can only grow as fast as and to the extent that members are willing to provide equity capital.

Practices Requiring Scrutiny

Several NGC practices have become problematic and are identified here to demonstrate how they conflict with operating on a sound cooperative basis. Some of these are interrelated.

1. *Ownership of Delivery Rights Outside of One's Own Production.* A former NGC decided to expand operations into a state that was not contiguous to it. Instead of selling delivery rights for supplying the new plant to producers surrounding it, many of the delivery rights were purchased by existing members in the distant state. This practice violates the basic tenants of operating on a cooperative basis, in which value is added to the production of one's own farming operation. Instead, it appears that return on investment was simply sought by processing someone else's raw commodities. This practice, as will be observed, is not too different from marketing co-ops' practice

of processing nonmembers' products instead of processing those under a marketing agreement with members.

2. *Off-market Purchases.* The provision for purchases "off the market" in NGCs was included because of the possibility of a seasonal drought, hailstorm, or disease problem that would make a member's delivery to fulfill the contractual obligation (delivery right) impossible. To keep the plant running at capacity, the NGC could purchase off the market in the member's name to keep operations going. In some situations, however, NGCs have made this a common practice, again losing the traceability of production from one's own farm through the co-op. This practice again smacks of operating more like an investor-owned firm (IOF) than a user-owned business.

3. *Leasing of Delivery Rights.* A recommended cooperative practice is that control should be vested in the hands of active producers. The 2001 payment-in-kind (PIK) program for sugar beet growers disclosed that many co-op members—especially older ones—had leased delivery rights to other producers. This presented many administrative problems for the USDA.

Program administration problems notwithstanding, the fact that delivery rights were leased shows that growers holding delivery rights while not actively producing themselves are doing so based on expected appreciation in value of those rights or for tax purposes regarding their estates. This property rights issue, not unlike farm program production quotas, requires active monitoring by boards of directors and needs policy direction. If direction is not provided, ownership in the co-op can end up in the hands of retirees rather than active producers. Further, a concentration on "delivery rights" can mask a significant problem when holders of the rights purchase from other producers for delivery to the co-op and, thus, essentially become the middlemen co-ops were designed to bypass.

4. *Splits Creating Shares That Exceed Production Capability.* Some successful NGCs have stock splits that create delivery rights exceeding members' capability of fulfilling without acquiring or renting more land. A board member of an NGC has suggested that this raises the need to find other ways of distributing earnings than simply through appreciable delivery rights. The point is well taken if high purchase prices preclude young farmers from becoming members; nevertheless, it leads to practices such as the leasing of delivery rights to other producers as previously addressed, or to inadequate reinvestment of capital in the co-op to keep it on the cutting edge of technology.

5. *Keeping Delivery Rights in the Hands of Active Producers.* Any time a property right is created that has value, a critical need exists to maintain it in the hands of active producers to preserve the "user-owned" character of a cooperative business. This is necessary to preclude ownership in the business by outside investors who have no interest in farming, and also to sidestep the

dissipation of shares among family members in settling estates. NGCs need well-defined board policies to preclude this type of outcome, which can potentially destroy the very character of the organization as a co-op.

Other practices requiring scrutiny by all co-ops are as follows:

- making fixed-term market obligations for final products when the market for the raw commodity becomes short, thus causing a wide price disparity for producers and losses for the business;
- hiring managers from outside of the industry who do not know the intricacies of the market;
- sourcing equity capital outside of memberships, resulting in conflicting goals and fiduciary responsibilities—it is difficult to serve two or more masters;
- board members micromanaging the business rather than devoting more time to strategic planning;
- engaging in large amounts of nonmember business;
- allowing the board chairman to also serve as chief executive officer, thus creating a lack of trust within the membership.

Correcting faulty practices in the NGC, and in the open membership co-ops, will go a long way toward enhancing their ability to survive and flourish, as well as to maintain their character as cooperative businesses. The New Generation "model" of vertical cooperation must be considered a work in progress that requires continual fine tuning. Much momentum and energy continues to be expended in developing opportunities for farmers to increase their incomes through value-added marketing. The preservation of farmer control of the marketing process and the opportunity to capture marketing margins will continue to be the main motivators for pursuing this strategy.

Summary

The development of effective forms of group action by farmers in marketing their products continues to be one of the biggest challenges facing the farm community as concentration in food manufacturing and distribution continues to grow. To fulfill their goals of income enhancement, more control over marketing conditions and terms of trade, and retaining their independence as autonomous business units, farmers have utilized professional associations and co-ops as two basic organizational types to represent their interests in the marketplace and before public bodies that influence their businesses. Pressure group theory presents a method for analyzing the interrelationships among these group action forms and the possibility of bringing a better understanding of how they are used structurally and functionally by farmers.

The California model of representation offers an excellent example of how producers can benefit from establishing farm gate prices through negotiations as well as achieving value-added earnings through effective cooperative marketing. Organizational efforts through a combination of both the horizontal and vertical levels holds the potential to better meet farm operators' goals. Furthermore, the interaction of these organizational types ensures that farmers continue to be the primary beneficiaries of group action initiatives established in their behalf.

NGCs will evolve as lessons and insights are gleaned from the first generation's experiences. Their contribution is in providing a more market-oriented approach for farmers; however, coordination between these co-ops to adopt an industry perspective and long-term strategic mission will add to their effectiveness. NGCs also represent a strategy for strengthening incentives for member commitment and control that have been deficient in some traditional co-ops. Yet, a few of the NGCs have at the same time created new disincentives for user-owner involvement and control. NGCs are at an early stage of the learning curve on how to apply principles and practices that expand opportunities while preserving the capture of benefits to active farmer-members.

Growth strategies through acquisition and conversion of IOFs to farmer-owned and controlled co-ops through new membership and through the organization of farmers to negotiate contract terms with corporate firms are each areas requiring further research and public attention. Important to this process is the assessment of new sanctions and institutional mechanisms that will strengthen farmers' hands in the marketplace as they traverse a rapidly changing food and agricultural system.

Acknowledgments

Appreciation is expressed to Don Frederick, Andy Jermolowicz, and Bruce Reynolds, who reviewed and commented on earlier drafts of this chapter.

References

Bakken, Henry, and Marvin Schaars. 1937. *Economics of Cooperative Marketing*. New York: McGraw-Hill.

Bekkum, Onno-Frank, and Gert Van Dijk. 1997. *Agriculture Co-operatives in the European Union*. Assen, The Netherlands: Van Gorcum.

Benedict, Murray. 1953. *Farm Policies of the United States, 1790–1950*. New York: Twentieth Century Fund.

Breimyer, Harold. 1965. *Individual Freedom and the Economic Organization of Agriculture*. Urbana: University of Illinois Press.

Bunje, Ralph. 1980. *Cooperative Farm Bargaining and Price Negotiations* (Cooperative information report 26). Washington, DC: USDA, Agriculture Cooperative Service.

Commons, John R. 1950. *The Economics of Collective Action*. Madison: University of Wisconsin Press.

———. 1957. *Legal Foundations of Capitalism*. Madison: University of Wisconsin Press.

"Co-op Resolution Raises Spirited Debates." 2001. *Farm Week* (Illinois Farm Bureau), December 10, 1.

Emelianoff, Ivan. 1942. *Economic Theory of Cooperation*. Ann Arbor, MI: Edward Brothers.

Frederick, Donald. 1993. *Income Tax Treatment of Cooperatives* (Cooperative information reports 44, parts 1–5). Washington, DC: USDA, Agricultural Cooperative Service.

Galbraith, John Kenneth. 1957. *American Capitalism: The Concept of Countervailing Power*. London: Hamish Hamilton.

Helmberger, Peter. 1964. "Cooperative Enterprise as a Structural Dimension of Farm Markets." *Journal of Farm Economics* 46: 603–617.

Hibbard, Benjamin. 1921. *Marketing Agricultural Products*. New York: D. Appleton.

Iskow, Julia, and Richard Sexton. 1990. "Status of Cooperative Bargaining for Fruits and Vegetables in the United States." In *Agricultural Bargaining: Issues for the 1990s* (ACS services report 28), 8–19. Washington, DC: USDA, Agricultural Cooperative Service.

Keillor, Steven. 2000. *Cooperative Commonwealth: Co-ops in Rural Minnesota 1859–1939*. St. Paul: Minnesota Historical Society Press.

Knapp, Joseph. 1969. *The Rise of American Cooperative Enterprise 1620–1920*. Danville, IL: Interstate.

———. 1973. *The Advance of American Cooperative Enterprise 1920–1945*. Danville, IL: Interstate.

———. 1979. *Edwin G. Nourse, Economist for the People*. Danville, IL: Interstate.

Larsen, Grace, and Henry Erdman. 1962. "Aaron Sapiro: Genius of Farm Cooperative Promotion." *Mississippi Valley Historical Review* 49 (September): 242–268.

Marcus, Gerald. 1994. *Farm Bargaining Cooperatives: Group Action, Greater Gain* (ACS research report 130). Washington, DC: USDA, Agricultural Cooperative Service.

Muhm, Don. 1998. *More than a Farm Organization: Farmers Union in Minnesota*. Rochester, MN: Lone Oak Press.

———. 2000. *The NFO—A Farm Belt Rebel: A History of the National Farmers Organization*. Rochester, MN: Lone Oak Press.

Mueller, Willard, Peter Helmberger, and T. Paterson. 1987. *The Sunkist Case*. Lexington: Lexington Books.

Nourse, Edwin G. 1922. "Economic Philosophy of Cooperation." *American Economic Review* 12 (December): 577–597.

———. 1928. "The Evolving Idea of Cooperation in the United States." *American Cooperation* 1: 13–23.

Olson, Mancur. 1965. *The Logic of Collective Action*. Cambridge, MA: Harvard University Press.

Patrie, William. 1998. *Creating "Co-op Fever": A Rural Developer's Guide to Forming Cooperatives* (Cooperative service report 54). Washington, DC: USDA, Rural Business-Cooperative Service.

Rasmussen, Wayne. 1991. *Farmers, Cooperatives and USDA: A History of Agricultural Cooperative Service* (Agricultural information bulletin 621). Washington, DC: USDA.

Rathbone, Robert. 1997. *Managing Your Cooperative's Equity* (Cooperative information report 56). Washington, DC: USDA, Rural Business-Cooperative Service.

Rogers, Richard, and Lisa Petraglia. 1994. "Agricultural Cooperatives and Market Performance in Food Manufacturing." *Journal of Agricultural Cooperation* 9: 1–12.

Sapiro, Aaron. 1920. *Cooperative Marketing*. Chicago: American Farm Bureau Federation.

Shaffer, James. 1979. "Some Arguments from the Testimony of the Michigan Agricultural Marketing and Bargaining Act Trial." In *Proceedings of the 23rd National Conference of Bargaining and Marketing Cooperatives* (ESCS-65), 22–28. Washington, DC: USDA, Economics, Statistics and Cooperatives Service.

Shannon, Fred. 1957. *American Farmers' Movements*. Princeton, NJ: Van Nostrand.

Stuckman, N. 1976. "Issues Emerging from the Michigan Experience: How the Public Views Agricultural Bargaining." In *Proceedings of the 20th National Conference of Bargaining and Marketing Cooperatives* (FCS special report 23), 83–88. Washington, DC: USDA, Farmer Cooperative Service.

Torgerson, Randall E. 1968. "The Cooperative Systems Approach to Improving Farm Incomes." Unpublished dissertation, University of Wisconsin–Madison.

———. 1970. *Producer Power at the Bargaining Table: A Case Study of the Legislative Life of S.109*. Columbia: University of Missouri Press.

———. 1971. *Farm Bargaining*. Oslo: Landbruksforlaget.

———. 1999. *A Critical Look at New Generation Cooperatives*. Presentation to the National and Pacific Coast Bargaining Conference, Reno, NV.

———. 2001. "A Critical Look at New-generation Cooperatives." *Rural Cooperatives* 68, no. 1: 15–19

———. 2002. *Strengths and Weaknesses of the Cooperative Movement*. Talk presented at the Marketplace of Ideas, January 9, Grand Forks, ND.

Torgerson, Randall E., Bruce J. Reynolds, and Thomas W. Gray. 1998. "Evolution of Cooperative Thought, Theory and Purpose." *Journal of Cooperatives* 13: 1–20.

Trechter, David, and Robert King. 2001. *The Impact of New Generation Cooperatives on Their Communities* (Research report 177). Washington, DC: USDA, Rural Business-Cooperative Service.

U.S. Department of Agriculture (USDA). 2001. *Food and Agricultural Policy: Taking Stock for the New Century*. Washington, DC: USDA, Office of the Secretary.

Utterstrom, Carl. 1980. *Organizational Vision, Ideologies and the Cooperative Myth: A Study of Mergers Among Farmer Cooperatives in Sweden*. Uppsala: Swedish University of Agricultural Sciences.

Woeste, Victoria. 1998. *The Farmer's Benevolent Trust*. Chapel Hill: University of North Carolina Press.

11

Measuring the Economic Impact of Producer Cooperatives

F. Larry Leistritz

Expanded processing of agricultural products in rural areas has been widely pursued as a strategy for rural economic development. Cooperatively owned processing facilities provide a way for producers to integrate forward and capture potential profits from processing and marketing their products. In addition, by adding value to farm products before they leave the area, new processing plants can create new employment opportunities and generate economic spinoffs in rural areas that have experienced economic stagnation or decline as a result of the long-term trends of farm consolidation (Leistritz 2000).

Consequently, the expansion of agricultural processing in rural areas usually receives broad-based support from commodity groups, rural development interests, and state political leaders (Walzer, Merrett, and Holmes 1999). This chapter examines the contribution of producer cooperatives to economic and community development in the areas where they are sited. First, the basic concepts and methods of economic impact analysis will be briefly reviewed. Then, the potential contributions of agriculture and agriculturally linked businesses to local economic development are examined, with an emphasis on the economic contribution of new value-added processing plants. Finally, specific issues associated with estimating the local economic contribution of a new producer co-op will be addressed.

Concepts and Methods of Economic Impact Analysis

The purpose of economic impact analysis is to estimate the changes in an area's level of economic activity (often measured by changes in employment, income, and gross receipts or value added by specific economic sectors) that might result from a specific project, program, or policy. The conceptual basis for economic impact analysis is *export base theory* (also known as *economic base theory*). A fundamental concept of export base theory is that an area's economy can be divided into two broad types of economic units. The *basic sector* is defined as those firms that sell goods and services to markets outside the area. The revenue received by these firms for their exports of goods and services is termed *basic income*. The remainder of the area's economy consists of those firms that supply goods and services to customers within the area. These firms are collectively referred to as the *nonbasic sector*, or sometimes as the *local trade and service* sector (Leistritz and Murdock 1981).

A second key concept in export base theory is that the level of nonbasic activity in an area is uniquely determined by the level of basic activity, and a given change in the level of basic activity will bring about a predictable change in the level of nonbasic activity. This relationship is known as the *multiplier effect*. Thus, export base theory emphasizes external demand for the products of the basic sector as the principal force determining change in the level of economic activity (Leistritz 1998).

The basis for the multiplier effect is the interdependence (or *linkages*) of the basic and nonbasic sectors in an economy. As the basic sector expands, it requires more inputs (e.g., labor and supplies). Some of the inputs are purchased from local firms and households. As firms in the nonbasic sector expand their sales to the basic sector, they, too, must purchase more inputs, and so on. Increased wages and salaries paid to labor and management by the basic sector, together with similar payments by the nonbasic sector, lead to increases in the incomes of area households.

Some of the additional income is spent locally for goods and services, some is saved, and some leaves the area as payments for imported goods and services (or as additional tax payments to government). These funds that flow out of the local area are termed *leakages*. To the extent that additional income is spent locally for goods and services, the output of local firms is increased and additional cycles of input purchases and expenditures result. This cycle of spending and responding within the local economy is the basis for the multiplier effect (Leistritz and Murdock 1981).

Export base theory is a subset of regional income theory. The regional income equation, which forms the basis for export base theory, is as follows:

$$Y = (E - M) + X' \qquad [1]$$

where:

Y = net area product or income; X' = area exports (assumed to be exogenously determined); E = expenditures; and M = imports.

Equation 1 simply states that area income is equal to domestic spending plus exports. Thus, exports are treated as the only source of autonomous demand for an area's products. The relationship presented in Equation 1 can be restated as follows:

$$Y = a - b + X' / 1 - (e - m) \qquad [2]$$

where:

e = marginal propensity to spend;
m = marginal propensity to import;
b = value of imports when $Y = 0$;
a = value of expenditures when $Y = 0$;
Y and X' are as previously defined.

The values of e, m, a, and b are assumed to be constant in a given area in the short run, although their values may vary substantially among areas. Thus, the level of exports (or basic income) determines the area's total income and output.

The effect of an additional dollar of exports on area income is shown by taking the derivative of Equation 2 with respect to X':

$$dY/dX' = 1/1 - (e - m) = K \qquad [3]$$

Because the value of $(e - m)$ is expected to lie between 0 and 1, the value of K in Equation 3 is expected to exceed 1. K is frequently termed the *export multiplier.*

The magnitude of the multiplier effect is determined by the proportion of a given dollar of additional income that is spent locally. High multiplier values are associated with high levels of local spending, which, in turn, imply a diversified, relatively self-sufficient economy. Leakages reduce the local multiplier effect (Richardson 1972).

When estimating the magnitude of secondary economic effects (resulting from the multiplier process) for a specific project in a given area, most analysts employ either an *export base model* (employment or income multipliers), or an *input–output (I–O) model* (Leistritz and Murdock 1981). In recent years, input–output models have been applied with increased frequency in impact assessment (Leistritz 1998).

Two reasons for the increased use of I–O models are (1) this technique provides more detailed impact estimates (e.g., business volume and employment by sector) than other approaches and can better reflect differences in expenditure patterns among projects; and (2) databases and data management systems are now available that enable development of I–O models tailored to local conditions but based largely or totally on secondary data sources. Commonly used I–O models of this type include IMPLAN, RIMS, and REMI (Leistritz 1998). Recent evaluations of these and similar I–O models are provided by Crihfield and Campbell (1991) and Rickman and Schwer (1995).

Economic Contribution of Agriculturally Linked Enterprises

Depressed agricultural commodity prices have created major financial hardships for many farm and ranch operators (Drabenstott and Smith 1996). Some farm families have been able to supplement their incomes through off-farm work, while others seek to increase their volume of production by farming more acres. Farm expansion is typically limited by the amount of farmland available, however, as well as by individual operators' reluctance or inability to finance expansion with borrowed capital. Off-farm employment opportunities may also be quite limited in agriculturally dependent rural areas because employment growth in these areas has generally been slower than in the nation's metro centers. In some cases, nonfarm employment has actually declined (Drabenstott and Smith 1996; Johnson 2001).

From a rural development perspective, the continuing trend of farm consolidation has meant there are fewer farm families to support small towns that serve as trade centers for agricultural areas. In addition, the large-volume farm operators that remain appear more likely to bypass local input suppliers, dealing directly with suppliers located in larger, more distant regional centers. These large-volume producers also may bypass local elevators to take advantage of slightly higher prices available at subterminal elevators or in other more distant markets (Barkema and Drabenstott 1996). As production of many major agricultural commodities becomes a high-volume, low-margin business, both producers and rural communities face severe challenges.

Producer co-ops offer a promising alternative for both farmers and rural communities (Merrett and Walzer 2001). For farmers, the co-ops offer an opportunity for them to integrate forward and participate in the processing and marketing of their products. This can be especially attractive because, on average, the returns in food processing typically exceed those in production of major crop and livestock commodities by a substantial margin (Williams and Merrett 2001).

While many processing co-ops require a substantial initial investment from producer-members, the potential returns may be several times those that would be expected from the investments needed to expand the farm. For example, prospective members of the Dakota Growers Pasta Company in North Dakota were required to invest a minimum of nearly $6,000 and commit at least 1,500 bushels of durum wheat for processing each year, making the average initial investment in this co-op nearly $12,000; however, the members have since received annual dividends of up to $1.00 per share (compared to an initial share cost of $3.90), which reflects the potential returns from a successful processing venture (Leistritz 2000). The members also have benefited from appreciation in the value of their shares.

Golden Oval

The Golden Oval co-op of Renville, Minnesota, offers another example of the benefits from a successful value-added venture (Holmes, Walzer, and Merrett 2000). This project was initiated by a local co-op elevator—Co-op Country Farmers Elevator—in an effort to add value to its members' corn. Shares initially sold at $3.50 per share, with each share carrying the right and obligation to deliver one bushel of corn each year. Golden Oval now has 411 members who deliver corn to feed 2 million laying hens.

In 1998, the members received a value-added payment of $1.58 per bushel for their corn, in addition to an average market price of $2.19. Thus, the members' payment (share of the co-op's profits) represented a premium of 72 percent over market prices. Alternatively, members received a return of 45 percent on their initial investment ($3.50 per share). The success of Golden Oval has been reflected in share prices. Shares are reported to have sold for up to $5.42; this increase in value has resulted in a more positive balance sheet for investors (Buschette 2000).

Successful value-added processing ventures also can provide substantial benefits to the communities where they are located. For example, Golden Oval employs approximately eighty workers in its Renville facility, where 2 million laying hens are housed in sixteen barns. Eggs leaving the laying barns travel by conveyor through a washing, breaking, and processing system, and within six hours, the liquid egg product is typically loaded on a tanker truck for shipment to customers. Golden Oval's expenditures within the local area amount to about $14 million annually, including payroll, shareholder payments, feed, supplies, and other operating expenses (Holmes et al. 2000). The local economic contribution of Golden Oval, together with those of several other value-added processors located in the Renville area, is credited with helping Renville maintain a healthy retail and service sector.

Dakota Growers Pasta Company

The Dakota Growers Pasta Company provides another example of the community benefits that can result from a successful producer co-op. Construction of the plant began in 1992 at a site near Carrington, North Dakota. Since beginning operations, the company's annual growth rate of 38 percent made it one of the five largest pasta producers in the nation by the late 1990s. The plant currently employs about 280 workers, roughly 13 percent of the total jobs in Foster County. Local leaders report that the plant draws workers from a forty–mile radius and that the advent of the plant marked the beginning of a new era in the community—a period characterized by residents' renewed belief in the community's future. This change in community attitude has been manifested in a willingness to invest in the community, including the local government making infrastructure improvements, business people improving their business places, and homeowners refurbishing their houses (Leistritz and Sell 2000).

Rather than leading to a major influx of workers and families, the Dakota Growers plant has stabilized the local population. Carrington's population grew by one person from 1990 to 2000, after showing a 14 percent decline from 1980 to 1990 (Leistritz and Sell 2000). Many of the plant jobs have been filled by workers from the surrounding area, and these jobs often represent a second income for a household. Enough Dakota Growers workers have moved to Carrington, though, to stimulate local housing demand and enhance local housing values. The stronger housing market, in turn, has increased residents' willingness to renovate, refurbish, and upgrade their properties.

The local retail sector was stimulated by the advent of Dakota Growers. Carrington's total retail sales (adjusted for inflation) increased by 16 percent from 1990 to 1998, after suffering a decrease of 37 percent during the 1980s. Businesses that appear to have succeeded most in recent years include motels, grocery and convenience stores, service stations, drug and hardware stores, the lumber yard, and auto dealers. The town gained a new auto dealership and a new grocery store since Dakota Growers was built.

Most local services have experienced only moderate changes in demand, consistent with the plant's role in stabilizing the local population. School enrollment (grades K–12) increased by about seventy-five students, or 12 percent, from 1991 to 1994, but this increase served only to replace part of the enrollment that had been lost during the 1980s (Leistritz and Sell 2000). The plant has enhanced the school district tax base as it comes onto the tax rolls at 20 percent per year and, when fully taxed, it will contribute about $75,0000 per year in school tax revenue.

The decision to locate the Dakota Growers plant in Carrington was the culmination of a classic recruitment competition in which twenty-nine towns submitted bids. Carrington's offer included (1) developing an industrial park; (2) donating the land (within the park) for the plant site; (3) providing a five-year abatement of local property taxes, after which the plant enters the tax rolls at 20 percent per year; (4) developing a rail spur; and (5) providing water and sewer with a three–year abatement (no cost) followed by a graduated scale working up to full cost. The total cost of this incentive package was estimated at $1 million, but local leaders feel the investment has been well worth the cost (Leistritz and Sell 2000).

Effects on Markets and Prices

While both Golden Oval and Dakota Growers illustrate the effects of adding value to an existing crop (corn and durum wheat, respectively), some agricultural processing initiatives provide opportunities for farmers to produce new, higher-value products. In other cases, the advent of large-scale processing operations has produced a noticeable effect on local market prices, a benefit that is shared by all area producers and not just those who deliver to the processing plant.

An example of the economic impact of shifting to a higher-value crop is the advent of irrigated potato production in central North Dakota (Coon and Leistritz 2001). This development of the potato industry resulted from several years of work by a group of area farmers and agribusiness leaders. Irrigated potatoes were selected as the crop with the best potential, and a plant to process the crop into frozen french fries and similar products was central to the development plan.

The farmers initially planned to build and operate the plant as a closed co-op (New Generation Cooperative [NGC]), but they determined that the combined capital requirements to install irrigation, grow and store potatoes, and build the plant were beyond their capabilities. Aviko, a company based in the Netherlands, joined the project, and the plant began operations in 1996. The plant now has thirty-three contract growers supplying irrigated potatoes from about 15,000 acres.

In analyzing the regional impacts of the potato project, Coon and Leistritz (2001) addressed both the economic effects of the processing activity and those of the shift from dryland crop production to irrigated potatoes. The potato processing activity was estimated to result in about $33.4 million annually in increased economic activity within North Dakota, while potato production would add another $22 million. The production impacts arise from the fact that (1) irrigated crops require substantially higher levels of inputs than dryland crops, and (2) because of rotation requirements, delivering potatoes from 15,000 acres means that about 41,250 acres of irrigated crops must be produced.

Irrigated potatoes require about $930 of production inputs (e.g., seed, chemicals, and fuel) per acre annually and produce a gross return of $1,320 per acre, compared to a gross return of $93 per acre and an input expenditure of $67 per acre for dryland wheat. About 40 percent of the total regional economic impact of the project can be attributed to the farm-level shift to higher-valued crops.

The initiation of a new processing project might have a positive effect on local commodity prices. This could be of special interest in regions like the Northern Plains, where local prices for wheat, corn, and other commodities typically have reflected a substantial discount compared to prices available at the major ports or processing centers (Egerstrom 2001).

A major processing plant can potentially affect the local basis (the difference between local cash prices and the price offered for the next expiring or "nearby" futures contract), thus enhancing the market situation for all area farmers and not just those who are members of the co-op. For example, the ProGold corn processing plant in North Dakota grinds more than 25 million bushels of corn annually, producing corn syrups, corn gluten meal, corn gluten feed, and corn germ (Leistritz 1997). The plant is estimated to raise corn prices by $0.10 to $0.15 per bushel within its multicounty draw area, resulting in an increase in income for area corn farmers of about $11 million annually (Leistritz 1997; Leistritz and Sell 2000).

Some NGCs are combining processing with innovative marketing to tap into specialized urban markets (Hilchey 2001). These organizations usually hope to achieve high returns from specialized or niche markets while avoiding the requirements for a large-volume operation to achieve economies of scale that are necessary to compete in mainstream food processing. An example of this marketing approach is the Mountain View Harvest co-op, headquartered in Aurora, Colorado. This wheat growers' co-op mills its own wheat flour and bakes specialty breads for the restaurant trade. The co-op has focused on "par baking" bread, which involves baking bread to within 10 percent of completion, then flash freezing the product and shipping it to restaurants and in-store bakeries where the baking of the product is completed. Through this process, restaurants are able to serve fresh-baked bread products with little investment in equipment or time.

Another example of a co-op that is focused on specialty products and markets is Superior Shores Agricultural Cooperative of Wisconsin. Superior Shores has attempted to build on the state's strengths in dairy and fruit production in developing new products targeted to health-conscious consumers (Hilchey 2001). While the co-op has test-marketed its products, further product development and commercialization have been impeded by market barriers, lack of adequate finances, and organizational issues. Slotting fees required by most chain stores have limited the co-op's access to this market channel.

While co-ops targeting specialized or niche markets do constitute a new wave of enterprises emerging around the country, the long-run viability of some of these enterprises is yet to be determined. Challenges confronting these co-ops include the time required to develop and commercialize a new product, the competing interests and needs of producer-members over time, and the adoption of value-added specialty food concepts by the mainstream food industry. Nevertheless, the potential benefits from successful development of a specialty or niche market appear sufficient to justify continued efforts in this direction.

Cooperatives as a Response to Increased Vertical Coordination

Current changes in the nature of agriculture are frequently described as the industrialization of agriculture (Barkema and Drabenstott 1996; Council for Agricultural Science and Technology 2001; Fulton and Andreson 2001). The most prevalent manifestations of these changes are increased consolidation and tighter vertical coordination within the agrifood value chain. Vertical coordination is achieved through several mechanisms, including contracts, joint ventures, strategic alliances, and mergers and acquisitions.

The industrialization of agriculture is often described as having begun with the poultry and vegetable sectors. During the 1990s, the pork sector experienced substantial changes in location and production practices, together with major increases in the level of vertical coordination. This coordination has been achieved through increased use of contracts as well as by direct ownership of multiple stages along the value chain (Fulton and Andreson 2001).

Increased reliance on contracts and similar forms of long-term negotiated relationships has changed the nature of risk for farmers and other decision makers in the agrifood chain, has changed the nature of power and control, and has increased the role of information. While decision makers may now face less risk with respect to the price, quality, and quantity of products they will be exchanging, they also face a significant new source of risk—relationship risk. More generally, many producers are concerned that, as a higher proportion of the regional production of a given commodity (e.g., hogs) is produced under contract or other long-term arrangement, independent producers may be placed at a disadvantage (Barkema, Drabenstott, and Novack 2001; Holz-Clause 2000). Thus, while the supply chains that are emerging in agriculture offer a system that may be more efficient and consistent in providing food products that meet consumers' changing demands, farmers and ranchers may have concerns about their role in the evolving food system.

NGCs are increasingly seen as a means by which producers can respond to the trends of concentration and integration in agriculture (Barkema et al. 2001; Fulton and Andreson 2001). NGCs provide producers with a mechanism for integrating around large processors. A co-op can serve as a competitive yardstick when it competes with investor-oriented firms (IOFs), provide an ensured market for farmers and ranchers to sell their product, and create a more competitive environment in the industry.

A recent example of the potential for NGCs is provided by U.S. Premium Beef (USPB), a co-op formed by cattle ranchers who wished to receive more value from their animals. The fed cattle delivered to USPB by its members are processed at two packing plants operated by Farmland National Beef, a subsidiary of Farmland Industries. Members are paid on a value-based grid system, which reflects the characteristics of each carcass. Profits from processing and marketing are returned to members through stock dividends. During its initial year of operation, USPB members experienced favorable returns from their investment. Furthermore, they see excellent prospects for the future as producers will be able to obtain information on individual carcass characteristics, which can potentially be very useful to guide herd management decisions (Holz-Clause 2000). In summary, USPB has developed a system to reward producers of cattle that yield high-quality meat products (Katz and Boland 2000). This system promises long-term benefits not only for members but also for the beef industry as a whole, as the rapid feedback of information should enable ranchers and cattle feeders to provide a product more closely matching consumers' preferences.

Estimating the Economic Impact of a New Producer Cooperative

Estimating the impact of a proposed producer co-op involves assessing both the direct impacts and the secondary effects of the new enterprise. In addition, it is important to decide on the relevant geographic area for evaluating the impacts (e.g., the state, the site county, and so on.).

Direct Impacts

The direct impacts are those changes in output, income, or employment that represent the initial or first-round effects of the project. For a new processing plant, these would include (1) expenditures for plant operation, such as payroll, employee benefits, utilities, and supplies; and (2) added returns for growers from producing a higher-value crop and/or from any share of the processing profits they may receive. As noted earlier, if a plant's requirements for the processed commodity are quite extensive relative to the local area production, the local basis can be affected, enhancing prices for all local producers. If this effect is estimated to be substantial, it may be included as part of the direct effects of the project.

The direct effects of a project should be estimated with respect to the impact area chosen. That is, if the goal is to determine the impact on the economy of the state, the direct effects should reflect expenditures made to and additional returns received by entities within the state. On the other hand, if the goal is to estimate the impact on the site county, then only expenditures to and receipts by entities within the county should be included.

The economic impacts of a new product or facility are often estimated both for the construction and start-up phase and for the subsequent operation of the facility. The construction and start-up phase expenditures represent a one-time stimulus to the area economy whereas the subsequent operations phase results in annually reoccurring expenditures. The identification of which expenditures are likely to accrue to entities within the study region is often especially significant with respect to project construction. For example, the total cost of constructing the ProGold corn processing plant in North Dakota was $261 million; however, only about 44 percent of this represented expenditures to entities within the project's region of influence (Leistritz 1997). Plant equipment alone amounted to about $70 million, virtually all of which was purchased outside the region.

The direct impacts from the operations phase are likely to include a higher proportion of expenditures within the site area or elsewhere in the state. The plant's payroll, utilities, and some types of supplies and services usually constitute local expenditures. Purchases of commodities to be processed may be localized or dispersed, depending on the location of member-growers and/or the plant's procurement practices. For example, the Aviko plant obtains a high percentage of its potatoes from a two-county area (Coon and Leistritz 2001). On the other hand, the members of the North American Bison Cooperative are distributed across several states and Canadian provinces; only 54 percent of the bison processed annually at the plant near New Rockford, North Dakota, are purchased from members within North Dakota (Sell, Bangsund, and Leistritz 2001).

The economic impact or contribution of an NGC can be substantially enhanced by the grower payments or dividends. These represent the profits from the processing activity, and for a successful venture they can be quite significant. For example, in the year 2000, the Dakota Growers Pasta Company made expenditures of about $17.2 million to entities within North Dakota (Reinhiller 2001). These expenditures included grower payments of about $4.5 million, or about 26 percent of the total direct impacts of the co-op. The grower payments (dividends) are estimated to result in another $9.3 million in secondary impacts within the state, for a total impact of $13.7 million. This is one measure of the economic benefit to the state of having the profits of the processing activity retained within the state.

Secondary Impacts

The secondary effects of a project can be further categorized into *indirect effects* (i.e., those that arise from the purchase of additional production inputs from other industries) and *induced effects* (i.e., effects of the additional household consumption that results from the additional income associated with industrial expansion). Economic impact analysis requires choosing a technique to estimate the secondary (indirect and induced) effects that the direct impacts will have on economic activity, income, and employment in the study area. Although other estimation methods are sometimes used, input–output (I–O) models have become the most commonly used technique.

Input–output analysis is a technique for tabulating and describing the linkages or interdependencies between various industrial groups (sectors) within an economy. The economy considered may be the national economy or an economy as small as that of a single county. To conduct an I–O analysis, it is first necessary to obtain an I–O model appropriate to the area being analyzed (i.e., a state, a site county, or a multicounty area). I–O models based on national coefficients and adjusted for local business patterns and regional trade flows are readily available at the local and state levels; two of the most widely used are IMPLAN and RIMS (Rickman and Schwer 1995).

Once the I–O model has been obtained, the direct effects are applied to the model's coefficients or multipliers to estimate the secondary and total (direct plus secondary) effects. For example, in the year 2000, Dakota Growers Pasta Company made direct expenditures totaling about $17.2 million to entities within North Dakota (Reinhiller 2001). These included $7.6 million in payroll, $4.5 million in grower payments, $1.6 million for utilities, and $1.1 million for worker benefits. When applied to the multipliers of the North Dakota Input–output Model, these direct effects (direct impacts) were estimated to result in a total statewide economic impact of $52.9 million. That is, the initial $17.2 million resulted in $35.7 million in secondary impacts, for a total economic contribution of $52.9 million. The annual economic contribution of this producer co-op included more than $23.2 million of added personal income and about $12 million in additional retail sales. These levels of added receipts by the various sectors of the state economy would support about 485 secondary jobs, in addition to the persons employed directly by the co-op. An analysis of the distribution of expenditures and commuting patterns of the plant workers indicates that nearly 50 percent of the economic impacts may be captured within the site county and almost 75 percent within the five counties surrounding the plant. Other examples of the use of I–O models to estimate the effects of new producer co-ops are provided by Leistritz (1997) and Sell et al. (2001).

Summary

Producer co-ops appear to have substantial potential as a means for farmers and ranchers to cope with the industrialization of agriculture. Co-ops provide a way for producers to integrate forward and participate in the processing and marketing of their products. In addition, new processing plants can create new jobs and economic opportunities in rural areas that have often experienced economic hardship as a result of farm consolidation and depressed commodity prices. Because efforts to stimulate development of new cooperative ventures often involve incentives or other assistance from local and/or state governments, local and state officials are interested in estimates of the projected economic impact or contribution of a new facility.

The main conclusion to be drawn here is that producer co-ops do have substantial potential to contribute to local and state economies. Their economic contribution may be enhanced if it results in substantial distributions of processing profits to their member-growers, enables members to produce higher value crops, or results in increases in the local price (basis) for an existing crop. A realistic assessment of this potential requires careful attention to defining the direct effects of the new facility, together with selection of an appropriate method (generally some form of input–output model) for estimating secondary impacts.

References

Barkema, Alan, and Mark Drabenstott. 1996. "Consolidation and Change in Heartland Agriculture." In *Economic Forces Shaping The Rural Heartland*, 61–76. Kansas City, MO: Federal Reserve Bank of Kansas City.

Barkema, Alan, Mark Drabenstott, and Nancy Novack. 2001. "The New U.S. Meat Industry." *Economic Review* (Federal Reserve Bank of Kansas City) 86, no. 2: 33–56.

Buschette, Patricia. 2000. "Golden Oval." In *New Generation Cooperatives: Case Studies*, ed. Mary Holmes, Norman Walzer, and Christopher D. Merrett, 33–42. Macomb: Illinois Institute for Rural Affairs, Western Illinois University.

Coon, Randall C., and F. Larry Leistritz. 2001. *Economic Impact of Production and Processing of Irrigated Potatoes in Central North Dakota* (Agribusiness and Applied Economics report no. 252). Fargo: North Dakota State University, Agricultural Experiment Station.

Council for Agricultural Science and Technology. 2001. *Vertical Coordination of Agriculture in Farming-dependent Areas* (Task force report no. 137). Ames, IA: Council for Agricultural Science and Technology.

Crihfield, John B., and Harrison S. Campbell, Jr. 1991. "Evaluation of Alternative Regional Planning Models." *Growth and Change* 22, no. 2: 1–16.

Drabenstott, Mark, and Tim R. Smith. 1996. "The Changing Economy of the Rural Heartland." In *Economic Forces Shaping the Rural Heartland*, 1–11. Kansas City, MO: Federal Reserve Bank of Kansas City.

Egerstrom, Lee. 2001. "New Generation Cooperatives as an Economic Development Strategy." In *A Cooperative Approach to Local Economic Development*, ed. Christopher D. Merrett and Norman Walzer, 73–90. Westport, CT: Quorum Books.

Fulton, Joan R., and Kevin Andreson. 2001. "Value Added Enterprises in the Rural Community." In *A Cooperative Approach to Local Economic Development*, ed. Christopher D. Merrett and Norman Walzer, 129–146. Westport, CT: Quorum Books.

Hilchey, Duncan. 2001. "Accessing Urban Markets Through New Generation Cooperatives." In *A Cooperative Approach to Local Economic Development*, ed. Christopher D. Merrett and Norman Walzer, 117–128. Westport, CT: Quorum Books.

Holmes, Mary, Norman Walzer, and Christopher D. Merrett, eds. 2000. *New Generation Cooperatives: Case Studies*. Macomb: Illinois Institute for Rural Affairs, Western Illinois University.

Holz-Clause, Mary. 2000. "U.S. Premium Beef." In *New Generation Cooperatives: Case Studies*, ed. Mary Holmes, Norman Walzer, and Christopher D. Merrett, 133–149. Macomb: Illinois Institute for Rural Affairs, Western Illinois University.

Johnson, Thomas G. 2001. "The Rural Economy in a New Century." In *Rural America at a Crossroads*, ed. Mark Drabenstott, 7–19. Kansas City, MO: Federal Reserve Bank of Kansas City.

Katz, Jeffrey P., and Michael Boland. 2000. "A New Value-added Strategy for the U.S. Beef Industry: The Case of U.S. Premium Beef Ltd." *Supply Chain Management: An International Journal* 5, no. 2: 99–109.

Leistritz, F. Larry. 1997. "Assessing Local Socioeconomic Impacts of Rural Manufacturing Facilities: The Case of a Proposed Agricultural Processing Plant." *Journal of the Community Development Society* 28, no. 1: 43–64.

———. 1998. "Economic and Fiscal Impact Assessment." In *Environmental Methods Review: Retooling Impact Assessment for the New Century*, ed. Alan Porter and John Fittipaldi, 219–227. Fargo, ND: International Association for Impact Assessment and Army Environmental Policy Institute.

———. 2000. "Agricultural Processing Facilities as a Source of Rural Jobs." In *Small Town and Rural Economic Development: A Case Studies Approach*, ed. Peter V. Schaeffer and Scott Loveridge, 115–121. Westport, CT: Praeger.

Leistritz, F. Larry, and Steve H. Murdock. 1981. *The Socioeconomic Impact of Resource Development: Methods for Assessment*. Boulder, CO: Westview Press.

Leistritz, F. Larry, and Randall S. Sell. 2000. *Agricultural Processing Plants in North Dakota: Socioeconomic Impacts* (Agricultural Economics report no. 437). Fargo: North Dakota State University, Agricultural Experiment Station.

Merrett, Christopher D., and Norman Walzer, eds. 2001. *A Cooperative Approach to Local Economic Development*. Westport, CT: Quorum Books.

Reinhiller, Liz. 2001. Personal communication from Liz Reinhiller, vice president, Dakota Growers Pasta Company, Carrington, ND.

Richardson, Harry W. 1972. *Input–output and Regional Economics*. New York: John Wiley.

Rickman, Dan S., and R. Keith Schwer. 1995. "A Comparison of the Multipliers of IMPLAN, REMI, and RIMS II: Benchmarking Ready-made Models for Comparison." *The Annals of Regional Science* 29: 363–374.

Sell, Randall S., Dean A. Bangsund, and F. Larry Leistritz. 2001. "Contribution of the Bison Industry to the North Dakota Economy." *American Journal of Alternative Agriculture* 16, no. 3: 106–113.

Walzer, Norman, Christopher D. Merrett, and Mary Holmes. 1999. "Agriculture and Local Economic Development." *Rural Research Report* 10, no. 10. Macomb: Illinois Institute for Rural Affairs, Western Illinois University.

Williams, Chris, and Christopher D. Merrett. 2001. "Putting Cooperative Theory into Practice: The 21st Century Alliance." In *A Cooperative Approach to Local Economic Development*, ed. Christopher D. Merrett and Norman Walzer, 147–166. Westport, CT: Quorum Books.

PART V

COOPERATIVES IN COMMUNITY DEVELOPMENT

12

Consumer Ownership in Capitalist Economies: Applications of Theory to Consumer Cooperation

Ann Hoyt

Economic theory assumes that consumers, acting as individuals, choose to consume products and services in a freely competitive marketplace that directly responds to their needs and wants. Early consumer cooperative theorists, especially in North America and Europe, rejected that notion and developed a different, more powerful role for consumers in industrialized capitalist economies.

Consumer Cooperation

A consumer co-op is a business owned and democratically controlled by consumers to provide themselves with goods and services on a not-for-profit basis. Consumers have organized co-ops in a wide variety of industries, including financial services, housing, food, insurance, utilities, child care, health care, recreational equipment, and funeral and memorial societies (Hoyt 1997).

Most of the estimated 120 million Americans in co-ops belong to a consumer co-op. The country's largest consumer co-op is Recreational Equipment, Inc. (REI), with 2 million active members. More than 80 million Americans belong to a credit union, more than 300 retail food co-ops exist in the country, and over 1.5 million families live in cooperative housing units (National Association of Housing Cooperatives 2002; National Cooperative Business Association 2002; Nolan, Swanson, Sumberg, and Gutknecht 2002).

Although there is tremendous variation in the types of consumer co-ops in the country, most researchers writing on the topic use the term *consumer co-op* to describe only retail food co-ops. Unless otherwise noted, that is the assumption of this article as well.[1]

This chapter traces the development of cooperative theory in relation to collective consumer action. The purpose is twofold: (1) to summarize the economic theory underlying consumer co-ops, and (2) to show that consumer co-ops offer equally important noneconomic benefits such as the promotion of social capital and the improvement of a community's quality of life. It also offers suggestions for further research.

The Cooperative Commonwealth

Consumer cooperation began as a response to the industrialization of the European and North American economies beginning in the mid-eighteenth century (Thompson 1994). Popular primarily in working-class communities where wages were low, consumer co-ops offered an alternative way to organize ownership and control of the distribution of consumer goods. They responded to the needs of the "new" working class who, through their co-ops, first understood their common roles as *consumers* (Furlough and Strikwerda 1999).

Early co-ops grew out of a cultural assumption of scarcity. Items sold in the co-ops were mainly basic foodstuffs and household supplies, including cloth, dry goods, and shoes. Owned and controlled by consumers, the co-ops "focused on selling goods that were 'honest,' unlike overpriced or shoddy commodities or adulterated foodstuffs sold by small shopkeepers or the emerging capitalist chain stores" (Furlough and Strikwerda 1999, 39).

As consumer co-ops grew into a widespread social movement, their activities were seen as an effort to counter injustices inherent in competitive capitalism, especially the inequitable distribution of resources between the rich and the poor and away from the working class. The strong tie between labor and consumer cooperation was crucial to the development of the cooperative movement and continues today in the perception of consumer co-ops as a "people's" movement.[2]

During the second half of the nineteenth century, the Knights of Labor considered cooperation to be an "essential part of labor reform" (Leikin 1999, 94). The important unique features of consumer co-ops—mutual ownership of economic resources, return of profits based on use, and democratic control of economic entities—became a "democratic model of the future society" (Furlough and Strikwerda 1999, 3).

Consumer cooperative theory, especially in Europe and North America, addresses the role of consumer co-ops in capitalist economies. Early cooperative theorists believed that capitalists were able to and did manipulate production and distribution systems in order to gain a larger share of the income and wealth generated by the technological advances of industrialization. In their view, consumers, as individuals, were unable to exert any control over the marketplace. Their only hope of influencing markets came from pooling their resources and acting collectively through a cooperatively owned system of retail, wholesale, and production businesses. Eventually, these consumer-owned businesses would dominate markets and cause the decline of capitalism. Co-ops would be the foundation of a new economic order, a cooperative commonwealth, which would correct the abuses of competitive capitalism.

Democratic socialists celebrated the absence of profits in cooperative economic transactions. They believed consumers' cooperation was destined to overthrow the profit-oriented capitalist system and would usher in a new age of consumer control of the economy. It is during this period that cooperation became linked with socialism and, in fact, became "one of the three pillars of socialism, along with trade unionism and political socialism . . ." (Furlough and Strikwerda 1999, 3).

In the writings of Sidney and Beatrice Webb (1921), cooperation was a step toward an ideal socialist state. It was, perhaps, the Webbs who most forcefully articulated the class-based appeal of consumer cooperation. They believed that class struggle was inevitable in industrial economies[3] and that consumer cooperation offered the working class a "way to win that struggle" (Donohue 1999, 120). Charles Gide, French economics professor and early proponent of consumer cooperatives, was convinced that only recognition of the "ultimate primacy" of the consumer and formation of a strong consumers' cooperative movement would create an industrial democracy in which wealth was equitably divided (Hoyt 1974). James Peter Warbasse (1923; 1939), first president of the Cooperative League of the United States (now the National Cooperative Business Association), wrote prolific treatises on the new age of peace, justice, and equality that would be the inevitable result of economic cooperation.

Cooperatives and the Capitalist Consumer

The association between consumer cooperation, quality of community life, community self-reliance, social change, democratic governance, collective political action, and economic justice has remained with the co-ops even though the strong ties to labor unions and socialism ended many years ago. Furlough and Strikwerda (1999) theorize that the decline of nineteenth-century consumer co-ops is directly tied to the stunning success of capitalism at creating the "capitalist consumer." Capitalism requires high and continuous levels of consumer purchasing to sustain mass markets for standardized goods and services. High levels of consumption require the creation of high levels of consumer demand. To sustain these levels of demand, it was imperative that the working class be both willing and able to consume the new goods being produced—that is, to become capitalist consumers.

A great success of capitalism was its ability to create a "commercialized consumer culture of advertising, department stores, national brands and chain stores that fostered individualist acquisitiveness, not collective solidarity or prudence" (Furlough and Strikwerda 1999, 38). Furlough and Strikwerda contend that during the interwar period, new generations of consumers found the "profit and pleasure-oriented" mass culture of capitalist consumption more appealing than the older cooperative culture based on values of frugality, collective responsibility, and community-based, noncommercial leisure activities. The co-ops' inability to adjust to the new consumerism and changing consumer needs and wants resulted in the decline of the consumer cooperative movement in many industrialized countries, especially the United States.

Since the early 1900s, Americans have embraced consumer co-ops with enthusiasm during such periods as the Great Depression and the early 1970s, and have greeted them with disinterest in periods such as the 1920s and the post–World War II years (Parker 1936). This waxing and waning of interest has varied among industries as well. For example, when women entered the workforce in large numbers in the 1970s and 1980s, interest in child-care co-ops increased dramatically while support for retail food co-ops dependent on volunteer labor declined.

Even so, while the consumer co-op did not thrive and become a dominant force in the distribution and sale of consumer goods, individual co-ops have survived, new co-ops have been developed, and the cooperative model has been applied to a full panoply of consumer goods and services. Interestingly, the commitments fundamental to the consumer co-op's "moral economy,"[4] as described by Furlough and Strikwerda (1999), have survived and are key to the opportunities for development of consumer co-ops in the twenty-first century. At the same time, when they have been confronted with a conflict between the "moral economy" and changing consumer needs and wants, co-ops have often been unable to change fast enough to remain competitive in their markets.

Economic Theories

As it became clear that consumer co-ops would not prevail over capitalism and create the cooperative commonwealth, economists began to study the economic impact that a co-op might have in competitive markets. We should note that most North American economic theories of cooperation have concentrated on analysis of agricultural marketing and supply co-ops (Staatz 1987). Consumer co-ops have not received the same level of attention, probably because individually they are not as large either in number, volume, or number of members as their agricultural counterparts; they do not have the same level of impact on their members' financial well-being; and they are not well-supported financially at the nation's universities.[5]

Economists first developed economic models of co-ops in the 1940s (Staatz 1987). Their work focused on the unique nature of the cooperative enterprise in a microeconomic framework (as opposed to analysis of cooperation as a sector or a system in macroeconomic models) and its potential for correcting a wide variety of economic conditions such as improving the general economic welfare by maximizing consumer surplus (Enke 1945); restoration of competitive equilibrium (Royer 1987); alternative and local distribution of wealth and the resulting stabilizing effects on the economy (Hamilton 1954); decentralization of economic decision making (Torgerson, Reynolds, and Gray 1997); correction of market failures (Torgerson et al. 1997); consumer protection (Sommer 1991); and performance as competitive yardsticks for consumers in oligopolistic food industries (Cotterill 1984).

Economic modeling is made more complex because there are different definitions of what a co-op is, and there is relatively little clarity about the objectives of co-ops (Royer 1987). This is especially true of consumer co-ops whose purposes may be economic, social, environmental, and political in nature. The broad nature of consumer cooperative objectives is illustrated in Table 12.1. Contrast these with the fundamental objective of an investor-owned firm (IOF), which is to maximize profits.

It should also be noted that with few exceptions (among them, Hoyt 1974; Kreitner 1978; and Mather 1968), little empirical work has been conducted to test the predictions of the theories described here in a consumer cooperative context. Very generally, the few studies that have been done confirm that cooperative prices tend to be lower than those of their competitors, and Hoyt (1974) presents some evidence that quality and selection of cooperative products may be superior. Mather (1968) is the only study that attempts to determine the actual (as opposed to theoretical) economic impact of a consumer co-op on its market. His results indicate that it may be "inadvisable" to reject the hypothesis that consumer co-ops act to lower overall prices in retail food markets. He does not find these results "wholly convincing" (134), however, and advocates further study.

Table 12.1

Selected Purposes of U.S. Retail Food Consumer Cooperatives

Cooperative	Economic goals	Social goals	Political goals	Environmental goals
Davis Food Co-op	To be fiscally sound; to support cooperative community activities	To be progressive; a model employer		To be an environmentally proactive business
Brattleboro	To provide quality products at reasonable prices	To create a fair and honest environment for employees, members, and the community		
Weaver Street Market	To be a vibrant, sustainable commercial center; to enable profits to stay in the community	To create opportunity for community interaction	To ensure that control stays in the community	To work in harmony with the environment
Sevananda		To empower the community to improve its health and well-being	To establish beneficial relationships with the local community and the global cooperative movement	To provide natural and organic foods
Mississippi Market		To educate consumers on the benefits of cooperative business practices	To provide leadership in influencing and developing public policy on agriculture and organically grown products	To promote the benefits of certified, organically grown food products
Williamson Street	To operate a financially sound retail grocery store	To support cooperative philosophy and values as an essential part of the enterprise	To enable workers to have participatory management and a humane work environment	

Sources: Brattleboro Food Co-op (2002); Davis Food Co-op (2002); Mississippi Market (2002); Sevananda (2002); Weaver Street Market (2002); Williamson Street Grocery Co-op (2002).

Note: These statements are excerpted from the co-ops' mission, vision, and values statements for illustrative purposes. In most cases, they do not include all of the purposes of the co-ops listed.

Cooperatives as Integrated Households

Ivan Emelianoff (1948) was the first economist to develop a rigorous theory of cooperative business, with extensions of his work developed by Robotka (1957) and Phillips (1953). While the primary focus of this work has involved agricultural co-ops, all three authors considered the theory to be applicable to consumer co-ops as well. Central to the theory is the assumption that co-ops are not independent, acquisitive firms that make entrepreneurial decisions and incur profits and losses.

Instead, consumer co-ops are seen as economic units comprised of individual consumer households that retain their independence even as they participate as members of the co-op. The co-op, *which has no independent economic identity*, represents the aggregated consumption functions of separate households, a "maximized household" (Emelianoff 1948, 248–249). Relationships among the cooperative members are characterized by group decision making (i.e., the co-op as an entity is not the decision maker). Goods and services are provided at cost, and the members share the risks of the venture in proportion to consumption of the services offered (Robotka 1957).

The common goal of the integrated households is to maximize economic returns to each of the individual associated households (Phillips 1953). Phillips showed that the optimum price and level of output needed to maximize returns to the co-op is the point at which the sum of the marginal costs in all plants (i.e., households and co-op) equals the marginal revenue in the co-op (Staatz 1987).[6] This is the same point at which firms in monopolistic or oligopolistic markets maximize profit. While this solution benefits cooperative members if all profits are returned to the members, it is not the optimum solution for consumers. This is due to the fact that less than optimum quantities are sold at higher than optimum prices (Enke 1945). Co-ops may choose to operate so as to maximize profit and not return those profits to members.[7] In those cases, the co-ops may or may not provide an increase in general welfare depending on how the retained profits are used in competitive markets.

Interestingly, the Emelianoff (1948) model may be useful to analyze the behavior and economic impact of food-buying groups, which are unincorporated affiliated households who order and distribute food as a group. No current statistics exist on the number of food-buying groups in the United States. Wholesalers who sell to them indicate there may be several thousand, ranging in size from fewer than five families to over forty. Unlike the *han* groups in Japan, which are described later in the chapter, these groups are usually not centrally organized and have little or no market power. They have little or no capital invested, make all decisions as a group, and seldom have any formal corporate identity. Their sole function is to pool orders from a group of consumers in order to generate sufficient quantity to justify reduced prices and/or delivery to a central location.

Little empirical work has been done on these co-ops, and it is usually felt that they have little competitive impact, if any, on their local markets. Interestingly, these co-ops require substantial volunteer labor from their members and keep costs as low as possible. Contrary to the predictions of the Emelianoff model, they price at the minimum price that will cover costs or the point at which average cost equals demand (average revenue).[8]

Cooperatives as Competitive Yardsticks

The first economist to analyze the co-op as an independent firm (as opposed to a vertical integration of aggregated households) focused on consumer co-ops. Stephen Enke (1945) was interested in the consumer co-op's potential to arrive at optimum pricing policies that enhance the *general* economic welfare—that is, prices that achieve maximum efficiency of economic resources *and* maximum financial profits (in contrast to traditional neoclassical theory of the firm, which holds that the sole goal of the firm is to maximize profits). The unique position of consumers as owners in a cooperative structure leads them to maximize the *total* utility they receive from the co-op. That utility is the sum of the utility they receive from the goods they consume at a certain quantity and price level plus their share of cooperative profits (returned in the form of patronage refunds). Note that there is a dynamic tension in this tradeoff for cooperative members. To increase profits, they must increase prices, which will reduce the utility of the goods they consume. If prices are reduced, utility increases, but profits that will be distributed as patronage refunds are reduced.

Enke (1945) showed that a consumer co-op's optimum price occurs at that point "where a decrease in the co-op's profits from a unit increase in output is exactly offset by the increase in members' consumer surplus" (149).[9] This is the point at which marginal cost and market demand intersect, which results in greater quantities being consumed at lower prices than in the Emelianoff model. At this point, the co-op's net earnings are less than they would be if profits were maximized, but the "sum of the co-op's net earnings and consumer surplus is greater" (Royer 1987, 12) than in any other condition.[10] Operation at the intersection of marginal cost and demand is the point at which resource allocation is most efficient and consumers' surplus is maximized.[11]

If the co-op operates in monopolistic or oligopolistic markets, pricing at the intersection of marginal cost and market demand results in higher output and lower prices than the competition and moves the levels of both output and price closer to those that would prevail under perfect competition (Staatz 1987). This is an important result that indicates consumer co-ops can have a positive competitive yardstick role in increasing the general welfare when they act to maximize consumer surplus. Cotterill (1984, cited in Staatz 1987, 81) points out that for a competitive yardstick co-op, investments must be analyzed in terms of the benefits they provide both members and nonmembers through their impact on lowering prices for all participants in a market. Consumer co-ops have had some excellent successes that are routinely cited as examples of the tremendous impact the introduction of a cooperative business can have in a monopoly situation.[12]

In addition to their potential to reduce overall market prices, consumer co-ops have provided numerous pro-consumer innovations that have become widely accepted in food retailing. These include unit pricing, bulk and bin sales, nutritional labeling, and sale of natural and organic foods.[13] This is another facet of the competitive yardstick role in which consumers are able to evaluate the performance of IOFs compared to co-ops and create demand for additional products and services based on models provided by consumer co-ops (Schomisch 1979).

An important consideration in the competitive yardstick model revolves around the consumer's perception of the patronage refund. If a cooperative member regards the patronage refund as a reduction in price, she or he will be motivated to consume at a higher level or move away from the equilibrium intersection of marginal cost and demand (Royer 1987, 14). In this situation, the Enke (1945) model is not stable.[14]

On the other hand, if a consumer sees the patronage refund as "windfall income," it would not be related to her or his demand function for cooperative goods, and would not create instability in the Enke model. Although there is no research on the perception of patronage refunds by cooperative consumers, one might expect that an annual refund based on a full year's purchases might be seen as windfall income.[15,16]

Minimum Pricing

The Enke (1945) model requires the co-op to balance price against consumer surplus; however, what would happen if the co-op were to decide to minimize surplus and provide goods at the lowest price possible? In this case, price would be set at minimum average cost and would equal the long-run equilibrium point under perfect competition. Fulton (2001) has shown that because consumer cooperative members are both owners and customers, pricing at minimum average cost does not result in maximum level of welfare for members. That would only occur if the demand curve intersected the average cost curve at its minimum point. If this were not the case, members' demand would exceed the quantity the co-op is able to provide at the minimum price, so the co-op must either restrict sales or raise the price to remain at the Pareto optimal solution.

Anderson, Porter, and Maurice (1979) extended Enke's work using a utility maximization framework to determine the impact of membership size on price and output of consumer co-ops. In their model, when consumer co-ops can control the number of members (and, hence, control demand) and they are organized to maximize the utility of each member, their optimum solution occurs at minimum average cost, the same long-run equilibrium position as the perfectly competitive firm. The co-op achieves this result by selecting the optimal membership size.[17]

In an effort to counteract the effects of limited start-up capital, new wave co-ops of the 1970s introduced two innovations in pricing: (1) member-labor discounts and (2) member-only discounts. The 1980s and 1990s brought a flurry of economic research on the implications of member-labor discounts, much of which expanded on the utility maximization framework introduced by Anderson et al. (1979). Caputo and Lynch (1991) looked at allocation decisions of consumers when there is an opportunity to barter labor for lower prices. In their model, consumer utility is a function of nondurable cooperative goods, nondurable noncooperative goods, leisure time, and member work hours. The primary result of their work is to demonstrate the possibility of upward sloping compensated demand functions for consumers who are able to barter labor hours for lower prices.[18]

A member-only discount at the point of sale results in a two-tiered pricing strategy in which it is presumed that nonmember prices are set at "regular" retail. In this case, nonmembers (who often make up to and exceeding 50 percent of retail sales in retail food co-ops) are clearly purchasing a combination of utilities or product/service attributes beyond the fundamental distinction of price.

In many cases, careful analysis of the financial performance of co-ops with a two-tiered pricing structure shows that price advantages offered to members are subsidized by nonmembers and may not be sustainable when an effective competitor enters the market.[19] Citing McGregor, Staatz (1987) notes that retaining surplus profits from nonmember trade for the benefit of members (either direct or indirect) gradually converts the co-op into an organization that has many IOF characteristics (82). In this case, Torgerson et al. (1997) predict that management will take a proprietary view of this equity and, presumably, manage it to maximize its own interests rather than those of the members. The need for strong member-controlled governance systems becomes especially important in these cases.

Economists who study co-ops ask questions regarding optimum combinations of price, quantity, and size. Their goal is to compare these optimums between co-ops and other forms of organization. In general, one can show that a firm whose goal is to maximize profit will sell the quantity of goods for which marginal cost equals price (Royer 1987, 4). It can also be shown that consumer co-ops can have beneficial economic impacts, not only for members, but also for the markets in which they operate.[20] In fact, co-ops are usually organized to correct a market failure (e.g., high prices, poor quality, unavailability of goods or services) that results from imperfect competition.

From a policy perspective, the most important economic characteristics of consumer co-ops may be their ability to allow a variety of options for consumer choice, each of which may result in maximized consumer welfare. These include using a patronage refund system to arrive at a maximum welfare equilibrium point, using member labor to offset diseconomies of scale that result from small store volumes relative to the competition, using a member-only point-of-sale discount system to provide direct competition on price, and using a member-labor option to barter labor hours for lower shelf prices.

Consumer Cooperatives and Social Capital

In addition to providing consumers with more choice, consumer co-ops may also offer less tangible but equally important benefits. During the past twenty years, sociologists and economists have articulated the value of *social capital* in economic transactions. Social capital is considered a factor of economic production in the same way as financial capital, human capital, physical capital, and natural resources are. It is, however, difficult to define the concept precisely as there is little agreement among social scientists (Robison, Schmid, and Siles 1999; Social Network Analysis 1999). Robert Putnam's (2000) widely used definition describes social capital as "connections among individuals, social networks and the norms of reciprocity and trustworthiness that arise from them" (19). These networks facilitate "cooperation for mutual benefit" (19). The positive consequences of social capital include "mutual support, cooperation, trust, and institutional effectiveness" (22). Robinson et al. (1999) describe it as the "service potentials derived from social relations" (5).

Empirical research shows that substantial benefits result from the presence of high levels of social capital in a community because collective problems tend to be solved more easily. Citizens who have worked together have developed a level of trust for and awareness of one another that facilitates the flow of information, "lowers transactions costs, and eases dilemmas of collective action" (Putnam 2000, 346).

Consumer co-ops have the potential to create significant increases in a community's social capital. Their fundamental purpose is dedicated to the good of the community or, at least, of the members. The cooperative principles are based on trust in the group, mutual self-help, and the members' ability to create greater benefits together than any one could create alone. In addition, many consumer co-ops currently are choosing creation of community as a primary mission of the co-op (see Table 12.1). In co-ops, citizen members learn social and civic skills and create social capital, particularly if they are active participants in the co-op either as staff or volunteers (Wylie 2001, 13, citing Spear n.d.).

Robert Putnam's (2000) quintessential illustration of the strong benefits of social capital—northern Italy—is described as being unusually successful at providing public services, promoting investment, and supporting successful economic development. Putnam ascribes this success to "rich networks of organized reciprocity and civic heritage" (346). An important part of this heritage is the interlocking network of small worker- and consumer-owned co-ops that flourish throughout the region.

Kenworthy (1997) supports the contention made by Putnam (2000) that cooperation among market participants is an important component of overall economic success; however, he criticizes Putnam's approach for placing too much emphasis on civic action and social capital as being critical to a healthy economy. Kenworthy has developed a list of nine types of economic cooperation that he assumes enhance economic welfare and progress. He contends that these activities grow out of the mutual advantages to both parties in the cooperative effort and are driven by business exigencies, not by the general level of trust extant in the society at large.

Kenworthy's (1997) perspective is useful because it focuses attention on the sequence of events that lead to economically beneficial cooperative action that improves the general welfare of market economies. He agrees with Putnam that cooperative actions among economic actors can be a beneficial complement to market competition and that trust among those actors can foster cooperation; however, the sequence that Putnam proposes—civic participation creates trust, which, in turn, inspires cooperation—does not appear to be a useful explanation for variations in economic performance among affluent countries. For our purposes, the more important possibility is that participation in a cooperative business creates social trust, which, in turn, fosters a willingness and ability to engage in other social and economic activities. That is, cooperation builds social trust that, in turn, inspires civic engagement and further cooperation.

Although there has been much empirical research to support Putnam's (2000) assertion of the economic value of social capital, little work has been done to document the social capital probably being created daily by consumer co-ops. Public opinion surveys repeatedly confirm that consumers trust cooperatively owned businesses more than other business forms (The Gallup Organization 1994; Hoyt 1995); that co-ops are dedicated to providing education to their members both on consumer and cooperative issues; and that co-ops constantly work to implement the principles of participatory democracy in their relationships with their members (International Joint Project on Cooperative Democracy 1995).

The thousands of people who have served on boards of directors of consumer cooperative businesses and credit unions have learned invaluable lessons about the responsibilities of governance, the challenges of representative democracy, and the need to make business decisions that consider the well-being of the community of members. Presumably, these skills are transferred to other areas of civic life as well.

There is also more general evidence that local associations and networks can influence local development in a positive way and improve the well-being of households (Feldman and Assaf 1999; Grootaert 1998). We should point out, however, that the value of social capital comes from its impact on the application of other forms of capital to the development process (Grootaert 1998).

In many ways, consumer co-ops are returning to the strategies of late-nineteenth-century co-ops, which were centers for locally generated consumer activity and community entertainment. Weaver Street Market (2002) in Carrboro, North Carolina, operates a natural foods grocery store and an Italian café. Community-sponsored activities listed on a recent Web page included a community art show, regular Sunday jazz brunches, free rabies clinics, a monthly "open bakery" when members can bake their own bread in the co-op's ovens, live theater presentations, and cooking classes.

In addition to sponsoring a wide variety of community events, North Coast Cooperative (2002) in Arcata, California, supports a Cooperative Community Fund, which has donated more than $833,000 to community causes since 1973. Funds have been used to support cooperative education, environmental protection, high-volume nonprofits, community events, scholarships, cooperative development, physical and emotional health programs, and programs for children and women. Lakewinds Natural Foods (2002) in Minnetonka, Minnesota, responded to members' priorities for a safe environment by opening Lakewinds Natural Home, a retail outlet for home products that are earth-friendly and without noxious odors or chemicals. These three examples show the wide variety of community-building activities that are conducted by consumer co-ops throughout the country, all of which contribute to each area's social capital resources.

Consumer Cooperatives and the Social Economy

Recent research on co-ops, especially in Europe and Canada, has focused on their role in the "social economy," broadly conceived as a third economic sector that lies between the private sector markets and government (Sanchez 2002). It includes co-ops, mutual associations, and nonprofit organizations (Wuelker 1995) that provide critical social services, among them health care, rural and urban utilities, higher education, child care, cultural activities, elder care, transportation services, and funeral services (Quarter 1992). It is generally believed that co-ops arise in these areas when there is a market or social failure in providing services (Lord and Mellor 1996; Stryjan 1994). The market may fail to provide the services needed, fail to provide affordable or reasonable cost services, or fail to provide services that meet consumers' expectations for quality. "Social failure" to provide services refers to the inability of individual households to provide the levels of care needed, mainly because of the entry of women into the paid labor force. Interestingly, in Japan, co-ops organized to provide welfare services are mainly seen as a replacement for family provision of care rather than as a replacement for government welfare services (Lord and Mellor 1996).

Borzaga and Santuari (1998) describe co-ops that operate in these areas as "social cooperatives," which "attempt to combine the product of collective goods with private-sector legal forms and managerial models" (75–76) in order to accomplish the social purposes of the organization. Consumer co-ops have traditionally operated in many of these areas; however, there may be a new potential for consumer cooperation that arises out of the massive social and economic changes brought about by technological innovation and globalization (Ebert and Noll 1999).

While the 1990s were characterized by economic growth and prosperity for some, the economic model based on full employment, mass consumption, and an extensive state welfare system resulted in highly concentrated unemployment in some areas, a persistent underclass, and increasingly high costs to support public welfare systems (Integra 1996). Declining public revenues and public will to support personal social services through taxation led to the privatization of many government services.

At the same time, the global economy offers large-scale, multinational companies an opportunity to relocate production facilities to countries with "the least regulation, low social taxes and a high degree of economic freedom" (Ebert and Noll 1999, 481). As companies relocate, communities lose a significant portion of their economic base in the form of jobs, taxes, and capital. Ebert and Noll describe the downward spiral effect when governments attempt to address economic dislocation. The ultimate result is failure to provide needed social services adequately through traditional methods of the welfare state (Wylie 2001).

In response, workers in and consumers of social services are organizing a variety of efforts to ensure that the services continue to be provided in a manner that meets their expectations for quality. Browne (1997) calls these efforts "networks of reciprocity" built on a combination of volunteerism, self-help, and workers' and consumers' co-ops. An essential value provided by co-ops is the opportunity for both consumers and providers to democratically participate in critical decisions regarding which services will be provided, at what cost, and at what level of quality (Lord and Mellor 1996).

Social co-ops are especially well developed in Italy. In 1995, co-ops in health care and social services represented 13 percent of Italian public spending in these areas. More than 200,000 people were served by nearly 2,000 co-ops, which employed 40,000 people. These co-ops functioned in three main areas: (1) integration of the disabled into the workforce, (2) provision of professional case work, and (3) provision of welfare and employment services (Borzaga and Santuari 1998).

Eastern Europeans have begun cooperative sheltered workshops for people with disabilities. In Sweden, there is a growing number of residential care co-ops for people with disabilities, a variety of cooperative care services for the elderly, co-ops that provide psychiatric care, and several thousand child-care co-ops. In fact, according to Pestoff (1998), co-ops are "one of the most important alternatives to the public provision of health care in Sweden" (102). The Migros Cooperative in Switzerland has developed senior housing co-ops and even a retail store specifically designed for elderly women (Co-op Suisse) (Wylie 2001).

Lord and Mellor's (1996) case study of the Fukushi Club in Japan gives another example of consumer co-ops' potential to provide personal care services. The Fukushi Club is an offshoot of the Seikatsu Club Consumers' Cooperative (SCCC), a federation of 26,500 small buying groups, or *han*, that serve 220,000 Japanese households. Over time, the *han* groups have expanded beyond their original concerns with food safety, the environment, and peace issues, which were articulated through a collective impact on production, distribution, and consumption of food products. In a model that seems remarkably similar to a twenty-first-century cooperative commonwealth, the *han* groups have developed a wide network of consumer and worker co-ops that provide child care, health care, and personal care and operate bakeries, cafés, and handcraft shops.

Originally financed by the Kanagawa branch of SCCC and begun in 1989, by 1993 the Fukushi Club had about 4,700 members—500 workers, and 4,200 consumers. Local women organized into a series of worker collectives and provided food purchase and delivery assistance, home meal preparation and delivery, and home care services. According to Lord and Mellor (1996), the fundamental principle is that the club has created a "system of 'participatory welfare' in which both care providers and care recipients are members and are actively involved in both the day-to-day and strategic decision-making of the organization" (206). Importantly, workers and consumers determine the services needed. The Fukushi Club intentionally seeks to "challenge the dominance of public sector professionals and government planners in determining both the content and the parameters of service provision" (211).

This empowered approach to personal social services is a critical factor in Pestoff's (1998) advocacy of privatization of social services through non-profit and voluntary associations (especially co-ops), cooperative self-management, and empowerment of citizens as coproducers.[21] He advocates a "social contract for welfare" that complements the current public provision of social services by creating a new environment that empowers both workers and clients to have a stake in the service and a meaningful voice in determining the nature of the service provided (249). In Pestoff's model, "citizens become members in social enterprises, where they participate directly in the production of the local services they demand, as users and producers of such services, and where they therefore become co-producers of these services" (25).[22]

It is also possible that economic benefits will result from use of the consumer co-op to provide services that result from efficiencies inherent in the model (Wylie 2001). These include partial reliance on volunteer (member) labor, which reduces wage expense; removal of the need to generate profits for outside investors; elimination of taxes on income generated from sales to members; and services designed based on member demand. It should also be noted that co-ops that provide social services operate in a business framework that may have multiple goals that are being maximized. Often, these goals will not be similar to those of IOFs in the same industry. As we saw earlier, in a cooperative business, consumers must balance the utility they receive from the co-op against the profits they will receive as owners. Unlike IOFs, the primary goal is not to maximize return on invested capital. Rather, the effort is designed not only to generate a satisfactory return on capital but also to provide the social service in the best manner possible.

While some U.S. consumer co-ops provide social services, especially child care, health care, home health care (provided by worker co-ops), and senior housing, there is no specific public policy designed to support development of co-ops as a part of an integrated provider strategy for social services, or to foster economic development. Historically, U.S. consumer co-ops have been organized to meet a specific consumer need (e.g., food, child care, housing, health care, and recreational equipment).

Cooperators have not generalized their model to create numerous affiliated co-ops to support the various needs of their members and their community. Models for a comprehensive cooperative development strategy in which specific-purpose co-ops are part of an "integrated system of regional development" (Quarter 1992, 102) exist in the Mondragon cooperatives in Spain; in the Emilia-Romagna region of Italy (Pestoff 1998); and, to a lesser extent, among the Evangeline cooperatives in Atlantic Canada (Wilkinson and Quarter 1996).

While the many lessons to be learned from these examples are beyond the reach of this chapter, there is one critical point that applies specifically to consumer co-ops. Historically, consumer co-ops have been just that—owned, capitalized, controlled, and patronized by consumers; however, the consumer co-ops in Mondragon (especially Eroski, a very large retail co-op), the Japanese *han*-based co-ops, and the new European social service co-ops have developed a broader "multistakeholder" ownership base.[23] In this model, cooperative members are drawn from both consumers and cooperative employees. The unique interests and goals of each are explicitly recognized in the membership requirements and organizational structure. The deep philosophical division between consumers and producers so strongly entrenched in the consumer cooperative movement by Beatrice Potter Webb may be losing power.

The idea is to see a co-op as a community institution in which many actors have an economic interest in its success. In this view, all the major stakeholders, *in their primary roles*, should be able to participate in democratic ownership and control, and share in the rights and responsibilities. Thus, there are categories of membership for consumers, workers, and possibly suppliers and financiers. One would expect that the level of interest and participation in a co-op varies with the level of economic "stake" each member had in the co-op.

The Weaver Street Market (2002) has instituted a multistakeholder model to create what they call a "hybrid ownership structure." The strategy was developed to involve workers more directly in the co-op's success and to provide incentives that would reduce turnover. The general manager has commented that, due to this structure, the program has created a more "dynamic and entrepreneurial organization." The co-op is owned by about 3,500 consumers and approximately 40 workers.

Share requirements differ for consumers ($75 for one adult and $135 for a two-adult household) and workers ($400). Workers receive dividends based on profits and participate in a gainsharing program. Consumers receive a 5 percent discount on about half the products in the store, as well as a number of additional benefits, and they are part of a vibrant and central community institution and not eligible for patronage refunds. The board has seven members—two elected by consumers, two elected by workers, two appointed by the board, and the general manager. The board makes all the decisions. There is no provision for member votes because of the complexity of the structure. Weaver Street Market (2002) is one of the most successful and most entrepreneurial of the natural foods consumer co-ops in the United States.

Opportunities for Further Research

In theory, consumer cooperation appears to have great potential to move imperfect markets toward more perfect competition. There is relatively little current and relevant empirical work at this time to support or refute theoretical predictions. Many of the research opportunities suggested by Mather in 1968 remain unstudied in 2002.

In order to more fully understand the economic potential of consumer cooperation, several research questions might be studied. Can it be shown through comparative empirical analysis, similar to Mather's (1968), that co-ops have the economic welfare effects predicted for them? What methods could be used to determine the welfare-enhancing effects of consumer co-ops? What, if any, are the characteristics of markets where co-ops have the potential to improve the general welfare? What are the most efficient ways to organize and sustain co-ops in these markets?

Trends toward strategic alliances among the food co-ops[24] may offer a research opportunity to adapt work done on agricultural co-ops as a nexus of contracts entered into by independent firms (Staatz 1987). Issues that could be addressed include levels and methods of capitalization required and valuation of investments made in the alliance, how to distribute residual claims among the participants, and decision-making rights among participants.

If one accepts that economies with deep reservoirs of social capital perform better than those that do not, or that societies with those same reservoirs provide a higher quality of life for their members, it would make sense for policymakers to consider strategies to develop social capital, just as they work to develop physical, financial, or human capital. One of those strategies could well be the intentional development of broad-based, locally owned, member-driven consumer co-ops in a wide variety of industries chosen by the member-owners based on their economic needs. While co-ops would be expected to provide economic benefits, the primary policy objective would be to create social capital. In this case, emphasis would be placed on member education, active democratic participation, strategic alliances with community institutions, community-based activities, and effective leadership training.[25]

The potential for future consumer cooperative growth may be greatest in the social economy; however, research is needed to develop methods to identify cooperative development opportunities in social services and to develop case studies of successful cooperative models in social services industries. It is also important to learn more about what factors are necessary for successful consumer cooperative development and survival. Is there a role for public support of co-ops? If so, are there models for effective public intervention—domestic or international? Should a cooperative development effort be designed to expand existing co-ops, or should an effort be made to develop co-ops in "new" communities where markets are imperfect? If the latter, what are the critical characteristics of these markets that would make them fertile ground for cooperative development? What specific support could public agencies provide, and what are the costs and benefits of each approach? Approaches that might be considered include direct financial support, loan guarantees, tax incentives, technical assistance, extension-based educational programs, assignment of VISTA volunteers, and expansion of cooperative development offices into urban areas.

Conclusions

Both economic theory and cooperative practice show that consumer co-ops can have a substantial impact on improving general economic welfare and overall quality of life for their members. Economic theory indicates consumer co-ops at least tend to move markets toward perfect competition and, at best, arrive at a Pareto optimal equilibrium that maximizes consumer welfare. Social capital theory indicates co-ops offer an effective opportunity to build a community's social capital. Finally, co-ops are playing a new role in providing consumer- and worker-directed critical social services, especially in situations when both government and IOFs have failed the market. The significant potential of the consumer cooperative model makes it an attractive opportunity for economic development research and public policy support.

Notes

1. A short history of a variety of U.S. consumer co-ops through 1980 can be found in Hoyt (1997).

2. Examples can be found in the vestiges of an early 1970s slogan that asserted "food for people, not for profit," and the still vibrant credit union mission of "people helping people."

3. Much of the Webbs's work focused on the relative merits of organizing the working class into producer versus consumer co-ops. Their strong support of putting labor's resources into organizing consumer co-ops (rather than producer co-ops) was

part of a major debate within the cooperative movement that "lasted for decades" (Furlough and Strikwerda 1999, 13). Major positions in the debate are described at length by Donohue (1999).

4. The cooperative concept of a moral economy assumes that consumer goods are more than the good itself, and consumption of them is inextricably tied to their social, political, and economic context. Thus, co-ops have made significant efforts to purchase goods produced under fair labor conditions (Furlough and Strikwerda 1999), are committed to consumer education about the products being sold, support consumer-friendly legislation, support local producers, and create significant consumer-oriented innovations in retailing.

5. To some extent, agricultural supply co-ops can be seen as similar to consumer co-ops, and the analysis of them can be generalized to consumer co-ops.

6. There are major criticisms of this theory based on assumptions regarding marginal productivity of cooperative and household resources and knowledge of the equilibrium levels of all the households in the co-op. Staatz (1987) points out criticisms of the vertical integration theory of Emelianoff–Robotka–Phillips, which, for maximization, requires equal marginal productivities of each resource allocated to the cooperative plant and of that resource in the member's household. In addition, the marginal productivity of the last dollar must be equal in every use within each firm. This Cournot–Nash assumption implies that the precise equilibrium point for an individual firm can be determined only if the equilibrium level of output of all other firms is given—a major weakness for a model that predicts a unique equilibrium (see Vitaliano 1978, 25).

7. Retaining member-generated profits may be strategically desirable if the co-op needs to accumulate capital for growth or expansion, pay off debt, build reserves, avoid price wars with competitors, or support community activities. Presumably, all of these options would have utility for the member-owners that offsets the reduction in their consumer surplus.

8. Building on the Enke model, Helmberger and Hoos (1962) developed this "zero surplus" solution for a "single firm" co-op.

9. Microeconomic theory assumes that consumer demand varies inversely with price. Thus, consumers would be willing to pay a higher price for the first unit consumed than for later units. Because producers are not able to price each unit consumed differently, however, consumers are able to purchase all the quantities consumed at the price of the last consumed unit. The difference between the last price and the higher prices that the consumer would have been willing to pay is called *consumer surplus*.

10. "Consumer surplus is the difference between what consumers would be willing to pay for a product and what they actually pay when a single price is charged for all units" (Royer 1987, 12).

11. Enke (1945) advocates greater public support for "certain" consumer co-ops that achieve a balance between consumer surplus and profit based on the social value of effective resource allocation through pricing policies based on this balance. This position may be worthy of further study as U.S. co-ops pursue federal legislation to support urban cooperative development.

12. The lightbulb monopoly in Sweden and CF Industries are two examples.

13. The natural foods market was initially developed in the 1970s and had a virtual monopoly on the market until the early 1990s. Entry of IOF retailers into the natural foods industry and increasing natural foods sales in traditional supermarkets have

created a multibillion-dollar industry. The role of co-ops in the development of that industry and their current potential for "correction" of market failures have yet to be studied.

14. Staatz (1987) assumes this will be the probable member interpretation (78). In this case, equilibrium can be reached only if the net margin is zero, a condition that is "inconsistent" with the Rochdale principle of noncompetition on retail price, with return to members of "overcharges" in the form of a patronage rebate.

15. Support for this contention comes from the experience of the North Coast Cooperative (2002) in Arcata, California. After shifting to a patronage refund system, the co-op offered members the option of receiving their patronage in cash or equity in the co-op, or donating it to the co-op's community fund. Relatively large numbers of members regularly choose to donate the funds. This special case of patronage refunds usage has resulted in substantial benefit to the greater Arcata community. Since 1973, the co-op has donated over $855,000 to a wide variety of local charitable causes.

16. It should be noted that if the long-run average cost curve is L-shaped, which Cotterill (1984) asserts is often the case, marginal cost equals average cost and "consequently the welfare-maximizing solution corresponds to the zero-surplus solution, leading to a stable welfare-maximizing equilibrium" (Staatz 1987, 82).

17. Ireland and Law (1983) extended the Anderson et al. (1979) model by creating a Cournot–Nash model of consumer co-ops.

18. Cotterill (1980) has commented on the difficulty of constructing utility functions for each cooperative member and then aggregating them into a "group utility function that can be maximized by the co-op. This exercise is very difficult and may be distracting from more basic questions concerning cooperative size and growth. What one needs to know is when will a consumer join or exit a co-op, not when his/her utility is maximized" (3).

19. This condition has created substantial financial losses and conflict within the membership at Gentle Strength Cooperative in Tucson, Arizona.

20. Under perfect competition, if the long-run price is driven to minimum average cost, markets are operating efficiently, and there are no market failures. Hence, there would be little reason to organize and support co-ops.

21. Pestoff (1998) also suggests that privatization can be accomplished through the market (resulting in commercialization and commodification of service) or through greater diffused, nonstructured community responsibility. Presumably, this community responsibility would be assumed by families and informal volunteers, resulting in "deprofessionalism" and feminization in the provision of these services.

22. Perhaps contrary to more traditional expenditures on social services, investment in the development of third-sector social service providers can also be seen as an investment in social capital represented by the "networks of reciprocity," democratic participation by stakeholders, and community trust that are fostered by the cooperative model (Pestoff 1998, 54).

23. Pestoff (1998) describes a federation of four health-care co-ops, which illustrates this concept. Located in Barcelona, Spain, Integral Health Cooperation includes a co-op of doctors, one for all other hospital workers, one for consumers and health insurance clients, and one central organization where they join forces and co-manage their integrated efforts.

24. Over eighty consumer co-ops have joined regional cooperative grocers' associations, which, in turn, belong to the National Cooperative Grocers Association (2002). The association provides opportunities for pooled purchasing, is developing a na-

tional cooperative identity (brand), has pioneered in developing common financial statements for use by members, and shares best practices.

25. This strategy departs from traditional reasons for organizing co-ops. Workers, producers, and consumers organized co-ops because the market failed to provide quality goods at fair prices—for example, affordable housing; access to financial services; reliable, parent-directed child care; living wage employment; prepaid health care; fair market prices for crops; rural utilities; and a host of other goods or services. If the motivation for starting co-ops is to build an economic resource (i.e., social capital), the entire psychology and motivation of the enterprise is different.

References

Anderson, Richard, Philip K. Porter, and Charles Maurice. 1979. "The Economics of Consumer-managed Firms." *Southern Economic Journal* 46, no. 1: 119–130.

Borzaga, Carlo, and Alceste Santuari. 1998. "Social Enterprise and New Employment in Europe." In *The Development of Social Enterprises*, ed. Marco Maiello and Carlo Borzaga, 71–92. Brussels: Regione Autonoma Trentino–Alto Adige/EC DG-V.

Brattleboro Food Co-op. 2002. *Our Mission.* Available at www.brattleborofoodcoop.com/frame1a.html (July 3, 2002).

Browne, Paul Leduc. 1997. *The Two Faces of the Social Economy.* Available at www.policyalternatives.ca/publications/regina.html (January 8, 2002).

Caputo, Michael, and Lori Lynch. 1991. "Implications of Endogenous Prices in Consumer Theory: The Case of Barter and the Consumer Cooperative." *Journal of Comparative Economics* 15, no. 3: 421–436.

Cotterill, Ronald. 1980. *Group Purchasing: An Analysis of Performance and Economies of Size in Preorder Food Cooperatives* (Agricultural Experimentation Station, journal article no. 9503). East Lansing: Michigan State University. Available at www.aae.wisc.edu/fsrg/publications/wp-42.pdf (January 22, 2002).

———. 1984. "The Competitive Yardstick School of Cooperative Thought." In *American Cooperation*, ed. Lisa L. Keller, 41–56. Washington, DC: American Institute of Cooperation.

Davis Food Co-op. 2002. *About the Co-op.* Available at www.daviscoop.com/about.htm#mission (July 3, 2002).

Donohue, Kathleen. 1999. "From Cooperative Commonwealth to Cooperative Democracy: The American Cooperative Ideal, 1880–1940." In *Consumers Against Capitalism? Consumer Cooperation in Europe, North America, and Japan, 1840–1990*, ed. Ellen Furlough and Carl Strikwerda, 115–134. Lanham, MD: Rowman and Littlefield.

Ebert, Werner, and Werner Noll. 1999. "Globalisation: New Demands on Public Enterprises." *Annals of Public and Cooperative Economics* 70, no. 3: 477–499.

Emelianoff, Ivan V. 1948. *Economic Theory of Cooperation.* Washington, DC: Edwards Brothers.

Enke, Stephen. 1945. "Consumer Cooperatives and Economic Efficiency." *The American Economic Review* 35, no. 1: 148–155.

Feldman, Tine Rossing, and Susan Assaf. 1999. *Social Capital: Conceptual Frameworks and Empirical Evidence: An Annotated Bibliography* (Social capital initiative working paper no. 5). Washington, DC: World Bank.

Fulton, Murray. 2001. *Class Notes for Economics 231.3: Consumer Cooperation* (Co-operative Pricing Notes, 7–34). Available at www.coop-studies.usask.ca/murray/Econ231/Econ231.html. (January 25, 2002).

Furlough, Ellen, and Carl Strikwerda. 1999. "Economics, Consumer Culture, and Gender: An Introduction to the Politics of Consumer Cooperation." In *Consumers Against Capitalism? Consumer Cooperation in Europe, North America, and Japan, 1840–1990*, ed. Ellen Furlough and Carl Strikwerda, 1–66. Lanham, MD: Rowman and Littlefield.

The Gallup Organization. 1994. *Awareness and Image of Business Co-operatives: A Survey of the American Public*. Lincoln, NE: Gallup Organization.

Grootaert, Christiaan. 1998. *Social Capital: The Missing Link?* (Social Capital Initiative Working Paper No. 3). Washington, DC: World Bank.

Hamilton, David. 1954. "Keynes, Cooperation and Economic Stability." *The American Journal of Economics and Sociology* 14, no. 1: 59–70.

Helmberger, Peter, and Sidney Hoos. 1962. "Cooperative Enterprise and Organization Theory." *Journal of Farm Economics* 44, no. 2: 275–290.

Hoyt, Ann. 1974. "An Analysis of a Food Buying Cooperative." Unpublished master's thesis, University of California at Berkeley.

———. 1995. "Marketing Member Involvement: The American Experience." In *The World of Cooperative Enterprise*, 39–47. Oxford: Plunkett Foundation.

———. 1997. "Consumer Cooperatives." In *Encyclopedia of the Consumer Movement*, ed. Stephen Brobeck, 188–194. Santa Barbara, CA: ABC-CLIO.

Integra. 1996. "The Social Economy: Potentials and Pitfalls." *Integra Review* (2). Available at www.iol.ie/EMPLOYMENT/integra/sepp.html (January 16, 2002).

International Joint Project on Co-operative Democracy. 1995. *Making Membership Meaningful: Participatory Democracy in Organizations*. Saskatchewan, Canada: Centre for the Study of Co-operatives, University of Saskatchewan.

Ireland, Norman J., and Peter J. Law. 1983. "A Cournot–Nash Model of the Consumer Cooperative." *Southern Economic Journal* 49, no. 3: 706–716.

Kenworthy, Lane. 1997. "Civic Engagement, Social Capital, and Economic Cooperation." *The American Behavioral Scientist* 40, no. 2: 645–656.

Kreitner, Philip. 1978. "The Theory of Economic Co-operation: U.S. New Generation Food Co-ops and the Co-operative Dilemma." Unpublished Ph.D. dissertation, University of Michigan, Ann Arbor.

Lakewinds Natural Foods. 2002. *Lakewinds Natural Foods*. Available at www.lakewinds.com/ (July 8, 2002).

Leikin, Steven. 1999. "The Citizen Producer: The Rise and Fall of Working-Class Cooperatives in the United States." In *Consumers Against Capitalism? Consumer Cooperation in Europe, North America, and Japan, 1840–1990*, ed. Ellen Furlough and Carl Strikwerda, 93–114. Lanham, MD: Rowman and Littlefield.

Lord, Anita, and Mary Mellor. 1996. "Women and the Cooperative Provision of Care: The Example of the 'Fukushi Club' in Japan." *Economic and Industrial Democracy* 17: 199–220.

Mather, Loys. 1968. *Consumer Cooperatives in the Grocery Retailing Industry*. Madison: University of Wisconsin–Madison.

Mississippi Market. 2002. *Co-op Info*. Available at www.msmarket.org/coop.htm (July 3, 2002).

National Association of Housing Cooperatives. 2002. *About NAHC and Housing Co-ops*. Available at www.coophousing.org/about_nahc.shtml (July 20, 2002).

National Cooperative Business Association. 2002. *Co-op Primer: Co-op Statistics.* Available at www.ncba.coop/stats.cfm (July 20, 2002).

National Cooperative Grocers Association. 2002. *About Us.* Available at www.nationalcoopgrocers.com (July 20, 2002).

Nolan, Peg, Walden Swanson, Kate Sumberg, and Dave Gutknecht. 2002. "Retail Operations Survey: Strong results, Debatable Future." *Cooperative Grocer* (101). Available at www.cooperativegrocer.com/cg2002/surveytxt2001.shtml (July 28, 2002).

North Coast Cooperative. 2002. *Cooperative Community Fund.* Available at www.northcoastco_op.com/cmunity.htm (July 8, 2002).

Parker, Florence, ed. 1936. *Consumers' Cooperation in the United States, 1936.* Washington, DC: U.S. Bureau of Labor Statistics.

Pestoff, Victor A. 1998. *Beyond the Market and the State: Social Enterprise and Civil Democracy in a Welfare Society.* Brookfield, VT: Ashgate.

Phillips, Richard. 1953. "Economic Nature of the Cooperative Organization." *Journal of Farm Economics* 35: 74–87.

Putnam, Robert. 2000. *Bowling Alone: The Collapse and Revival of American Community.* New York: Touchstone.

Quarter, Jack. 1992. *Canada's Social Economy.* Toronto: Jack Lorimer.

Robison, Lindon, Allan Schmid, and Marcelo Siles. 1999. *Is Social Capital Really Capital?* (Staff paper no. 99–21). East Lansing: Department of Agricultural Economics, Michigan State University.

Robotka, Frank. 1957. "A Theory of Cooperation." In *Agricultural Cooperation: Selected Readings,* ed. Martin Abrahamson and Claud Scroggs, 121–142. Minneapolis: University of Minnesota Press.

Royer, Jeffrey S. 1987. *Cooperative Theory: New Approaches* (ACS service report no. 18). Washington, DC: USDA, Agricultural Cooperative Service.

Sanchez, Alfonso. 2002. *Social Economy Organizations in a World in Transition.* Available at www.2uhu.es/alfonso_vargas/cretavar.html (July 9, 2002).

Schomisch, Thomas P. 1979. *Edwin G. Nourse and the Competitive Yardstick School of Thought* (UCC occasional paper, no. 2). Madison: University Center for Cooperatives, University of Wisconsin–Madison. Available at: www.wisc.edu/uwcc/info/ocpap/edwin.html (July 10, 2002).

Sevananda. 2002. *Our Mission.* Available at www.livingnaturally.com/retailer/store_templates/ret_about_us.asp?storeID=c5g13s77a6gb8p0JT1p2q4xbhr8bfxx2 (July 3, 2002).

Social Network Analysis. 1999. *Definitions of Social Capital in the Literature.* Available at www.analytictech.com/networks/definitions_of_social_capital.htm (October 10, 2001).

Sommer, Robert. 1991. "Consciences in the Marketplace: The Role of Cooperatives in Consumer Protection." *Journal of Social Issues* 47, no. 1: 135–148.

Spear, Roger. n.d. *The Co-operative Advantage.* Milton Keynes, UK: Co-op Research Unit.

Staatz, John. 1987. "Recent Developments in the Theory of Agricultural Cooperation." *Journal of Agricultural Cooperation* 2: 74–95.

Stryjan, Johanan. 1994. "The Formation of New Cooperatives: Theory and the Swedish Case." *Economic and Industrial Democracy* 15, no. 4: 51–80.

Thompson, David. 1994. *Weavers of Dreams.* Davis: University of California at Davis.

Torgerson, Randall E., Bruce J. Reynolds, and Thomas W. Gray. 1997. *Evolution of Cooperative Thought, Theory and Purpose*. Madison: Center for Cooperatives, University of Wisconsin–Madison. Available at www.wisc.edu/uwcc/info/torg.html (November 19, 2001).

Vitaliano, Peter. 1978. "The Theory of Agricultural Enterprise: Its Development and Present Status." In *Agricultural Cooperatives and the Public Interest* (North Central regional research publication 256), ed. Bruce Marion, 21–42. Madison: Research Division, College of Agricultural and Life Sciences, University of Wisconsin–Madison.

Warbasse, James Peter. 1923. *Cooperative Democracy: Attained Through Voluntary Association of People as Consumers*. New York: Macmillan.

———. 1939. *Cooperation as a Way of Peace*. New York: Harper and Brothers.

———. 1950. *Cooperative Peace*. Superior, WI: Cooperative Publishing Association. Available online: http://abob.libs.uga.edu/bobk/coopp.html (June 23, 2002).

Weaver Street Market. 2002. *Weaver Street Market*. Available at www.weaverstreet market.com/events.html#opendoor (July 8, 2002).

Webb Sidney, and Beatrice Webb. 1921. *The Consumers' Cooperative Movement*. London: Longmans, Green.

Wilkinson, Paul, and Jack Quarter. 1996. *Building a Community-controlled Economy: The Evangeline Co-operative Experience*. Toronto: University of Toronto Press.

Williamson Street Grocery Co-op. 2002. *Willy Street Co-op*. Available at www.willystcoop.com/wsc_coop.html (July 3, 2002).

Wuelker, Hans-Detlaf. 1995. *The Social Economy and Co-ops: A German Perspective*. Available at www.wisc.edu/uwcc/icic/orgs/ica/pubs/review/vol-88–2/21.html (July 9, 2002).

Wylie, Lloyd. 2001. *European Social Cooperatives: A Survey and Analysis of Current Developments* (Occasional paper no. 6). Victoria: British Columbia Institute for Co-operative Studies, University of Victoria.

13

The Business of Relationships

Greg MacLeod

Introduction

In *Bowling Alone*, Robert Putnam (2000) has brought to light a fact that most American economists have largely ignored—that human relationships are the underpinning of all economic activity. In traditional economic theory, there has been scant recognition of human purpose as being economically significant in relationships within an enterprise or in the relationship of the enterprise with the community. Admittedly, research on transaction costs does focus on elements of trust, but this only applies to empirical relations between and within firms (e.g., Williamson 1980). Following standard empirical methods, neoclassical economics recognizes only quantifiable factors that can be measured and translated easily into systems that can be manipulated logically. Neoclassical economics is modeled upon the physical sciences, which are based on the discovery of observables, which follow systematic laws such as supply and demand; personal relationships and attitudes are considered "external" to the equations.

The fact that human elements are excluded is very significant in light of Putnam's (2000) work, demonstrating that the basic stability and viability of all structures in society depends on personal relationships. This insight is extremely important for those interested in the reform of the global corporate system. It is especially useful for those involved in the cooperative sector of business because the explicit basis of a cooperative is fundamentally "social" capital, whereas the basis dominant in conventional corporations is "financial" capital. The key question is whether it is the human relationship or the financial relationship that dominates in a system.

Putnam (2000) defines social capital as "the relationships, networks and norms that facilitate collective action" (6). He has marshaled a compelling case for its importance in a range of social and economic outcomes and then documents a dramatic decline in social capital during the last two decades in the United States. He found some striking correlations such as the following: (1) high social capital goes with high tolerance of racial differences, (2) violent crime is rarer, and (3) health is better in states with high social capital (Putnam 2000, 2001).

"Social" capital is different from "human" capital, which is expressed as an individual contribution, an economic behavior easily measured. In contrast, social capital focuses on networks and relationships within and between them. Putnam (2000) points out that economic stability, indeed civil society itself, is at risk when social capital declines radically and, from his analysis, it appears that the result is a consequential decline in economic capital. One obvious example is the kind of labor disputes that arise out of poor relationships between workers and management.

Whether the relationship is between groups in a society or between nations, problems and conflicts arise when relationships become unbalanced. The twenty-first century has begun with an increasing chasm between the system of international business and the concerns of the ordinary citizen (Went 2000), a division highlighted in recent years by widespread public protests directed toward corporate globalization. In the year 2001, unease seemed to have reached a climax at the Summit of the Americas in Quebec, where thousands of people from all over North America gathered in an enormous outcry against the abuses of free trade (Stiglitz 2001).

Eighteen months earlier, a similar protest took place in Seattle, and May Day 2001 demonstrations in Europe were a further sign of discontent, with half a million Germans taking to the streets in protest. In July of the same year, we saw violence and death in Genoa during the meetings of the G8 countries. It is true that extremists were involved in all of these events; however, from such widespread discontent we know that there is a basis in fact for a deep reappraisal of our economic relationships.

A related symptom of disorder in this new century is the increasing number of large corporate mergers with resulting layoffs of hundreds of thousands of employees (Korten 2001). To have "belonged" to a firm for twenty years means little in this business environment, for relationships between employees and the enterprise are more and more tenuous. Massive layoffs, then, may be seen as a consequence of business relationships based on a flow of capital and subject to fluctuations in a world system of stock exchanges. Employee mistrust has increased in light of corporate malfeasance by companies such as Enron and WorldCom, among others, which caused massive layoffs and financial loss for workers (Cave 2002; Krugman 2002). The broader point is that capitalism and democracy operate on the principle of trust. If people cannot trust the economic and political institutions within society, then democracy and the operation of markets are at risk (Sen 1999).

In contrast, it will be shown later why the multibillion-dollar Mondragon cooperative complex has never had layoffs in its fifty–year history. The faults of our global economic system are best seen in terms of relationships at various levels: among employees, among enterprises, and in the relationship of the corporate system to its ambient society (Drucker 1993). In this perspective, the cooperative movement assumes major importance because it is about improving relationships. Thus, this chapter underlines the critical role of positive relationships for the very survival of our democratic societies and points out how the cooperative movement is founded on a kind of relationship in which human values are primary.

As Melnyk (1985) pointed out, however, much of the cooperative sector has become overinstitutionalized with the result that it has not adapted to the needs of today. As the need for reform increases in the face of global economies, pressure is mounting for a reexamination of the basic concept of the co-op as a business entity. On the positive side, a variety of empirical cases of cooperative businesses are presented in this chapter that are innovative and point in the direction of healing broken relationships between individuals and societies. Finally, it is suggested that social reformers should consider the cooperative sector as a powerful potential ally for positive change in the world—a sleeping giant that needs to be awakened and challenged (Quarter 1993).

Four Relationships

While Putnam (2000) considers social relationships of all sorts, the humanistic language of his economic analysis is strikingly similar to the language of the old cooperative movement. Those relationships involving businesses will be discussed next. Among the endless types of relationships that exist, just four have been selected to help illustrate various approaches to cooperative development:

1. internal relationships;
2. the enterprise and wider society;
3. enterprise to enterprise;
4. workers to the enterprise itself.

Each of these relationships will be addressed, with consideration to how they relate to typical global corporations. Then, a cooperative example will be presented, showing how each cooperative approach can correct problematic aspects of these relationships. No cases are models of perfect relationships. One or the other of the four relationships will dominate in each case, although some exemplify several of the relationship types. A variety of cases will be examined in order to show possible direction for improvement and reform.

Internal Relationships

The exploitative nature of the relationship between the owner of capital and the worker is the classical criticism of capitalistic business. As Karl Marx (1867 [1986]) illustrated, workers became tools of owners in the nineteenth century—a master–slave relationship, so to speak. While the abuses of the old system have been largely overcome (although sweatshops still exist), a new postindustrial society has not made a profound difference in the relationships between stakeholders in the business corporation. Some individuals in the business control while others are controlled.

Today, large corporate systems are often technocratic and impersonal (Marcuse 1964) and control is usually more powerful than the systems of the nineteenth century (MacIntyre 1984). Because of these lopsided relationships, the concept of worker-owned enterprises has become important. The cooperatives of Yugoslavia, under Tito, as well as those of the Basque nation in Spain, were organized in response to this problem. The most famous of these is Mondragon, which received a United Nations prize as one of the fifty best social economic innovations in the world. Much can be learned from this amazing history (MacLeod 1997; Morrison 1991; Whyte and Whyte 1988).

The Mondragon co-ops started in the 1950s when a group of young engineers began working for a traditional industry in Mondragon, Spain. Inspired by the humanistic principles of their local pastor, they found that the business was in conflict with their personal values and they resigned, deciding to set up their own business based on their own egalitarian values. Establishing a small company to manufacture kerosene stoves, they agreed that all employees would be owners, sharing in both the responsibility and the rewards.

In their new worker co-op, they agreed that no one would earn more than three times the salary of the lowest paid. If a junior member earns $20,000 per year, then the president cannot earn more than $60,000. The idea of wages being determined by a set ratio between the highest paid and the lowest paid was a standard to be maintained in all the future Mondragon cooperatives.

In this new kind of co-op, worker candidates are required to purchase a share, which today equals approximately one-half of their yearly salary. The share entitles the worker to vote in the choice of the board of directors, which, in turn, hires a general manager. This process avoids the kind of alienation from company management experienced by employees who have no control whatsoever over corporate decision making. There are no layoffs in Mondragon—workers effectively have a guarantee of lifetime work. This is a far cry from the precarious position of most workers employed by Fortune 500 companies that lay people off in harmony with fluctuations in the stock market.

When the stove factory became profitable, the founders expanded and hired more members, always as associates and voting members. Soon they required more money for expansion, which was difficult to obtain, so their mentor, Don José María Arizmendiazzieta, suggested that they form a cooperative bank. They did this, setting up branches in the villages, avoiding larger cities because they assumed that the city provided less social solidarity and support. Of course, small town, rural life is not automatically more democratic. The experience with fish barons and village merchants showed how rural people can be subservient. The difference in Mondragon is that the local college and the discussion groups organized by Don José Maréa helped ensure a level of social consciousness. Social capital in itself does not automatically translate into democratic structures. Leadership and education are essential.

The cooperative bank, or credit union, soon became successful. Leaders did not, however, promote them as places to save money but, rather, as a way to create businesses and jobs for the children in their communities. Their early motto was "Savings or Suitcases," referring to the brain drain that in the past forced their children to leave—a subtle message that capital drain was the cause of the brain drain (Mathews 2000). In a sense, they were building on local social capital. Most of rural and small town North America, too, has declined radically with the outflow of young people moving to the larger cities for work and education (Drabenstott and Smith 1996). Rarely do they return.

Most North American credit unions are conceived as consumer co-ops, providing a service to member-consumers of capital. In contrast, Mondragon leaders saw capital as being a part of production, and they departed from tradition by viewing the credit union as a productive force. Following the philosophy of worker participation, they required employees of the credit union to be voting members alongside client members. Because the challenge was job creation through business development, and in contrast with North American credit unions, key clients are cooperative businesses. This is reflected on boards of directors, the memberships of which are half employees and half business clients.

By the year 2001, the Mondragon Cooperative Corporation (MCC) had grown into a large complex made up of four divisions (Mondragon n.d.):

1. *Corporate:* 15 Enterprises. These are responsible for planning and development, including the university.
2. *Finance:* 6 Enterprises. These include the Caja Laboral, or Credit Union, along with insurance and social security.
3. *Industrial:* 80 Enterprises. These include the factories, which produce a range of products such as auto parts, industrial equipment, and household appliances.
4. *Distribution:* 10 Enterprises. These are organized into two sectors. One is retail, which has hundreds of branches, including superstores. The other is agrifood, with a range of businesses from dairy and livestock feed to greenhouses.

During the last five years, the MCC has created more than 20,000 jobs—an incredible statistic in view of the large-scale layoffs repeatedly announced by global stockholder companies in large and small centers around the world. This multibillion-dollar complex of companies is now a global force and clearly an outstanding success by any business standard; however, leaders acknowledge a dilemma in trying to do business in the global system, which is not cooperatively organized. A problem is that most of the cooperative sector in the world is oriented to consumer businesses, and very few co-ops are involved in the industrial sector. In order to ensure markets, they have entered into joint ventures and partnerships with a variety of private capitalistic corporations around the world.

Despite rapid growth, the MCC has been able to maintain its founding principles in its home territory. Today, the wage ratio is in the range of six to one, compared with the original ratio of three to one. The democratic principles are the same, however. The individual members of each cooperative enterprise elect a board of directors and that board chooses a manager, although final power rests with the general assembly, which can convoke a special meeting and dismiss the manager. Individual workers know that they have ownership.

Outside commentators have noted that Mondragon factories require less middle management than a conventional factory and that there is a high level of self-motivation, which is reflected in higher productivity (Thomas and Logan 1982), an indicator that workers are less alienated. Still, in any system, management tends to concentrate on efficiency and production so that the human welfare of the workers can easily be neglected. The Social Council established in all Mondragon co-ops is seen as a countervailing force to management. It is similar to a labor union in that it negotiates working conditions, wages, and benefits, representing another tool to protect worker rights.

During the 1990s, the major change was the establishment of the Congress as a structure to unify all of the various parts of the Mondragon system in order to provide unified strategies for competition in the global system. It is structured according to principles of representative democracy; the different cooperative enterprises elect 350 delegates who constitute the supreme authority on policy and general direction. There is an administrative board made up of managers, but important decisions must be approved by the general assembly. Agreements are made such that when a worker becomes redundant in one co-op, that worker has the right to claim the first available job in another factory in the same sector. Of course, the worker must accept retraining.

With increasing size and complexity, much of the earlier type of leadership has been replaced by a technocratic system, something that seems almost inevitable in modern, globally competitive business, just as there has been a gradual shift away from innovation as such toward the need to satisfy customers (Cheney 2001). Despite such an imperative, Mondragon has maintained a strict adherence to the principles of both direct and indirect democracy—the worker members are conscious of the fact that they do have the final say. More than any other known corporate business system in the world, Mondragon's leaders have gone to great lengths to design systems with democratic and fair relationships between all participants.

Cooperative Advantage

In their analysis of Mondragon, Thomas and Logan (1982) conclude that the internal structure of the Mondragon co-ops provides an advantage in efficiency—less supervision is required on the shop floor than in similar stockholder factories. There is a low turnover of workers, so the workforce provides an accessible pool of potential managers.

Another empirical measure of efficiency is the time lost through labor unrest and strikes—Mondragon has had only one minor strike during its fifty-year history. The fact that Mondragon has received the General Motors prize for excellence in production of auto parts is an indicator of a superior workforce (Mondragon 2000). Most of all, the MCC has been able to deliver thousands of jobs each year, so the local county has avoided many of the unemployment problems present in other parts of Spain.

The Business Enterprise and the Society

Criticism of the corporate reality has been a major topic in the United States during this century (Krugman 2002; Stiglitz 2001). Business corporations have become extremely powerful, as predicted by Berle and Means (1932

[1967]), the first major analysis to point out the danger of concentrating economic power in a manner that could eventually compete on equal terms with the nation-state.

While traditionalists have claimed that families are the building blocks of society, Don José María (MacLeod 1997), a co-founder of the Mondragon complex, admitted that business corporations have replaced families as the building blocks of society (Azurmendi 1987; Thurow 1996). In this age of megabusinesses, the corporation itself is an agent of social change. The fact that the same television programs with the same advertisements are carried all over the world is an indication of their influence. One of the biggest entertainment business successes of the first years of the twenty-first century were the Harry Potter books and films. The company that produced the movie, and that controls most of the product rights, is AOL–Time Warner—one of a new kind of conglomerate that combines both communication and content. With yearly revenues of $40 billion, they connect half of all U.S. Internet users; have more than a million subscribers in Latin America; and their magazine division has millions of subscribers for titles that include *Time*, *Sports Illustrated*, and *Fortune Magazine* as well as some leading magazines in Britain (Barber 1996; McChesney 1999). They have an obvious impact on culture all over the world. Furthermore, as consolidation increases among media companies, democracy is at risk as the diversity of editorial viewpoints is reduced. For example, can NBC News—a General Electric subsidiary—objectively cover the business practices of General Electric, which produces a range of civilian and military products?

While global corporations can bring positive benefits to local societies (Novak 1981; Rugman 2000), this author, Soros (1997), and Reich (1992) argue that those benefits are short-term. Over time, corporations merge so that economic power becomes more and more concentrated. *Le Monde Diplomatique* ("Supplement sur l'avenir" 1999) reported that 200 business corporations controlled 30 percent of the assets of the world. This economic centralization has been matched by a demographic centralization (Tables 13.1 and 13.2) that might be termed "massification."

In having moved from the industrial to the postindustrial—and now to the knowledge economy controlled by huge global corporations—we have a new context in which to consider the role of business in this new century. Demographic and economic massification eventually causes a cultural massification, exemplified by the uniformity of popular music and clothing styles around the globe. Megacorporations have workforces in the hundreds of thousands scattered throughout the world. Because of their power and influence, they set the tone for business in general—they set the rules of the game—and, with the fall of the communist bloc, it is becoming clearer that there is only

Table 13.1

Economic Massification: Megacorporations (annual sales: US$7,592 trillion)

Country	No.	Sales (in trillions)	Percentage
United States	74	2,776	36.5
Japan	41	1,830	24.1
Germany	23	958	12.6
Others	62	2,028	26.8
Totals	200	7,592	100.0

Source: "Supplement sur l'avenir" (1999).

Table 13.2

Demographic Massification: Megapoles (cities with 15+ million inhabitants)[a]

City	1995 population (in millions)
Tokyo	26.8
São Paulo	16.4
New York	16.3
Mexico City	15.5
Bombay	15.1

Source: "Supplement sur l'avenir" (1999).

[a]*Le Monde Diplomatique* ("Supplement sur l'avenir" 1999) predicts that there will be thirty-three megapoles by 2015.

one economic game in the world. Those areas of the globe that are not in the game suffer from unacceptable levels of poverty, disease, and famine.

Over and over again we have seen that global corporations follow the needs of their own internal structure and not those of the society where they are located. According to Friedman (1980), the purpose of each enterprise must be egoistic. If migrating from one country to another can increase shareholder value, then most business corporations will do so. The result is often unemployment and economic depletion for the communities abandoned. Vast areas of North America, such as Saskatchewan, Colorado, Nebraska, and Kansas, are being depopulated because of corporate business evolution (Drabenstott and Smith 1996; Kristof 2002). The correlation is clear. The population figures in Table 13.2 match the increasing concentration and centralization of corporations in Table 13.1.

The typical global corporation does not profess to be dedicated to the development of the United States, France, or Japan; its expressed purpose is the increase of share value. If a society does benefit, then, it is by accident, not on purpose. Wal-Mart is found in many countries, but its presence is not motivated by a desire to benefit that country—the impact on the ambient society is not of great concern except so far as it would affect public relations and customer attitudes. While Friedmanites (disciples of Milton Friedman and laissez-faire capitalism) see this as virtue, others see it as a perversion of what traditional society intended business corporations to be (Davis 1905).

Business writers from within the corporate system, such as Mark Scott (2000), warn that the egoism of corporations is self-destructive, but solutions from the corporate establishment simply call for new visionary mission statements that are practically religious in tone. Such solutions are superficial because the stock market share system makes such visionary changes impossible. Change must be much more profound than updating a mission statement—it must involve different basic legal structures.

Co-ops are business groups incorporated under law and, strictly speaking, they can be called corporations; hence, Mondragon (n.d.) has tended to use the term "cooperative corporation." A look at the historical sources of the corporate concept shows that today's co-ops are closer to the original organizational practices than are many Fortune 500 corporations. Earlier enterprises were clearly set up for social purposes, to be of service to the general society that granted them legitimacy and privilege. Davis (1905) traces the origins of the corporate form from the monasteries of the seventh century, to the guilds and boroughs in Renaissance times and later, and to trading associations. Gower (1969) clearly indicates that corporations are creatures of law—that the original intent was an "association of a number of people for some common object or objects" (3). He is highly critical of the ownership of corporations by shareholders, calling it a legal fiction; the real associates are managers and employees. Because law tends to lag behind society, Gower calls for reform of corporate law, which is long overdue.

Because incorporated bodies are created by law to be responsible to the enabling society, the relationship of the corporation to society is the most fundamental of all business relationships (Ryan 1983). These may be exploitative, with advantage to one side, or they may entail mutuality. Moses Coady, a Canadian cooperative pioneer, attacked relationships that were unequal, suggesting "in every cooperative venture a bilateral contract is required for real business; and nothing is business in the real sense where the contract is unilateral and one party can take all the traffic will bear" (Laidlaw 1971, 98).

While some see co-ops as turned inward and benefiting only the members, the main tradition in the world has been to see the cooperative sector as serving society in general. Professor Yuichiro Nakagawa (2000), of Mejii University in Tokyo, says there is no raison d'être for the cooperative movement if it is not community-based well-being. This tradition of commitment to the wider mission of social-economic reform was always present, with frequent references to the ideal of the cooperative commonwealth (Craig 1993; Laidlaw 1971).

The cooperative movement has been different from the mainstream economy in that it proposed a different set of relationships for doing business (Fairbairn and MacPherson 2000; MacPherson 1995). Robert Owen promoted co-ops in response to the abuses of nineteenth-century business. (Quarter 2000). In a similar way today, communities feel abandoned by the global corporate system, and development groups are now organizing businesses for the specific purpose of service to the larger community. These new business structures reverse economic decline in their region in a cooperative manner. This difference in purpose makes them radically different in their relationship with local society. It is important to note that the difference is not simply in stated purposes, but is reflected in the basic legal structure.

Cape Breton

One small example is New Dawn Enterprises on Cape Breton Island, Nova Scotia, Canada (MacLeod 1985). It is very small in comparison with Mondragon, but its dominant emphasis is also service to the local community, driven by the closure of local coal mines and chronically high unemployment. A group of social activists organized as a development co-op to initiate businesses in response to social needs. Legally, it is a not-for-profit corporation similar to a 501(c)3 organization in the United States. This small group of a dozen people had no capital, so they borrowed money to buy an abandoned retail store as a headquarters for handicraft projects, renovating the building's second floor to create five small apartments. Much sweat equity by volunteers raised the value of the building, and the rents paid the mortgage, providing equity for the foundation to make more purchases of property.

With the economic declines, new dentists tended to avoid the area, and people had long waits to receive treatment. New Dawn decided to build dental clinics, offering "turn-key" deals to prospective dentists. Soon the dental shortage was resolved, and New Dawn made a profit in the process. As these small ventures succeeded in business terms, New Dawn moved into the construction of apartment buildings with the help of low-interest government mortgages. Soon, a care facility for seniors was added along with a home-care service for the infirm. All that began in 1974. Just twenty-five years later, New Dawn is still operating without government grants, has more than CA$15 million in assets, employs almost 200 people, and is still actively developing new businesses.

Within the local community, New Dawn was an innovation. Co-ops tended to follow the tradition of being a retail co-op, a financial co-op, or a marketing co-op. New Dawn was none of these. It was multifunctional and flexible. Although the overarching purpose was community improvement, the group adopted many of the flexibility and growth principles more typical of large business corporations. The relationship is fundamentally different from most other approaches, however. The local community is not treated as a means of profit for the cooperative corporation; rather, it is treated as the reason for the provision of services. It is a difference of ends and means.

After fifteen years of experience with New Dawn, some leaders realized that the drain of capital from the area was a key obstacle to business development and employment. They organized the BCA (Banking Community Assets) Financial Group as a holding company and an investment co-op. Raising half a million dollars in the local community, they managed to secure a matching interest-free loan from government. When a small local credit union could not finance a new building, BCA stepped in and designed a community center, with the credit union as a tenant, along with other tenants, such as Tim Horton's donuts, to pay off the mortgage.

When an industrial plumbing company went bankrupt, BCA lent the employees money to buy the assets. That company has expanded with great success, and the BCA group has taken over several other bankrupt companies, reorganizing them to subsequently become successful. This is important because bankruptcies occur frequently in communities under economic stress.

A new government program in Canada allows a tax credit for investors in approved community companies, and the BCA Investment Cooperative has raised more than $1 million in fourteen months, offering such incentives to investors. In 2002, the BCA group will manage almost $3 million. Hundreds of jobs have been created, and hundreds of local citizens have bought shares. The typical appeal by investment companies is to promise the highest possible returns, regardless of where the money is directed. BCA's appeal has been different and successful. A reasonable financial return is promised, but the main appeal is to serve the local community rather than the anonymous stock market.

As more communities become economically depleted with both capital and young brains drained away, the future of local communities will depend on the capacity of local leaders to create structures dedicated to the local good and not to distant shareholders. This reinforces local relationships. Small town and rural North America are especially threatened by the new, centralized economy, and co-ops must be developed as a kind of economic infrastructure to help local society to survive. The federal government of the United States seems to have recognized this role of society-building through a federal Department of Agriculture program that provides up to $5 million in matching funds for groups willing to organize co-ops in rural America (Harrison and Oldroyd 2002).

Cooperative Advantage

The Italian economist Stefano Zamagni (2000) of the University of Bologna says that Western governments have not acknowledged the important contribution of co-ops to the development and preservation of societies. He points to measurable indicators of social well-being in Emilia Romagna, which has the highest percentage of co-ops in Italy:

- unemployment in the Emilia Romagna region is 4 percent;
- social capital is higher because there is more participation in networks and federations;
- the high level of joint venturing and networking in this region has resulted in a high rate of business success, and wages are almost double those in other regions of Italy;
- social stability is greater in this area, with low outmigration and a higher level of job creation than in other areas of Italy.

David Erdal (1999) provides a comparison of towns in Italy with co-ops versus those without co-ops. In several areas, including health, he found that the towns with a high percentage of cooperative business had a much better record. There has not been enough empirical study done to come to a definitive conclusion, but evidence is mounting that the cooperative way of doing business brings significant nonmonetary advantages to local societies (Zamagni 2000).

Enterprise to Enterprise

The conventional wisdom of business has been based on competition, which, to be fair, has brought benefits to society; however, it can also be destructive, especially in communities under economic stress. Businesses that are big and powerful will usually destroy those that are smaller and weaker—a fact glaringly evident in the family farm sector. It has been extremely difficult for family farmers to compete with large agri-industries, and whole communities can be destroyed when a very large business corporation dominates a sector. As is often said, big fish eat little fish, and the socioeconomic challenge for many communities is small enterprises collaborating and working together for local survival.

Table 13.3

Cooperatives in Quebec

Members	1,400,000
Enterprises	2,200
Employees	31,000
Annual sales	CA$6.2 billion
Assets	CA$3.2 billion

Source: Perron (2000, 1).

In recognition of this reality, the International Cooperative Alliance has stressed "cooperation among cooperatives" as a key principle for development. It is a principle largely neglected by most co-ops. In general, they have tended to be turned inward for their own growth and development as well as for service to their members. It is now clear that the social impact of the cooperative sector could be greatly multiplied through commercial mergers and joint venturing. Mondragon is obviously a classic example in which the unification of diverse cooperative enterprises triggered a staggering growth rate, but there are many other examples.

Quebec

For many years, the province of Quebec, with a population of 7.5 million, has been the strongest region for cooperative businesses in Canada. The statistics for 1999 do not include credit unions and cooperative insurance companies (see Table 13.3, Perron 2000).

With such a high level of infrastructure, it is not surprising that Quebec has the most innovative cooperative structures in Canada. Innovation is difficult unless supportive resources are available, and worker co-ops are especially difficult to establish because, in most cases, workers do not have the resources to take ownership. Mondragon has maintained a high level of enterprise creation because their unified structure served as a platform for launching new initiatives. Without that structure, Mondragon might never have grown the way it has. Based upon the idea of intercooperation, Quebec leaders developed a strategy to unify co-ops from different sectors. In the 1980s, this strategy took the form of regional development co-ops whereby in specific regions credit unions, retail co-ops, forestry co-ops, and so on, were invited to form an umbrella structure to promote new development (Côté and Gratton 1994).

After much experimentation, four regional development co-ops were established with the help of government assistance and contributions from cooperative members. These development co-ops received two kinds of financial support from the Quebec government: (1) basic core funding for a minimal staff, and (2) a matching grant for the money they were able to raise in their region. Because of rising unemployment in Quebec, the province linked funding to job creation. Along with providing a grant of CA$2,000 to the co-op group for each job created, the province provided CA$1,200 for each job saved.

The most successful regional development co-op is called La Coopérative de Développement Régional de Québec–Appalaches (CDRQA), which serves the region around Quebec City. Its stated mission is "To organize cooperatives from all the sectors as one group, to promote and develop cooperative businesses and to represent the cooperative movement at the regional level" (Côté and Gratton 1994, 6).

More than 500 co-ops are members of this regional co-op, including credit unions, retail co-ops, and worker co-ops, among other enterprises. They have participated in developing at least 163 such enterprises, involving more than 3,000 employees. Of these, 77 percent still function after ten years. The business activities involved include forestry, agriculture, housing, food services, educational services, television cable systems, funerals, and leisure activities. Examples range from a group of ambulance drivers who formed a co-op to purchase their own ambulances, to farmers and forestry workers. In the field of agriculture, Unicoop is one of the best examples. It was formed in 1986 from a merger of three co-ops involved in a variety of activities from milling flour to providing farm supplies. With five co-ops as members, it now has approximately 750 producer members and 250 employees (Perron 2000).

Solidarity Co-ops. While most co-ops in Canada have a single category of membership—either producers or consumers—Quebec has developed a mixed model, somewhat similar to the Mondragon co-ops—called solidarity co-ops. Producers, employees, and consumers who have common needs can be members of the same co-op. Each member category is assigned a minimal representation in the board meeting. For example, home service co-ops offer services to people suffering from physical handicaps. The membership includes employees, users of the service, and partners in the area such as social clubs and organizations for the handicapped. Using this same kind of structure of mixed membership, a group of eighty citizens in Notre Dame du Rosaire raised CA$50,000 to purchase a local restaurant and turned it into a successful solidarity co-op (Perron 2000).

In the new economy, small towns frequently lose businesses for a variety of reasons—for example, an owner growing old without a successor, a parent company closing out the local branch plant, or a company simply going bankrupt. Solidarity co-ops and worker co-ops are very useful as rescue mechanisms in such cases. One example in Quebec was the company called Promo Plastik, a manufacturer of plastic promotion articles such as dolls, decals, credit card sleeves, and other items. When it was about to close, six workers formed a worker co-op and purchased the plant to keep it in their hometown, Saint Jean Port-Joli; otherwise, the machinery would have been moved to a major city. In 1998, the company produced the effigy-mascot for the French soccer team in the World Cup.

Worker Shareholder Cooperatives. While most organizers are familiar with worker co-ops, the modified version found in Quebec is not commonly understood. In this version, the workers do not own 100 percent of the business, and the co-op usually occurs when a privately owned business is having difficulty. In such a case, workers form a co-op and purchase a percentage of the business, becoming partners with management instead of simply being employees, or resorting to full-blown worker cooperative ownership. While such co-ops usually form to resolve a business problem, sometimes they are initiated for very positive reasons.

Maska Workers' Cooperative is such a case. This company designs and produces specialized pulleys for industry. With encouragement from the owner, the employees decided to organize into a worker co-op. The eighty-five–member group purchased 12 percent of the shares so that they could become partners in the enterprise. This company ranked among the fifty best-managed private companies in Canada in a contest organized by Arthur Andersen and the *Financial Post* (Perron 2000).

Emilia Romagna

Besides Mondragon, the other famous European example of cooperation between co-ops is Emilia Romagna in Northern Italy. We will refer to this highly organized region as simply Emilia. In Mondragon, the relationships between co-ops are strictly formalized. One is either in or out of the system. If a member enterprise borrows from the cooperative bank (Caja), it is obliged to sign a contract of association according to which it cannot borrow from another bank and must be open to audits by the Caja. Emilia is not tightly organized in this manner. In contrast, the kinds of cooperation in this northern Italian region depend more on consensus and traditional relationships than upon legal structures, yet the cooperative system is much more widespread in Emilia than in the Basque area of Spain.

The Emilia region has one of the highest percentages of small firms in the world. With a population of 4 million, there is one business enterprise for every five workers. Ninety percent of the businesses have fewer than 20 employees, and only five companies have 500 or more. While many of these businesses are family-owned, they tend to form co-ops for various purposes, ranging from marketing to design. Emilia is quite striking in that the whole economy seems to be organized around natural relationships—people like to do business with their neighbors.

In Emilia, cooperatively organized businesses account for 40 percent of the gross domestic product. There are more than 8,000 co-ops in the region, and they are structured in various ways. Some are very large, like the cooperative retail chain Nordest, which has 396,000 members and 3,300 employees. Besides the huge hypermarkets, the region also hosts small stores and twenty-one travel agencies, representing assets of $1 billion. There are also a variety of sectoral co-ops for such products as shoes and textiles. Most of the cooperative system is made up of small units, however, such as the 4,000 social co-ops, which provide services such as home care, recreation, and care for the socially disadvantaged. There is even a cooperative village for the treatment of drug addicts.

The variety of business relationships in this region is amazing. Some are very formal. The Lega (*Lega Nazionale delle Cooperative e Mutue*) is a federation of co-ops one of whose roles is to help start new co-ops. To make this possible, they have established the Co-op Fund. Every member co-op contributes 3 percent of its earnings, and this centralized capital is then used for investment in cooperative development. A second-level co-op, to which members contribute, is a central guarantee fund from which members may borrow and receive a partial guarantee that lowers the interest rate paid.

Sometimes cooperation is based on informal agreements. An example would be a competition for a contract to supply a large quantity of furniture. There could be as many as ten small companies bidding, but the winning enterprise will subdivide the work among other small furniture companies in the area. Thus, small companies can act like large companies through cooperation. These sharing arrangements often take the form of a flexible manufacturing network (Piore and Sabel 1984).

Cooperative Advantage

The advantage of structured networking is quite obvious. Where it has been tried seriously, the evidence is incontrovertible that relationships among co-ops bring positive growth and wealth creation. Several cooperative businesses working together can achieve much more than when each works independently. As stated above, the low unemployment rates in the immediate Mondragon area and Emilia province, as well as the high job creation record of the Quebec consortium, are convincing examples of empirical evidence.

In most of the cases under discussion, it is clear that the co-ops were formed on the basis of existing social relationships. This is significant in light of recent research on social capital (Helliwell 2001; Putnam 2001). While multinational corporations can weaken the social fabric of a community, co-ops tend to build on and even strengthen local social relationships. The cooperative formula may become one of the most important instruments available to slow down the dangerous deterioration of social capital referred to by Putnam (2000).

Worker to the Enterprise Itself

Following the research of Putnam (2000), it does appear that workers see themselves as isolated individuals with little institutional linkage—work has become a place where one earns money. According to the tradition of most Western religions, work should be the institution through which workers contribute to society and find meaning in their lives. In the classical notion of a business corporation (Davis 1905), the worker plays a social role through the medium of such institutions. A place of work should provide an opportunity to participate in service to society; however, in the modern technocratic business corporation, there is little room for personal input. This is true not only for lower employees but also for middle management. As U.S. Chief Justice John Marshall (1819) stated it,

> A corporation is an artificial being, invisible, intangible, and existing only in contemplation of the law. Being the mere creature of law, it possesses only those properties, which the charter of creation confers upon it, either expressly, or as incidental to its very existence. These are such as are supposed best calculated to effect the object for which it was created.

The corporation is more than its members; the whole is greater than the sum of its parts. Gower (1969) describes a corporation as an association of persons acting for a particular end. Davis (1905) says that society always needs such subsidiary bodies to develop and meet its needs. Corporations could be enabling structures to permit local societies to survive and prosper, however; and while many people appeal to corporations to become "good corporate citizens," most corporations do not recognize service to society as their primary function (Reich 1992).

The large modern business corporation leaves little room for personal input in a larger social mission. In fact, the corporation often contradicts the good intentions of employees who do feel concern for the poor and unemployed but who have little impact on the decision-making apparatus of their employers. Hence, there is a dissonance between the individual will and the will of the corporation to which the individual belongs—a situation worsened by recent revelations of fraudulent corporate behavior (Krugman 2002). The public rightly blames the whole corporation, but the typical employee is usually completely unaware of the decisions that are being made by a small group of managers "at the top." The typical employee is completely at the mercy of the top managers, as are millions of shareholders.

In our concern for worker rights and community benefit, we often forget that the corporation, whether cooperative or joint stock, is an entity in its own right with corporate responsibilities greater than those of the persons within it. The corporate entity is given legal status as a corporate person and should be seen as a citizen serving a civil society. The worker can then gain dignity and satisfaction in contributing to the effectiveness of this relationship—the contribution of the individual employee to society mediated by the corporation itself. This is the ideal and the norm, even though unethical management can subvert it. As the dangers of corporate misbehavior become more evident, the advent of socially oriented cooperative corporations becomes more and more necessary for civil society. The cooperative approach encourages workers to participate as conscious partners and members, not as cogs in a machine where the worker at the bottom has neither knowledge of nor control over decisions made by the managers at the top.

While capitalistic joint stock corporations drain off capital continually, co-ops such as Mondragon, where 20 percent of earnings are retained, build in protections for the co-op itself. Year after year, this builds up and constitutes social equity, which does not belong to any of the members. It is intended to keep the co-op itself strong and able to serve the society better. New Dawn Enterprises is much smaller, but the same principle is used. All retained earnings are kept permanently as social equity. Salaries are paid, but no single individual member owns New Dawn capital. It is a kind of community trust.

Cooperative Advantage

A good argument can be made that the cooperative structure makes a business stronger. According to a study done in Quebec, the survival rate of co-ops is much higher than that of privately owned stockholder companies (Table 13.4).

Perron (2000) states that the average American firm loses half of its clients every five years, half its employees every four years, and half of its shareholders every year. This instability is estimated to reduce efficiency by 25 to 50 percent—hardly conducive to building teams of workers united in a shared mission to serve society. Instead of being a medium for participation

Table 13.4

Survival Rate of Cooperatives Compared to Private Enterprises

	After 3 years	After 5 years	After 10 years
Private enterprises	No data	36 percent	20 percent
Cooperatives	No data	64 percent	46 percent
Cooperatives supported by CDRQA	98 percent	84 percent	77 percent

Source: Perron (2000).

in the wider society, the business corporation becomes simply an impersonal place where one earns money.

In addition to providing a more stable labor force, the cooperative structure encourages capitalization and reinvestment. The accumulation of capital to be owned by the co-op is called social equity because it enables the corporate entity to better exercise its social responsibility. It belongs to the enterprise as such and not to the members. The concept of social equity is not well understood because of the strong North American accent on individual ownership.

Social equity enriches the cooperative corporation itself—not only the individual owners. It is a powerful technique for growth and new enterprise creation, and it explains why Mondragon never has bankruptcies. Government policy can be an influence in this regard. In Italy, co-ops can avoid taxation by reinvesting 80 percent of earnings back into expansion and development. This money is called nondivisible assets—it cannot be drawn out by individual members and has made the Mondragon and Emilia co-ops extremely strong.

Conclusions

There is, in fact, a concentration of global corporate power, with 200 corporations controlling 30 percent of the assets in the world. Most social activists oppose this massive control by profit-seeking conglomerates (Dobbin 1998). Serious reformers should look to the cooperative movement as a counterweight to the global business colossus. If cooperative enterprises in small communities adopted the emerging methods of Emilia, Quebec, or Mondragon, growth and diversification would ensue. If we are really serious about the dangers of the global corporations, then we should also become serious about developing the cooperative sector as an alternative. When we consider the size of the corporate sector around the world, it is not unreasonable to set a goal for the cooperative sector by which it would control 30 percent of the world's assets.

Diversification does not happen by itself. As seen in Quebec, Emilia, and Mondragon, diversification comes from within (Côté and Gratton 1994). It did not start with leaders from outside the cooperative system. New enterprises can develop if existing cooperative enterprises come together to form launching platforms for innovation. Of course, all changes come down to leadership and, in the above cases of innovation within the cooperative system, a team of four or five people with vision and commitment took the lead—often at great personal risk. It is entrepreneurship, but not the kind of entrepreneurship that depends upon one getting the better of the other. This is social entrepreneurship, where the local society benefits from the energy and talent of those so gifted.

What this boils down to is an ecology of business, a sustainability. True financial capital is built upon social capital, depends upon it, and has its source in it. If financial capital is mobile, then it absorbs and uses social capital and moves on, leaving behind a depleted society. To be sustainable, financial capital must feed back into the social capital and, as more financial capital is developed, social capital will be reinforced.

This process can be compared to the life of a forest. The trees grow and depend upon the soil, the ground underneath, whence they sprung. If we cut the trees off from their source and move them away, then we have two effects: (1) the trees are now dead, even if useful for manufacture, and (2) the soil is dead—once we remove all the trees—because the soil dries up and dies. Co-ops and neocooperatives admit that, by their very structure, they depend upon social capital as the soil in which they become rooted. While increasing their wealth and financial capital, they give back strength and life to the community and, in the cases examined here, the co-ops did give vitality to the local communities from which they sprang. Much of our world needs to be revitalized, and the cooperative philosophy appears to be the best tonic.

In the history of humankind, we have had terrible disasters such as plagues and wars. Somehow humanity has had the courage and strength to reorganize and rebuild. In the world of today, we often hear it said that the problems are too great, and that there is nothing we can do. History has shown that there is always something we can do. Being hopeful is part of being human, as Camus (1942) tried to tell us in the *Myth of Sisyphus*. When we lose hope, we have lost our humanity. I believe that hope triggers action, and this action does not take a great deal of effort. There is always something a few people can do to improve their local community by working together. That is how most successful cooperative corporations began.

References

Azurmendi, José. 1987. *El hombre cooperativo*. Mondragon, Spain: Caja Laboral Popular.

Barber, Benjamin. 1996. *Jihad vs. McWorld: How Globalism and Tribalism are Reshaping the World*. New York: Ballantine Books.

Berle, Adolfe, and Gardiner Means. [1932] 1967. *Modern Corporation and Private Property*. New York: Macmillan.

Camus, Albert. 1942. *The Myth of Sisyphus and Other Essays*. New York: Vintage Books.

Cave, Damien. 2002. "The New Gilded Age and Its Discontents: Nobel Prize-winning Economist Joseph Stiglitz Talks About the Corporate Looting Spree and Bush's Woeful Mismanagement of the Economy." *Salon.com*, July 3. Available at www.salon.com/tech/feature/2002/07/03/stiglitz/ (December 2001).

Cheney, George. 2001. *Managed Democracy: The Shape of Employee Participation in the Customer Driven Firm*. Ithaca, NY: Cornell University Press.

Côté, Daniel, and Andrée-Anne Gratton. 1994. *La coopérative de développement régional de la région de Québec*. Montréal: Centre d'Etudes en Cooperation, Ecole des Hautes Etudes.

Craig, John G. 1993. *The Nature of Cooperation*. Montreal: Black Rose Books.

Davis, John P. 1905. *Corporations: A Study of the Origin and Development of Great Business Combinations and Their Relation to the Authority of the State*. Vols. 1 and 2. New York: Burt Franklin.

Dobbin, Murray. 1998. *Democracy Under the Rule of Big Business*. Toronto: Stoddard.

Drabenstott, Mark, and Tim R. Smith. 1996. *The Changing Economy of the Rural Heartland*. Kansas City, MO: Federal Reserve Bank of Kansas City.

Drucker, Peter. 1993. *Post Capitalist Society*. New York: Harper Business.

Erdal, David. 1999. "The Psychology of Sharing: An Evolutionary Approach." Unpublished dissertation, University of St. Andrews.

Fairbairn, Brett, and Ian MacPherson. 2000. *Canadian Cooperatives in the Year 2000*. Saskatoon: Center for the Study of Cooperatives, University of Saskatchewan.

Friedman, Milton. 1980. *Free to Choose*. New York: Harcourt Brace.

Gower, L.C.B. 1969. *The Principles of Modern Company Law*. London: Stevens and Sons.

Harrison, Alison, and Taylor Oldroyd. 2002. "$5 Million in Rural Cooperative Development Grants to Foster Economic Development in 19 States." Press Release, August 26. Washington, DC: USDA. Available at www.usda.gov/news/releases/2002/08/0354.htm (December 2001).

Helliwell, John. 2001. Guest editor, Special Issue on Social Capital. *Canadian Journal of Policy Research* 2, no. 1: 1–93. Available at www.isuma.net/v02n01/index_e.shtml (December 2001).

Korten, David. 2001. *When Corporations Rule the World*. 2d ed. West Hartford, CT: Kumarian Press.

Kristof, Nicholas. 2002. "America's Failed Frontier." *New York Times*, September 3. Available at www.nytimes.com/2002/09/03/opinion/03KRIS.html (December 2001).

Krugman, Paul. 2002. "The Outrage Constraint." *New York Times*, August 23. Available at www.nytimes.com/2002/08/23/opinion/23KRUG.html (December 2001).

Laidlaw, Alex. 1971. *The Man from Margaree: Moses Coady.* Toronto: McClelland Stewart.

McChesney, Robert. 1999. "The New Global Media: It's a Small World of Big Conglomerates." *The Nation,* November 29, pp. 11–13. Available at www.past. thenation.com/issue/991129/1129mcchesney.shtml (December 2001).

MacIntyre, Alasdair. 1984. *After Virtue.* Notre Dame, IN: University of Notre Dame Press.

MacLeod, Greg. 1985. *New Age Business.* Ottawa: Canadian Council on Social Development.

———. 1997. *From Mondragon to America.* Sydney, Nova Scotia: University College of Cape Breton Press.

MacPherson, Ian. 1995. *Cooperative Principles for the 21st Century.* Geneva, Switzerland: International Cooperative Alliance.

Marcuse, Herbert. 1964. *One Dimensional Man.* Boston: Beacon Press.

Marshall, John. 1819. *Dartmouth College v. Woodward.* 4 Wheat 518, 636, 41. Ed. at 629.

Marx, Karl. [1867] 1986. *Capital: A Critical Analysis of Capitalist Production.* Vol. 1. New York: International Publishers.

Mathews, Race. 2000. *Credit Unions in the New Millennium: The Regional and Rural Economic Development Option.* Paper presented at the Credit Union Historical Co-operative Convention, Albury-Wodonga, Australia.

Melnyk, George. 1985. *The Search for Community: From Utopia to a Cooperative Society.* Montreal: Black Rose Books.

Mondragon. n.d. Web site for Mondragón Corporación Cooperativa. Available at www.mondragon.mcc.es. (December 2001).

———. 2000. *2000 Annual Report.* Available at www.mondragon.mcc.es/ingles/ficheros/memoriaeng2000.pdf (December 2001).

Morrison, Roy. 1991. *We Build the Road as We Travel.* Philadelphia: New Society Publishers.

Nakagawa, Yuichiro. 2000. "Development of French Cooperative Thought in Britain." *Bulletin of the Institute of Social Sciences* 22, no. 4. Tokyo: Mejii University.

Novak, Michael. 1981. *Toward a Theology of the Corporation.* Washington, DC: American Enterprise Institute for Public Policy Research.

Perron, Gerard. 2000. *Cooperation: A Winning Formula.* Quebec City: Regional Development Cooperative of Quebec–Appalachia.

Piore, Michael, and Charles Sabel. 1984. *The Second Industrial Divide: Possibilities for Prosperity.* New York: Basic Books.

Putnam, Robert. 2000. *Bowling Alone: The Collapse and Revival of American Community.* New York: Simon and Schuster.

———. 2001. "Social Capital Measurement and Consequences." *ISUMA: Canadian Journal of Policy Research* 2, no. 1: 41–53. Available at www.isuma.net/v02n01/putnam/putnam_e.shtml (December 2001).

Quarter, Jack. 1993. *Canada's Social Economy.* Toronto: Lorimer.

———. 2000. *Beyond the Bottom Line: Socially Innovative Business Owners.* Westport, CT: Quorum Books.

Reich, Robert B. 1992. *The Work of Nations.* New York: Vintage Books.

Rugman, Alan. 2000. *The End of Globalization.* New York: Amacom.

Ryan, Tim. 1983. "The Legitimacy of the Large Modern Business Corporation and the Roman Catholic Social Teaching Tradition." Unpublished Ph.D. thesis, University of Toronto—St. Michaels College, Toronto, Ontario.

Scott, Mark C. 2000. *Re-inspiring the Corporation: The Seven Seminal Paths to Corporate Greatness*. New York: John Wiley.

Sen, Amartya. 1999. "Democracy as a Universal Value." *Journal of Democracy* 10, no. 3: 3–17. Available at http://muse.jhu.edu/demo/jod/10.3sen.html (December 2001).

Soros, George. 1997. "The Capitalist Threat." *Atlantic Monthly* 297, no. 2: 45–58. Available at www.theatlantic.com/issues/97feb/capital/capital.htm (December 2001).

Stiglitz, Joseph. 2001. "Thanks for Nothing." *The Atlantic Monthly* (3): 36–40. Available at www.theatlantic.com/issues/2001/10/stiglitz.htm (December 2001).

"Supplement sur l'avenir." 1999. *Le Monde Diplomatique* (December). Available at http://mondediplo.com/1999/12/.

Thomas, Henk, and Chris Logan. 1982. *Mondragon: An Economic Analysis*. London: Allen and Unwin.

Thurow, Lester. 1996. *The Future of Capitalism: How Today's Economic Forces Shape Tomorrow's World*. New York: W. Morrow.

Went, Robert. 2000. *Globalization: Neo-liberal Challenge, Radical Response*, trans. by Peter Drucker. London: Pluto Press.

Whyte, William Foote, and Kathleen King Whyte. 1988. *Making Mondragon*. Ithaca, NY: Cornell University, ILR Press.

Williamson, Oliver. 1980. "The Organization of Work: A Comparative Institutional Assessment." *Journal of Economic Behavior and Organization* 1, no. 1: 5–38.

Zamagni, Stefano. 2000. "Economic Reductionism as a Hindrance to the Analysis of Structural Change." *Structural Change and Economic Dynamics* 11, nos. 1–2: 197–208.

About the Contributors

Lee Egerstrom is the agribusiness writer for the *Saint Paul Pioneer Press*, a former Washington correspondent for Knight-Ridder newspapers, and a past president of the National Association of Agricultural Journalists. He authored *Make No Small Plans* (1994), which raised international awareness of New Generation Cooperatives forming on the northern Great Plains. He is co-author, with Gert van Dijk and Pieter Bos, of *Seizing Control: The International Market Power of Cooperatives* (1996).

Brett Fairbairn is professor of history at the University of Saskatchewan, Canada, and directs the Centre for the Study of Co-operatives. He teaches and researches the history of co-ops; agrarian, democratic, and social movements; and related subjects. He has published many books and articles on the history of co-ops in Germany and Western Canada, and on community economic development. His most recent co-edited book is *Canadian Cooperatives in the Year 2000: Memory, Mutual Aid, and the Millennium* (2000).

Joan Fulton is an associate professor in the Department of Agricultural Economics at Purdue University and engages in teaching, research, and extension. Her research examines the impact of organizational structure on the efficiency of agribusiness firms, with special emphasis on co-ops. Recent research projects include the impact of producer investment in value-added processing activities, alternative contracting arrangements in the production of specialty grains, and success factors associated with business reorganization via mergers/acquisitions and joint ventures/strategic alliances.

Peter Goldsmith is an assistant professor of agribusiness in the Department of Agricultural and Consumer Economics, and co-director of the Center for Global Supply Chain Studies at the University of Illinois–Champaign-Urbana. He earned the 1997 Edwin G. Nourse award for outstanding doctoral research on co-ops. His research interests include organizational strategy focusing on structural change and adaptation processes in agriculture, biotechnology and its impact on agriculture, and entrepreneurship and innovation. He has published numerous articles in scientific journals and in the popular press.

Mark J. Hanson is an attorney with Lindquist and Vennum, PLLP, a law firm in Minneapolis, where he directs the Agribusiness and Cooperative Group within the firm. He has extensive experience in starting co-ops and counseling mergers, acquisitions, and joint ventures. He is licensed to practice in state and federal courts in Minnesota and Wisconsin and has authored many legal journal articles on agricultural credit and financing, surface water preservation and use, and groundwater protection.

Ann Hoyt is on the faculty of the Department of Consumer Science at the University of Wisconsin–Madison and is the director of the Urban Cooperative Institute. She has also worked for the University of Wisconsin Center for Cooperatives. She has national experience in promoting co-ops and currently serves on the Board of Directors for the NCBA—the National Cooperative Business Association. She serves as an affiliate of the UW–Cooperative Extension and conducts research on consumer co-ops and cooperative finance.

F. Larry Leistritz is Distinguished Professor of Agricultural Economics at North Dakota State University. His research has focused on regional economic development issues and on the economic impact of agricultural and resource development projects, programs, and policies. He has undertaken several studies of the economic impact of New Generation Cooperatives in North Dakota and has authored or co-authored many books, journal articles, and research reports. He is past president and director of the International Association for Impact Assessment and of the Western Agricultural Economics Association.

Greg MacLeod is a professor of philosophy at University College of Cape Breton (UCCB) where he also directs the Tompkins Institute. He is an ordained priest and is the founding chairperson of New Dawn Enterprises, a community development organization with an annual budget of $6 million employing 175 people. He also founded BCA Holdings, a community venture–finance company with assets of almost $2 million dollars. He has authored numerous books, journal articles, and reports.

Christopher D. Merrett is an associate professor of geography at the Illinois Institute for Rural Affairs and the Department of Geography at Western Illinois University. He researches local responses to globalization, with a specific focus on co-ops and cooperative development. He has written two books, many journal articles, and numerous reports examining the effectiveness of New Generation Cooperatives as a tool for local community development. Most recently, he has written on social justice issues.

Jeffrey S. Royer is professor and head of the Department of Agricultural Economics at the University of Nebraska–Lincoln, where he teaches and conducts research in agricultural marketing and agribusiness management. He served with the Agricultural Cooperative Service of the U.S. Department of Agriculture, where he led the agency's program of research, technical assistance, and education in financing co-ops. He has worked in cooperative finance, taxation, and theory and is the author of numerous technical and popular publications. He received the USDA Distinguished Service Award and the National Society of Accountants for Cooperatives Silver Pen Award.

David J. Schaffner is a professor in the Department of Agribusiness, California Polytechnic State University, San Luis Obispo. He specializes in futures, options, and their use in price risk management. He has been a visiting professor at the Institute of Agribusiness, Santa Clara University, and at Massey University, New Zealand, and has taught executive short courses on the futures market in Australia. He has published a textbook, numerous articles, and reports on food marketing and strategic planning activities.

Randall E. Torgerson has served as head of the USDA's Cooperative Service for twenty-six years, directing programs of research, technical assistance, and education about the cooperative method of doing business. Prior to that time, he was administrator of the Farmer Cooperative Service, USDA, and was staff economist to the administrator of the Agricultural Marketing Service, USDA. He helped establish the Missouri Institute of Cooperatives, a statewide cooperative association, and served as its executive secretary. He is the author of two books and many articles in the field of group action in agriculture.

Norman Walzer is a professor of economics and founding director of the Illinois Institute for Rural Affairs at Western Illinois University. He has published extensively on rural community and economic development, local public finance, and Brownfields issues. His most recent work has been on New Generation Cooperatives as an economic development policy. He serves on many boards and commissions and works with local and state agencies on a variety of rural development issues.

Kim Zeuli is currently an assistant professor in the Department of Agricultural and Applied Economics at the University of Wisconsin–Madison, and an associate director of the University of Wisconsin Center for Cooperatives. She has served on the faculty in the Department of Agricultural Economics at the University of Kentucky. She has been actively engaged in research on cooperatives and other approaches to rural development.

Index

M

Mad Cow Disease. *See* Bovine
    spongiform encephalopathy(BSE)
Madison, WI 37
Maine 86, 219
Management 9, 11–12, 28, 32, 41–42,
    45, 49, 54–56, 58, 70–72, 75–76,
    78–79, 81, 85, 88, 101, 117, 134,
    147, 159, 180, 182, 184, 186–87,
    192–93, 195–96, 209–10, 212, 216,
    228–29, 231, 233, 236, 248–49,
    256, 274, 280, 291, 294–95, 305,
    307–8
Managers 10, 41, 55, 71–73, 76, 78–79,
    82, 87, 134–35, 138, 160–61, 183,
    192, 195–96, 243, 296, 299, 308
Manitoba 34–35, 44, 47
Maritime Co-operative Services 41
Market failure 53, 269, 275
Market power of suppliers. *See* Porter,
    Michael
Marketing pool 159
Marshall, Thurgood 307
Marx, Karl 293
Maska Workers' Cooperative 305
Massachusetts 37, 77, 98
Meat packing 30
Member labor 275
Membership 11–13, 25, 37–38, 43, 54–
    56, 61–66, 77, 80, 83, 97, 99–101,
    103, 108, 111, 113, 117, 123–24,
    126, 128, 135, 137, 139, 166–68,
    170, 172–79, 194, 208–12, 219, 229,
    232, 235, 238–41, 243–44, 274, 281,
    294, 304
Membership Commitment. *See* Loyalty;
    Free-rider problems
Mergers 3, 5, 11, 43, 46–48, 65, 84, 148,
    255, 291, 303
Michigan 98, 108, 210, 216, 218–20,
    231–32
Michigan Agricultural Cooperative
    Marketing Association (MACMA)
    232
Michigan Agricultural Marketing and
    Bargaining Act of 1972 218

Midwest (U.S.) 29, 31–32, 63, 83, 103,
    108, 180, 228, 231
Milk. *See* Dairy foods
Miners/Mining 28–29, 40
Minimum pricing 273
Mining communities 28, 40
Minneapolis, MN 43, 72
Minnesota 4, 30, 42, 72, 83, 98, 102, 108–
    9, 120, 148, 155, 180, 211, 251, 277
Minnesota Corn Processors 148
Minute Maid 213
Mississippi Market 270
Missouri 31, 42, 73, 83, 107, 108
Modernism 23–24, 26, 46
Mondragon Cooperative Corporation
    (MCC) 15–16, 281, 292–97, 299–
    300, 303–6, 308–10
Monopoly/monopolistic 13, 27, 29, 30–
    31, 35, 47, 49, 57, 165, 169, 172–73,
    175, 178, 234, 271–73
Monopsonistic (collusive oligopolistic) 5,
    135, 220
Montana 86
Mountain Equipment Co-op 43
Mountain View Harvest Cooperative 254
Multiplier effect 14, 240, 248–49
Mutual associations 73, 278
Mutual fire-insurance companies 27

N

N.O. Nelson Company 39
National Conference of Commissioners
    on Uniform State Laws in 1925 102
National Cooperative Bank 42
National Cooperative Business
    Association (NCBA) 25, 38, 43–45,
    265, 267
National Cooperative Grocers Association
    (NCGA) 7
National Corn Growers 238
National Council of Farmer Coopepratives
    (NCFC) 8, 58
National Farmers Union 231
National Foundation for Women Business
    Owners 86
National Pork Producers Council 238